PRICE EXPECTATIONS
IN
RISING INFLATION

IGNAZIO VISCO

Banca d'Italia

1984

NORTH-HOLLAND
AMSTERDAM · NEW YORK · OXFORD

ISBN 0 444 86836 4

Publishers:

ELSEVIER SCIENCE PUBLISHERS B.V.
P.O. BOX 1991
1000 BZ AMSTERDAM
THE NETHERLANDS

Sole distributors for the U.S.A. and Canada:

ELSEVIER SCIENCE PUBLISHING COMPANY, INC.
52 VANDERBILT AVENUE
NEW YORK, N.Y. 10017

Library of Congress Cataloging in Publication Data

Visco, Ignazio.
    Price expectations in rising inflation.

    (Contributions to economic analysis ; 152)
    Revision of thesis (Ph.D.)--University of
Pennsylvania, 1981.
    Bibliography: p.
    Includes index.
    1. Inflation (Finance) 2. Rational expectations
(Economic theory) I. Title. II. Series.
HG229.V57 1984   332.4'1   83-27162
ISBN 0-444-86836-4

PRINTED IN THE NETHERLANDS

INTRODUCTION TO THE SERIES

This series consists of a number of hitherto unpublished studies, which are introduced by the editors in the belief that they represent fresh contributions to economic science.

The term "economic analysis" as used in the title of the series has been adopted because it covers both the activities of the theoretical economist and the research worker.

Although the analytical methods used by the various contributors are not the same, they are nevertheless conditioned by the common origin of their studies, namely theoretical problems encountered in practical research. Since for this reason, business cycle research and national accounting, research work on behalf of economic policy, and problems of planning are the main sources of the subjects dealt with, they necessarily determine the manner of approach adopted by the authors. Their methods tend to be "practical" in the sense of not being too far remote from application to actual economic conditions. In addition they are quantitative rather than qualitative.

It is the hope of the editors that the publication of these studies will help to stimulate the exchange of scientific information and to reinforce international cooperation in the field of economics.

The Editors

To Bianca,
Giuliana, Francesca, Caterina

PREFACE

This study is a revised version of my Ph.D thesis submitted to the University of Pennsylvania in 1981. Chapters 4 and 6 have been especially revised.

Professors Albert K. Ando, Lawrence R. Klein and Roberto S. Mariano served as my dissertation committee and offered many comments and suggestions at various stages of this work. Professor Ando agreed to be my dissertation advisor. I am particularly indebted to him for his continuous interest in my progress, his advice, and his friendship. I am also very grateful to Professor Klein who always generously gave of his time to discuss the results of this study. Professor Mariano made many useful remarks not only during his reading of a first draft of this book but also during numerous discussions which helped to clarify my ideas and understanding.

I started to be interested in examining the process of expectations formation when I wrote my thesis for the *Laurea* in *Economia e Commercio* at the University of Rome in 1971, under the supervision of Professor Federico Caffè, to whom I will always be grateful. I first discovered the *Mondo Economico* surveys, which are the primary input to this work, while writing a paper for a course offered by professor F. Gerard Adams, during my first Ph.D. year at the University of Pennsylvania in 1972. Professor Adams offered at the time many suggestions which have proven fruitful during the years. When I returned to Italy after completion of my course requirements, in 1974, I started working in the research department of the Bank of Italy from which I took a leave of absence between July 1975 and January 1976. During this period I was back to Philadelphia, with a dissertation fellowship of the Economics Research Unit, to which I am grateful. The first chapters of this work were substantially conceived at that time. In 1977 I first met the late Bruno Pagani, the editor of *Mondo Economics*, and Gerolamo Fiori, the present editor. From them I learned many details on the surveys and obtained a precious body of data. With them and with my former colleague Vittorio Conti, presently of Banca Commerciale Italiana, there has been in the recent years a continuous cooperation which has led to the changes which have characterized the surveys. I am most grateful to the staff of *Mondo Economico*, and wish to express my admiration for having started in 1952 the collection of such useful information on expectations.

I also want to thank Ignazio Angeloni, Giorgio Bodo, Sergio Calliari, Giuseppe Marotta, Renato Filosa, and Asher Tishler for their help and comments at various stages of this work. I also received assistance from Doug Battenberg, Flavio Capra, Jared Enzler, Stephen Franklin, Rita Iacoboni, Donald Mullineaux, and especially Anna Scocco to whom I am grateful, and I have benefited from the editing of Elmer Luke, who has helped me to improve very much the English content of this work. The drawings have been skillfully prepared by Sandro Montozzi and Raimondo Urbanetti.

I am thankful to the Bank of Italy for having allowed me to go to Philadelphia between July and October 1981 when my dissertation, of which this book is an outgrowth, was materially written. Also, most of the computer work was performed at the Bank of Italy, taking advantage of the Speakeasy computer language, which I have found particularly suited to the empirical analysis which I have conducted.

Needless to say that I take full responsibility for what is written in this book, without implicating anyone of the above mentioned individuals and institutions.

Finally, I must admit that it is likely that this work would not have been completed were it not for the continuous incitement I received from many persons: among them, my parents, my professors, Ando and Klein, and my friends, Vittorio Conti and Renato Filosa. My greatest debt is however to my wife Bianca for her understanding, support and continuous encouragement during the long period this work has been in the making. To her and our daughters this effort is dedicated.

Ignazio Visco

August 1983

CONTENTS

CHAPTER 1

INFLATION EXPECTATIONS: THE DIRECT APPROACH

> It is perhaps only through personal interviews with individuals
> that we may measure their expectations and obtain quantitative
> variables that econometricians were previously disposed to cast
> into unknown residual disturbances.
>
> Lawrence R. Klein (1955, p. 243)

1.1. The Importance of Direct Estimates of Inflation Expectations

This study is concerned with the analysis of inflation expectations measured
by means of semiannual surveys conducted by the Italian economic magazine *Mondo Economico* within a panel of Italian businessmen and economic experts.

Economists have always recognized that the anticipations of economic
agents, whether consumers or businessmen, play a central role in the
decisions they make. In the works of Fisher (1930), Keynes (1936), and
Hicks (1939) – to cite three of the major contributions to economic thinking
in the first half of this century – substantial importance is attributed to the
expectations[1] of economic decision makers. For a long time, however,
expectations have been considered to be "unobservable" variables. In
Keynes' *General Theory*, they were even considered to be determined
sometimes by the "animal spirits" of businessmen, so that on many occasions they could probably not be related to other observed phenomena, nor
could they be generated within a rational, optimizing framework.[2] In

---

[1] In the present context anticipations and expectations are synonyms. The latter term has
gained, however, large popularity in the most recent years and it will be used throughout most
of this study. As many writers have pointed out, this might create some confusion when one
considers the "rational expectations hypothesis" according to which individual anticipations
are equal to the "true" mathematical expectations conditional on the available information set.
This appears to be, however, a minor problem and the present warning should suffice for what
follows.

[2] See, also Keynes (1937), Shackle (1952, 1955) and the discussion in Ozga (1965). The fact
that at times expectations could probably not be related to other observed phenomena, nor
could they be generated within a rational probabilistic framework, does not imply that
economic agents do not have any view about the future. It makes however of primary
importance the investigation of the actual process of expectations formation through the
analysis of *direct* observations on expectations. Such observations also appear very fruitful for a
correct interpretation of Knight's (1921) famous distinction between "risk" and "uncertainty".
Under risky situations economic agents can form probabilities; this becomes impossible as one
moves towards a world of "total" uncertainty. One can think that in this process the variances
of individual probability distributions increase towards infinity so that direct measures of the
dispersion of individual expectations appear very fruitful in characterizing the above distinction
which is probably more one of degree rather than of substance.

general, however, their effects were only studied in an indirect manner, using *a priori* interpretative frameworks in which they were linked to other variables measured statistically.[3] Two logically separate moments of analysis were therefore joined: the moment when the scheme on which the economic agents base their expectations is detected, and the moment when the effects of these expectations on their decisions (that is, on other economic variables) are analyzed. This makes practically impossible any discrimination among alternative hypotheses. It becomes very difficult, in evaluating empirical results, to distinguish between expectation effects and, say, adjustment effects. The logic and the dynamics of the estimated economic relationships are likely to be substantially affected by arbitrary, unchecked initial assumptions.

This is so not only when simple schemes of expectations formation are hypothesized, such as the extrapolative or the adaptive ones (in general distributed lag models on the "history" of the variable to be predicted), but also in the case of sophisticated assumptions such as that of "rational" expectations.[4] According to this hypothesis, economic agents make the best possible use of all the information available to them to anticipate future events relevant for their individual decisions. Without direct observations on these expectations, however, models in which the latter are assumed to be "rational" will in general not be distinguishable from (that is, will be "observationally equivalent" to) those in which other hypotheses are embedded.[5] The conditions for the identification of "rational expectations models" (restrictions on the generating process of exogenous variables and disturbances) appear to be so strong that the only solution which might be feasible is that of utilizing direct observations on expectations. These can be used to verify alternative hypotheses of formation; they will be particularly useful in breaking the "joint" condition on the generating mechanism and on the effects of the anticipations of economic units on their own actions. It is indeed clear that the ultimate goal of the adoption of direct data on expectations in empirical studies (and eventually in the macroeconometric models) is dependent on their ability to improve one's understanding of observed phenomena in the economic world. Survey-based expectations must therefore satisfy a number of requirements. They have to be representative of the expectations of the population of the economic agents

---

[3] See, for instance, Klein's (1972) review.

[4] The "rational" expectations hypothesis will be considered in detail in Chapter 5. Muth (1961) is generally credited with its introduction in the economic literature. The implications of the predictability of economic policy actions were however clearly outlined in a seminal paper by Grunberg and Modigliani (1954). For two recent surveys, see Poole (1976) and Shiller (1978).

[5] Pesaran (1981).

whose decisions are being considered. They must therefore come from well-organized surveys with well-formulated questions and a sufficiently large number of respondents. The structure of the surveys has to be checked continually and, when necessary, updated to keep pace with economic and other changes which take place in the real world. Furthermore, the transformation of the original survey answers into quantitative estimates of expectations variables should depend on a limited number of possibly weak initial assumptions.

These characteristics are present at a satisfactory level in the surveys which will be discussed in this study. One of the most interesting features of these inquiries is that they started about thirty years ago so that sufficiently long time series are available for the empirical analysis. Their structure and characteristics will be examined in detail in the following sections of this chapter, after a brief review, in Section 1.2, of other surveys on inflation expectations which have recently been considered in the literature.

Anticipations of sales, capital expenditures and inventory changes have been collected by many private and governmental agencies and have been often utilized in the empirical work.[6] The pioneering efforts of George Katona have produced important even if controversial evidence on consumer attitudes, intentions, and anticipations – which also have been thoroughly examined and used in applied research.[7] Only in the last decade, however, sufficient attention has been dedicated to direct evidence on inflation expectations.[8] It is no surprise that this has occurred at a time when inflation has become a substantial, often dramatic, phenomenon which has produced large changes also in the industrialized economies for which price stability has been observed over many years since World War II. Even if inflation expectations have only recently become a popular topic, one can, however, still benefit from the early pioneering contributions with survey-based anticipation variables which have been published in the fifties and the sixties on phenomena not directly related with inflation. The

[6]Many surveys have been considered, the most popular being, in the United States, the Railroad Shippers' forecasts, the inquiries by the Department of Commerce–Securities and Exchange Commission, the Dun and Broadstreets survey and those by McGraw-Hill and Fortune. In Europe, considerable attention has been given to the monthly surveys of the IFO-Institute in Munich. Among others, see Modigliani and Sauerlander (1955), Modigliani and Weingartner (1958), Bossons and Modigliani (1960), Ferber (1953, 1958, 1960), Hastay (1954, 1960), Friend and Bronfenbrenner (1955), Friend (1958), Hart (1960), Cohen (1960), Eisner (1956, 1958), Foss and Natrella (1960), Levine (1960), Pashigian (1964, 1965), Anderson (1952), Anderson, Bauer and Fels (1954), Theil (1952, 1955, 1961).

[7]On the SRC surveys, see Katona (1958, 1960) and the exchange between Tobin (1959) and Katona (1959) on the forecasting capacity of consumers' attitudes. See also, Katona and Mueller (1953), Klein and Lansing (1955), Lansing and Whitey (1955), Mueller (1957, 1960), Schweiger (1955), Juster (1959, 1960), Okun (1960), Hymans (1970), Taylor (1974).

[8]For a recent survey, see Chan-Lee (1980).

pioneering efforts by Klein, Modigliani, and a number of other talented economists,[9] who have made use of survey data in the econometric estimation of economic relations, should still be followed for many important applications which could prove useful to one's understanding of the way decisions take place in the complex economic environments of our societies. The present study, like many contributions on the measurement and analysis of inflation expectations, finds its motivations in the same considerations which have characterized those earlier efforts: the improvement of our knowledge of economic behavior, the purpose of increasing our ability to forecast economic activity, the understanding of the causal relations which characterize modern economies, and the testing of alternative theories on the effects of policy measures and environmental changes on the actions of economic units.

The analysis of the channels through which inflation expectations affect other economic variables will, however, not be pursued in this work. It will first be considered the problem of obtaining reliable estimates of expected inflation from the answers to *Mondo Economico* surveys (Chapter 2). These estimates will then be evaluated, examining their forecasting accuracy, over different periods, for different groups of respondents and different price indices, comparing them with those from other surveys on inflation expectations and studying their properties at turning points of the inflation process (Chapter 3). In Chapter 4 the forecasting performance of the respondents to these surveys will be compared with that of the forecasts generated by alternative predictors of inflation, and in Chapter 5 the hypothesis of "rational" expectations will be investigated. The formation of inflation expectations will be considered in Chapter 6, and in the last chapter general remarks will be advanced on the results which have been obtained and the many lines of future research opened by the availability of this direct evidence on expectations of price changes.

This study, therefore, represents the necessary first step that must be taken before the effects of inflation expectations on other variables such as interest rates, production decisions, and wage and price changes can be fruitfully investigated. This first step is not a small one and many pages have thus been devoted to what one might still consider a preliminary investigation. The investigation, it is hoped, will contribute to an understanding of what inflation expectations are, how they differ among persons, and how they are generated.

---

[9]Besides those cited in Footnotes 6 and 7, see the contributions by Klein (1954), Modigliani and Cohen (1958, 1961), Adams (1964), Adams and Green (1965), Adams and Klein (1972), Adams and Duggal (1974), Friend and Adams (1964), Friend and Thomas (1970), Jorgenson and Stephenson (1969), Eisner (1965), Evans and Green (1966), Carlson (1967), Lovell (1967), Hirsch and Lovell (1969), Juster (1969), Juster and Wachtel (1972c), Conti (1975).

1.2. A Brief Review of Direct Sources on Inflation Expectations

In the last decade many articles have been published where use has been made of survey-based inflation expectations. Some of the major surveys considered in these articles will be briefly reviewed in this section. In the last section of this chapter, characteristics of these surveys will be compared with those of *Mondo Economico* opinion polls.

Various surveys contain direct information on inflation expectations. Estimates of the expected inflation rate can be obtained by extracting and summarizing (or aggregating) this information from the individual answers to questions on the expectations of the economic agents interviewed. Two types of surveys must be considered: the *qualitative* and the *quantitative*. To the latter belong those conducted since 1946 by the financial columnist Joseph Livingston whose reports have appeared in the two Philadelphia newspapers, the *Bulletin* and the *Inquirer*. These data have been used in studies on the formation of inflation expectations (Turnovsky (1970)), on the "Fisher effect" on interest rates (Pyle (1972), Gibson (1972)), on the "expectations-augmented" Phillips curve (Turnovsky and Wachter (1972), Turnovsky (1972), Gordon (1971)). They have been thoroughly examined and revised by Carlson (1977a). Many are skeptical about the success of these surveys in approximating the expectations of the general public or even of businessmen only. The surveys are in fact conducted on a small panel (averaging about fifty) of business and academic economists. The respondents are therefore very specialized, and it is not clear whose expectations they might be representative of. Furthermore, over the many years of Livingston's surveys, the panel has necessarily undergone substantial changes in its composition, which cannot be understated given the small number of participants. An impressive collection of papers has, however, been produced which make use of these data to examine the formation and rationality of inflation expectations, their effects on various variables of interest, and the role played on economic relations by uncertainty on future inflation (measured by the dispersion of expectations across the respondents).[10]

---

[10] Livingston's surveys also consider anticipations of other variables besides prices. The latter, however, have been most extensively examined and utilized in empirical works on expectations. Besides those mentioned in the text, see the studies by Severn (1973), De Milner (1975), Pesando (1975), Carlson (1975, 1977b, 1979, 1980), Cargill (1976, 1977), Brinner (1976), McGuire (1976a, 1976b), Lahiri (1976, 1977, 1980, 1981), Lahiri and J. Lee (1979a, 1979b, 1981a, 1981b), Lahiri and Y. Lee (1981), Foster (1977), Holden and Peel (1977), Mullineaux (1977, 1978, 1980a, 1980b), Pearce (1979), Maital (1979), Holmes and Kwast (1979), Cukierman and Wachtel (1979, 1982), Levi and Makin (1979, 1980, 1981), Barnea, Datan and Lakonishok (1979), Zarnovitz (1978, 1979), Lakonishok (1980), Resler (1980), Jacobs and Jones (1980), Hafer and Resler (1980, 1982), Tanzi (1980, 1982), Bomberger and Frazer (1981), Figlewsky and Wachtel (1981), Brown and Maital (1981), Keen (1981), Amihud (1981), Taylor (1981), Mitchell (1981), Mitchell and Taylor (1982), Figlewsky (1983).

As it has been observed, Livingston's surveys are of a quantitative nature. The interviewees are in fact required to provide precise forecasts. Since 1966 the question on expected changes of the consumer price index asked to the consumers interviewed by the Survey Research Center of the University of Michigan have also been of the quantitative type.[11] In the preceding years, however, qualitative questions were raised.[12] Mueller (1959) provided a first descriptive analysis of the answers concerning expectations of price changes. Shuford, Juster, Wachtel, and De Menil were the first researchers to utilize these expectation estimates in econometric studies on consumer behavior and wage determination. They also considered the problems of transforming the qualitative answers in quantitative estimates of expected inflation and of linking them to the post 1966 data. Many studies have since followed these initial efforts.[13]

Total qualitative surveys, in which questions concerning the expected price level for a given future period are usually classified in the four "up", "same", "down", and "don't know" categories, are those conducted monthly by Gallup in the United Kingdom and by the IFO-Institute für Wirtschaftforschung in Germany. The Gallup surveys are conducted among consumers and have been studied first by Carlson and Parkin (1975). The IFO-Institute surveys concern industrial enterprises and have been utilized for the study of the formation of inflation expectations first by Knöbl (1974). The problems which are faced in obtaining quantitative estimates from these surveys will be examined in great detail in Chapter 2.

Other surveys have also been object of investigation in recent years. These will be discussed as necessary in the following chapters.

---

[11]Until the third quarter of 1977 consumers were asked "closed-end" questions. That is, even if the interviewees were free to produce any answer which they considered to be appropriate, for those who anticipated price increases the questions contained hints on a number of possible answers. Data from these closed-end questions were coded in a number of contiguous categories, but the distribution of answers was clearly multimodal. Since the third quarter of 1977 a major change was introduced and consumers were asked an "open-end" question, that is they were requested to produce, if they anticipated a price increase, a precise estimate of the future percentage change of prices, without any suggestion of possible values contained in the question. See also Footnotes 34 and 35 for further details and comments.

[12]A qualitative question (that is, whether the interviewees expected prices to go up, stay the same or go down) has always been asked to the consumers participating to the SRC surveys. Since the second quarter of 1966 they were also asked to produce quantitative estimates, as mentioned in the preceding footnote. Between the fourth quarter of 1951 and the first quarter of 1961, those who did not expect prices to stay the same were also asked an additional qualitative question. In particular, they were asked whether they expected that next year prices would be a lot (or a little) higher (or lower) than at the moment the survey was taken.

[13]See Shuford (1970), Juster and Wachtel (1972a, 1972b), Juster (1974), Juster and Taylor (1975), Juster and Comment (1978), De Menil (1974), De Menil and Bhalla (1975), Wachtel (1977a, 1977b), Fackler and Stanhouse (1977), Sheffrin (1978), Cukierman and Wachtel (1979), Van Duyne (1980), Fishe and Lahiri (1981), Curtin (1982), Fields and Noble (1981), Noble and Fields (1982), Noble (1982), Fischer and Huizinga (1982).

1.3. The Mondo Economico Opinion Poll

Beginning in the second semester of 1952, the Italian economic magazine *Mondo Economico* has systematically conducted semiannual surveys among four categories of economic agents. The objective of these surveys has been to gather specific information, from a sufficiently large panel of qualified and informed persons, on their expectations of changes in prices and demand variables.

A few points should first be raised before going further into the details of the surveys (a list of which is given in Table D.1 of the Data Appendix):[14]

(a) The surveyed people do not constitute a random sample; they have been instead selected by the editors of *Mondo Economico* with the intention of assembling a *panel* of individuals that should change only gradually through time and who should belong to four main categories of economic agents: that is, managers and executives in the sector of industrial *production*; in the world of *finance*, credit, insurance, and the stock exchange; in the field of *commerce*; and finally, general *experts* in economic affairs.

(b) The surveys are conducted by means of an anonymous *mail* questionnaire and the interviewees are asked to answer questions on the expected changes of aggregate demand, of the total consumption of nondurables and durables, of fixed investment, of exports, of the general levels of the wholesale and consumer price indices,[15] as well as a question on the evolution of the stock exchange market. In more recent years questions on exchange and interest rates have been included.

(c) The answers to each question, with the exception of that on the stock market, have to fall in one of a number of *pre-selected intervals* (the bottom and top ones being, of course, open intervals).

(d) The surveys have been conducted from 1952 until the end of 1980 every six months, with the questionnaires being mailed out during the last two or three weeks of June and December of each year, and coming back by the first one or two weeks of July and January.

(e) Until the end of 1977 the time horizon of the surveys has covered only the six months following the date in which each survey has been conducted (that is, expectations have been surveyed at the end of the first semester for the second semester of the same year, and at the end of the second semester

---

[14] For a recent survey of the purposes and results of the opinion poll over the years, see: Mondo Economico, "Il sondaggio semestrale di *Mondo Economico* 24 anni dopo", no. 7, February 21, 1976. See also the reports published each semester by *Mondo Economico* jointly with the results to the surveys. Some general observations, both on the structure and on the results of the surveys – even if they are synthetic and based on a small number of inquiries – are contained in Di Fenizio (1961).

[15] Up to the survey for the first semester of 1977 also a question on the cost of living index (a more limited consumer price index) was advanced.

for the first semester of the next year). In more recent years both the time span covered by these inquiries as well as their frequency has been changed; details are given below.[16]

(f) A report is issued by *Mondo Economico* after each survey, summarizing the main statistical results on the anticipations of the total of the respondents, and including some explanatory comments by the interviewees.

In the next section general remarks and observations on the composition of the panel of respondents and on the number and percentage of answers by class of respondents will be advanced. The 1952–1977 and the 1978–1980 series of inquiries will then be considered in some detail, with brief comment on the new series which has started in the first quarter of 1981.

1.4. General Remarks on the Number and the Composition of Participants and Respondents to the Mondo Economico Surveys

As stated above, the sample of people interviewed by *Mondo Economico* consists of a *panel* of qualified agents in the *production*, *finance*, and *commerce* sectors in addition to some economic *experts*. It is not, therefore, a group of randomly sampled interviewees but is instead a group of "informed" individuals arbitrarily selected by *Mondo Economico* on the basis of their qualifications. Also, this panel has been only gradually modified over time with the sole intent to maintain "on active service" (so to speak) "a well selected group, in terms of functions, preparation and experience of its members, so that it could answer on good grounds interesting questions concerning the evolution of the economic situation and the attitudes of economic policy".[17]

Table D.2 contains the number of the questionnaires dispatched for each survey and the percentages of returned over dispatched questionnaires, for the total as well as for the four categories of interviewees.[18] Table D.3 reports the number of returned questionnaires and offers an absolute and percentage breakdown by categories of respondents.

----

[16] See also Conti and Visco (1978).

[17] Mondo Economico, "Cosa si attendono gli ambienti economici nel prossimo semestre? (risposte a un questionario di *Mondo Economico*)", no. 22, May 31, 1952, supplement, p. 1 (translated from Italian).

[18] These unpublished data have been kept by *Mondo Economico* since the survey for the second semester of 1954. They have been checked for consistency with the percentages of answers falling in each interval for each question contained in the questionnaires. These percentages have also been used to reconstruct, by means of a trial and error procedure, the figures for the returned questionnaires relating to the first four surveys missing from the *Mondo Economico* files. See also Footnote 24.

Initial examination of these data immediately reveals two occasions of substantial revision in the number of questionnaires sent out by *Mondo Economico* – in the early and late seventies. Until the first semester of 1971 between 750 and 1,000 questionnaires were dispatched, 250 to 300 of them being returned; since the second semester of 1971 the number of dispatched questionnaires was raised to more than 1,300 and the number of those returned also increased for a few semesters (with a maximum of 408 out of 1,492 for the first semester of 1973), before falling back to the earlier levels. When the second series of inquiries began (second semester of 1978), the number of mailed questionnaires was further increased, again with only a minor and transitory rise in answers.

At least two explanations can be advanced to justify the fact that a permanent increase in answers has not taken place: first, the new members of the panel were in general unwilling to participate, so that only the questionnaires filled by those participating from the beginning continued to be returned; and second, the rise in the number of dispatched questionnaires coincided with a gradual reduction in the number of answers of long-time panel members who continued to participate only nominally and who then ceased to provide answers at some point. It is this latter indication which seems to account best for the results following the first major change, that is, if one expects that after twenty years many of the "qualified agents" might have reached the age of retirement. The increase in the number of dispatches, and therefore of panel participants, was then made very timely, anticipating what could have been a natural decline of the answers in terms both of their number and their quality. On the other hand, the former explanation is plausible enough for the change that occurred at the start of the second series of surveys, given also the fact that the questionnaire became more difficult to complete.[19]

As regards the distribution of questionnaires *mailed* to the four categories of panel members, the production sector has received on average about 45 percent (passing from 47 percent to 42 percent between 1952 and 1966, coming back gradually to 47 percent in the following years with some peaks of about 50 percent at the first major change in the number of dispatched questionnaires, and staying at about 53 percent after the start of the second series of surveys in 1978); the finance sector has been sent about 20 percent (with maximum oscillations of about 3 points above and below); the number of questionnaires mailed to the commerce sector has, on the other hand, fallen over the years from about 25 percent to about 15 percent; and experts have received between 10 percent and 15 percent.

[19]Further details on the second series of answers are given in Section 1.6. See also Section 1.7 for a brief description of the third survey series and a summary of the results of a special preparatory questionnaire on the identity of panel participants sent out in September 1980.

The number of answers *returned* to *Mondo Economico*, as indicated earlier, has presented less variation than that of the dispatched questionnaires; over the whole sample, it has been on average 280 with a standard deviation of 41, a maximum of 408 in the first semester of 1973, and a minimum of 173 in the first semester of 1954. Also the percentages of returned questionnaires present considerably less variability than those of the dispatched ones, suggesting that the latter might contain some noise not included in the former.[20] Besides, one can observe that while the percentage of questionnaires returned from the commerce sector is always larger than that of those dispatched to that sector, the opposite seems true for the finance sector; furthermore, while the production sector tends to present a percentage of return generally smaller in the first years and larger in the last years than the percentage out of the total of dispatched questionnaires, an opposite trend is evident for those interviewees identified as experts. These observations indicate as well that certain direction biases which *Mondo Economico* incurred (willingly or not) when changing the panel (mainly the two occasions in which it was substantially increased) have not been reflected in the answers.

1.5. *The First Series of Mondo Economico Surveys (2nd Semester 1952 to 2nd Semester 1977)*

Until the second semester of 1977 the questionnaire employed by *Mondo Economico* for the semiannual surveys on expectations remained practically unchanged, both as regards the objects of the inquiries and the way the questions were posed. The former included five demand variables (percentage changes in real terms over the next six months) and three general price indices (also percentage changes over the next six months). While there were questions on wholesale prices since the first survey (for the second semester of 1952), results for the other two price indices are available from the second semester of 1956 only.[21]

---

[20] It might have been the case that, on the two occasions in which major changes in the panel took place, new participants were just added to the mailing list without a careful consideration of their qualifications; on these occasions mainly the number of individuals in the production and experts categories were substantially increased.

[21] Examining the first reports published by *Mondo Economico* in the early fifties, it would appear from the references made therein that a question on "retail" prices had also been asked (even if the official statistics on consumer prices only started in 1954, various indices on retail prices for a number of goods and a cost of living index were being published since many years). There is however no trace in *Mondo Economico* files of the answers to this possible question and only with the survey for the second semester of 1956 did answers to questions on the consumer price index and the cost of living index start to be collected and published. With the survey for

For each variable the interviewee was asked to choose the interval which he judged had the highest probability of including the actual rate of change over the next semester with respect to the previous one. The pre-selected answers and the intervals corresponding to them (always published with a statement emphasizing that the interviewee was required to give a quantitative, even if not exact answer) were for the price questions[22] the following:

"up a lot"	(5% or more)
"up a little"	(between 2% and 4%)
"no change"	(between −1% and 1%)
"down a little"	(between −4% and −2%)
"down a lot"	(−5% or less)
"don't know"	

Two observations can be made at this point: first, the fact that the pre-selected intervals were symmetric, in the sense of equally allowing for answers of positive and negative sign, was clearly due to the non-inflationary situation of when the surveys were started (and to the fact that there were actual instances of reduction in the general level of prices); and second, the finite limits of the two open intervals (±5 percent on a semiannual basis) were judged sufficiently large in absolute terms to encompass most of the possible answers concerning the rate of change of prices.

---

the second semester of 1977 the question on the cost of living index, which was giving results similar to those of the one on the consumer price index, was suppressed.

[22]Up to the 10th survey (for the first semester of 1957) the intervals were slightly different, in the sense that they were contiguous. The three middle intervals were in fact "between 2% and 5%", "between −2% and 2%" and "between −5% and −2%", respectively. For the survey for the second semester of 1977, partially to cope with the high inflation conditions, the intervals for the *consumer* price index were changed to the following:

"up a lot"	(8% or more)
"up a little"	(between 4% and 7%)
"no change"	(between −1% and 3%)
"down a little"	(−2% or less)
"don't know"	

Only the intervals referring to the questions on the price levels are considered here, since this work is concerned with inflation expectations only. For the first series of surveys the intervals for the demand questions have been different than those for the price questions. The main difference consisted in they being wider, so that from the answers to these questions estimates of the rates of change expected *on average* by the respondents to the surveys less precise than those for the price indices considered in the next chapters can be obtained.

Besides the questions on demand and price variables, the interviewees were also asked to disclose, even if only qualitatively, their anticipations on the stock exchange market and, if they deemed it appropriate, to express in writing their opinions on the current economic situation, briefly stating their reasons. These opinions and reasons were also used by the *Mondo Economico* staff to prepare their after-survey reports and some of them, in complete or abridged form, were actually published; they constitute a useful reference, for certain peculiar periods, for what the anticipations expressed by respondents were founded on.

As stated earlier, four categories[23] of informed and qualified persons make up this panel. For the first series of surveys, however, only the total answers were published for each interval as percentages, without decimals and summing to 100. The breakdown by categories, however, has been kept by *Mondo Economico*, even if always in percentage form, generally with one decimal. Given the absolute number of total answers for each category, reported in Table D.3, it has been possible to reconstruct[24] the actual number of answers falling in each interval for each category of respondents; these data are useful, on the one hand, to increase the precision of the estimates obtained in Chapter 2 and, on the other, to compute goodness of fit statistics for particular distributions interpolating the percentage frequencies, also considered in Chapter 2.

Tables D.4 through D.6 of the Data Appendix, for wholesale prices, and Tables D.7 through D.9, for consumer prices, report for the "total", the "production", and the "other" respondents the breakdown of these answers

---

[23]As can be seen from Table D.3 the answers of economic experts were collected only starting with the second survey.

[24] This has been done multiplying the percentage figures by the total number of answers, made available by *Mondo Economico* since the second survey of 1954, and rounding the obtained figures to the nearest integer. A check was also performed summing the answers of the four categories, computing the percentages for the "new" total figures and comparing them with those published by *Mondo Economico*. It was found that for the first four surveys for which data on the number of answers *were* available (starting with the fifth survey, that for the second semester of 1954), these data overestimated (in any case by not much) the actual figures on which the percentages were computed, very likely because they included "late arrivals". The total number of answers was then accordingly reduced for these surveys so to coincide with that on which the actual percentages were computed (and these are the ones appearing in Table D.3). For the first four surveys for which data on total numbers of answers *were not* kept by *Mondo Economico*, a trial and error procedure was adopted, as mentioned in Footnote 18. It was so discovered that for the first two surveys the total "don't know" answers (the only published ones) were larger than those obtained summing the "don't know" answers of the four categories. A possible reason for this result might be that a number of questionnaires which were returned unanswered were not allocated among the four categories but were rightly included among the "don't know" answers at the total level (a policy followed afterwards also at the single category level). To reconcile the categorical answers with the total ones, the figures for the total "don't know" answers presented in Table D.4 for these two surveys have been appropriately modified so as to coincide with the sum of answers at the detailed level. This has no consequence for estimates of the average expected rates and of the standard deviations considered in the next chapter, according to the methodology there followed.

over the six classes (including "don't know"), up to the second semester of 1977. The "other" respondents' answers are comprised of the answers of the "finance", "commerce", and "experts" respondents.

The analysis here has been conducted not only with regard to the total but also to the two large subgroups of interviewees, the *more homogeneous* one composed of people working in the industrial sector ("production") and the *less homogeneous but of approximately equal size* one composed of people working in the other three sectors ("other"). A comparison of the results obtained with respect to these separate subsamples is valuable for the purposes of both locating general biases in the sample as a whole and analyzing the dispersion of information, the forecasting accuracy, and the formation mechanisms of the expectations of two rather different groups of persons (whose only common characteristic is that *Mondo Economico* has considered them as good representatives of the "informed and qualified individuals" who operate in the business world).

From the details of Tables D.4 through D.9, a few remarks can be made with respect to the two observations put forward at the beginning of this chapter.[25] The symmetry of the pre-selected intervals was probably an appropriate choice for the fifties; afterwards, however, a negligible number of answers fell in the intervals containing expectations of large reductions (over 5 percent on a semiannual basis) of the general price level. Similarly, while the bottom limit for the upper open-ended class appeared reasonable enough for the fifties and the sixties, it was clearly too low with regard to the inflationary conditions which followed the 1973 oil crisis. More desirable would have been to make this change in the questionnaires somewhat before 1978, when it actually took place along with the other changes that are discussed below.

1.6. The Second Series of Mondo Economico Surveys (1st Semester 1978 to 2nd Semester 1980)

The motivation for embarking on a new series of surveys at the end of 1977[26] was provided by the observation, discussed in the previous section,

[25]A further comment might be made with respect to the number of answers falling in the "don't know" class. Even if more details are contained in Section 2.2, one can already notice that after having reached peaks of about 10 percent of the total answers during the fifties pos sibly because the survey was then still new and the respondents were not used to reveal (maybe not even to form!) their expectations, and also because there was not yet a very discernible upward trend in prices—this kind of answers fell during the sixties and the seventies to negligible figures, amounting, for wholesale prices, to percentages of the total answers between 0 and 2 percent (with an exception of 3 percent of the second semester of 1964), and, for the consumer prices, to percentages between 3 and 5 percent (with exceptions of 6 percent for the second semesters of 1968 and 1970).

[26]*Mondo Economico* decided to introduce the changes discussed in this chaper after a number of meetings with Vittorio Conti, of the Research Department of the Banca Commer-

that the high inflationary conditions which characterized the Italian economy after 1973 had rendered the questionnaire ineffective. Other factors were also taken into account, and the following changes took place beginning with the fifty-second survey, that of the first semester of 1978:

(a) The horizon of the surveys was doubled, so as to cover a whole year. The questions continued to investigate semiannual rates of change in the same demand and price variables considered in the first series of surveys, but the anticipated changes were no longer limited to the first semester after the survey; now they were also relative to a semester beyond.

(b) A new qualitative question,[27] was introduced concerning expected appreciation or depreciation of the Italian currency with respect to those of "the other industrialized nations".

(c) The width of the intervals for answering questions on the demand variables was reduced considerably: their number was increased to 8 for aggregate demand and 10 for its components (including the "don't know" class).

(d) The intervals for the price questions were augmented. The upper class remained open, but a finite bottom limit of 11 percent on a semiannual basis was established. For the two price indices the pre-selected intervals then became:[28]

"up very very much"   (11% or more)
"up very much"   (between 8% and 10%)
"up a lot"   (between 5% and 7%)
"up a little"   (between 2% and 4%)
"no change"   (between −1% and 1%)
"down a little"   (between −4% and −2%)
"down a lot"   (−5% or less)
"don't know"

Two intervals were then added, for changes in prices, to the ones considered in the first series of surveys. Apparently, it was felt that, unless

---

ciale Italiana, and the present writer. Changes in the panel were also introduced, as discussed in Section 1.4, mainly increasing the number of individuals to whom the questionnaires were forwarded.

[27] Pre-selected quantitative intervals were in fact not attached to the proposed qualitative answers (four for the first survey and six afterwards). It was considered, in fact, that respondents might find it rather difficult to compute percentage changes of the exchange rate with respect to an average – not better identified – basket of currencies.

[28] For consumer prices, the two bottom intervals were lumped together under the heading: "down" (−2% or less).

the country was going to be trapped in an unfortunate hyper-inflation state, the open interval had a sufficiently high bottom limit so that answers falling in it would not constitute a significant problem.[29] The doubling of the horizon was an important innovation for two reasons: the ability to measure longer term expectations and, since the questions referred to two non-overlapping semesters (where the second for a survey would become the first for the next one), the possibility to study the process of revisions of expectations[30] and to test for their consistency, a further necessary condition of rational expectations besides the more commonly tested efficiency condition.

Tables D.10 through D.12 and D.13 through D.15 contain the results of this second series of surveys, for wholesale and consumer prices, respectively, and for the first and second semester following the date in which the surveys took place.

It might be observed that the number of answers falling in the upper open-ended intervals, while never being extremely large, reached in certain situations peaks of 15 percent for wholesale and 22 percent for consumer prices. The presence of an upper open-ended class, therefore, still constituted an obstacle for an accurate measurement of the mean and other moments of the distribution of expectations over the participants to the panel of *Mondo Economico*. The above figures, however, do not lead to problems comparable to those inherent to the first series of surveys after 1972. A solution was found when the questionnaire for the third series of surveys was designed. This will be briefly discussed in the next section.

1.7. The Third Series of Mondo Economico Surveys (from 1st Quarter 1981)

Starting with the first survey of 1981 several substantial changes have been introduced.[31] These changes, which were preceded by a careful analysis of the identity of the participants in the panel, amounted to the following:

(a) A revision in the frequency of the surveys so that they are now conducted every three months (March, June, September, and December).

---

[29] Obvious space constraints on the questionnaire were also a limit to further expansion of intervals.

[30] This "revision" refers to the changes in the rates of inflation for a given future period expected at two different moments in time. A well-known theoretical example of such revisions is given by the "error learning" principle introduced by Meiselman (1962) in the literature on the term structure of interest rates.

[31] These changes were carefully studied in a series of meetings between the staff of *Mondo Economico*, Vittorio Conti for the Banca Commerciale Italiana, and the present writer for the Banca d'Italia.

(b) A consequent revision of the time span to which expectations should refer.

(c) The introduction of new questions and the revision of old ones.

(d) Necessary revisions in the width of the intervals (for questions on quarterly changes) and the opportunity for the interviewee to give a precise answer if his anticipated rate of change were to fall in an open-ended class.[32]

(e) A revision in the panel, subsequent to the above mentioned analysis on the identity of its participants, which was conducted in September 1980.

The availability of quarterly information on expectations is an important adition to general statistical information, and it should prove particularly fruitful when this body of data is used for the analysis of behavioral phenomena involving short-term expectations. In order, however, to maintain continuity with respect to the previous two series of surveys, questions, for aggregate demand and the two price indices, inquiring of the expected changes for the semester following the date of the survey and the next (formally asking for semiannual rates of change) were to be continued in June and December of each year. The main innovation for these questions, therefore, was to ask the interviewees whose answers would fall in an open interval to produce an exact figure, so that the open class problem would be solved without arbitrary assumptions.

Besides these semiannual questions, panel participants are now asked to answer questions referring to changes in the first and in the second quarter following the survey date. They are explicitly asked for a quarterly rate of change, and the questions refer to the same demand and price variables of the two preceding series of surveys. Given that these answers now concern quarterly changes, the width of the pre-selected intervals has been reduced by one-half with respect to that of the intervals for the semiannual surveys.

A question has been added on the lending rate of interest (measured by the "prime rate") for which exact forecasts of the average level are requested for both the two quarters following the survey date. The question on the rate of exchange has also been modified; while it still asks only for qualitative answers ("strong depreciation", "mild depreciation", "no change", "mild appreciation", "strong appreciation", "don't know"), it has been split into two questions: the first considers the rate of exchange of the Italian lira with respect to the U.S. dollar, and the second with respect to an average of the other EEC currencies.

Finally, the inquiry conducted in September 1980 has allowed a revision of the mailing list, resulting in the following. The persons to whom the

---

[32]Also the qualitative statements ("up very much", "up a lot", etc.) which were attached to each pre-selected quantitative interval were suppressed; the upper interval for the semi-annual questions on prices, which used to be during the second series of surveys "11% or more" was replaced by the statement "if over 11% state how much".

TABLE 1.1

RESULTS OF THE SPECIAL 1980 SURVEY ON THE IDENTITY
OF THE MONDO ECONOMICO PANEL

	Production	Finance	Commerce	Experts	Total
Period of time belonging to the panel					
- less than 5 years	50.5	47.1	29.0	71.8	52.9
- 5 to 10 years	32.8	38.2	32.3	11.3	27.6
- more than 10 years	16.7	14.7	38.7	16.9	19.5
	100.0	100.0	100.0	100.0	100.0
Participation to the panel					
- regular answer	63.8	66.7	58.3	53.4	60.7
- irregular answer	36.2	33.3	41.7	46.6	39.3
	100.0	100.0	100.0	100.0	100.0
Form of answer					
- individual	69.3	68.1	41.3	83.9	69.2
- with associates	30.7	31.9	58.7	16.1	30.8
	100.0	100.0	100.0	100.0	100.0
Reading of Mondo Economico					
- usual	78.5	87.5	86.9	85.7	83.1
- unusual	21.5	12.5	13.1	14.3	16.9
	100.0	100.0	100.0	100.0	100.0
Age					
- under 30	1.0	1.4	---	1.6	1.1
- 30 to 45	22.6	13.7	6.2	56.4	28.1
- 45 to 55	33.3	27.4	39.9	20.6	29.4
- over 55	43.1	57.5	56.9	21.4	41.4
	100.0	100.0	100.0	100.0	100.0

questionnaires had been sent, received a special questionnaire, asking for general identity answers (some of which are summarized in Table 1.1).[33] Specific comments on the survey, mainly with respect to the opportunity of moving the frequency from six to three months were requested. The interviewees were also asked to return the questionnaire unanswered, if they wished not to be a part of the survey, so that they could be dropped from the mailing list.

[33]Among other characteristics which are self-evident in Table 1.1, one is worth emphasizing, that is the fact that more than one-half of the respondents were participating to the panel since less than 5 years. It is therefore confirmed what has been said in Section 1.4, that is, gradual changes in the actual participation to the panel have occurred thanks to the timely modifications in the mailing list (especially in the early and in the late seventies), with sufficient increases in its length which have gradually compensated for the natural self-exclusion of older participants. Only with this special inquiry the latter have been singled out, so that it has been possible to skim efficiently the list of participants.

TABLE 1.2

DIFFERENCES BETWEEN THE LAST SURVEY OF THE SECOND SERIES
AND THE FIRST SURVEY OF THE THIRD SERIES OF MONDO ECONOMICO
OPINION POLLS

	Survey for		
	2nd Semester 1980		1st Quarter 1981
	(Percentage of)		
	Dispatched Questionnaires	Returned Questionnaires	Dispatched Questionnaires
Categories			
Production	53.9	48.8	47.5
Finance	16.3	17.5	19.0
Commerce	13.5	14.8	14.2
Experts	16.3	18.9	19.3
	100.0	100.0	100.0

Of 1,850 dispatched questionnaires, 59 came back simply because of wrong addresses or unknown addressees, 174 were returned blank, 417 were compiled, and 1,200 never came back; it can be observed that this composition reflects rather closely the one of Tables D.2 and D.3. The 1,200 who did not answer were then contacted, if possible, by telephone, and 47 more persons indicated willingness to participate in the panel.

This special inquiry, then allowed for a cleaning of the mailing list and a better knowledge of the panel participants. Although it reduced considerably the total number of persons in the panel, new participants were added to the revised mailing list, each one checked and chosen on the basis of sector of activity, age, territorial and other characteristics. The present panel is thus composed of about 600 persons, the difference in its composition with respect to the last survey of the second series being shown in Table 1.2.

As a final point it should be mentioned that 90.7 percent of the respondents indicated that the proposed change in the frequency of the surveys was an appropriate innovation.

1.8. General Remarks and Comparison with Other Surveys on Inflation Expectations

One cannot speak of an "expected rate of inflation" without defining at least three aspects. First one must decide who are the *economic agents* whose expectations will be studied. Naturally, different people have different expectations and this difference is not only dependent on the "economic" area to which certain agents belong (consumers and producers, traders and entrepreneurs, etc.) but also may exist within homogeneous categories. Second, one must define the *period* to which the expectations refer. Third, the *type of price index* must also be established.

Finally, two further points must be made here:

(a) The same persons may hold uncertain probabilistic expectations; in this case it must be made clear whether the inflation rate expected by a person means the expected value or some other synthetical measure of the subjective distribution of the probabilities as seen by that person.
(b) Assuming that the inflation rate (given the index and period) expected by an individual is either a precise value or a measure of central tendency of his subjective probability function, it must be made clear whether the general term "expected inflation rate" is meant as an *aggregate estimate*, such as the arithmetic average of individual expectations, or as something else (such as some other measure of central tendency, that is, median or mode).

In the present work the estimates presented refer to two indices (consumer and wholesale prices); expectations are those of "informed" economic agents (to be specific, businessmen in production, commerce, the banking and financial world, and economic experts); the period to which the expectations refer is six months; and finally, series reported in the next chapter and utilized throughout this work should be interpreted as rates of change of prices expected on average by these economic agents. In other words, the estimates of Chapter 2 will summarize the various individual expectations, without neglecting the fact that these persons have different expectations and that it is therefore important to consider their dispersion around the aggregate synthetical index which constitutes "the" expected rate of inflation.

One important characteristic of *Mondo Economico* surveys is their quantitative nature. As observed in the preceding sections the respondents' answers have to fall into one of a set of pre-selected intervals. Only the limits of the open-ended classes are unknown. This constitutes a substantial difference with respect to qualitative surveys of the kind Carlson and Parkin (1975) have considered. As it will be shown in the next chapter, many difficulties arise in the latter case when transforming the answers to these surveys into quantitative measures of inflation expectations. If instead of asking the respondents to choose among a number of pre-selected intervals, they were asked to provide precise forecasts, one would have not only quantitative surveys but also quantitative answers out of which it would be very easy to calculate average, standard deviation, etc. This is the case of Livingston's surveys and since 1977 those of the SRC of the University of Michigan.[34] Against obvious advantages such as the simplicity of the processing of answers and the removal of the problem of open-ended intervals, there are, however, in this case some drawbacks as well. The most evident is that, very likely, economic agents are not prepared to provide precise answers concerning their expectations. In particular, their probabilistic nature is neglected. Pre-selected intervals – possibly with the solution to the open intervals problem adopted for the third series of *Mondo Economico* surveys – can facilitate the collection of answers on individual expectations.[35] It is likely that one could obtain more interesting information from surveys which requested the respondents to add to exact anticipations of future values of the relevant variables an evaluation of the odds they would give to their estimates. It might be of interest to examine, for a number of "pilot" surveys, how the interviewees would react to this kind of questions. The risk is, of course, that many respondents might feel that they are asked to provide too many and too detailed answers so that the number of returned questionnaires could turn out to be insufficient.

---

[34] Between 1948 and 1966 the quarterly SRC surveys were, as it has been already observed, strictly qualitative. Between 1966 and 1977 the quantitative answers were coded in intervals similar to those of the *Mondo Economico* questionnaires. On seven occasions, between 1973 and 1977, the SRC sample was divided randomly in two parts. To the first half the standard closed-end question (containing a number of hints) was asked; the consumers who were in the second half of the sample were instead requested to provide a precise answer (if they expected prices to increase) and no suggested values or ranges of response were advanced to them. Different results, in terms of the distribution of answers, were obtained and the distribution from the open-end questions was judged by the SRC researchers (see Juster and Comment (1978)) to be more convincing than that of the answers to the closed-end questions. The former question was then introduced permanently in the questionnaire starting with the survey conducted in the third quarter of 1977. The question became then similar to that of Livingston's surveys. However, it still referred to expected percentage *changes* of consumer prices, while Livingston has always asked for expectations of price *levels*.

[35] As observed, between the second quarter of 1966 and the second quarter of 1977 also the answers to the SRC surveys were coded in contiguous intervals similar to those of *Mondo Economico* questionnaires. In the latter case, however, the intervals are pre-selected and respondents only have to choose the one which they expect will contain next semester inflation rate. In the former case, the respondents gave instead a precise answer and all the answers were then coded by the SRC in contiguous intervals. The suggestions contained in the questions strongly influenced the respondents and the answers tended to concentrate about the suggested values. When the answers were grouped in the intervals set *ex post* by the SRC, their distribution continued, however, to present an irregular pattern. This led to the change introduced in 1977 and discussed in Footnotes 13 and 34. An accurate linkage between the two series of answers to the SRC surveys has been produced by Juster and Comment (1978), who have also considered and advanced solutions to the problem of adjusting the data prior to 1966 to make them consistent with the quantitative data available since then.

CHAPTER 2

THE MEASUREMENT OF INFLATION EXPECTATIONS

2.1. The Measurement of the Expected Rate of Inflation from Survey Data: General Remarks and the Case of Qualitative Surveys

As we have seen in the preceding chapter, existing direct information on individual expectations is available under a wide spectrum of survey characteristics. The unifying link among these survey data is likely only that of its relation to anticipations of the rate of change (or of the level) of a number of variables of interest. These data generally take the form of frequencies, from the distribution among the respondents to the surveys, of central tendency measures of their individual subjective probability distributions on (transformations of) the given variables.

The objective most researchers have pursued has been to estimate, on the assumption that the individual answers concern a given location parameter of each person's subjective distribution, the first one or two moments of the distribution of these parameters among the respondents. A further necessary assumption has been made concerning the shape of the latter distribution. Given these often implicit hypotheses, the final results of the measurement process have been time series of the average expected level or rate of change of the variable of interest and, when possible, of the dispersion of the individual expectations around this estimate of a central tendency measure of their distribution. These estimates have then been used to analyze different mechanisms of expectation formation, to test for accuracy and unbiasedness, to verify specific macroeconomic propositions.

Most of the time this is the only practical way to make use of these data; even in those cases where precise individual answers are available (the Livingston data, for example), hypotheses should be made as to how the answers relate to the individual subjective distributions. Likely, the only improvement in the use of the data would be toward the minimization of aggregation problems.[1]

Where it is possible, however, an effort should be made to determine the nature of the dependence of the "final product" – which is generally a much used statistical time series – on the assumptions used to derive it. Generic explicit or implicit assumptions such as "normality" of distributions or

---

[1] For an interesting recent attempt in this direction, see Figlewski and Wachtel (1981).

"constant dispersion" of individual parameters over time have simply too much effect on certain variables in some instances for them to be accepted without question.

This chapter will be concerned primarily with extracting information of macroeconomic relevance – to be used in the following chapters – out of the answers on inflation expectations of the *Mondo Economico* questionnaires of informed and qualified Italian businessmen.[2] As stated earlier, these answers are available in the form of frequencies for pre-selected quantitative intervals, the main problem being that of open-ended class difficulties. The measurement of the "average expected rate of inflation" and of its standard deviation will be considered in the following sections. Here the problem will be introduced and the difficulties which characterize a large number of available surveys on price expectations will be outlined. These are surveys which have received wide attention[3] and from which widely used measures of inflation expectations have been obtained.[4]

[2] The returned questionnaires have been kept in their entirety since 1979. It will then be possible in the future to perform cross-section analyses of the answers to different questions by the individual respondents.

[3] These surveys include the Gallup poll on consumer price expectations in the United Kingdom examined by Carlson and Parkin (1975), and Smith (1982); the monthly EEC surveys on enterprise expectations for a number of relevant variables as well as assessments of current conditions (conducted by national institutes such as IFO-Institute für Wirtschaftsforschung in Germany, INSEE in France and ISCO in Italy, on a uniform basis since the early sixties and since the mid seventies also collected in the United Kingdom): expectations on selling prices have been examined for Germany by Knöbl (1974) and for Germany, France and Italy by Praet (1981), while demand and price expectations for Italy have been used by Conti (1975) and Carlucci (1982) respectively, and output and price expectations have been considered by Batchelor (1981, 1982) for a number of European countries; the ACMA/Bank of New South Wales survey analyzed by Danes (1975) for price expectations of Australian manufacturing firms and by Hall (1980); the price and cost expectations data collected in the United Kingdom by the Confederation of British Industry, discussed by Parkin, Sumner and Ward (1976), Smith (1978), Tompkinson and Common (1981) and Pesaran (1983); the selling price expectations of the New Zealand Institute of Economic Research Quarterly Survey of Business Opinion considered by Hall and King (1976); the data on consumer price expectations coming from the SRC of the University of Michigan and examined in their *qualitative* form (the only one available until 1966) by Shuford (1970), De Menil (1974), De Menil and Bhalla (1975) and Juster (1974). A qualitative survey on consumer expectations is also conducted three times a year in the EEC by national institutes since 1972. The question on price expectations is also of a qualitative nature but it concerns *changes* in the rate of inflation and has more than three possible answers. It has been recently examined by Papadia and Basano (1981) and Papadia (1982).

[4] A method of analysis of the answers to surveys of this kind which differs from that of obtaining aggregate synthetic measures of the expected rate of inflation and then examining their properties and effects, has been followed by Koenig, Nerlove and Oudiz (1981); it consists in testing log-linear probability models of the relationship between expectations and realizations or expectations and past forecasting errors, directly utilizing the original answers to the questionnaires. This is a very interesting and accurate approach to the problem even if it has obvious limitations, which are a direct consequence of the limited quantitative content of this kind of surveys. It has to be emphasized, however, that the reservation advanced in the text

In the present case, answers are available for a question such as "Do you expect prices to increase, remain constant or decrease over the next three months?"[5] The answers to this type of survey fall in each period t, into four classes with the following percentage frequencies:

P_{1t} in "up"

P_{2t} in "same"

P_{3t} in "down"

P_{4t} in "don't know"

with

$$\sum_{i=1}^{4} P_{it} = 1.$$

Carlson and Parkin will be followed in the outline of a possible procedure to obtain the "final results":[6]

(a) Assume that at time t each person has a subjective probability distribution of the percentage change of prices, y, expected for the following period; this subjective probability distribution $f_t(y)$ may vary among persons and in time.

(b) Assume the existence of an interval of price changes sufficiently close to zero for the "same" (no change) class to be chosen by the interviewees.[7]

---

concerns mainly the questions on price expectations, while very useful seem to be those on deviations of certain variables from the levels which are considered to be "normal" by the enterprises participating to these inquiries and those on production plans. A further interesting way of relating anticipations and realizations for this kind of data, making use of probit and logit analysis, is that suggested by Dramais and Waelbroeck (1979). Another elaborate method for obtaining estimates of the aggregate expected rate of inflation has been proposed by Fishe and Lahiri (1981); it is, however, dependent on the joint estimation of a model of formation of these expectations. Very recently Pesaran (1983) has come up with an interesting method which can be used in the case of those surveys which not only ask for the expectations of future price changes but also for the assessments of actual past changes.

[5] In certain surveys, as it is the case for the question on selling prices of the monthly EEC inquiries, the published answers are weighted by sales or value added ratios.

[6] This method is most often associated with the names of Carlson and Parkin (1975) but it was independently worked out by Shuford (1970), De Menil (1974), Juster (1974) and Knöbl (1974). A first detailed formulation, together with other interesting results, is however to be found in Theil (1952) who carefully analyzed the results of the IFO-Institute monthly surveys (the so-called "Munich Business Test Method" for which see Anderson (1952)).

[7] This interval was called by Theil "indifference interval"; its existence is justified by the fact that the variable of interest is the rate of change of a price index constructed from a "bundle" of goods, some prices of which may fall, other rise and other again remain stable. Alternatively, its existence may be justified by identifying it with what experimental psychologists call the "difference limen", i.e., "the increment in physical stimulus necessary to produce a just noticeable difference in sensation" (Osgood (1953), quoted in Carlson and Parkin (1975, p. 126)).

At time t this interval falls between $-\delta_t$ and $+\delta_t$, and hence the answers forecasting stability of price, P_{2t}, will correspond to expectations concerning y that fall within the interval $\pm\delta_t$.

(c) Suppose that each individual replies on the basis of a "fair bet", that is, if x is the median (at time t) of $f(y)$, defined as

$$\Pr(y < x) = \int_{-\infty}^{x} f(y)\,\mathrm{d}y = \tfrac{1}{2},$$

the interviewee will reply:

"up" if $x \geq \delta_t$,
"same" if $-\delta_t < x < \delta_t$,
"down" if $x \leq \delta_t$.

(d) Considering now the total of answers, the (*average*) expected rate of inflation may be defined as the average of the medians of individual subjective distributions of possible rates of inflation in the next period. In other words, one looks at the distribution for all individuals, $g(x)$, defined from the values of x expected in period t for the next period.[8] Assuming that δ_t is common to all individuals, one can easily deduce for each period the average (μ) and the standard deviation (σ) of the rates of inflation expected by each person from the percentages obtained for the answers different from the "don't know" ones,

$$F_i = P_i/(1 - P_4), \qquad i = 1, 2, 3.[9]$$

[8]Alternatively one could start from here, as do Shuford, Knöbl, Juster and De Menil, and assume that each individual forecasts a precise value of y for the following period, so that $y = x$ and the expected rate of inflation is defined as the mean of the distribution $g(y)$ among the values of y forecast by the interviewees at time t for the subsequent period. Actually, the assumption that individual answers refer to medians rather than means could cause some difficulties for the test of rational expectations propositions, in the case of skew probability distributions (since the expected value of the medians is not the median of the expected values, as it holds instead for the means). In any event the relation between subjective and "objective" expectations is rather complex, and it is difficult to argue that in a "rational expectations" world the two have to coincide; as a matter of fact this is instead very likely a rash proposition (see for example the recent paper by Swamy, Barth and Tinsley (1982)).

[9]This implies that the entire "don't know" category is neglected. In such a case one could first assume that those who did not express any view about the future rate of inflation did so because they were not able to locate a measure of central tendency in their subjective probability distributions because, for example, of very large second moments. The second assumption would then be that, had they had more precision in their prior beliefs so to express a definite view, their answers would have fallen in the three other classes in the same proportions of the answers of those who expressed a positive reaction. This hypothesis, even if questionable, is probably to be preferred to the one followed by Carlson and Parkin, which is discussed at greater length in the next section.

(e) One can then write

$$F_{1t} = \Pr(x \geq \delta_t) = \int_{\delta_t}^{\infty} g(x)\,dx = \int_{z_{1t}}^{\infty} h(z)\,dz = 1 - H(z_{1t}), \qquad (2.1)$$

$$F_{3t} = \Pr(x \leq -\delta_t) = \int_{-\infty}^{-\delta_t} g(x)\,dx = \int_{-\infty}^{z_{2t}} h(z)\,dz = H(z_{2t}), \qquad (2.2)$$

where

$$z_t = (x_t - \mu_t)/\sigma_t, \qquad (2.3)$$

$H(z_t)$ being the cumulative distribution of z_t and $h(z_t)$ its density function. Then

$$z_t = z_{1t} \quad \text{when} \quad x_t = \delta_t, \qquad (2.4)$$

$$z_t = z_{2t} \quad \text{when} \quad x_t = -\delta_t, \qquad (2.5)$$

so that from (2.3),

$$z_{1t} = (\delta_t - \mu_t)/\sigma_t, \qquad (2.6)$$

$$z_{2t} = (-\delta_t - \mu_t)/\sigma_t, \qquad (2.7)$$

and these equations can be solved for μ_t and σ_t to obtain for the survey for period t,

$$\mu_t = -\delta_t(z_{1t} + z_{2t})/(z_{1t} - z_{2t}), \qquad (2.8)$$

$$\sigma_t = 2\delta_t/(z_{1t} - z_{2t}). \qquad (2.9)$$

In order to calculate μ_t and σ_t it is necessary to make at least two more assumptions concerning (1) the distribution of x_t, and hence of z_t; and (2) the value of the parameter δ_t (in this case, a scale factor as can be seen from (2.8) and (2.9)).

One extremely simple hypothesis concerning the distribution of x_t (and hence also z_t) is the normal distribution. This in effect is the only hypothesis adopted so far,[10] especially because of its simplicity and the availability of tables, which are of considerable help in numerical calculations. Given this

---

[10] Only very simple distributions can be used which can be identified by two points in the cumulative distribution space. For a brief comparison between the normal and the uniform distributions see the Appendix at the end of this chapter. A log-normal distribution has been recently used by Wachtel (1977a) not for the rate of inflation x_t (which can also be negative), but for its somewhat arbitrary transformation $100 + x_t$. In a very recent paper, Batchelor (1981) also takes into account skewness characteristics; see, however, the comments, also contained in the Appendix to this chapter, to his interpretation of Carlson and Parkin's approach.

hypothesis, one can compute immediately the values of z_{1t} and z_{2t} (the abscissa values for the frequencies $1 - F_{1t}$ and F_{3t} of the cumulative standard normal distribution).

In addition, all authors assume that δ_t is constant in time[11] (as well as the same among persons). In some cases, it is arbitrarily fixed *a priori*; Carlson and Parkin use instead an estimate

$$\hat{\delta} = -\left(\sum_{t=1}^{T} p_t \right) \bigg/ \sum_{t=1}^{T} [(z_{1t} + z_{2t})/(z_{1t} - z_{2t})], \qquad (2.10)$$

which is a consequence of arbitrarily assuming $\sum \mu_t = \sum p_t$ $(t = 1, \ldots, T)$, where μ_t is the (average) expected rate of inflation defined in (2.8), p_t is the actual rate, and T is the total of information (surveys) available.

There are many problems associated with such a procedure of obtaining quantitative measures out of this kind of qualitative surveys. Those which appear to be the most relevant are the following:

(a) The assumption of a normal distribution of the rates of change of prices expected by the individual interviewees, even if it is naturally only made for the sake of simplicity, is highly questionable. There are strong implicit constraints on the shape of this distribution, such as its symmetry and the implicit allowance for the expected rate of inflation not to possess finite upper and lower bounds (as a matter of fact, the rate of inflation has an obvious lower bound at -100 percent; the $-\infty$ left limit might not, however, be thought to be "very distant" from -100 percent, but it *certainly* is very distant from what a reasonable person would naturally think the maximum percentage reduction in the general level of prices to be!).

(b) Because the first and second moments of a normal distribution are highly nonlinear transformations of the original frequencies, even moderate sampling fluctuations in certain regions of the frequency space can produce substantial and disturbing movements in the estimates of these moments.

(c) These difficulties are aggravated by the fact that, for these surveys, only two points are available to identify the cumulative distributions. This

---

[11] This hypothesis was justified for instance by Carlson and Parkin (1975, p. 129) – apart from motives such as "simplicity" and "lack of evidence to the contrary" – on the grounds of what is known in experimental psychology as Weber's law, i.e., the observed fact that "the fraction by which a stimulus must be increased (or decreased) in order for the change to be just perceptible is constant regardless of the absolute magnitude of the stimulus" (Osgood (1953, p. 75)).

amounts to exact identification in the case of a normal. On one hand, then, sampling variations appear to have larger importance; on the other, the symmetry constraint and the ignorance of the fact that actual frequencies are effectively equal to zero over wide regions of the abscissa line have a strong potential for producing biased estimates. Observe that if more points were available, even if for all these reasons the normal might be on certain occasions a poor interpolating function of the actual frequency distribution, it could have sufficient flexibility at least to produce estimates of the first moment not too distant from the "true" parameters (that is, the estimate of σ_t could be quite far away from the true standard deviation – for all the reasons mentioned – even if the estimates of μ_t fell in a "sufficiently small" neighborhood of μ_t).

(d) The value hypothesized for δ_t plays an important role in the arbitrariness of μ_t. There is no reason why it should be 1, 1.5, or 2 percent, etc. Nor is it clear why it should be constant among all persons and, in particular, over time.[12] Different values of δ, if assumed constant over time, simply shift the whole series up or down; the use of a "wrong" δ can then produce an upward or downward biased estimate of the (average) expected rate of inflation. The procedure adopted by Carlson and Parkin (equation (2.10)) to compute δ also seems highly arbitrary. Behind (2.10) lies the assumption that throughout the period considered the expected inflation rates are on average equal to the actual rates. But this is a *very* bold hypothesis of unbiasedness of expectations, one that should be tested rather than assumed *a priori*. Moreover, the existence of even a few "spurious" cases of inflation that are seriously under- or over-estimated might wholly vitiate the estimate of δ obtained by the above procedure.

Some of this points, along with others, are further investigated in the Appendix to this chapter. By way of conclusion to these introductory remarks, however, it should be pointed out that it is not so much the methodology here outlined that should be subject to criticism; there is indeed a problem not only with the method but with the very nature of these qualitative surveys. Surveys of this kind cannot but offer, in the case of phenomena such as price changes, very limited and superficial information, especially for periods of high rates of inflation. One should thus use with caution the estimates of expected price changes obtained from these surveys

---

[12] It would be much different (and probably better) if the limits were given *a priori* in the questionnaire so that the "no change" class would reflect the view of the interviewer, who is after all interested in evaluating these answers according to his own criteria; much arbitrariness in the procedure outlined in the text would then disappear and one could try to use some outside information (collected for example from "pilot surveys") to choose a proper interpolating distribution.

along the lines of the procedure explained above. The large number of published articles (and the equally large number of unpublished but circulating papers) in which use is made of these data,[13] leads one to suspect that not enough attention is being paid to these problems. They also indicate a high demand for direct estimates of anticipated inflation. It is hoped, therefore, that the present effort will take into account a superior and more revealing series of surveys of individual expectations and will produce a significant contribution to the set of estimates of expected changes in prices.

2.2. The Measurement of the Expected Rate of Inflation: Quantitative Surveys and the Mondo Economico Data

Two kinds of "quantitative" surveys can be considered. In the first, precise estimates of individual expected rates of inflation are collected. One might think, as in the case treated in the foregoing section, that these are estimates of the medians of the subjective probability distributions. More likely, though, when a person is asked to reveal a central tendency measure from his subjective distribution, another measure, most probably the mode, would be picked up. In the second kind of surveys, the interviewees are only asked to indicate a pre-selected interval which they deem the more likely to contain the future rate of inflation. These surveys are therefore similar to those considered in the previous section, but *not being of a qualitative nature* it is not necessary to make arbitrary assumptions on the limits of the "no change" class (the indifference interval). Furthermore, when more than only one interval is available for the "up" answers, the surveys are more suited to treat the case of inflation expectations and fewer problems in choosing an interpolating distribution occur. In this case also it is reasonable to assume that an answer will fall in each interval when it will contain the median of

---

[13] Besides the works by Shuford (1970), Carlson and Parkin (1975), Knöbl (1974), Juster (1974), De Menil (1974), Danes (1975), Hall and King (1976), Parkin, Sumner and Ward (1976), Smith (1978, 1982), Praet (1981), Batchelor (1981, 1982) to which reference was made in Footnote 3, at least the following published articles, to the writer's knowledge, make extensive use of series of expected inflation measured with the technique (or variants thereof) outlined in the text: Juster and Taylor (1975), Holden and Peel (1977, 1979), Valentine (1977), Sheffrin (1978), Saunders (1978), Foster (1979), Batchelor and Sheffrin (1980), McDonald and Woodfield (1980), Mills (1981) and Severn (1983). A very critical comparison between the series obtained using this technique for the answers to a short (20 quarters) quantitative Australian survey and the actual sample means of these answers is provided by Defris and Williams (1979a).

the subjective probability distribution. In such a fashion, the fact that a precise estimate is not required is probably a virtue and not a deficiency.[14]

To the first set belong Livingston's survey and since 1977 the one by the Survey Research Center of the University of Michigan;[15] to the second, as shown in the previous chapter, the one considered throughout this work, that is, the semiannual survey by *Mondo Economico*. For the former, one can use without particular problems the individual answers to estimate the sample moments corresponding to the "population" distribution.[16] In the present consideration of the latter case, the main objective of this chapter is to obtain satisfactory estimates of the first two moments of the distribution of the expected rate of inflation among the respondents to the panel of *Mondo Economico*.[17]

To proceed in this task, two initial steps have been taken:

(a) The classes containing the individual answers (see Tables D.4 through D.15) have been transformed into continuous intervals; for example, those falling in the class "between -1% and 1%" have been assumed to cover the interval "-1.5% to 1.5%", those in the class "between 2% and 4%", the interval "1.5% to 4.5%" and so on;[18] and

(b) The answers have been standardized by excluding from the total the percentages for class *ND* ("don't know"). In this way it has been assumed

---

[14]See the discussion in Section 1.8. The request of precise forecasts from the participants to a survey should probably be accompanied by a request of revealing also the odds that each respondent would assign for his answer to be confirmed; such information could prove very useful both in aggregating individual answers and in studies which consider the effects on behavior of different degrees of subjective uncertainty.

[15]See, for the former, Turnovsky (1970) and Carlson (1977a), and, for the latter, Juster and Comment (1978); more extensive references are contained in Footnotes 10 and 13 to Chapter 1. Similar surveys, not only on prices, have been recently considered and utilized in papers by Zarnovitz (1969, 1978, 1979, 1982), Su and Su (1975), Su (1978), Pesando (1976), Hudson (1978), Defris and Williams (1979b), Williams and Defris (1980), Horne (1981), Friedman (1979a, 1980), Saunders (1980, 1981), Leonard (1982), De Leeuw and McKelvey (1981). The predictions of a private forecasting enterprise have also been considered by Jonson and Mahoney (1973) as representative of the price expectations of Australian businessmen.

[16]In certain instances it is difficult to understand what is the "parent" generation of a given sample. This is certainly the case of the survey most considered until now, that is Livingston's which is conducted over a panel of about fifty non-steady participants ("informed business economists").

[17]As it has been repeatedly observed in Chapter 1 these respondents belong to a population of businessmen (entrepreneurs, bankers, managers) and for a small percentage general economic experts.

[18]It is then implicitly assumed that being the limits of the pre-selected intervals rounded to the nearest integer, a respondent with a possible answer of, say, 1.4 percent would have chosen the class "between -1% and 1%", and one with an answer of 1.6 percent the class "between 2% and 4%".

that the distribution of these answers is equal to that of those who gave a positive reaction.

The treatment of the "don't know" answers deserves some further comment. The implicit assumption is that those who did not express an opinion did so because of the low degree of confidence in locating a first moment of their subjective distribution (that is, their second moments were very large). It has then been assumed that, had they had more precision, they would have picked up any of the possible intervals in the same proportion of those who were able to locate their central tendency measures. Carlson and Parkin (1975) followed a different route. They assumed that the "don't know" answers were of two kinds: those of the individuals "incapable of developing any view about what will happen to prices"[19] (a percentage α_t of ND_t) and those of people capable of expressing a positive reaction $(1 - \alpha_t)$ but with less than one-half of their subjective distribution lying in *any* of the possible ranges. They excluded α_t of ND_t from the total (in the case of *Mondo Economico* surveys, it is likely that none of those participating to the panel can be thought to be "incapable of developing any view about prices" so that $\alpha_t = 0$); for the percentage $(1 - \alpha_t)$ Carlson and Parkin, however, formally considered that "don't know" was an indication that x (the median of the subjective probability distribution on the future rate of inflation) was such that

$$- \delta_t < x < \delta_t \quad \text{and} \quad \Pr(- \delta_t < x < \delta_t) < \tfrac{1}{2}.$$

But one sees immediately that this actually assumes that the "no change" class was not picked up only because, due to a high level of dispersion of the subjective distribution, not "enough" of it covered the range $\pm \delta_t$. However, this is just *one* possible case; in fact, as Carlson and Parkin spelled out, a "don't know" answer would be given if less than one-half of the distribution lay in *any* possible range. To implement these steps empirically, they assumed at first $\alpha_t = \alpha$ (constant) and ran the regression

$$\text{"don't know"} = \alpha + \beta \text{ "no change"} + u_t, \tag{2.11}$$

obtaining significant positive estimates for α, β and evidence of first-order serial correlation ("evidence against our assumption of a constant α")[20] which they corrected in the usual way.

All this seems unconvincing. The only correct point with regard to this procedure is the fact that if the probability of x falling in a given interval

[19]Carlson and Parkin (1975, p. 125).
[20]Carlson and Parkin (1975, p. 125).

was less than one-half, *any* interval could have been picked up *even if* the median of the distribution lay in the "no change" class. Therefore, it is not necessarily the case that to the "no change" interval was assigned the highest probability, as it is not the case that to each interval was assigned equal probability. This is precisely the message of the low Durbin–Watson statistics which indicate "first-order serial correlation". This simply highlights the obvious misspecification present in (2.11), which should also have on the right-hand side the answers falling in the other feasible ranges as

TABLE 2.1

RESULTS OF REGRESSIONS OF "DON'T KNOW" ON "NO CHANGE" ANSWERS

Variable	Period	α	β	R^2	DW	F	T
Wholesale (total)	5202–7702	4.425 (1.814)*	.029 (1.571)	.048	.468	2.468	51
Wholesale (production)	5202–7702	2.439 (1.766)*	.035 (1.414)	.039	.164	1.723	51
Wholesale (other)	5202–7702	2.313 (2.010)*	.020 (1.313)	.034	.468	1.998	51
Wholesale (total)	5202–8002	3.650 (1.988)*	.034 (2.125)*	.076	.481	4.517*	57
Wholesale (production)	5202–8002	2.075 (1.838)*	.039 (1.880)*	.060	.619	3.535*	57
Wholesale (other)	5202–8002	1.835 (1.946)*	.025 (1.907)*	.062	.487	3.638*	57
Consumer (total)	5602–7702	8.326 (4.675)**	.069 (3.248)**	.205	.681	10.548**	43
Consumer (production)	5602–7702	3.575 (3.567)**	.093 (3.466)**	.227	.950	12.014**	43
Consumer (other)	5602–7702	4.736 (4.754)**	.050 (2.343)*	.118	.899	5.488*	43
Consumer (total)	5602–8002	6.558 (4.267)**	.084 (4.312)**	.283	.645	18.595**	49
Consumer (production)	5602–8002	2.902 (3.454)**	.106 (4.426)**	.294	.931	19.594**	49
Consumer (other)	5602–8002	3.664 (4.202)**	.066 (3.336)**	.191	.833	11.130**	49

OLS regression: "don't know" = α + β "no change" + u.

Note

Absolute values of t-statistics are reported in parentheses under each coefficient estimate.
* Significant at the .05 level (one-tail test for t-statistics).
** Significant at the .01 level (one-tail test for t-statistics).
The t and F-tests are for the hypothesis α=0, β=0; R^2 is the (unadjusted) determination coefficient; DW is the Durbin-Watson statistic; T is the number of observations.

distinct regressors, with obvious unsurmountable estimation difficulties being due to built-in collinearities.

Equation (2.11) has been estimated with the *Mondo Economico* data to see how the estimates would look. The results are reported in Table 2.1. The very low levels of the DW and R^2 statistics, the fact that for wholesale prices the estimates of β have very low t-statistics, the implausible levels of the estimates of α which exceed for a large number of cases the *total* of the actual "don't know" answers, all indicate that the present judgment about such a representation is very much supported by the data.

It is therefore possible to conclude that the strategy of subtracting all the "don't know" answers from the total before computing the percentage frequencies is the only reasonable one. This amounts to assuming that a relation between the former and the answers lying in each of the feasible ranges is a linear one with coefficients β_i ($i = 1, \ldots, n$ where n is the number of intervals) equal to the percentages of these answers out of the total *net* of the "don't know" ones. In any case, a different treatment of these answers would not produce relevant changes in the estimates considered in the next section.[21]

2.3. The (Average) Expected Rate of Inflation and the Standard Deviation of Individual Expectations: Distribution Hypotheses and Results

Having considered the problems raised by the treatment of the "don't know" answers, one can now concentrate on the more relevant question of how to obtain estimates of the expected rate of change of prices, that is, the mean and the standard deviation of the distribution of the individual expectations of the participants in the panel. It must be noticed that for the first series of surveys there are four points (corresponding to the abscissa values -4.5, -1.5, 1.5, and 4.5 percent) available to identify the cumulative frequency distribution.[22] For the second series of surveys, the points are six for the wholesale and five for the consumer price index; these correspond to abscissa values of -4.5 (for wholesales prices only), -1.5, 1.5, 4.5, 7.5 and 10.5 percent.

---

[21] See Chapter 1, Footnote 25. Preliminary estimates of a series of expected inflation (using the piecewise uniform distribution to be considered in the next section), under alternative hypotheses (such as (i) $\beta_i = \beta$ for all i and (ii) $\beta_i = 0$ for all i except k ("no change"), $\beta_k = 1$) were not very different from those considered in the text. It is interesting to observe that in his revision and extension of Carlson and Parkin's estimates, Smith (1982) treats the "don't know" answers in the same way as is done here, not having been able to find any stable relationship between these answers and the "no change" ones.

[22] For the second semester of 1977, and for the consumer price index only, there are only three points and they correspond to abscissa values of -1.5, 3.5 and 7.5 percent.

The aim is to use this information in a simple but adequate way to approximate the "real" distribution of individual expected rates with a theoretical distribution (which *would not* require many parameters, because of the scantiness of available data) and to compute the mean and the standard deviation. Two distributions will be considered: the piecewise uniform and the normal.[23]

A general formulation of the problem is the following: given the abscissa values x_i, $i = 1, 2, \ldots, n$, and the corresponding cumulated percentage frequencies $G(x_i)$,[24] find for a given distribution function $g(x)$ the mean and standard deviation, μ and σ. One can write:

$$G(x_1) = 1 - F_1 = \int_{-\infty}^{x_1} g(x)\,dx = \int_{-\infty}^{z_1} h(z)\,dz = H(z_1),$$

$$G(x_2) = 1 - F_1 - F_2 = \int_{-\infty}^{x_2} g(x)\,dx = \int_{-\infty}^{z_2} h(z)\,dz = H(z_2),$$

$$\vdots \tag{2.12}$$

$$G(x_{n-1}) = F_{n+1} + F_n = \int_{-\infty}^{x_{n-1}} g(x)\,dx = \int_{-\infty}^{z_{n-1}} h(z)\,dz = H(z_{n-1}),$$

$$G(x_n) = F_{n+1} = \int_{-\infty}^{x_n} g(x)\,dx = \int_{-\infty}^{z_n} h(z)\,dz = H(z_n),$$

where the F_i are the percentage answers for each interval, and

$$z_i = (x_i - \mu)/\sigma, \tag{2.13}$$

$h(z)$ being the density function of the standardized variate z_i, and $H(z)$ its cumulative distribution.

2.3.1. The Piecewise Uniform Distribution

Most obvious would be to interpolate exactly the points $(G(x_i), x_i)$ and then compute the mean and standard deviation of this interpolating distribution. This can be done only if the left and right limits of this distribution

---

· [23] Preliminary estimates with a number of alternative distributions were considered (for the first set of surveys and up to the first semester of 1975) in Visco (1976); besides the normal and the piecewise uniform, a linear, a piecewise linear and a uniform distribution were tried. While the analysis conducted in this section is dependent to some extent on the results obtained in that paper (which considered only the total of answers), there is a major difference in the method of deriving the normal estimates, as it will be pointed out in what follows.

[24] Notice that there are n known ordinate values of the cumulative distribution, one less of the known areas of the density function; obviously a time subscript, referring to each survey, should accompany these values: it has been deleted for simplicity.

are known, that is, those values x_0 and x_{n+1} such that $G(x_{n+1}) = 0$ and $G(x_0) = 1$, which amounts to having solved the problem posed by those answers falling in the open-ended intervals. Thus:

$$G(x) = \begin{cases} \alpha_i + \beta_i x, & i = 1, 2, \ldots, n+1 & \text{for} \quad x_i \leq x \leq x_{i-1}, \\ 1 & & \text{for} \quad x_0 < x, \\ 0 & & \text{for} \quad x < x_{n+1}, \end{cases} \tag{2.14}$$

The density function would then be

$$g(x) = \begin{cases} \beta_i & \text{for the same intervals of (2.14)}, \\ 0 & \text{elsewhere}, \end{cases} \tag{2.15}$$

and obviously

$$\begin{aligned} \beta_i &= [G(x_{i-1}) - G(x_i)]/(x_{i-1} - x_i) \\ &= F_i/(x_{i-1} - x_i), \qquad i = 1, 2, \ldots, n+1. \end{aligned} \tag{2.16}$$

It is easy to show that

$$\mu = \int_{x_{n+1}}^{x_0} x g(x) \, dx = \sum_{i=1}^{n+1} F_i w_i, \tag{2.17}$$

where

$$w_i = (x_{i-1} + x_i)/2. \tag{2.18}$$

Similarly,

$$E(x^2) = \int_{x_{n+1}}^{x_0} x^2 g(x) \, dx = \sum_{i=1}^{n+1} F_i v_i, \tag{2.19}$$

where

$$v_i = (x_{i-1}^3 - x_i^3)/3(x_{i-1} - x_i). \tag{2.20}$$

The standard deviation is then easily obtained as

$$\sigma = [E(x^2) - \mu^2]^{\frac{1}{2}}. \tag{2.21}$$

From (2.17) it is evident that the mean of the piecewise uniform distribution is just the sample weighted average of the mid-points of the $n+1$ intervals containing the individual answers. One must allow, however, in computing the standard deviation, for the fact that there is a built-in "uncertainty" margin in such surveys, strictly connected to the size of the intervals. Equation (2.20) can in fact be rewritten as

$$v_i = w_i^2 + (x_{i-1} - x_i)^2/12 = w_i^2 + \sigma_i^2, \tag{2.22}$$

where σ_i^2 is the variance of the uniform distribution defined over the range $x_{i-1} - x_i$. Even if all answers lay in a single interval, say the ith, σ^2 would be non-zero, as one can see from

$$\sigma^2 = \sum_{i=1}^{n+1} F_i\left(w_i^2 + \sigma_i^2 - \mu^2\right) = w_i^2 + \sigma_i^2 - w_i^2 = \sigma_i^2. \tag{2.23}$$

The estimate of the variance of the piecewise uniform distribution will therefore have an upward bias between 0 and $\sigma_i^2 = 0.75$ percent for all i.[25]

Two solutions have been considered for the open-ended intervals problem. In both cases the lower interval has been considered to be of length equal to the closed ones, so that $x_{n+1} = -7.5$ percent.[26] If the same assumption for the upper open-ended interval is made, the estimates of the mean and the standard deviation of the individual expected rates of change of prices could be obtained from (2.17) and (2.21): in such a case, of course, $x_0 = 7.5$ percent for the first series of surveys[27] and $x_0 = 13.5$ percent for the second. Such estimates will be called *PU*. It is obvious that while *PU* could provide a satisfactory approximation for those cases in which F_1 was relatively small (that is, when few answers lay in the upper open-ended interval), it would probably do poorly when F_1 is large. This is so for a number of surveys of the first series: specifically, between 1973 and 1977, a large percentage of respondents anticipated price increases higher than 4.5 percent per semester. This problem seems instead negligible for the post-1977 surveys: the bias due to the assumption that the open-ended upper interval was of length equal to the closed intervals would probably be very small.

One way to obviate such a difficulty is depicted in Figure 2.1. Under the assumption of a piecewise uniform distribution, the uniform for the second

[25] Since $x_{i-1} - x_i = 3$ percent (except for the special case of the second semester of 1977 for the consumer prices, and under the assumption of equal length for the open and the closed intervals)

[26] For consumer prices, $x_{n+1} = -5.5$ for the second semester of 1977 and $x_{n+1} = -4.5$ percent for the second series of surveys. The equal length assumption appears to be the easiest and more reasonable one to make for the lower open-ended interval. In any event, since a negligible percentage of people anticipates possible future reductions of the general level of consumer prices for the second series of surveys, an alternative assumption would not produce results sensibly different than those obtained here.

[27] For consumer prices, $x_0 = 11.5$ percent for the second semester of 1977.

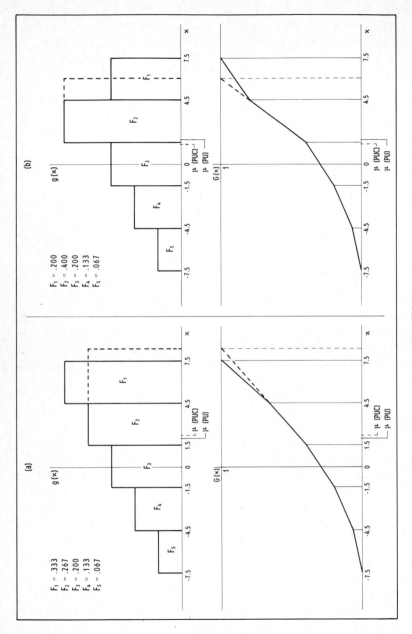

FIGURE 2.1
EXAMPLES OF THE PIECEWISE UNIFORM DISTRIBUTION AND
CORRECTION FOR THE UPPER OPEN-ENDED INTERVAL

interval has been assumed to hold also for the first, that is, the upper open-ended interval has been closed by extrapolating the segment which joins the points $(G(x_2), x_2)$ and $(G(x_1), x_1)$. In the example of Figure 2.1 (part (a)), one would obtain $x_0 = 8.24$ rather than 7.5 percent so that it would be $\mu = 2.125$ rather than 2 percent. In general,

$$x_0 = x_1 + (x_1 - x_2) F_1 / F_2, \tag{2.24}$$

and (2.17) and (2.19) would be computed accordingly. With this correction to the PU estimates, series for μ and σ for the two price indices and three groups considered (that is, "total", "production", and "other") were obtained and were labeled as PUC.

It should be noted in this regard that if the area F_1 is smaller than the area F_2 (that is, fewer people forecast large increases than moderate ones) the PUC correction produces a lower mean than in the first case (that is, $\mu(PUC) < \mu(PU)$ as one can see from part (b) of Figure 2.1), although the difference is generally small. Instead, in the case where F_1 is larger than F_2, the PU mean might underestimate considerably more than the PUC one the actual rate of inflation. The correction just proposed would appear to be an arbitrary procedure, and to some extent it is. Consider, however, that if the distribution of answers in the F_1 interval was really uniform, then the average obtained with PUC when $F_1 > F_i$ (all $i = 2, \ldots, n + 1$) would be the *highest* value obtained if F_1 retains its characteristics of being the *modal* category of the answers to the survey. This would appear to exclude the search for a limit to the upper open-ended interval larger than that given by (2.24).

Since there could be a possible downward bias, however, when $F_1 < F_2$, another set of piecewise uniform estimates, PUM, for which the PUC correction is applied only when $F_1 > F_2$, has been considered.

Before examining the results, an alternative hypothesis for the interpolating distribution will be considered.

2.3.2. The Normal Distribution

Under the assumption that the distribution of the individual (median) expected rates of inflation is normal, the set of equations (2.12) can be used to obtain for given F_i ($i = 1, 2, \ldots, n + 1$) and x_i ($i = 1, 2, \ldots, n$), the corresponding z_i values of the standard normal distribution. If the sample were exactly interpolated by a normal distribution, (2.13) would hold exactly for every i. That is, the system of equations

$$x = \mu + \sigma z, \tag{2.25}$$

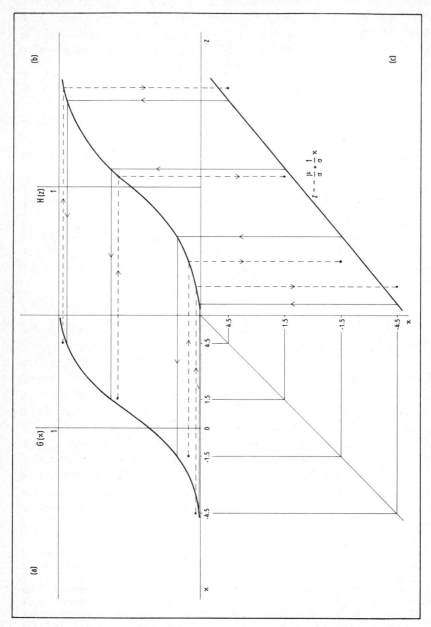

FIGURE 2.2

EXAMPLE OF THE ESTIMATION OF THE PARAMETERS OF THE
INTERPOLATING NORMAL DISTRIBUTION

where $z = (z_1, z_2, \ldots, z_n)'$ and $x = (x_1, x_2, \ldots, x_n)'$, would contain, for $n > 2$, more equations than unknowns, these equations being linearly dependent. We could pick up two sets of z_i and x_i at a time and end up always with the same values of μ and σ. Even if the true distribution was normal, however, sample variability would produce a system of equations such as

$$z = \alpha + \beta x + u, \tag{2.26}$$

where u is a random error. Equation (2.26) has been estimated by ordinary least squares, and estimates $\hat{\alpha}$ and $\hat{\beta}$ have been obtained. The mean and standard deviation of the interpolating normal distribution have therefore been obtained as $\mu = -\hat{\alpha}/\hat{\beta}$, $\sigma = 1/\hat{\beta}$.

Figure 2.2 illustrates the steps which have been followed. From the n cumulated sample frequencies $G(x_i)$ (quadrant (a)), the abscissa values of the standard normal distribution, z_i, have been computed (quadrant (b)), and they have been regressed on the x_i's (quadrant (c)); the interpolating normal distribution given in quadrant (a), which has mean $\mu = -\hat{\alpha}/\hat{\beta}$ and standard deviation $\sigma = 1/\hat{\beta}$, obviously corresponds to the fitted values of the z_i (again passing via the standard normal of quadrant (b)).

A number of points should be considered:

(a) While the estimates of α and β are best linear unbiased ones, the computed μ and σ do not have necessarily similar properties. Indeed, only if the error term u in (2.26) were normally distributed, $\hat{\alpha}$ and $\hat{\beta}$ would be maximum likelihood estimates, carrying over their properties to the transformed values μ and σ. For u to be normal, however, the original errors in the sample frequencies (that is, the difference between the cumulated frequencies $G(x_i)$ – the four points in the quadrant (a) in the example of Figure 2.2 – and the corresponding points on the interpolating normal distribution) should be so distributed that equating these frequencies to those of the standard normal distribution, $G(x_i) = H(z_i)$, would produce *normally distributed* estimates, z_i, of the "true" standardized transformations of the x_i values! All this, obviously, is conditional on the assumption that the true interpolating distribution is normal.[28]

[28]Since the errors are related to the z_i it seemed better to perform a least squares regression on (2.26) and then obtain μ and σ as nonlinear transformation of the estimates, rather than to run a regression such as $x = \mu + \sigma z + u$ which would be linear in μ and σ but for which there would be no clear interpretation for the residual u. This is the equation estimated in Visco (1976), where the six different possible sets of μ and σ (for the first series of surveys and the total of answers) were also computed and compared, which could be obtained from the solution of the six systems of two equations in two unknowns which can be derived from (2.25). In that paper, all zero entries were arbitrarily approximated by a small figure so that the computation of six sets of the four components of z was always possible. A further set of estimates was also computed, on the assumption that the distribution was only normal around the average μ and

(b) In the present data, there are a few anomalous cases of a non-zero entry F_i followed by a zero entry F_{i-1}; these cases have been solved by grouping F_i with the nearest non-zero entry with an obvious reduction in the number of intervals, and therefore of points in the cumulative distribution space on which to perform the interpolation.[29]

(c) In the first series of answers, for a number of cases only three non-zero F_i values were available; in these cases, the situation has two equations in two unknowns for system (2.25) which can then be uniquely solved in terms of μ and σ; this has been done, with the obvious consequences that, first, the information that some F_i were actually zero has not been used,[30] and second, no test on the goodness-of-fit of the normal interpolations has been performed.[31]

(d) In the first series of answers, in a few cases only two non-zero F_i values were available.[32] This case is discussed at length in the Appendix to this chapter with reference to its more common occurrence in the qualitative surveys discussed in Section 2.1. An *ad hoc* procedure has been followed, obtaining first an estimate of σ by linear interpolation of the values for the preceding and the following surveys and then solving (2.25) – which consists in such a case of only one equation in μ and σ, only one component of z being known – to obtain the corresponding estimate of μ.

The possibility that – in accordance with the results outlined in Section 2.1 and in the Appendix to this chapter with reference to the much more troublesome case of qualitative surveys – sampling errors could be amplified, for F_i very small, by the non-linearity of the normal transformation was worrisome. One further set of estimates was therefore computed grouping

---

that this average lay into the same class of the median of the distribution (with some correction for those cases when the median fell in the upper class). These estimates were therefore obtained with a method similar to that used by Modigliani and Sauerlander (1955) to estimate the expected change in sales from data collected by the economic magazine Fortune. In Visco (1976) it was found that they were always very close to those obtained from regressions of x on z.

[29] As one can see from Tables D.4–D.15 generally 1 and at most 2 answers lay in the i th interval followed by 0 in the $(i-1)$ th; this occurred in the first series of surveys only for consumer prices ("total": 6602, 7302; "production": 6602, 7701; "other": 7302) and only for wholesale prices in the second series ("total" and "production": 7902; "other": 7802; all for the second semester after the date of the survey).

[30] Obviously there is a loss of information in all those cases in which one or more F_i is equal to 0 so that the number of z_i that is possible to compute is accordingly reduced and the regression estimates of (2.26) are based on less than n points.

[31] See Section 2.4.

[32] This occurred only in the second semester of 1973 for consumer prices (for both categories of respondents and therefore for the total) and only for the "other" respondents in the second semester of 1968 (for wholesale prices).

the "small" F_i with the neighboring ones: the rule followed was to have, for each interval, at least four answers for the total, and three for each of the two subgroups considered in this work. The set of estimates so obtained was then labeled *NR2*, *NR1* being the estimates obtained from the original data.[33]

2.3.3. The Statistical Results

The results for the four sets (*PUC, PUM, NR1, NR2*) of estimates of the average expected rates of change of prices and of the standard deviations are presented for the wholesale price index in Tables D.16 through D.18 of the Data Appendix (for the "total", "production", and "other" respondents); they are computed as semiannual percentage rates, refer to the semester following the date of the survey and cover the 57 semesters between the second of 1952 and the second of 1980. Similarly, Tables D.19 through D.21 contain the results for the consumer price index, for a total of 49 semesters (between the second of 1956 and the second of 1980).

In this section the differences between these various estimates will be considered. The analysis, while limited to the results for the total of respondents, leads to similar conclusions as those for the two categories into which the total has been divided; a detailed comparison between the estimates of the "production" and those of the "other" respondents will be the object of Section 2.5.

In Figures 2.3 and 2.4 the *PUC* and *PUM* estimates and the *NR1* and *NR2* estimates are plotted together for the wholesale and the consumer price index, respectively. It is immediately evident that the *PUC* and *PUM* estimates of the average expected price changes are practically coincident also when the upper open-ended class correction of the *PUC* series is not applied to the *PUM* ones: in fact, the excess of the latter over the former is

---

[33] The grouping of a "small" F_i with a larger neighboring area, which has been done to obtain the *NR2* estimates, does not reflect the belief that the information contained in F_i was of poor quality: as a matter of fact, the very important notion that F_i was sometimes almost empty has been utilized in the first set of estimates (*NR1*) and has been sacrificed in the second, in order to minimize the problems due, in the case of a normal, to possibly large effects of, even small, sample variability. However, in a few cases a "small" F_i has *not* been added to the next frequency because one would have obtained less than three areas in the density space, and correspondingly less than two ordinates of the cumulative distribution, so that it would not have been possible to estimate μ and σ even by an exact solution of (2.25). Similarly, the second set of estimates has been kept equal to the first also for the cases considered in points (c) and (d). The same has been done in a few cases (wholesale prices: "other", 6102, 6201, 6701) when the *NR2* estimates would have been strongly at odds with the data, due to the anomalous effects of the grouping (i.e., the neglect of some information) for particular values of the original frequencies.

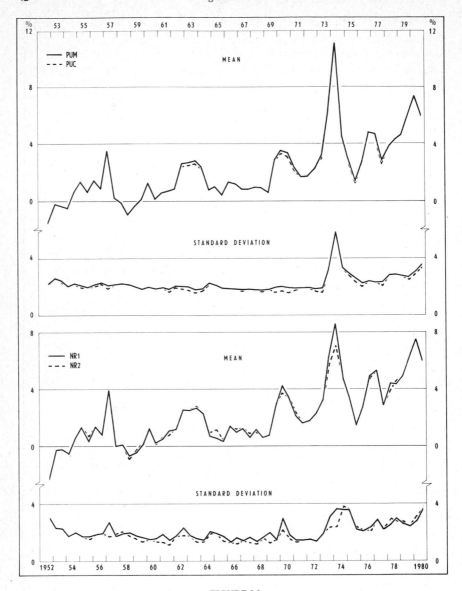

FIGURE 2.3

EXPECTED RATE OF CHANGE OF WHOLESALE PRICES: ESTIMATES FROM THE
PIECEWISE UNIFORM AND THE NORMAL DISTRIBUTION HYPOTHESES

Note: Semiannual percentage changes for the total of respondents to the Mondo Economico
opinion poll.

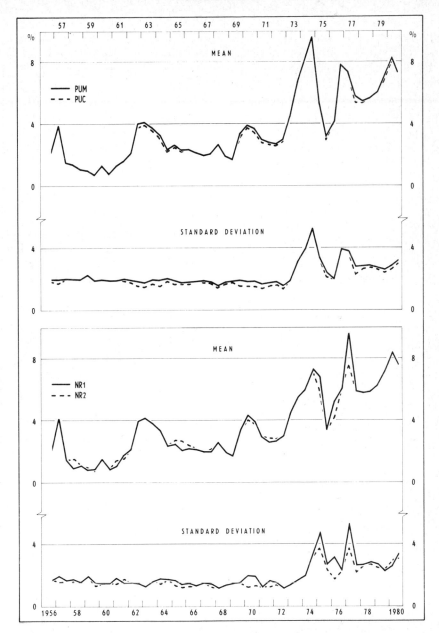

FIGURE 2.4
EXPECTED RATE OF CHANGE OF CONSUMER PRICES: ESTIMATES FROM THE
PIECEWISE UNIFORM AND THE NORMAL DISTRIBUTION HYPOTHESES

Note: Semiannual percentage changes for the total of respondents to the Mondo
Economico opinion poll.

in these instances absolutely negligible. Also the *NR1* and *NR2* estimates seem to be rather similar. On two occasions (1st semester 1974 for wholesale and 1st semester 1977 for consumer prices), however, positive differences of 1.5 and 2 percentage points – of the former over the latter occur, exemplifying the amplification by the normal transformation of even very small differences in observed frequencies.

Larger are the differences between the estimates of the standard deviations, especially so for the two normal interpolations. Here again, up to the second series of surveys, the *NR1* estimates are much more irregular than the *NR2* ones, reflecting once more the problems that small changes in certain areas of the frequency distribution can have on the overall results. Even so, however, it appears that all these estimates tell a very similar story. One observes that the correlation coefficients among the means are all very large: for the whole sample the minimum value of these correlations is equal to 0.962 for wholesale prices (*NR2* vs. *PUC*) and to 0.948 for consumer prices (*NR1* vs. *PUC*). The correlation among the standard errors is less pronounced – as one would have expected even before computing these

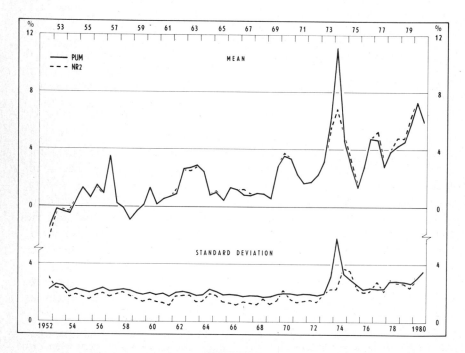

FIGURE 2.5

COMPARISON BETWEEN ESTIMATES OF THE MEAN AND THE STANDARD DEVIATION OF EXPECTED WHOLESALE PRICE CHANGES FROM THE PIECEWISE UNIFORM AND THE NORMAL DISTRIBUTION HYPOTHESES

Note: Semiannual percentage changes for the total of respondents to the Mondo Economico opinion poll.

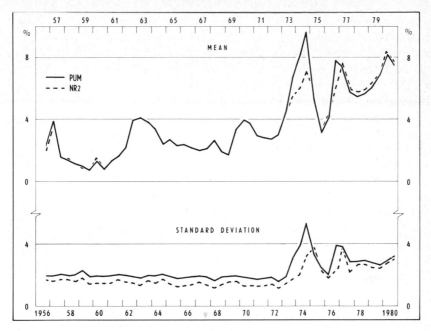

FIGURE 2.6
COMPARISON BETWEEN ESTIMATES OF THE MEAN AND THE STANDARD DEVIATION
OF EXPECTED CONSUMER PRICE CHANGES FROM THE PIECEWISE UNIFORM
AND THE NORMAL DISTRIBUTION HYPOTHESES

Note: Semiannual percentage changes for the total of respondents to the Mondo Economico opinion poll.

estimates. The minimum value here is equal to 0.704 (*NR1* vs. *PUC*) and 0.645 (*NR2* vs. *PUC*), for consumer and wholesale prices. The main differences arise when the least information is available, that is, for the period between the first oil crisis and the beginning of the second series of surveys. It appears that the main differences between the normal and the piecewise uniform estimates are those for *NR1* for consumer prices and for *NR2* for wholesale prices. In both cases, however, substantial differences concern only the standard deviations.

These results emerge neatly from Figures 2.5 and 2.6: what is impressive is the similarity – with *very few* exceptions[34] – between the piecewise

---

[34] These exceptions are: for wholesale prices only that of the first semester of 1974, where the correction adopted for the upper open-ended interval in the case of the piecewise uniform distribution substantially raises the estimate of μ (still well below, however, the actual rate of inflation in that semester!); for consumer prices in the first and the second semester of 1974 and in the second semester of 1976, again for the above mentioned reason and also, for the last case, for the unreliability of the normal estimates when almost all answers are concentrated in two intervals only.

uniform and the normal estimates of the average expected rates of inflation. On average, while basically replicating the same movements, the standard deviation of the piecewise uniform is higher than that coming from the normal distribution. A possible reason for this difference is the fact that, in computing the former estimates, a lower bound has been added to the weighted sample variance (σ_i^2 in (2.23)).

2.4. Tests of the Normal Hypothesis and of the Piecewise Uniform Correction, and the Selection of "Best" Estimates of the Means and Standard Deviations of Individual Expected Rates of Inflation

Before discussion of the problem of selecting the set of estimates of μ and σ on which to continue this study of survey measured inflation expectations, brief comments will be made on some tentative but suggestive results on, first, the goodness-of-fit of the normal interpolations, and, second, the reasonableness of the *PUC* correction for the upper open-ended intervals.

2.4.1. Goodness-of-Fit Tests for the Normal Distribution Assumption

Given the measures for μ and σ obtained from the least squares estimates of the system of equations (2.26), the next step is that of evaluating how good is a normal distribution for interpolating the observed frequencies. In many cases, however, for the first series of surveys, only three frequencies are available: in those cases they exactly identify – as for the qualitative surveys considered in Section 2.1 and in Appendix 2.1 – any distribution completely characterized by only two moments, such as is the normal. As a consequence, it is not possible in these instances to proceed to any test of goodness-of-fit. Furthermore, since in any case only between four and five (exceptionally six) intervals are available, to which correspond non-zero observed frequencies, one should limit the analysis to those cases for which the theoretical frequencies are not too small. Given the fairly adequate size of the samples considered here (only the total of answers will be examined), one can reasonably apply, when possible, a standard chi-square goodness-of-fit test. The statistic that has been computed for such a test is

$$CHI2 = (NT - ND) \sum_{i=1}^{n+1} (F_i - \hat{F}_i)^2 / \hat{F}_i, \qquad (2.27)$$

where NT and ND are, respectively, the total and the "don't know" answers to the survey, F_i are the $n+1$ *observed percentage frequencies* (they sum to one and correspond to the n points in the cumulative distribution space which have been used for the interpolation), and $\hat{F}_i$ are the *theoretical percentage frequencies* obtained from the estimates of μ and σ.

The statistic given in (2.27) has been computed for all the surveys for which the *minimum* $\hat{F}_i$ (*MF*) was greater or equal than 4.[35] The results for the wholesale and consumer price indices are presented in Tables 2.2 and 2.3, respectively. As one can see, in many occasions it was not possible to compute *CHI2*; in particular this was the case for the very large increases in prices which followed the first oil crisis. Out of 63 observations for the wholesale and 55 for the consumer prices (including the expectations of two semesters ahead available for the second series of surveys), the test was performed only fourteen (24.5%) and nine (16.4%) times respectively, for the *NR1* estimates, and twenty-seven (47.7%) and twenty (36.4%) times respectively, for the *NR2* ones.

The results, even if limited, do not favor the normal hypothesis. This is especially so for the most recent period of high inflation when more intervals are available to perform the test. It is likely that in these cases the distribution of answers tends to be skewed to the right so that a symmetric distribution such as the normal could fail to provide an accurate interpolation. It should be remembered that the normal has long tails, making the approximation to the standard deviation especially poor – a finding supported by the results of Section 2.3.3 which show large similarities between estimates of the mean using piecewise uniform and normal approximations, and rather large differences between the estimates of the variance.

Table 2.4 summarizes the results. Even in the most favorable situations ($MF \geq 4$), the *CHI2* statistics exceed the critical values (at the 1 percent significance level) 21 and 30 percent of the time for the *NR1* and *NR2* estimates for wholesale prices, and 67 and 65 percent of the time for consumer prices. The limits of these tests notwithstanding, the results here

---

[35]As it has been observed in Section 2.3.2, two sets of normal estimates have been obtained: the first, from the interpolation of *all* observed frequencies, no matter how small; the second, of the frequencies grouped so that in each interval lay at least four answers. It is possible that in both cases, even when more than three non-zero frequencies were available, the resulting *theoretical* frequencies would be smaller than what a reasonable *rule of thumb* would suggest as adequate for a chi-square goodness-of-fit test (say 5, as most textbooks in mathematical statistics recommend). The test has therefore been performed only when the minimum theoretical frequency was found to be larger than 4 and the results have been separately examined for both cases when it was larger than 4 and larger than 5, respectively, without substantial differences. The fact that on many occasions the *CHI2* statistics have not been computed does not necessarily imply that the normal was a poor interpolator of the "true" distribution, but only that there was not enough information in the sample (as it was the case when only three areas were available) to proceed to such a test – besides the information necessary for the interpolation.

TABLE 2.2

GOODNESS OF FIT TESTS FOR THE NORMALITY HYPOTHESIS:
WHOLESALE PRICES

	NR1				NR2		
Semester	MF	CHI2	DF	Semester	MF	CHI2	DF
5301	4	2.51	2	5301	4	2.51	2
5302	4	5.94(*)	2	5302	4	5.94(*)	2
5501	7	5E-5	1	5402	4	.47	1
5601	11	2.64	1	5501	7	5E-5	1
6001	4	.25	1	5601	11	2.64	1
6201	7	25.00(+)	1	5602	6	1.01	1
7102	5	2.41	1	5801	4	2.27	1
7201	5	.01	1	5802	6	.39	1
7601	7	5.64(**)	1	6001	4	.25	1
7702	6	2.39	1	6201	7	25.00(+)	1
7902	8	23.45(+)	2	6402	6	5.81(**)	1
8001	4	5.06(*)	2	7102	5	2.41	1
8002	5	17.49(+)	3	7201	5	.01	1
7802(^)	4	5.86(*)	2	7402	10	.99	1
				7502	26	1.85	1
				7601	7	5.64(**)	1
				7702	6	2.39	1
				7802	4	25.95(+)	2
				7901	5	14.66(+)	2
				7902	8	23.45(+)	2
				8001	42	.16	1
				8002	5	17.49(+)	3
				7802(^)	4	5.86(*)	2
				7902(^)	4	15.89(+)	2
				8001(^)	9	17.29(+)	2
				8002(^)	8	20.23(+)	2
				8101(^)	17	1.54	2

Note

The semesters are those for which expectations are formed at the end of the previous se-
mester, and for (^) at the end of two semesters before.
MF   =   minimum frequency of the theoretical distribution;
CHI2 =   chi-square statistic;
DF   =   degrees of freedom.
(*)   Significant at the .10 level.
(**)   Significant at the .05 level.
(+)   Significant at the .01 level.

obtained call for a general rejection of the normality hypothesis.[36] When a
sufficient number of observations from the third series of *Mondo Economico*
surveys becomes available, it will be possible to base this conclusion on
firmer grounds. It will then also be possible to obtain results on a larger
number of surveys on which *CHI2* statistics could be calculated (or similar

[36] Even if in all the surveys for which it was not possible to compute *CHI2* statistics the
normal hypothesis *was not* rejected, the results of Tables 2.2 and 2.3 would imply an overall
rejection at the 1 percent significance level 4.8 and 12.7 percent of the times (*NR1* and *NR2*
with $MF \geq 4$) and 4.8 and 9.5 percent of the times (*NR1* and *NR2* with $MF \geq 5$) for wholesale
prices; for consumer prices the rates of rejection would be even higher, that is 10.9 and 23.6
percent (*NR1* and *NR2* with $MF \geq 4$) and 7.3 and 21.8 percent (*NR1* and *NR2* with
$MF \geq 5$). A rejection of the normal distribution hypothesis – even if somewhat less substantial
than in our case – was also supported by the findings of Carlson (1975) for the expectations (on
the price *levels*) of the individuals interviewed by Livingston.

TABLE 2.3

GOODNESS OF FIT TESTS FOR THE NORMALITY HYPOTHESIS:
CONSUMER PRICES

	NR1				NR2		
Semester	MF	CHI2	DF	Semester	MF	CHI2	DF
5602	4	15.62(+)	1	5602	4	15.62(+)	1
5702	9	1.08	1	5702	9	1.08	1
5802	4	2E-5	1	5809	4	2E-5	1
6001	6	7.53(+)	1	5901	6	6.82(+)	1
6102	4	4.63(**)	1	6001	6	7.53(+)	1
7801	9	28.80(+)	2	6101	4	.62	1
7802(^)	13	13.08(+)	2	7501	6	9.39(+)	1
8001(^)	4	34.25(+)	2	7502	6	3.22(*)	1
8002(^)	56	16.85(+)	2	7801	9	28.80(+)	2
				7802	14	25.69(+)	2
				7901	9	31.93(+)	2
				7902	24	35.02(+)	1
				8001	23	3.86(**)	1
				8002	7	3.16	2
				7802(^)	13	13.08(+)	2
				7901(^)	15	15.38(+)	2
				7902(^)	9	18.56(+)	2
				8001(^)	26	39.85(+)	1
				8002(^)	56	16.85(+)	2
				8101(^)	12	7.36(**)	2

Note

The semesters are those for which expectations are formed at the end of the previous se-
mester, and for (^) at the end of two semesters before.
MF = minimum frequency of the theoretical distribution;
CHI2 = chi-square statistic;
DF = degrees of freedom.
(*) = Significant at the .10 level.
(**) = Significant at the .05 level.
(+) = Significant at the .01 level.

tests could be performed), given the availability of a sufficient number of non-empty intervals; in addition, given that, in this series of surveys, the upper and lower intervals are closed by the respondents, one can then classify *completely* the individual answers and perform tests involving symmetry and kurtosis measures. Obviously, alternative hypotheses using other distributions can then be investigated.

2.4.2. A Tentative Test of the "Correction" for the Piecewise Uniform Distribution in the Case of Large Frequencies in the Upper Open-Ended Interval

The rejection of the normal distribution as an accurate interpolator for the true distribution of individual expectations does not imply that the estimates of the mean based on the normal approximation are also inaccurate. As a matter of fact, these estimates are rather close, as it has been shown in

TABLE 2.4

GOODNESS OF FIT TESTS FOR THE NORMALITY HYPOTHESIS,
WHOLESALE AND CONSUMER PRICES: SUMMARY RESULTS

	Significance Level	Number of Tests Performed (A)	Number Exceeding Critical Value (B)	(B/A)
WHOLESALE				
NR1				
MF $\geq$ 4	.10	14	7	.50
	.05	14	4	.29
	.01	14	3	.21
MF $\geq$ 5	.10	9	4	.44
	.05	9	4	.44
	.01	9	3	.33
NR2				
MF $\geq$ 4	.10	27	12	.44
	.05	27	10	.37
	.01	27	8	.30
MF $\geq$ 5	.10	19	8	.42
	.05	19	8	.42
	.01	19	6	.32
CONSUMER				
NR1				
MF $\geq$ 4	.10	9	7	.78
	.05	9	7	.78
	.01	9	6	.67
MF $\geq$ 5	.10	5	4	.80
	.05	5	4	.80
	.01	5	4	.80
NR2				
MF $\geq$ 4	.10	20	16	.80
	.05	20	15	.75
	.01	20	13	.65
MF $\geq$ 5	.10	17	15	.88
	.05	17	14	.82
	.01	17	12	.71

Section 2.3.3, to the estimates obtained by weighting the percentage frequencies with the midpoints of each interval (that is, using a piecewise uniform distribution). The only significant differences can be found when the correction for the open-ended upper interval implies a substantial modification of the original *PU* estimates, obtained under the assumption of equal length for all possible intervals.

With the second set of surveys more information is available, that is, more classes in which the individual answers can lie. Thus, even if only for tentative and *post hoc* evidence, one might see how the correction performed to obtain the *PUC* estimates (or the *PUM* ones, if the correction is applied only when $F_1 > F_2$) would have worked in the case of the surveys taken between 1978 and 1980. In these surveys, the percentage frequencies F_4 correspond to the "1.5%–4.5%" interval; the first three classes have therefore been grouped together so that $A = F_1 + F_2 + F_3$ and $B = F_4$ in the second series of surveys correspond to F_1 and F_2 for the first. These two frequencies have been reported, for the two price indices and the three groups of individuals considered in this work, in Table 2.5. For the first series, only those surveys in which F_1 was greatest making the upper open-ended intervals a serious problem, have been selected.

TABLE 2.5

FIRST TWO PERCENTAGE FREQUENCIES IN THE SECOND SERIES OF SURVEYS,
RECLASSIFIED ACCORDING WITH THE FIRST SERIES CLASSIFICATION,
AND IN SELECTED SURVEYS OF THE FIRST SERIES

	TOTAL		PRODUCTION		OTHER	
			WHOLESALE PRICES			
	A	B	A	B	A	B
			1st series of surveys			
7302	67.86	28.57	70.63	27.78	65.58	29.22
7401	83.67	15.14	82.05	16.24	85.07	14.18
			2nd series of surveys			
7801	35.85	47.17	33.80	50.70	38.21	43.09
7802	41.34	48.94	39.05	48.52	43.75	49.38
7901	49.10	41.92	48.48	43.03	49.70	40.83
7902	70.45	27.92	68.32	30.43	72.79	25.17
8001	82.91	16.00	80.62	18.60	84.93	13.70
8002	66.55	27.24	61.70	29.79	71.14	24.83
			CONSUMER PRICES			
	A	B	A	B	A	B
			1st series of surveys			
7302	71.11	28.52	69.75	30.25	72.19	27.15
7401	76.61	22.18	77.12	22.03	76.15	22.31
7402	79.31	16.96	80.73	13.76	77.69	19.83
7501	61.04	30.31	62.39	29.36	59.84	31.15
7602	75.09	22.46	72.39	25.37	77.48	19.87
7701	73.49	24.16	73.76	24.82	73.25	23.57
			2nd series of surveys			
7801	61.80	34.83	56.64	41.26	67.74	27.42
7802	66.16	30.21	59.41	37.06	73.29	22.98
7901	73.65	24.55	70.30	28.48	76.92	20.71
7902	87.14	12.22	87.12	12.88	87.16	11.49
8001	91.97	7.66	91.41	7.81	92.47	7.53
8002	83.79	14.14	80.85	17.02	86.58	11.41

Note

A = F_1 and B = F_2 for the 1st series of surveys; A = $F_1 + F_2 + F_3$ and B = F_4 for the 2nd series of surveys.
The data for the 1st series of surveys only refer to those cases for which $F_1 > 60$.

TABLE 2.6

WHOLESALE PRICES - TEST OF THE CORRECTION FOR THE UPPER OPEN-ENDED INTERVAL
IN THE CASE OF THE PIECEWISE UNIFORM DISTRIBUTION

SEM	PUM	PU1	PU2	PUM1	PUM2	P12
			TOTAL			
7801	3.838	3.555	3.426	.926	.893	1.038
7802	4.258	3.903	3.806	.916	.894	1.025
7901	4.572	4.186	4.312	.916	.943	.971
7902	5.844	5.065	6.675	.867	1.142	.759
8001	7.342	5.455	10.655	.743	1.451	.512
8002	5.917	4.717	6.158	.797	1.041	.766
			PRODUCTION			
7801	3.782	3.528	3.359	.933	.888	1.050
7802	4.047	3.746	3.631	.925	.897	1.031
7901	4.564	4.164	4.256	.912	.933	.978
7902	5.720	5.012	6.288	.876	1.099	.797
8001	6.977	5.395	9.426	.773	1.351	.572
8002	5.489	4.489	5.481	.818	.998	.819
			OTHER			
7801	3.902	3.585	3.520	.919	.902	1.018
7802	4.481	4.069	3.994	.908	.891	1.019
7901	4.580	4.207	4.369	.919	.954	.963
7902	5.980	5.122	7.188	.857	1.202	.713
8001	7.664	5.507	12.132	.718	1.583	.454
8002	6.322	4.933	6.923	.780	1.095	.713

Note

The entries of each column refer to computations of (or related to) the mean of the
expected rates of change of wholesale prices, respectively for the total, the "produc
tion" and the "other" respondents. In particular:

PUM = piecewise uniform distribution (see text Section 2.3.1 and Tables D.16-D.18);
PU1 = piecewise uniform distribution with the answers for the 3 upper intervals
("5%-7%", "8%-10%" and "11% or more") grouped together and the mean computed
as if they lay in the interval "4.5%-7.5%";
PU2 = as PU1, but with the upper limit x_0 of the interval "4.5%-x_0" obtained with
the correction discussed in the text (as for the case of answers to the first
series of surveys);
PUM1 = PU1/PUM;
PUM2 = PU2/PUM;
P12 = PU1/PU2.

In Tables 2.6 and 2.7 the following series, for the second set of surveys,
have been computed and reported:

(1) In the first columns are the *PUM* original estimates of Tables D.16
through D.21.
(2) In the second columns are the estimates (*PU1*) that would have been
obtained from the frequencies *A* and *B* (and the other necessary to reach
unity) if the upper open-ended interval had been closed at 7.5 percent.

TABLE 2.7

CONSUMER PRICES - TEST OF THE CORRECTION FOR THE UPPER OPEN-ENDED INTERVAL
IN THE CASE OF THE PIECEWISE UNIFORM DISTRIBUTION

SEM	PUM	PU1	PU2	PUM1	PUM2	P12
			TOTAL			
7801	5.438	4.753	5.470	.874	1.006	.869
7802	5.619	4.858	6.039	.865	1.075	.804
7901	6.018	5.147	7.356	.855	1.222	.700
7902	6.868	5.595	13.609	.815	1.982	.411
8001	8.201	5.748	20.923	.701	2.551	.275
8002	7.397	5.431	11.624	.734	1.571	.467
			PRODUCTION			
7801	5.266	4.636	4.953	.880	.941	.936
7802	5.294	4.659	5.196	.880	.982	.897
7901	5.836	5.055	6.603	.866	1.131	.766
7902	6.810	5.613	13.143	.824	1.930	.427
8001	7.875	5.719	20.389	.726	2.589	.280
8002	7.213	5.340	9.888	.740	1.371	.540
			OTHER			
7801	5.637	4.887	6.381	.867	1.132	.766
7802	5.963	5.068	7.475	.850	1.254	.678
7901	6.195	5.237	8.369	.845	1.351	.626
7902	6.932	5.574	14.188	.804	2.047	.393
8001	8.486	5.774	21.409	.680	2.523	.270
8002	7.570	5.517	14.073	.729	1.859	.392

Note

The entries of each column refer to computations of (or related to) the mean of the expected rates of change of <u>consumer</u> prices, respectively for the total, the "production" and the "other" respondents. In particular:

PUM = piecewise uniform distribution (see text Section 2.3.1 and Tables D.19-D.21);

PU1 = piecewise uniform distribution with the answers for the 3 upper intervals ("5%-7%", "8%-10%" and "11% or more") grouped together and the mean computed as if they lay in the interval "4.5%-7.5%";

PU2 = as PU1, but with the upper limit x_0 of the interval "4.5%-x_0" obtained with the correction discussed in the text (as for the case of answers to the first series surveys);

PUM1 = PU1/PUM;

PUM2 = PU2/PUM;

P12 = PU1/PU2.

(3) In the third column are the estimates (*PU2*) obtained closing this interval as shown in Section 2.3.1 (they are therefore the analog of the *PUC* series).

(4) In the last three columns are the ratios *PU1/PUM*, *PU2/PUM* and *PU1/PU2*, respectively.

These tables, especially the figures reported in the fourth and fifth columns, tend to support the proposition that the correction of the upper open-ended intervals would have produced results similar to those of the

PUM estimates on the frequencies which are available since the first semester of 1978. Only for the last three surveys for the consumer price index the *PU2* estimates would have been wildly off the mark. In such cases, however, the *A* and *B* frequencies are very different from all the cases of interest that we have encountered in the first series of surveys, being much larger and much smaller, respectively, as one can see from the entries of Table 2.5. In the other three surveys, where much more similar results in terms of the frequencies have been obtained, the *PU2/PUM* ratio is very much in the neighborhood of 1. The same applies for wholesale prices: only on one occasion is this ratio somewhat larger than 1, that is, in the first semester of 1980 (1.651 for the total of answers). In this case, however, *A* and *B* are similar to those which occurred in 1974 (first semester). This might suggest the estimate for that semester to be too high, that is, the adjustment has overcorrected a possible *downward* bias. In that semester, however, Italy experienced the highest rate of increase of prices after 1947 in the wholesale index – something like 58 percent on an annual basis. Hence, even if the estimated average expected rate of inflation was too high (for about two to three points, according to the *ex post* evidence for the first semester of 1980), a forecasting error of nearly 15 percent on a semiannual basis would still exist!

In any event only for this single estimate for both the wholesale and consumer price indices the correction adopted could be – according to the evidence of Tables 2.5 through 2.7 – somewhat inaccurate. Thus, this correction still appears the most reasonable procedure for dealing with instances in which too many answers are concentrated in the upper open-ended interval in the first series of the *Mondo Economico* surveys.[37]

2.4.3. Selection of the "Best" Estimates

We have now reached the point where a choice has to be made between the four sets of estimates of μ and σ, for the two price indices and the two groups of persons considered, reported in Tables D.16 through D.21. As has been seen, the estimates of the means do not seem to differ from each other. The normal assumption, however, has not performed well in the goodness-of-fit tests of Section 2.4.1.

Without resorting too much to an *ad hoc* choice, one can compare the properties of these estimates as predictors of the actual changes in prices. This is not to say that a "minimum error of prediction" criterion is

---

[37]Results similar to those of Tables 2.6 and 2.7 have been obtained for the estimates of the standard deviation.

TABLE 2.8

WHOLESALE PRICES – PRELIMINARY TESTS OF ACCURACY: ROOT MEAN SQUARE ERRORS

PERIODS	R M S E				% R M S E			
	PUC	PUM	NR1	NR2	PUC	PUM	NR1	NR2
				TOTAL				
5202-7202	.965	.983	1.018	1.008	1.139	1.160	1.203	1.191
5202-7702	3.411	3.396	3.619	3.809	1.276	1.270	1.354	1.426
5202-8002	3.345	3.327	3.519	3.698	1.060	1.054	1.115	1.172
7301-7702	7.451	7.406	7.909	8.357	.733	.729	.778	.822
7301-8002	6.122	6.080	6.439	6.792	.675	.670	.709	.748
7801-8002	2.726	2.676	2.511	2.571	.375	.368	.346	.354
				PRODUCTION				
5202-7202	.972	.988	1.037	1.095	1.148	1.167	1.224	1.194
5202-7702	3.457	3.440	3.548	3.819	1.293	1.287	1.327	1.429
5202-8002	3.399	3.380	3.463	3.724	1.077	1.071	1.097	1.180
7301-7702	7.556	7.507	7.734	8.370	.743	.739	.761	.824
7301-8002	6.225	6.180	6.322	6.838	.686	.681	.697	.753
7801-8002	2.860	2.813	2.628	2.814	.394	.387	.362	.388
				OTHER				
5202-7202	.982	1.002	1.056	1.035	1.150	1.183	1.247	1.223
5202-7702	3.369	3.356	3.830	3.842	1.250	1.255	1.432	1.437
5202-8002	3.298	3.281	3.709	3.722	1.045	1.040	1.175	1.179
7301-7702	7.344	7.302	8.381	8.419	.723	.719	.825	.829
7301-8002	6.022	5.982	6.795	6.828	.654	.659	.749	.753
7801-8002	2.613	2.564	2.463	2.488	.350	.353	.339	.342

Note

The entries refer to the absolute and percentage root mean square errors of the predictions of the actual price changes, as measured by the average expected changes obtained under the various distribution hypothesis.

TABLE 2.9

CONSUMER PRICES – PRELIMINARY TESTS OF ACCURACY: ROOT MEAN SQUARE ERRORS

PERIODS	R M S E				% R M S E			
	PUC	PUM	NR1	NR2	PUC	PUM	NR1	NR2
TOTAL								
5602-7202	1.090	1.155	1.165	1.142	.627	.664	.670	.656
5602-7702	1.496	1.518	1.613	1.731	.467	.474	.504	.541
5602-8002	1.538	1.545	1.612	1.717	.407	.409	.426	.454
7301-7702	2.388	2.347	2.589	2.929	.298	.293	.323	.365
7301-8002	2.189	2.135	2.271	2.517	.274	.267	.284	.315
7801-8002	1.809	1.727	1.604	1.613	.228	.217	.202	.203
PRODUCTION								
5602-7202	1.114	1.177	1.192	1.179	.640	.676	.685	.678
5602-7702	1.461	1.485	1.767	1.778	.456	.464	.552	.556
5602-8002	1.534	1.542	1.770	1.786	.405	.408	.468	.472
7301-7702	2.253	2.217	2.957	3.001	.281	.276	.369	.374
7301-8002	2.154	2.104	2.581	2.627	.270	.263	.323	.329
7801-8002	1.979	1.903	1.785	1.840	.249	.239	.225	.232
OTHER								
5602-7202	.848	.843	.875	.888	.624	.660	.648	.667
5502-7702	1.156	1.175	1.143	1.258	.484	.489	.487	.555
5602-8002	1.181	1.190	1.150	1.252	.413	.415	.409	.461
7301-7702	2.174	2.104	2.029	2.480	.316	.310	.311	.376
7301-8002	1.869	1.802	1.717	2.004	.281	.274	.271	.319
7801-8002	1.362	1.299	1.196	1.211	.208	.199	.186	.186

Note

The entries refer to the absolute and percentage root mean square errors of the predictions of the actual price changes, as measured by the average expected changes obtained under the various distribution hypothesis.

necessarily the best possible one. There are, however, reasons to believe that the choice of one of these four sets of estimates which had poor forecasting properties could be viewed with suspicion, unless it is convincingly justified, something that could not be done easily.

In Tables 2.8 and 2.9, for various periods, the root mean square errors of prediction are reported (they are also expressed, for each price index, as ratios to the averages of the actual rates of change of prices over the periods of interest). Virtually identical results have been obtained using an alternative descriptive statistic such as the mean absolute error.

While the results are substantially similar for the four sets of estimates – as was to be expected – the best overall performance is given by the *PUM*

TABLE 2.10

CORRELATION MATRICES FOR THE MEANS AND THE STANDARD
DEVIATIONS OF EXPECTED CHANGE OF PRICES   (PUM AND MIX)

A.   WHOLESALE PRICES: 5202-8002

		TOTAL		PRODUCTION		OTHER		
		PUM	MIX	PUM	MIX	PUM	MIX	
TOTAL	PUM	1.	.999	.996	.995	.997	.996	
	MIX	.987	1.	.994	.996	.996	.996	
PRODUCTION	PUM	.989	.975	1.	.999	.985	.984	correlation among the means
	MIX	.975	.981	.986	1.	.985	.985	
OTHER	PUM	.994	.989	.967	.955	1.	.999	
	MIX	.982	.984	.954	.959	.990	1.	

correlation among the
standard deviations

B.   CONSUMER PRICES: 5602-8002

		TOTAL		PRODUCTION		OTHER		
		PUM	MIX	PUM	MIX	PUM	MIX	
TOTAL	PUM	1.	.999	.993	.995	.993	.994	
	MIX	.991	1.	.990	.993	.995	.996	
PRODUCTION	PUM	.973	.962	1.	.999	.976	.974	correlation among the means
	MIX	.974	.976	.910	1.	.978	.978	
OTHER	PUM	.981	.974	.994	.916	1.	.999	
	MIX	.972	.981	.901	.919	.991	1.	

correlation among the
standard deviations

estimates for wholesale prices and by the *PUC* estimates for consumer prices (the *PUM* estimates come very close). When subperiods are considered individually, however, the *PUC* have the lowest prediction errors until the end of 1972 (that is, before the high upsurge of prices in the more recent years), while for the remaining years of the first series of surveys the *PUM* are the best predictors. It seems then that a fixed limit for the upper open-ended intervals of 7.5 percent in years of moderate inflation might be too high an estimate. Surprisingly, in the second series of surveys, the normal estimates (particularly the *NR1*) appear to be slightly superior.

On this basis the study here proceeds by utilizing as measures for the expected changes in prices the *PUM* estimates and estimates obtained combining those which performed best in predicting the actual changes over the three periods considered. These have been labeled *MIX*.

From Table 2.10 it is clear that these two sets of estimates have very high correlations – particularly those of the means. The minimum correlation coefficient for the estimates of the means is that between the *PUM* estimates of the "production" group and the *MIX* estimates of the "other" group for consumer prices – equal to 0.974. The minimum correlation for the estimates of the standard deviations is instead equal to 0.901 (still between the

TABLE 2.11

CORRELATION MATRICES BETWEEN MEANS
AND STANDARD DEVIATIONS (PUM AND MIX)
TOTAL RESPONDENTS

A. WHOLESALE PRICES: 5202-8002

		mean		stand. dev.	
		PUM	MIX	PUM	MIX
mean	PUM	1	.999	.732	.671
	MIX		1	.739	.678
stand. dev.	PUM			1	.987
	MIX				1

B. CONSUMER PRICES: 5602-8002

		mean		stand. dev.	
		PUM	MIX	PUM	MIX
mean	PUM	1	.999	.834	.790
	MIX		1	.841	.800
stand. dev.	PUM			1	.991
	MIX				1

same two series). Most of the results which follow have been derived both for the *PUM* and the *MIX* estimates; they are always very similar, so that those for only one set of estimates will often be reported.

As a final point, the relation that occurs between the measures of the average expected rates of inflation and those of the standard deviations among the respondents is of interest. From Table 2.11, one sees clearly that there are indeed quite high positive correlations. A graphical display of this result is given in Figure 2.7. After 1972 increases in the rate of inflation expected on average by the respondents to the surveys are accompanied by a *larger* dispersion of their responses, accounting for *all* the correlation shown in Table 2.11. One cannot thus conclude that whenever there is an

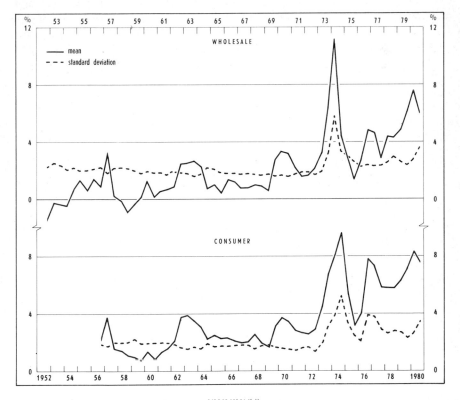

FIGURE 2.7
RELATION BETWEEN THE MEAN AND THE STANDARD DEVIATION
OF EXPECTED RATES OF CHANGE OF PRICES

Note: Semiannual percentage changes for the total of respondents to the Mondo Economico opinion poll (MIX estimates).

expected acceleration in prices there is an increase in the standard deviation of the individual expectations, and vice versa. The substantial constancy of the latter through the fifties and sixties seems to suggest that this observed correlation for the most recent years is probably due to a third factor such as, for example, conditions of more irregular, less steady growth of the economy.

2.5. Comparison between the Expectations of the "Production" and the "Other" Groups

The expectations of the "production" group versus those of the "other" group of respondents in the surveys will be briefly examined here. The plots of the means and standard deviations for the two price indices considered are given in Figure 2.8 and in Figure 2.9.

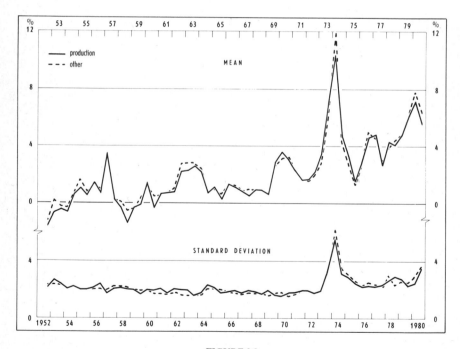

FIGURE 2.8

COMPARISON BETWEEN THE ESTIMATES OF THE MEAN AND THE STANDARD DEVIATION OF EXPECTED WHOLESALE PRICE CHANGES OF "PRODUCTION" AND "OTHER" RESPONDENTS

Note: Semiannual percentage changes for the total of respondents to the Mondo Economico opinion poll (MIX estimates).

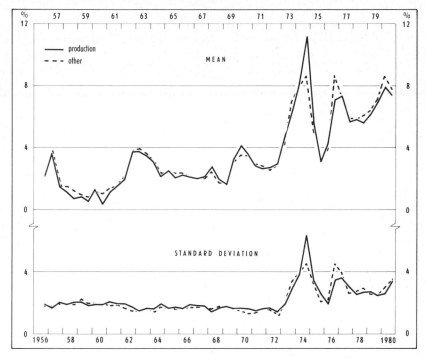

FIGURE 2.9
COMPARISON BETWEEN THE ESTIMATES OF THE MEAN AND THE STANDARD DEVIATION
OF EXPECTED CONSUMER PRICE CHANGES OF "PRODUCTION"
AND "OTHER" RESPONDENTS

Note: Semiannual percentage changes for the total of respondents to the Mondo Economico opinion poll
(MIX estimates).

It is perhaps surprising to observe that these estimates are so similar over
two different non-overlapping groups of individuals. The differences present
in these plots are quite small and systematic patterns are not self-evident.
The only one which might be singled out, but with exceptions, concerns a
general tendency of producers (that is, people who are nearer to selling
rather than retail prices) to anticipate smaller increases for wholesale prices
and larger increases for consumer ones.

The information content of the series for these two groups is quite similar,
however. A test of such a proposition can be easily performed by regressing
the difference between the rate of inflation expected on average by one
group and that expected by the second group on the latter and then on the
former. If the difference in information content were negligible, one should
not obtain a rejection of the joint hypothesis that the intercept and the slope

TABLE 2.12

TEST OF DIFFERENTIAL INFORMATION CONTENT OF THE RATE OF CHANGE
OF PRICES EXPECTED BY "PRODUCTION" AND "OTHER" RESPONDENTS (MIX)

	α	β	γ	F	R^2	SER	DW	T
WHOLESALE 5202-8002	-.065 (.901)	-.028 (1.229)		3.59*	.12	.40	2.00[+]	57
	-.129 (1.796)		.001	2.76	.09	.40	2.09[+]	57
CONSUMER 5602-8002	-.100 (.726)	.012 (.377)		.37	.02	.51	1.74[+]	49
	-.258 (2.007)		-.056 (1.878)	2.08	.08	.49	1.69[+]	49

OLS regressions:

MIX(PRODUCTION) - MIX(OTHER) = α + βMIX(PRODUCTION) + u

MIX(PRODUCTION) - MIX(OTHER) = α + γMIX(OTHER) + u.

Note

Absolute values of t-statistics are reported in parentheses under each coefficient estimate.
* Significant at the .05 level.
+ Does not reject the hypothesis of absence of first order serial correlation.
The t and F - tests are for the hypotheses α=0, β=0, and α=0, γ=0; R^2 is the (unadjusted) determination coefficient; SER is the standard error of the regression; DW is the Durbin-Watson statistic; T is the number of observations.

coefficient are equal to zero and there should be no evidence of serial correlation among the residuals. The results of this test, reported in Table 2.12, are in total agreement with the advanced hypotheses, as one can see from all the test statistics computed.

One can conclude therefore that the two groups of respondents to the *Mondo Economico* opinion polls, that is, those in the industrial sector, on one side, and those belonging to the finance or the trade sector or general economic experts, on the other side, appear to have practically the same expectations – on average – concerning the future changes in wholesale and consumer prices. Furthermore, the dispersion of the individual expectations is also quite similar for the two groups, as can be seen from Figures 2.8 and 2.9. This finding gives a larger amount of generality to the *Mondo Economico* panel than one might have thought earlier. It, moreover, affords one to concentrate for some of the more burdensome tests presented in future chapters, on only the evidence referring to the total of the respondents.

2.6. Summary of the Results

This chapter has highlighted the problems of measuring "the" expected rate of inflation from direct survey data and of obtaining numerical estimates of the rates of change of wholesale and consumer prices expected by the respondents to the *Mondo Economico* surveys, as well as of the dispersion of their individual expectations.

In Section 2.1 and the Appendix to this chapter, the method proposed by Carlson and Parkin (1975) – and many others, with a surprising first treatment about thirty years ago by Theil (1952) – to deal with qualitative survey data is considered extensively. Many problems are associated with such a method, but it seems that all are dependent on the limited information content of these surveys, at least for what concerns a variable such as the inflation rate. These problems are obviously not present in "pure" quantitative surveys, where the interviewees are asked to advance precise numerical estimates of their expectations. If one chooses not to ask the interviewees to accompany their answers with a statement on the odds which they would assign to these precise estimates (out of their subjective probability distributions), surveys which ask the respondents to select the interval containing the actual future rate of inflation might be preferable. The *Mondo Economico* opinion poll is of this type.

After a brief discussion of the treatment of the "don't know" answers, two sets of estimates have been obtained. The first has been derived interpolating the sample frequencies with a piecewise uniform distribution. The second set uses instead the hypothesis that these frequencies might be interpolated by means of a normal.

In the case of the piecewise uniform distributions, an assumption has to be made concerning the limits of the open-ended intervals. This assumption has limited effects on most of the surveys taken over the period considered, but it is crucial in obtaining reliable estimates for some of the first series of surveys (for the years between 1973 and 1976), when – due to the high rate of inflation prevailing in Italy and to the inadequacy of the questionnaire – more than 50 percent of the answers were contained in the upper open-ended interval. A correction to a piecewise uniform based on the hypothesis that all intervals had equal length has therefore been considered, and two sets of estimates have been obtained. The first set of estimates has this correction applied to those surveys with over half of the answers falling in the upper open-ended class.

Under the hypothesis of a normal distribution, estimates of the mean and the standard deviation of the individual expectations have been obtained by means of a regression between the points on the abscissa line of the space of the standard normal distribution – obtained from the original frequencies –

and the corresponding points on the abscissa line of the space of the sample distribution, which are the known limits of the pre-selected intervals that had to be chosen by the interviewees. Also in this case two sets of estimates were obtained, corresponding to different groups of the original answers made in order to reduce possibly serious effects of sampling variability.

Modest differences emerge between the two sets of estimates out of each of the two distribution assumptions. Most impressive, however, is the similarity between the piecewise uniform and the normal estimates of the average expected rate of inflation. Only in one or two occasions do significant differences take place, that is, in 1974 and 1976, when the former distribution produced higher estimates than the latter, probably because of a significant skewness in the "true" sample distribution and the role played by the correction to the piecewise uniform. Somewhat larger differences are present among estimates of the standard deviation: the normal estimates are more volatile and somewhat below those from the piecewise uniform assumption.

Tests were then performed, when possible, to assess the goodness-of-fit of the normal distributions and the reliability of the correction for the upper open-ended intervals applied to the piecewise uniform distribution. In the latter case encouraging results were obtained; the tests point to the acceptance of the corrected piecewise distribution and to the general rejection of the normal interpolation. It is likely that this result does not apply with equal strength to the estimates of the average expected rate of change of prices which do not vary much in response to the choice of alternative distribution assumptions. The results of the tests of goodness-of-fit are instead related to the volatility of the estimates of the standard deviation of the distribution over the individual respondents.

To select the estimates on which to continue this work, the choice has been based on the accuracy with which the estimated expected rates of inflation did forecast the changes in prices that actually occurred. A comparison between root mean square errors of prediction was performed over the whole sample and various subperiods, resulting in only slight differences for the four sets of estimates considered. On this basis, however, the piecewise uniform, modified only when the upper open-ended class contained over 50 percent of the answers, (*PUM*) gave the best overall performance; also a series was constructed out of the "best" estimates for the various subperiods (*MIX*). Very minor differences characterize the *PUM* and *MIX* estimates, and indeed the results discussed in the following chapters hold equally for both.

Finally, the average expected rates estimated separately for the "production" and the "other" respondents to the surveys are also very similar to each other. It appears from the tests performed in Section 2.5 that the information content of the series for these two groups is practically the same. Also the dispersion of the individual expectations is quite similar for the two groups. One can therefore conclude that the whole *Mondo Economico* panel represents a fairly homogeneous population and the whole panel as a unit can be used, particularly when a large number of computations will be performed for the more burdensome tests of the following chapters.

Appendix to Chapter 2

Further Notes on the Estimation of the Expected Rates of Inflation from Qualitative Surveys

As it has been observed in Section 2.1, there are a number of problems with the so-called Carlson–Parkin method used to obtain quantitative estimates from qualitative surveys. It has already been emphasized that these problems are a direct consequence of the characteristics of these surveys. It has also been outlined that not only are there very weak justifications for supposing the scale parameter δ_t in (2.8) and (2.9) to be constant, but also that there are no reasons whatever to assume it equal among individuals. Furthermore, estimates *à la* Carlson and Parkin given by (2.10) impose a very strong unbiasedness condition for the expectations over the sample period, a condition which should rather be tested than assumed *a priori*.[38] Even if δ_t were constant and known *a priori*, still other difficulties are self-evident. With only two data points it is obviously impossible to test for the goodness of fit of a given interpolating distribution. The normal, however, has at least the following disadvantages: (1) it is a symmetric distribution; (2) it produces in certain occasions results which could be considered "counterintuitive"; (3) it does not allow independent estimates of the mean, μ_t, and the standard deviation, σ_t, of the rate of inflation among the respondents when no answers fall in one of the three possible intervals; (4) finally, but probably most important, the estimates might be very inaccurate for certain regions of the frequency space (and it is likely that in the case of a variable such as the rate of inflation these situations are not exceptional).

---

[38]It might even be the case that for some people a zero value in the indifference interval could not coincide with its center (being more indifferent, say, towards negative than towards positive price changes) so that we would have $\delta_1 < x < \delta_2$ instead of $-\delta < x < \delta$.

Even if it might be reasonable to consider a unimodal distribution,[39] there is also at least some good *a priori* reason to assume that, with a sensible upward trend in prices, the distribution of answers might be skew to the right. The degree of skewness will probably be low on average, but certainly there are situations in which a strong inflationary climate prevails and the asymmetry becomes relevant.[40] With only two points in the distribution space, there are simply no degrees of freedom to allow a sufficient departure of the variance of the interpolating normal distribution from the "true" one, which could at least permit to obtain a reasonably close estimate of the mean. Using Livingston's data Carlson (1975) was able to show that some occasions of skewness do actually exist: a lognormal did not provide notable improvements,[41] but *a scaled log t-distribution* gave satisfactory results.[42] In this case, however, there is a third parameter to estimate, i.e., the number of degrees of freedom of this transformed *t*-distribution (equal to six for Carlson's best estimates). For the qualitative surveys which we are considering, there are not enough observations to estimate other parameters besides μ and σ.

Passing to the "counterintuitive" results, it can be proved that in the case of a normal distribution, when the "up" answers are above 50 percent of the total, the estimate of the mean increases when the "down" answers increase (and conversely, switching the "up" and the "down").[43] This case is very frequent for surveys of the nature (and on the variable) of those we are considering; with a constant δ, the reduction in the "no change" answers causes an increase in the variance and shifts the mean to the right. This is so not only for a normal but also for other distributions as well (for example, the uniform) and is a direct consequence of having only three

---

[39]"...Since respondents to the survey are exposed to similar information and public prognostications, we would expect at any given time a unimodal distribution around the 'consensus' rate" (Carlson and Parkin 1975, pp. 128–129).

[40]See the discussion in Foster and Gregory (1979).

[41]The lognormal has been later used by Wachtel (1977a) for the SRC surveys, again without finding results substantially different from those given by a normal interpolation. Wachtel did use the relations: $\mu_x = [\exp(\mu_y + \sigma_y^2)] - 100$, $\sigma_x^2 = (\mu_x + 100)^2[\exp(\sigma_y^2) - 1]$, where the subscripts refer respectively to the normal (x) and to the lognormal (y) distributions; he therefore arbitrarily assumed the quantity $(100 + x)$ to be lognormal, where x is the expected rate of inflation.

[42]The scaled *t*-distribution provides greater peakedness than the normal and the logarithms impart also skewness. Since the original answers to Livingston's surveys concern the *level* of prices, the logarithmic assumption does not suffer from the arbitrariness of Wachtel's (see previous footnote).

[43]See the excellent, much quoted but still unpublished paper by Carlson and Ryder (1973), which has been considered also for some of the other points examined in this Appendix.

possible intervals *and* of assuming a constant δ. Thus, the "counterintuitive" result is only a consequence of possibly too stringent assumptions and too limited data.

A third difficulty occurs for those occasions when the percentage of the respondents who answer "down" is zero ($F_3 = 0$, in the notation of Section 2.1). This occurs fairly frequently in periods of heavy inflationary pressures, when it may happen that of all those replying, less than 0.5 percent (the data being generally rounded to the nearest percentage point) anticipated a decrease in the following period. (Even if we knew an exact non-zero figure, there would still be great difficulties due to the sampling fluctuations to be discussed next.) In this case, on the assumption of a normal distribution, (2.2) loses significance and (2.7) cannot be used. It is therefore necessary to resort to *ad hoc* procedures. That adopted by Carlson and Parkin involved neglecting (2.7) and considering (2.6) which can be rewritten as follows:

$$\mu_t = \delta_t - z_{1t}\sigma_t. \tag{A.1}$$

With a given value of δ_t, one could therefore estimate μ_t only if he had some *a priori* information concerning σ_t. On these occasions, Carlson and Parkin have made σ_t equal to the highest estimate obtained in the previous or subsequent surveys "on the grounds that the variance of the distribution, when no one expects prices to fall will be at least as large as at other times within a few months of the survey".[44] However, it is obvious that this procedure, and other similar ones, is extremely arbitrary. An empty interval could in fact imply, for instance, a lower dispersion of the answers, not a higher one, since it could be considered an indication of larger agreement among respondents.[45] In any case, when $F_3 = 0$, the method described in Section 2.1 cannot be satisfactory; reasserting what has been said, in an inflationary context these surveys are simply not informative enough.

The last point to be considered hinges upon the strong nonlinearity of the transformation of the original frequencies necessary to obtain the moments of a normal distribution; obviously, when the nonlinearity becomes severe, even small sampling variations might produce large changes in the estimates of these parameters. This point has been outlined and emphasized by Carlson and Ryder (1973); they determined approximate confidence regions for F_1 and F_3 and looked at the potential variation in estimates of μ_t/δ_t around the central point. The main results of their exercise were the

---

[44] Carlson and Ryder (1973, p. 9).

[45] Other serious problems following from such *ad hoc* procedures have been outlined by Foster and Gregory (1979).

TABLE 2.13

EXAMPLES OF ESTIMATES OF THE MOMENTS OF A NORMAL AND A UNIFORM DISTRIBUTION IN SITUATIONS OF SMALL CHANGES IN THE "DOWN" ANSWERS

(percentage)

	case 1			case 2			case 3		
	F_1	F_2	F_3	F_1	F_2	F_3	F_1	F_2	F_3
a	94	5.5	0.5	96	3.5	0.5	10	89.5	0.5
b	94	5	1	96	3	1	10	89	1
c	94	4.5	1.5	96	2.5	1.5	10	88.5	1.5

	case 1 μ		σ		case 2 μ		σ		case 3 μ		σ	
	normal	uniform	normal	uniform	normal	uniform	normal	uniform	normal	uniform	normal	uniform
a	4.049 (−19.5)	17.000 (− 8.6)	1.961 (−24.3)	10.497 (− 9.1)	5.250 (−25.8)	27.286 (−13.8)	2.427 (−30.1)	16.496 (−14.3)	0.335 (15.5)	0.106 (4.9)	0.518 (−6.5)	0.645 (−0.6)
b	5.028	18.600	2.591	11.547	7.080	31.667	3.472	19.245	0.290	0.101	0.554	0.649
c	6.057 (20.5)	20.556 (10.5)	3.252 (25.5)	12.830 (11.1)	9.358 (32.2)	37.800 (19.4)	4.773 (37.5)	23.094 (20.0)	0.257 (−11.4)	0.096 (−4.9)	0.579 (4.5)	0.652 (0.5)

Note

The figures in parentheses below the a and c estimates are percentage differences with respect to the b estimates. It has been assumed that $\delta = 1$ (alternatively, the estimates refer to μ/δ and σ/δ).

following: when the "no change" class (F_2) is relatively large, sampling variations have moderate effects; these become much more dramatic as the sum $(F_1 + F_3)$ tends to unity and are rather disturbing for those surveys the results of which have been rounded to the nearest percentage point.

For example, a rounding that makes F_3 equal to 1 percent rather than 0.5 or 1.5 can produce for high levels of F_1 very different estimates of these two parameters, for only one point variation in the answers falling in the "down" class (see Table 2.13). For the case of $F_3 = 0.01$, there are differences with respect to the mean – for $F_1 = 0.94$ and $F_1 = 0.96$, respectively – of about 20 and 30 percent; larger percentage differences apply for the values of σ. These differences are somewhat reduced when a large F_2 area is present, as one can see from case 3 of Table 2.13.

In any event, these fluctuations are much higher than those one could get from using a different interpolating distribution such as the uniform, as the same table shows.[46] In such a case it is easy to prove that[47]

$$\mu_t = \delta(F_{1t} - F_{3t})/F_{2t}, \tag{A.2}$$

$$\sigma_t = \delta/(F_{2t}\sqrt{3}), \tag{A.3}$$

so that F_{1t} changes linearly, for given μ_t and σ_t, with F_{3t} rather than non-linearly as is the case for a normal distribution; this is shown in Figure 2.10 (part B) where the contours for μ/δ are represented for the two distributions in the (F_1, F_3) space.[48]

To obviate such problems of sampling variations associated with the normal distribution, Carlson and Ryder proposed two estimators for $(\mu/\delta)_t$ derived from the normal under the hypothesis that $(\sigma/\delta)_t$ was respectively (i) constant or (ii) determined by an adaptive adjustment process. This second measure passed some rather weak tests; to estimate μ_t one needs however a time series for either σ_t or δ_t from some other source and the

---

[46] Notice that also in the case of a uniform one gets the apparently counterintuitive result that if $F_1 > 0.5$, an increase in F_3 produces an increase in the mean, *compensated* by an increase in the variance of the distribution.

[47] As one can see from part A of Figure 2.10 the uniform is defined by $G(x) = \alpha + \beta x$, $x \in [a, b]$, so that $g(x) = \beta = 1/(b - a)$ for $x \in [a, b]$ and $g(x) = 0$ elsewhere. Since we know two points on the $G(x)$ line, it is straightforward to see that $\beta = F_2/2\delta$ and $\alpha = F_3 + F_2/\delta$, so that for $G(x) = 0$ and $G(x) = 1$, $a = -\alpha/\beta$, $b = (1 - \alpha)/\beta$ and from $\mu_t = (a + b)/2$ and $\sigma_t = (b - a)/\sqrt{12}$, (A.2) and (A.3) follow.

[48] This figure is adapted from Figure 1 of Carlson and Ryder (1973) who drew it for the case of a normal distribution. Notice that when only the region delimited by the thick lines is feasible (as it is the case when the "same" answers are at least so numerous as *either* the "up" *or* the "down" answers, a rather likely situation), the nonlinearity of the contours for the normal distribution is much more serious; notice also that this nonlinearity disappears for μ/δ equal to 0 or ± 1.

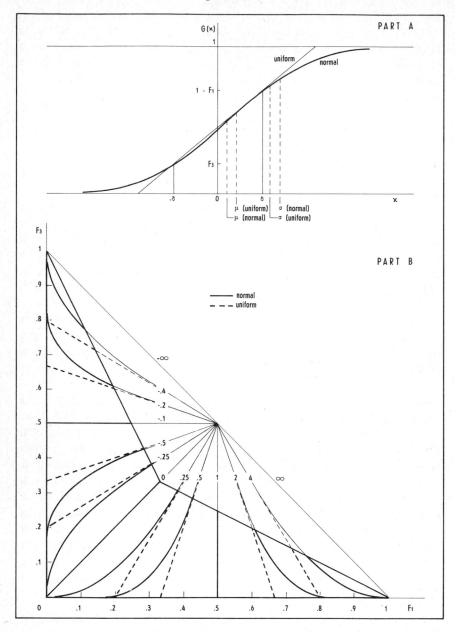

FIGURE 2.10
NORMAL AND UNIFORM DISTRIBUTIONS AND CONTOURS
FOR THE μ/δ RATIO IN THE (F_3, F_1) SPACE

implied stability of $(\sigma/\delta)_t$ is also not very convincing.[49] As a matter of fact it appears that the assumptions behind these estimators are as restrictive as those necessary to consider the so-called "balance" (or Theil[50]) statistic as a satisfactory proxy for μ_t. The balance is defined as the difference between the percentage of "up" and the percentage of "down" answers, that is,

$$BAL_t = F_{1t} - F_{3t}. \tag{A.4}$$

It can be seen from (A.2) and (A.3) that for a uniform distribution,

$$\mu_t = k_t BAL_t \quad \text{where} \quad k_t = \sigma_t\sqrt{3}. \tag{A.5}$$

A necessary and sufficient condition for k_t to be constant so that μ_t is proportional to BAL_t is therefore σ_t constant;[51] for σ_t to be constant however, from (A.3) δ/F_{2t} has to be constant and for a constant δ we would need F_{2t} constant too. These conditions show incidentally that, even if we were willing to assume a *uniform* distribution, the balance (a very much used synthetic measure for these surveys) would be a reasonable indicator only for those situations in which the "same" answers are roughly constant.

Before closing this appendix, a few comments might be raised on a recent interesting article by Batchelor (1981), who offers a somewhat different criticism to Carlson and Parkin's approach and proposes an alternative method.

Batchelor considers the choice of the normal distribution to be *the* necessary assumption in the Carlson and Parkin framework; he then claims that their approach rests on three critical empirical assumptions: "First, the subjective probability distributions of all respondents are identical in form and independent. Second, the reporting threshold is identical for all respondents. Third, over a sequence of surveys, at $t = 1, 2, \ldots, T$, say, expectations are unbiased".[52] He then so continues: "they [Carlson and Parkin] argue that the first assumption means the distribution g can be considered normal according to the Central Limit Theorem".[53] But rather than rely on a special case of this theorem for sums of independent, identically distributed random variables such as the one leading to an asymptotically normal distribution, Batchelor suggests that one should instead consider the more general case leading to a distribution that lies in the class of stable probability laws.

---

[49]See the discussion in De Menil (1974, app. A.1).

[50]After the extensive analysis of these indicators summarized for example in Theil (1961, 1966).

[51]See Carlson and Ryder (1973) and, more than twenty years before, Theil (1952).

[52]Batchelor (1981, p. 201).

[53]Batchelor (1981, p. 201).

Only if the component distributions have finite first and second moments do these random variables tend to the normal. But typically stable distributions can be totally described in terms of *four* parameters which play roles similar to moments (so that Θ_3 is an inverse measure of skewness and Θ_4 an inverse measure of peakedness). Only when Θ_4 takes its extreme value of 2 do the stable distributions have finite variance and we would obtain a normal distribution completely characterized by two moments only. Batchelor then investigates the skewness and kurtosis issues considering the distribution of changes of elementary price indices (components of the general index), and obtains estimates of Θ_3 and Θ_4 which he uses to estimate the expected rates of inflation "along the lines of the Carlson–Parkin method except that different abscissae a_t and b_t [z_{1t} and z_{2t} in the notation of this book] are obtained from the cumulants of the non-normal laws".[54]

It should be noticed, however, that Carlson and Parkin, as Shuford, Juster, De Menil and *almost* all the other authors who used this method, have considered surveys raising to the interviewees questions on the expected change of a *general* price index, that is an *aggregate* measure of inflation. They were interested in obtaining estimates of the sample mean of the rates of change of this price index expected by the respondents to the surveys. In doing so there was no reason to assume, and obviously they *did not* assume, equal subjective probability distributions among the respondents nor to rely on any central limit theorem on such *equal* subjective distributions. As it has been observed, one actually had simply to assume that the respondents chose a given class when they had a sufficiently high degree of belief that a location parameter of their subjective distribution function – that they considered appropriate, for example the median – would have fallen in that class. One then *defines* the average expected rate of change of prices as the sample mean of these location parameters. Since frequencies over only three intervals (once the indifference limen has been identified) are available in the space of the density function to find the sample distribution out of which this mean can be estimated, the choice of a normal comes out from simplicity considerations, not from any appeal to a central limit theorem. If instead of having only three areas of the density function one had the individual answers – as is the case with the Livingston's surveys and the new series of the SRC ones – the sample mean could be computed without any problems, and if one had a larger number of intervals, with known limits, in which the individual expectations fell with given corresponding frequencies – as is generally the case with the *Mondo Economico* surveys – the sample mean could be computed by a weighted average of the mid-points of these intervals. While it is reasonable to rely on

[54] Batchelor (1981, p. 207).

central limit theorems to make inferences concerning the (asymptotic) distribution of the sample mean (when the sample is large), they simply do not tell anything about the distribution of individual forecasts (out of the subjective distribution) of a given aggregate variable, such as the change in a general price index.[55]

Even if there are good reasons to believe that the normal is not an adequate interpolating distribution in this case, with only two points in the space of the cumulative distribution we cannot consider the estimation of moments higher than the first two; furthermore, there is no evidence – since the economic data cannot be replicated – about the distribution of the *actual* change of an *aggregate* price index at any given moment in time.

There is however a case for which Batchelor's suggestion could be quite useful: this is when one considers surveys relating not to expectations about aggregate variables, but collecting instead individual anticipations of single firms or entrepreneurs about their *own* prices (or other variables at a *micro* level). This is actually the case empirically studied by Batchelor. While there still is no apparent reason why these individual expected rates should have a distribution around the aggregate rate (of which they are individual components) which could (or should) be identified by the use of a central limit theorem,[56] it seems however appropriate to rely on analyses of the distribution of actual individual price changes, such as that of Vining and Elvertowsky (1976) considered by Batchelor, in order to obtain the outside information needed to estimate – out of only two points of the cumulative distribution – the expected change in the average level of the individual prices. However, one has to be very careful, in these cases, that two conditions be at least approximately satisfied: (i) the weights used in these

---

[55] There are also some other unjustified claims in Batchelor's paper. It is not true that Carlson and Parkin developed their technique *building* on earlier work by Theil (1952) as he asserts on page 200. While Theil's work was certainly very imaginative and contained a complete analysis of the method proposed by Carlson and Parkin, Shuford, Juster, Knöbl and De Menil, no reference to it was made by any of these authors. Batchelor also asserts (p. 203) that in Carlson's (1975) analysis of the distribution of Livingston's data, Carlson did not consider skew distributions. As it has been mentioned, as a matter of fact the most satisfactory distribution is the one he calls "scaled log t-distribution": "To impart skewness as well as peakedness to the distribution, the logarithms of the observations are assumed to have a scaled t-distribution" (Carlson (1975, p. 753)).

[56] Using the same kind of data Batchelor used, Knöbl (1975) justifies the use of a normal distribution, claiming that "since the number of individuals asked is large, the expected rate of price change over all individuals can be assumed as normally distributed" (p. 86). Also in this case, where the expectations refer to individual prices rather than to an aggregate index, the implicit reference to a central limit theorem is faulty, as noticed by Carlson (1975, fn. 1); a more reasonable argument, but one that could indeed be tested as shown by Batchelor, is that concerning the distribution of individual *actual* price changes: if this was normal and many firms were randomly interviewed, then one could reasonably assume that their expected rates of change would also be normally distributed.

surveys to aggregate the answers of individual firms should be equal to those needed to obtain the change in the aggregate price level out of the changes in its individual components; (ii) the actual individual prices – by necessity they also, to some extent, aggregate – used to determine the kurtosis and asymmetry characteristics to be utilized in the estimation of the expected rate of change, should be those set by the firms considered in the surveys.

In any event, also in this case serious problems are present. The more relevant one is very likely that to obtain a numerical estimate of the rate of change of the aggregate price index expected by the firms participating in the survey equal limits for the "no change" class have to be assumed *for all prices for all firms* (and not only for all respondents for the same aggregate, as it is the case with surveys on the change of a general price index). This is certainly not appropriate if one considers that elementary price indices might be in certain cases very volatile (so that a larger "no change" interval should be considered), while in other cases they could be very smooth. This problem is likely to be even more important than that of the arbitrariness with which the length of what could be called the "average indifference limen" is determined, which is not reduced, in Batchelor's analysis, with respect to that of Carlson and Parkin's procedure.[57]

This too, to conclude, is a problem which stems out of the qualitative nature of these surveys; there is probably very little one could do with these data in addition to the analysis that is possible to implement along the lines of log-linear probability models of the kind considered by Koenig, Nerlove and Oudiz (1981).

[57]While Carlson and Parkin obtain estimates of the limits of the "no change" class on the basis of the assumption that over the sample period the expected rate is on average equal to the actual, Batchelor obtains them by assuming that the mean square difference between the two rates is a minimum. One should observe, however, that the generalization of an *ad hoc* assumption still remains *ad hoc* and one cannot claim *a priori* the latter to be superior to the former. In a later paper – Batchelor (1982) – the above criterion is also used to estimate the thresholds, within a framework identical to that of Carlson and Parkin, necessary to obtain quantitative estimates of enterprise expectations on output and price changes for a number of European countries. While Batchelor claims that making use of such a criterion does not imply the *a priori* assumption of unbiased expectations, it is easy to show that this is an obvious consequence of his criterion and estimation method.

CHAPTER 3

EVALUATION OF INFLATION EXPECTATIONS, 1: ACCURACY ANALYSIS

3.1. Preliminary Analysis and General Remarks

In this chapter the rates of change of prices expected (on average) by the respondents to the *Mondo Economico* opinion poll will be compared with the actual rates of change. The comparison is of interest not only for the light it sheds on the reliability of persons in the surveys, but also on a number of features which characterize their expectations. Together with the comparison of alternative predictors of inflation, the subject of the next chapter, this analysis is propaedeutical to further investigation on issues such as the "rationality" and the "formation" of inflation expectations.

The actual rates of change of prices considered in this chapter are the rates of change of semiannual averages of the monthly indices. As a matter of fact, the questions put to the interviewees ask for their expectations on the rate of change *in* the next semester *with respect to* the previous one. Even if the change between the average indices for the two semesters is not what is explicitly referred to, it seems reasonable that it is the most obvious object of these questions, and of the corresponding answers. Such a presumption is reinforced by the preliminary results of Table 3.1 which show that, at least in terms of mean square errors of prediction, the comparison of the expected rates of inflation with the actual rates of change of semiannual averages of monthly price levels is more favorable than that with rates of change between the last months of the semesters of interest.[1]

In Tables D.22 through D.24 and D.25 through D.27 the actual changes, respectively in wholesale and consumer prices, are reported together with the measures of expected inflation obtained in the previous chapter (that is, estimates *PUM* and *MIX*). The tables also contain the standard deviations of individual expectations, computed jointly with the (average) expected rates as well as the anticipation errors, that is, the differences between actual and expected rates. Table D.28 contains the definitions of all the variables.

---

[1] The percentage changes for each of the six months of each semester with respect to the corresponding month of the previous semester are compared in Table 3.1 with the expected changes; root mean square errors of prediction are computed for various periods (for the choice of the periods see Section 3.4). The same is done for percentage changes between the average indices of each semester and it is clear that the latter generally outperform all the others. Among the former, the fourth and fifth months rates of change do generally best, as it should be expected if what the respondents are actually predicting is the change in the average index.

Ignazio Visco

TABLE 3.1

ROOT MEAN SQUARE ERRORS OF PREDICTION FOR VARIOUS PRICE CHANGES

Period	PCS	PCS6	PCS5	PCS4	PCS3	PCS2	PCS1
			WHOLESALE PRICES				
5202-7202	.983	1.236	1.134	1.122	1.193	1.389	1.643
5202-8002	3.327	3.511	3.360	3.574	3.774	3.842	3.780
5801-7202	.975	1.209	1.194	1.162	1.188	1.202	1.334
5801-8002	3.671	3.856	3.711	3.948	4.160	4.185	4.057
7301-8002	6.080	6.325	6.076	6.502	6.863	6.902	6.631
			CONSUMER PRICES				
5602-7401	1.290	1.335	1.375	1.432	1.462	1.398	1.396
5602-8002	1.506	1.576	1.560	1.557	1.723	1.790	1.754
5801-7401	1.285	1.271	1.383	1.425	1.470	1.401	1.405
5801-8002	1.516	1.552	1.576	1.561	1.743	1.814	1.780
7402-8002	1.986	2.102	1.985	1.862	2.296	2.581	2.490

Note

The root mean square errors have been computed for the errors of predic - tion given by the difference between the actual changes in prices listed below and the expected ones for the total of the respondents to the Mondo Economico surveys (MIX). All rates have been considered on a semi-annual basis.

PCS = percentage change of the <u>average</u> of the six monthly indices of each semester with respect to the average of the preceding semes- ter;

PCS1 = percentage change between the <u>first</u> month of each semester and the first month of the preceding semester;

PCS2 = percentage change between the <u>second</u> month of each semester and the second month of the preceding semester;

PCS3 = percentage change between the <u>third</u> month of each semester and the third month of the preceding semester;

PCS4 = percentage change between the <u>fourth</u> month of each semester and the fourth month of the preceding semester;

PCS5 = percentage change between the <u>fifth</u> month of each semester and the fifth month of the preceding semester;

PCS6 = percentage change between the <u>sixth</u> month of each semester and the sixth month of the preceding semester.

The characteristics of these series will be discussed in the next section, but a brief look at some general statistics is helpful here. The sample means and standard deviations have been computed both for the actual and the expected rates of change of prices, and are reported in Table 3.2 for various sub-periods. It is interesting to observe that while the means did not differ significantly over the period preceding the first oil crisis, large differences are present in more recent years, especially for the wholesale price index.[2]

[2] Experiments were also performed on the wholesale price index considering it net of a number of items related to oil, energy and agricultural products. This was done on the presumption that respondents might consider producer prices, which would only indirectly incorporate changes in the prices of these goods (the wholesale price index does instead directly weigh also the prices of a number of raw materials, generally imported). It was felt that this might partly explain the large anticipation errors in forecasting wholesale price changes in the

More interesting is that the standard deviations with respect to these means[3] are always smaller for the expected series than for the actual.[4]

A preliminary qualitative test on the accuracy of the respondents' forecasts over the years of the *Mondo Economico* surveys is presented in Table 3.3. This table gives for each survey the percentage of answers falling into the interval which contained the change in prices which actually occurred. It can be seen that on most occasions more than 50 percent of the answers lay in the right intervals throughout the period considered, even if there were numerous oscillations and frequently only a very few interviewees succeeded in anticipating correctly the class containing the actual rate of inflation.[5] While the evidence is still preliminary, it gives at least some idea of the general degree of accuracy of these expectations; in particular, it confirms that even if *on average* the expectations of the panel were not very far from being quite accurate, the dispersion of inflationary expectations about the average rate is quite high. This implies that the interviewees either were not exposed to the same information or, more likely, did not make the same use of this information regarding the inflationary process. It also reflects considerable uncertainty *among* the economic agents interviewed, probably also as a reflection of uncertainty at the individual level. While the present study is mainly concerned with inflation expectations at the aggregate level, this finding cannot be easily dismissed; the dispersion of individual expectations will be briefly considered in the analysis of the last chapters when aggregation and uncertainty problems will be addressed. It is clear, however, that it must eventually deserve special attention given the implications that it can have for theoretical work on the subject.

---

more recent years. In a number of occasions the root mean square errors for the net indices were lower than those for the general wholesale price index. The differences, however, were not large enough to request for a separate analysis for these indices; looking at the plots of percentage changes of the general index and of those net of oil and/or other energy and agricultural products, one observes very similar patterns and very similar anticipation errors both in timing and magnitude.

[3] These standard deviations were computed in the usual way, i.e., as $[\sum(X_t - \overline{X}_t)^2/(T-1)]^{\frac{1}{2}}$ where X_t is the series of interest and $\overline{X}_t$ is its sample mean over the period $t = 1,\ldots,T$. Therefore, for the expected changes they provide a measure of the variability of the estimates of the (average across individuals) expected rate of change of prices in the sample period and are *not* to be confused with the sample deviations of the individual expectations computed in the previous chapter jointly with the average expected rates.

[4] It is well known indeed that for "optimal" predictors the variance cannot be larger than that of the series to be predicted. See, for example, Granger and Newbold (1977, pp. 285–286) and, for specific references, Mincer and Zarnowitz (1969), Hatanaka (1975a), Samuelson (1976), all dealing with "stable" stochastic processes.

[5] On average the answers lying in the right class have been 53 and 55 percent for wholesale and consumer prices respectively, with a standard deviation in both cases approximately equal to 18 percent.

TABLE 3.2

MEANS AND STANDARD DEVIATIONS OF ACTUAL AND EXPECTED PRICE CHANGES

Period	Mean (A)			Standard Deviation (B)			(B)/(A)		
	Actual	Expected (PUM)	Expected (MIX)	Actual	Expected (PUM)	Expected (MIX)	Actual	Expected (PUM)	Expected (MIX)
				WHOLESALE PRICES					
5202-7202	.85	1.09	1.04	1.42	1.20	1.15	1.68	1.10	1.10
5202-8002	3.16	2.12	2.11	4.98	2.28	2.31	1.58	1.08	1.10
5801-7202	1.04	1.29	1.24	1.58	1.12	1.07	1.51	.87	.86
5801-8002	3.84	2.50	2.49	5.33	2.31	2.34	1.39	.92	.94
7301-8002	9.08	4.75	4.84	5.95	2.29	2.30	.66	.48	.48
				CONSUMER PRICES					
5602-7401	2.17	2.71	2.62	1.92	1.54	1.52	.88	.57	.58
5602-8002	3.78	3.68	3.64	3.36	2.27	2.32	.89	.62	.63
5801-7401	2.30	2.73	2.64	1.96	1.59	1.57	.85	.58	.59
5801-8002	3.98	3.75	3.72	3.37	2.31	2.36	.85	.62	.63
7402-8002	8.24	6.36	6.45	2.24	1.74	1.75	.27	.27	.27

Note

All rates are expressed on a semi-annual basis. The expectations refer to the total of respondents to the Mondo Economico surveys.

TABLE 3.3

RIGHT FORECASTING OF THE CLASS CONTAINING THE ACTUAL CHANGE IN PRICES

Semester	WHOLESALE TOT	WHOLESALE PRO	WHOLESALE OTH	CONSUMER TOT	CONSUMER PRO	CONSUMER OTH
5202	28.9	27.3	30.8			
5301	51.6	49.0	53.9			
5302	55.0	51.2	58.1			
5401	60.5	54.8	64.9			
5402	53.4	51.4	55.2			
5501	49.3	55.9	44.2			
5502	64.2	65.1	63.5			
5601	43.3	40.9	45.1			
5602	50.6	46.7	53.8	25.6	24.4	26.6
5701	10.2	7.7	12.1	5.6	4.2	6.7
5702	58.3	61.8	55.9	45.1	47.4	43.5
5801	58.5	56.9	59.5	48.7	41.9	52.9
5802	36.0	44.5	30.0	56.2	60.0	53.5
5901	21.8	25.2	19.5	47.4	54.7	42.3
5902	73.5	78.7	69.3	67.4	71.2	64.4
6001	52.9	47.6	56.7	39.9	39.8	39.9
6002	72.0	69.6	73.9	62.8	68.7	58.4
6101	70.7	61.8	76.9	54.3	51.4	56.2
6102	74.3	70.6	76.8	48.6	49.0	48.3
6201	25.8	24.8	26.7	60.6	55.3	64.8
6202	66.3	58.4	72.8		56.6	62.8
6301	68.0	60.0	74.3	37.9	34.9	40.1
6302	73.4	72.0	74.6	59.9	60.0	59.8
6401	68.8	63.0	72.9	69.7	64.6	73.2
6402	56.8	55.4	57.8	59.4	59.3	59.5
6501	51.9	46.8	55.7	72.6	73.1	72.2
6502	71.2	76.2	67.1	70.7	66.4	74.1
6601	56.2	56.1	56.2	24.5	25.4	23.7
6602	60.5	59.8	61.1	31.1	30.4	32.1
6701	72.7	69.6	74.8	57.8	57.4	58.1
6702	68.5	69.8	67.3	30.9	29.7	31.8
6801	66.3	65.1	67.3	16.9	11.0	21.8
6802	71.4	72.6	70.2	39.7	35.0	44.4
6901	22.9	26.6	19.6	46.4	46.0	46.7
6902	69.6	70.7	68.7	66.5	64.6	68.0
7001	25.8	31.2	21.7	62.7	54.7	68.8
7002	9.4	11.8	7.5	67.8	65.0	70.1
7101	67.4	63.8	70.1	78.6	76.9	79.8
7102	44.0	44.3	43.6	76.5	76.7	76.2
7201	51.9	51.8	51.9	72.3	67.7	76.6
7202	66.2	64.9	67.4	82.1	80.7	83.4
7301	17.7	22.5	13.4	50.3	54.4	46.5
7302	67.9	70.6	65.6	71.1	69.7	72.2
7401	83.7	82.0	85.1	76.6	77.1	76.1
7402	52.1	53.1	51.2	79.1	80.7	77.7
7501	41.6	39.3	43.6	61.0	62.4	59.8
7502	41.9	42.4	41.5	28.1	30.0	26.4
7601	17.1	18.7	15.7	43.2	45.4	41.3
7602	54.4	52.1	56.6	75.1	72.4	77.5
7701	53.4	54.4	52.5	73.5	73.8	73.2
7702	55.4	53.6	21.7	64.1	62.3	65.9
7801	47.2	50.7	43.1	44.9/61.8	42.0/56.5	48.4/67.7
7802	48.9	48.5	49.4	47.1/66.2	43.5/59.4	50.9/73.3
7901	8.1/49.1	7.3/48.5	8.9/49.7	52.1/73.7	52.1/70.3	52.1/76.9
7902	14.9/70.5	13.7/68.3	16.4/72.8	23.8/87.1	21.5/87.1	26.4/87.2
8001	32.4/82.9	29.5/80.6	34.9/84.9	21.9/92.0	16.4/91.4	26.7/92.5
8002	36.5/66.5	36.2/54.6	36.9/71.1	29.7/83.8	27.0/80.8	32.2/86.6

Note

The figures correspond to the percentages of those who accurately forecast the class containing the rate of change of prices occurred during the semester to which the forecast refers. The percentages only cover those who expressed an opinion, the "don't know" answers having been excluded. For the second series of surveys -- which start with the first semester 1978 -- when two figures are reported, the first refers to the class of the new questionnaire and the second to the group of classes which would have contained the actual change in prices, had the old questionnaire been retained.

3.2. *Actual vs. Anticipated Rates of Change of Prices*

In Figures 3.1 and 3.2 the expected rates are compared with the actual rates of change of semiannual averages of monthly price levels for wholesale and consumer prices, respectively.

One observes that the average expectations generally follow the actual changes fairly closely, except for certain periods. For the first semester of 1957 the answers all indicate a marked increase in prices (outcome of the influence of the Suez crisis which had just broken out, as evidenced in comments attached to the individual answers), an increase which did not in fact take place. It is worth noting how expectations immediately came back into line with the actual change in prices in the next semester.

The periods with largest errors are, however, more recent. For the wholesale prices there was a substantial underestimation of the upsurge which immediately preceded the first oil crisis of 1973 and of its effects (in

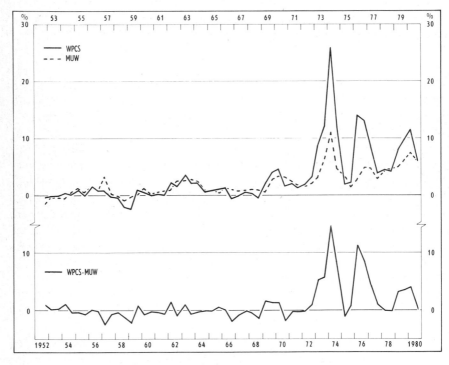

FIGURE 3.1
ACTUAL AND EXPECTED RATES OF CHANGE OF WHOLESALE PRICES

Note: WPCS is the actual semiannual rate of change of the wholesale price index; MUW is the average rate of change of wholesale prices expected by the total of respondents to the Mondo Economico opinion poll (MIX estimates).

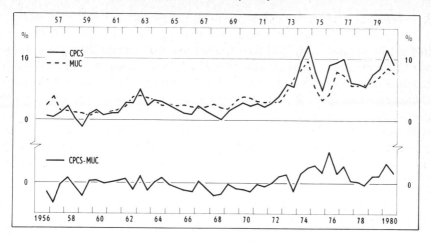

FIGURE 3.2
ACTUAL AND EXPECTED RATES OF CHANGE OF CONSUMER PRICES

Note: CPCS is the actual semiannual rate of change of the consumer price index;
MUC is the average rate of change of consumer prices expected by the total of
respondents to the Mondo Economico opinion poll (MIX estimates).

the first semester of 1974, wholesale prices increased by almost 26 percent
with respect to the previous semester). It might be worth mentioning that
before 1973 – for the entire period over which the surveys took place –
wholesale prices increased at the most, from one semester to the other, of
4.6 percent! A substantial underestimation was also observed during 1976:
while for the first semester the respondents to the survey did not forecast the
unprecedented crisis of the exchange rate market (which was actually closed
for more than one month about three weeks after the survey took place),
they were also unable to anticipate the effects on the wholesale price index
brought about by the subsequent devaluation of the Italian lira. Finally,
even if less dramatic, a further period of positive anticipation errors took
place between the first semester of 1979 and the first semester of 1980, in
connection with the crisis in Iran and the second oil crisis.

A similar story, even if on a smaller scale, holds true for the consumer
price index. One can observe a slight overestimation of the actual changes
between 1965 and 1970. The errors connected with the first oil crisis are
much smaller than those observed for wholesale prices and appear to begin
only with a lag of one year or so with respect to those for the wholesale
index, that is, in the second semester of 1974. Again in 1976–77 and in
1979–80, the respondents to these surveys anticipated changes in the
consumer price index somewhat smaller than those which actually took
place.

From the most recent episodes one can discern that when substantial oscillations in the rate of inflation take place, even "informed" persons are unable to anticipate very substantial increases. Once these have taken place, however, and the rate of inflation declines, the expected rates follow quite closely, indicating that the tendency to underestimate the actual price changes is not constant and that there are strong co-movements in the actual and expected series.

Before discussion of some synthetic measures of the accuracy of these forecasts, it is of interest to consider the plots in Figure 3.3. In the first plot the anticipation errors for both the changes in the wholesale and in the

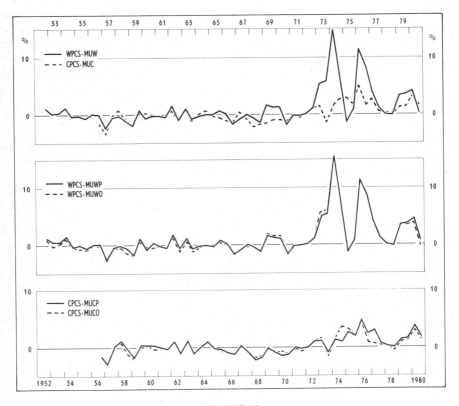

FIGURE 3.3

ANTICIPATION ERRORS OF WHOLESALE AND CONSUMER PRICE CHANGES

Note: WPCS and CPCS are the actual semiannual rates of change of the wholesale and consumer price indices; MUW, MUWP and MUWO are the average rates of change of wholesale prices expected by the total, "production" and "other" respondents to the Mondo Economico opinion poll (MIX estimates); MUC, MUCP and MUCO are the average rates of change of consumer prices expected by the total, "production" and "other" respondents to the Mondo Economico opinion poll (MIX estimates).

consumer price indices (total of answers) are considered jointly, allowing one to evaluate the less satisfactory performance of *Mondo Economico* panel in anticipating the wholesale rather than the consumer price indices in more recent years. On intuitive grounds, it would seem that forecasting changes in the consumer price index is, in general, easier, since such changes tend to lag behind those in the wholesale index as well as have a substantially smaller time variability. As can be seen from Table 3.2, over the period 1958–80 standard deviations of 5.3 percent for wholesale and 3.4 percent for consumer price changes correspond to almost identical means of 3.8 percent and 4 percent.

The second and third plots of Figure 3.3 confirm what was concluded in Section 2.5, that is, the very similar performance of the anticipations of the two groups of persons into which this study has divided the panel of *Mondo Economico*. While in the most recent years there is a larger tendency to underestimate actual changes on the part of the "production" respondents (but very likely not significant enough), on only very few occasions, and only for the consumer price index, there were sensible differences. These occasions appear to be three: the absolute differences being of 0.74 percentage points in the second semester of 1960, 1.5 percentage points in the second semester of 1976, and a large one of 2.53 percentage points in the second semester of 1974 when the correction for the upper open-ended interval might have exaggerated the true difference.

3.3. The Evaluation of Forecasting Accuracy

Figures 3.1 through 3.3 show that actual and expected rates of inflation do indeed follow a similar pattern over the period for which there is statistical evidence. Before 1973 no signs of systematic errors of anticipation can be found. As these signs are much more present in recent years, some discussion of synthetic and illustrative measures of the forecasting performance of the (average of the) respondents to the *Mondo Economico* surveys is called for here.

There are many descriptive statistics which have been proposed in order to evaluate predictive success or failure,[6] each of which has something to be recommended but none of which is completely satisfactory. They do, however, provide a general qualitative flavor of the characteristics of the series of forecasts to be evaluated. The main inconvenience of these measures is that it is not known which values one should assume in order to

---

[6]For specific discussions on the evaluation of economic forecasts, see Theil (1961, 1966), Klein (1971) and Granger and Newbold (1977).

conclude how accurate these forecasts are. The strategy of considering not only one but a number of these statistics, of comparing their values over different periods and among different variables, of using them to examine the differences between such forecasts and alternative predictors of the series of interest, of looking at the properties of the time series of the errors of prediction, must then be relied upon. The last two subjects will be considered in depth in Chapter 4 (comparison with alternative predictors) and Chapter 5 (error analysis and tests for unbiasedness and rationality). In the next sections the first two points will be addressed as well as the behavior of the series of expected rates of change of wholesale and con-

TABLE 3.4

DEFINITIONS OF ACCURACY MEASURES AND RELATED STATISTICS

$$AM = \sum_{t=1}^{T} A_t/T \quad \text{(arithmetic average of actual rates of inflation, } A_t);$$

$$EM = \sum_{t=1}^{T} E_t/T \quad \text{(arithmetic average of expected rates of inflation, } E_t);$$

$$ME = AM - EM \quad \text{(mean error of prediction)};$$

$$MAE = \sum_{t=1}^{T} |A_t - E_t|/T \quad \text{(mean absolute error of prediction)};$$

$$RMSE = \left[\sum_{t=1}^{T} (A_t - E_t)^2/T\right]^{1/2} \quad \text{(root mean square error of prediction)};$$

$$\%MAE = MAE/AM ;$$

$$\%RMSE = RMSE/AM ;$$

$$UTC1 = \left[\sum_{t=1}^{T} (A_t - E_t)^2 / \sum_{t=1}^{T} A_t^2\right]^{1/2} \quad \text{(Theil's inequality coefficient, 1)};$$

$$UTC2 = \left[\sum_{t=1}^{T} (A_t - E_t)^2 / \sum_{t=1}^{T} (A_t - A_{t-1})^2\right]^{1/2} \quad \text{(Theil's inequality coefficient, 2)};$$

$$VNR = T \sum_{t=2}^{T} \left[(A_t - E_t) - (A_{t-1} - E_{t-1})\right]^2/(T-1) \sum_{t=1}^{T} \left[(A_t - E_t) - \sum_{t=1}^{T} (A_t - E_t)/T\right]^2$$

(von Neumann's ratio);

$$RHO = V(A_t, E_t)/\left[V(A_t, A_t)V(E_t, E_t)\right]^{1/2} \quad \text{(correlation coefficient between } A_t \text{ and } E_t);$$

$$PM = V\left[(A_t - E_t), (A_t - E_t)\right]/V(A_t, A_t)$$

$$UM = ME^2/MSE \quad \text{(bias proportion of MSE)};$$

$$UR = \left[V(E_t, E_t)^{1/2} - RHO \cdot V(A_t, A_t)^{1/2}\right]^2/MSE \quad \text{(regression proportion of MSE)};$$

$$UD = (1 - RHO^2) \cdot V(A_t, A_t)/MSE \quad \text{(disturbance proportion of MSE)};$$

where:

T = number of observations

$V(y,z) = E(y - Ey)(z - Ez) \quad$ (E is the expected value operator)

MSE = mean square error of prediction ($= RMSE^2$) .

sumer prices in anticipating turning points or exceptional events. It must be pointed out, however, that an accurate examination of the series and corresponding errors plotted in Figures 3.1 through 3.3 offers great benefit and frequent reference will be made to such.

The measures considered to evaluate the forecasting performance of the inflation expectations formulated by the respondents to the *Mondo Economico* surveys are defined in Table 3.4. As can be seen, mean errors, mean absolute errors, and (root) mean square errors of prediction will be computed. The last two will also be evaluated as ratios to the average of the actual rates of change of prices, so that forecasts for different time periods and over different price indices will also be compared. Two estimates of Theil's inequality coefficient[7] will also be computed, one to evaluate the predictive performance with respect to a prediction of *no change* of the price level (*UTC1*) and the other with respect to a prediction of *equal change* of the price level to what actually occurred in the semester preceding the date of the survey (*UTC2*). A simple test on the randomness of the anticipation errors will be performed on the basis of von Neumann's ratio,[8] against the null hypothesis of first-order serial correlation in the series of errors. The correlation coefficients between actual and expected changes will be estimated[9] and a related measure (*PM*), that is, the ratio between the variance of the anticipation errors and the variance of the actual changes,[10] will also be presented. Finally, one of the two standard decompositions of the mean square error of prediction will be performed, considering, first, the proportion of this error measure due to bias in the forecasts (as described by the difference in the means of the actual and expected series), second, that due to the deviation from one of the slope of the regression line between the actual and the expected changes in prices, and third, that due to remaining random components of the actual series.[11]

---

[7] These inequality coefficients which can be used to discriminate against "naive" alternative forecasts – such as the "no change in the level" or "no change in the rate of change" – do not suffer from the inconveniences associated with the first inequality coefficient proposed by Theil (1961, p. 32), which were pointed out by Granger and Newbold (1973).

[8] Von Neumann (1941), tabulated by Hart (1942).

[9] Provided the forecasts are unbiased, "the best forecast will be the one most correlated with actual values" (Granger and Newbold (1977, p 286))

[10] Obviously, $0 \leq PM \leq 1$ and, when the forecast and the anticipation error series are uncorrelated (which is a necessary condition for optimal forecasts), $PM = 1 - RHO^2$ (where *RHO* is the correlation coefficient between the actual and predicted values). The use of this measure as a criterion for judging forecasting performance has been suggested by Granger and Newbold (1977, pp. 286–287).

[11] The set of proportions based on the alternative decomposition of the mean square error advanced by Theil (1961, p. 34) is not considered here, since Granger and Newbold (1973) have convincingly demonstrated the impossibility of a clear interpretation of these quantities.

3.4. The Predictive Accuracy of the Inflation Expectations of the Respondents to Mondo Economic Surveys

The accuracy measures and the other statistics described in the last section (defined completely in Table 3.4) have been computed for the two price indices considered in this study, with reference to the inflation expectations of the total respondents to *Mondo Economico* surveys and of those of the two groups ("production" and "other") in which they have been divided. The results are presented in Tables 3.5 and 3.6 for the wholesale and consumer price indices, respectively.[12]

The analysis has been performed not only for the whole sample period (second semester 1952 to second semester 1980 for wholesale, and second semester 1956 to second semester 1980 for consumer prices), but also for four sub-periods.[13] The latter have been chosen so as to split the sample period in two parts: the first, before the effects of the first oil crisis were reflected in the price indices and the second, after. As can be seen from Figure 3.2, substantial anticipation errors for consumer price changes only started with the second semester of 1974, so that the first sub-period has been closed with the survey for the first semester of that year. For wholesale prices, instead, substantial prediction errors were committed also in 1973; technically only a part of the error for the *second* semester of that year could be attributed to the oil crisis (the Yom Kippur war started on the 6th of October). Other large shocks, however, hit the Italian economy for the first time after more than twenty years of steady growth and mild inflation: in January and February the Italian lira left the "snake" and there was a substantial depreciation with respect to the stronger European currencies (accompanying that of the U.S. dollar); and in the next months large increases in the costs of production came from the simultaneous rise of world prices for raw materials and agricultural products and of the cost of labor, when most national labor contracts were renewed. These shocks were then followed and amplified by the energy crisis. It seems natural then to include 1973 in the second sub-period for wholesale prices and in the first for consumer prices, on which these shocks produced their effects only with a lag. Since, as observed, a large error was also committed in the first semester of 1957 when price increases connected with the Suez crisis were anticipated but did not occur, the analysis has also been performed starting

---

[12] These tables report the results obtained on the basis of the *MIX* estimates of the average expected rates of change of prices; very similar results have been obtained with the *PUM* estimates.

[13] These are also the sub-periods considered in Tables 3.1 and 3.2.

TABLE 3.5

MEASURES OF THE ACCURACY OF FORECASTS - WHOLESALE PRICES
COMPARISON BETWEEN ACTUAL AND EXPECTED RATES OF CHANGE

	5202-7202	5202-8002	5801-7202	5801-8002	7301-8002
			TOTAL		
AM	.847	3.157	1.045	3.838	9.076
EM	1.041	2.106	1.240	2.491	4.835
ME	- .195	1.050	- .195	1.348	4.240
MAE	.765	1.789	.798	2.056	4.413
RMSE	.965	3.310	.971	3.655	6.053
%MAE	.904	.567	.764	.536	.486
%RMSE	1.139	1.049	.930	.952	.667
UTC1	.589	.565	.518	.561	.563
UTC2	.718	.861	.705	.863	.873
VNR	1.939	.863	2.097	.889	1.385
RHO	.742	.876	.801	.884	.760
PM	.454	.404	.374	.416	.562
UM	.041	.101	.040	.136	.491
UR	.010	.380	.041	.409	.126
UD	.950	.519	.919	.456	.383
T	41	57	30	46	16
			PRODUCTION		
AM	.847	3.157	1.045	3.838	9.076
EM	.962	2.031	1.171	2.423	4.772
ME	- .115	1.126	- .126	1.415	4.304
MAE	.759	1.804	.769	2.060	4.482
RMSE	.972	3.361	.947	3.706	6.149
%MAE	.897	.572	.736	.537	.494
%RMSE	1.148	1.065	.906	.966	.678
UTC1	.594	.573	.505	.569	.572
UTC2	.723	.874	.687	.875	.887
VNR	2.043	.921	2.305	.947	1.466
RHO	.737	.869	.801	.882	.767
PM	.474	.411	.364	.423	.581
UM	.014	.112	.018	.146	.490
UR	.038	.360	.015	.404	.148
UD	.948	.527	.967	.450	.362
T	41	57	30	46	16
			OTHER		
AM	.847	3.157	1.045	3.838	9.076
EM	1.106	2.157	1.294	2.530	4.848
ME	- .260	1.000	- .249	1.308	4.227
MAE	.793	1.809	.833	2.077	4.411
RMSE	.982	3.269	1.011	3.612	5.966
%MAE	.937	.573	.797	.541	.486
%RMSE	1.160	1.036	.968	.941	.657
UTC1	.600	.558	.540	.554	.555
UTC2	.731	.850	.734	.853	.361
VNR	1.876	.823	1.960	.850	1.346
RHO	.738	.879	.789	.883	.763
PM	.456	.397	.397	.408	.534
UM	.070	.094	.061	.131	.502
UR	.002	.387	.047	.401	.108
UD	.928	.519	.892	.468	.390
T	41	57	30	46	16

Note

For the definitions see Table 3.4. MIX estimates for the expected rates of change.

TABLE 3.6

MEASURES OF THE ACCURACY OF FORECASTS - CONSUMER PRICES
COMPARISON BETWEEN ACTUAL AND EXPECTED RATES OF CHANGE

	5602-7401	5602-8002	5801-7401	5801-8002	7402-8002
			TOTAL		
AM	2.174	3.782	2.304	3.980	8.236
EM	2.623	3.639	2.640	3.717	6.451
ME	- .450	.143	- .336	.263	1.785
MAE	.889	1.138	.815	1.101	1.829
RMSE	1.116	1.496	.982	1.450	2.234
%MAE	.409	.301	.354	.277	.222
%RMSE	.513	.396	.426	.364	.271
UTC1	.387	.297	.327	.279	.262
UTC2	.849	.861	.742	.821	.870
VNR	1.771	.980	1.898	1.000	1.790
RHO	.844	.924	.882	.934	.782
PM	.290	.201	.229	.183	.389
UM	.163	.009	.117	.033	.638
UR	.008	.269	.025	.288	.000
UD	.829	.722	.857	.679	.362
T	36	49	33	46	13
			PRODUCTION		
AM	2.174	3.782	2.304	3.980	8.236
EM	2.593	3.615	2.611	3.695	6.447
ME	- .419	.167	- .307	.285	1.789
MAE	.890	1.130	.821	1.096	1.796
RMSE	1.119	1.493	.994	1.450	2.222
%MAE	.409	.299	.356	.275	.218
%RMSE	.515	.395	.431	.364	.270
UTC1	.388	.297	.331	.279	.261
UTC2	.851	.859	.751	.821	.865
VNR	1.694	.928	1.777	.935	1.636
RHO	.838	.918	.873	.927	.795
PM	.299	.199	.240	.182	.374
UM	.140	.012	.096	.039	.648
UR	.001	.210	.007	.221	.005
UD	.859	.777	.897	.741	.346
T	36	49	33	46	13
			OTHER		
AM	2.174	3.782	2.304	3.980	8.236
EM	2.650	3.671	2.666	3.749	6.499
ME	- .477	.111	- .362	.232	1.737
MAE	.903	1.147	.827	1.108	1.821
RMSE	1.128	1.525	.989	1.477	2.289
%MAE	.416	.303	.359	.278	.221
%RMSE	.519	.403	.429	.371	.278
UTC1	.391	.303	.329	.285	.269
UTC2	.858	.877	.748	.836	.891
VNR	1.841	1.089	1.999	1.125	1.877
RHO	.845	.919	.884	.928	.724
PM	.291	.210	.228	.192	.478
UM	.178	.005	.134	.025	.576
UR	.012	.252	.035	.270	.002
UD	.810	.742	.832	.705	.422
T	36	49	33	46	13

Note ˙

For the definitions see Table 3.4.　MIX estimates for the expected rates of change.

from the first semester of 1958 to exclude that error for which an immediate explanation was available.

The results of Tables 3.5 and 3.6 will be evaluated comparing: (1) the general predictive performance of the inflation expectations over the various periods considered, (2) the relative performance of the "production" and the "other" respondents' expectations, and (3) the performance of the expectations of wholesale and consumer price changes. The predictive accuracy of the expectations from the *Mondo Economico* surveys will then be compared with that of the expectations collected from other surveys on expected inflation.

3.4.1. Predictive Performance over Various Periods

In the whole sample period (second semester 1952 to second semester 1980 for wholesale, and second semester 1956 to second semester 1980 for consumer prices), the expected price changes were more efficient (under a mean square error criterion) than the "naive" predictions of no change or equal change of the price levels with respect to the previous semester, as can be seen from Theil's inequality coefficients, *UTC1* and *UTC2*. The prediction errors were such that the hypothesis of positive first-order serial correlation cannot be rejected (as shown by the *VNR* statistics). The correlation coefficients between the actual and the predicted series are rather high (88 percent and 92 percent for the wholesale and consumer prices, respectively); the *PM* statistics show, however, that the variance of the errors was 40 percent of that of the actual wholesale price changes and half as much for the consumer price changes. There is evidence of bias in the predictions, due for the most part to a substantial difference from unity of the slopes of the regressions of actual on expected price changes. These results hold true also for the sample which starts with the first semester of 1958, even if a small improvement in the overall predictive accuracy is obtained (compare the figures for *%RMSE* and *%MAE*, which show a reduction in the two measures of prediction errors in terms of the average actual inflation of the periods considered).[14]

Splitting the sample in two sub-periods, however, a different picture results. In particular, over the first period, no serial correlation in the errors and no bias in the prediction of actual changes result. Almost all the

---

[14]Also the correlation coefficients are higher in this case; observe however that for the wholesale prices the increase of *RHO* is accompanied by an increase in *PM* which points to a larger correlation between the expected series and that of the anticipation errors.

difference between actual and expected inflation seems due to random components (see the *UD* terms of the *MSE* decomposition, which for both price indices are very near to one, even if for consumer prices it appears from *UM* that there has been an overall, though mild, overestimation of actual changes). A general improvement in the results is obtained for the periods starting after the Suez crisis. For more recent years, after the first oil crisis, only sixteen and thirteen observations are available, for the wholesale and consumer price indices, respectively. The statistics obtained should therefore be considered with some care. It appears that from the von Neumann ratios, the hypothesis of first-order serial correlation can be rejected; it is clear, however, that there is a substantial understatement of the inflationary experience of the seventies, as it was already noticed from the plots considered in Section 3.2 (see, in particular, Figure 3.3). The values of the *UD* terms are indeed, for both indices, smaller than 40 percent. In both sub-periods there is strong correlation between actual and predicted price changes; the *PM* statistic shows, however, that for wholesale prices there are signs, in the more recent period, of correlation between the forecasts and the anticipation errors.[15] Also, in both sub-periods Theil's inequality coefficients indicate similar degrees of efficiency of the expectations of the *Mondo Economico* panel with respect to the "naive" alternatives. Finally, even if, as shown in Figures 3.1 and 3.2, larger absolute errors were committed in forecasting the higher more recent rates of inflation, a somewhat unexpected result occurs: both absolute and mean square errors indicate that in the second periods there is a significant reduction in the size of the unanticipated inflation when this is compared with the actual inflation record. For example, the root mean square errors have been equal for the wholesale price index to 0.965 in the first period and to 6.053 percentage points in the second; as ratios of the average actual rates of inflation, however, they passed from 1.139 to 0.667. For the consumer price index, a root mean square error of 1.116 in the first period has been followed by one of 2.234 in the second; for the ratios with respect to the actual inflation from the second semester of 1956 to the first semester of

---

[15]Comparing the *PM* statistics with $PM^* = 1 - RHO^2$ – which is what one would get if the necessary condition for optimality (under a mean square error criterion) of prediction did hold – one obtains the following results:

	Wholesale Prices			Consumer Prices	
	PM	*PM**		*PM*	*PM**
5202–7202	0.454	0.449	5602–7401	0.290	0.287
7301–8002	0.562	0.422	7402–8002	0.389	0.388
5202–8002	0.404	0.233	5602–8002	0.201	0.146
5801–7202	0.374	0.358	5801–7401	0.229	0.222
5801–8002	0.416	0.219	5801–8002	0.183	0.128

1974, a figure of 0.513, reduced to 0.271 in the more recent years, is observed.

3.4.2. *Predictive Performance of "Production" and "Other" Respondents*

The comparison between the expectations of the two groups of respondents does confirm, as it was expected, what the analysis of Section 2.5 and the plots of Figure 3.3 had indicated: there is no evidence of significant differences between these expectations. Indeed, as one can see from Tables 3.5 and 3.6, the statistics computed for the total of respondents are always very similar to those computed for the two separate groups. The only difference that seems to emerge is that of a slightly higher accuracy of the forecasts of the "production" respondents for consumer prices both in the first and in the second sub-periods and for wholesale prices in the first period only. This is particularly evident for the latter price index for the semesters between 1958 and 1972.

3.4.3. *Expectations of Wholesale vs. Consumer Price Changes*

Comparing the expectations of wholesale prices and those of consumer prices, one immediately observes that the latter are much more accurate, both in absolute terms and relative to the actual changes. There is also a general higher correlation between actual and anticipated consumer price changes and, as it was to be expected given the substantially higher variability of wholesale prices (displayed, for example, in Table 3.2), much higher values of the *PM* ratios are obtained for the latter. The relative efficiency of the expectations of the *Mondo Economico* respondents, in predicting actual price changes, with respect to the "naive" alternative predictors, is not very different, however, for the two price indices. This is particularly so when the hypothesis of changes in the price level equal to those occurring in the previous semester is considered as a yardstick. The *UTC2* coefficients are, over the entire sample, equal to 0.861 for both price indices; they are practically the same for the more recent period and actually better for wholesale prices in the first period. The decomposition of the mean square error indicates an overall small bias, over the entire sample, for the consumer price expectations. This is mainly a result of two different stories for the two different sub-periods. In fact, the wholesale price expectations have for the first sub-period higher *UD* ratios (and therefore lower relative bias) than those for consumer price changes. The largest changes in the pattern of the wholesale price index, which is more exposed than the

TABLE 3.7

COMPARISON OF THE FORECASTING ACCURACY
OF RESPONDENTS TO DIFFERENT SURVEYS

	Horizon	Frequency	AM	ME	RMSE	%RMSE	T
		CONSUMER PRICES					
Mondo Economico (Italy)	6 months	semi-annual					
5602-7401			4.43	-.91	2.29	.52	36
7401-8002			17.20	3.85	4.81	.28	13
5602-8002			7.82	.35	3.16	.40	49
SRC U. of Michigan (USA)	12 months	quarterly					
4901-6701			1.72	.15	2.14	1.25	73
6702-7804			6.07	.48	1.97	.32	47
4901-7804			3.42	.34	2.08	.61	120
Livingston (USA)	8 months	semi-annual					
4801-7302			2.69	1.43	2.37	.88	52
7401-8002			9.32	2.43	3.44	.37	14
4801-8002			4.10	1.65	2.63	.64	66
Gallup (UK)	6 months	monthly					
6101-7312			5.75	.67	3.51	.61	156
IAESR (Australia)	12 months	quarterly					
7401-7704			14.02	-.37	3.34	.24	16
		WHOLESALE or PRODUCER PRICES					
Mondo Economico (Italy)	6 months	semi-annual					
5202-7202			1.72	-.45	1.93	1.12	41
7301-8002			19.31	9.35	13.57	.70	16
5202-8002			6.66	2.30	7.37	1.11	57
Livingston (USA)	8 months	semi-annual					
4801-7302			2.10	1.16	3.04	1.45	52
7401-8002			9.31	1.70	3.60	.39	14
4801-8002			3.63	1.27	3.17	.87	66
BEA (USA)	12 months	annual					
1971-1980 (sales prices)			7.55	1.88	3.84	.51	10
1971-1980 (capital goods prices)			9.15	.97	2.35	.26	10

Note

Actual and expected rates of change of prices have been considered for all surveys on yearly basis.
For the definitions, see Table 3.4.

Sources

Mondo Economico: Tables D.22 and D.25 (expected rates = MIX);   SRC - University of Michigan: Juster
and Comment (1978), Table 7 (revised estimate);   Livingston: Carlson (1977), Tables 1 and 2, updated
with slight revisions by Donald J. Mullineaux of the Federal Reserve Bank of Philadelphia;   Gallup:
Carlson and Parkin (1975), Table in Appendix;   IAESR: Defris and Williams (1979), Table 1;   BEA: De
Leeuw and McKelvey (1981), Table 1.

consumer index to shocks of international nature such as the ones which have dominated in the recent past, can probably account for the results obtained over the whole sample period.

3.4.4. Comparison with Other Surveys on Inflation Expectations

As it has been observed at the beginning of this section, it is difficult to gauge from the simple examination of summary measures such as those of Tables 3.5 and 3.6 the general level of accuracy with which the respondents to the surveys have forecast the actual changes in prices. One can only perform relative comparisons; to evaluate the general reliability of persons who participate in the surveys, one should probably compare their predictions with those generated in alternative ways; in the next chapter some of these comparisons will be performed.[16] Here a different analysis will be attempted: the forecasting performance of the inflation expectations of the *Mondo Economico* respondents will be compared with that of expectations from other surveys among different individuals and for different countries.

The results of this comparison are presented in Table 3.7. Without going into details, since the table is sufficiently clear, it has to be at first emphasized that widely different results for different countries could be expected *a priori* since the inflation pattern of Italy and the United Kingdom are, for example, very dissimilar to that of the United States. The forecasts of businessmen are, furthermore, likely to be based on quite different information sets than those of households or people in general. The evidence presented in Table 3.7 is, nonetheless, extremely interesting. A surprising similarity emerges in the performance of the different expectation series, as it is measured by the root mean square errors divided by the average actual rates of inflation (all these expectations are for short-term horizons – six to twelve months – and have been expressed on a yearly basis to facilitate comparison).

On the basis of the figures of Table 3.7 it is possible to conclude that the forecasts of the Italian businessmen collected by *Mondo Economico* do relatively well when compared with those of other persons for other countries.[17] One has also to remember that the inflation pattern, for the periods

[16] The results of Tables 3.5 and 3.6 do however confirm, as it has been mentioned, that the expectations of the respondents to *Mondo Economico* surveys are more accurate than the predictions which one would have obtained had he used the two "naive" alternatives.

[17] In Table 3.7 expected rates of inflation measured from quantitative surveys and, for the U.K., also from qualitative ones have been considered. The accuracy measures have been computed for various sub-periods – when it was possible and when the "history" of inflation was such to produce different results. The expectations series are those published in the

considered in this comparison, has probably been for Italy more complex and more difficult to predict than those experienced by the other countries considered in Table 3.7.

3.5. *The Anticipation of Turning Points*

Economists have long been interested in studying both the turning point properties of economic time series – given their main interest in the business cycle – and in evaluating forecasts at turning points (see Theil (1961, 1966) and Zarnovitz (1972) for two widely quoted references). Yet, there is no consensus on the definition of a "turning point" and there is even some disagreement among economists and applied econometricians, on one side, and statisticians and time series analysts on the other, on the usefulness of giving them special attention as far as forecasts are concerned. It is clear that if one is to minimize expected loss functions of a quadratic or similar form, one might regard as inferior a forecast which would do systematically worse than the one generated under the above criterion, even if it did consistently catch all the turning points experienced in reality.[18] If, however, economic policy is influenced more by the realization of a turning point than by, say, large errors in anticipating rates of change of a given variable,

---

relevant studies (references are contained in Table 3.7); for the Livingston's data the series have been used kindly made available by Donald J. Mullineaux of the Federal Reserve Bank of Philadelphia, who has updated, along the lines of Carlson's (1977a) study, the results published by this author (with some revisions also with respect to the published series, which account for some further minor inconsistencies, besides those discovered by Carlson). For the accuracy measures the expectations have been compared with the following actual price changes (all referring to the same periods to which the expected changes refer): for the IAESR and BEA surveys, those published in the articles by Defris and Williams (1979b, table 1) and DeLeeuw and McKelvey (1981, table 1); for the SRC surveys, the percentage changes between the consumer price index for a given quarter and the same quarter of the previous year; for the Livingston's data, the percentage changes in the consumer and the producer (wholesale) price indices for the months of June and December of each year with respect to the month of October of the previous year and the month of April of the same year, respectively; for the Gallup surveys, the percentage changes between the retail price index for a given month t and that for month $t-6$ (these data differ from those published by Carlson and Parkin (1975), which are not comparable in this respect with their series of expected price changes, as observed by McDonald and Woodfield (1980, fn. 4)).

[18] Two leading textbooks in time series analysis (Box and Jenkins (1970) and Granger and Newbold (1977)) do not even discuss the subject of turning points and a third (Nelson (1973, p. 211)) claims that "once the loss associated with [prediction] errors has been specified, then conditions for optimal predictions may be stated, for example, in minimization of mean square error. Thereafter, turning-point errors are of no special interest in and of themselves". For a contrary view and an interesting attempt at predicting the turning points of a time series, see Wecker (1979).

equal in sign to those in previous periods, it would probably be necessary to consider a different criterion when generating forecasts. These are but two extreme examples; nonetheless, one cannot dismiss so easily an investigation of the performance of a given forecast in anticipating the turning points which did actually occur as is done by many modern time series analysts.

The definition of a turning point is of course somewhat arbitrary and necessarily reflects the subjective beliefs and interests of the single investigator. One might, for example, define a turning point in a time series as an observation that is followed by at least two realizations in the opposite direction. For the present purposes, since semiannual changes in prices are the concern, turning points are defined as the *first* change observed in the sign of the *difference* of two successive price changes (turning point in the rate of change). Due to obvious problems in "discriminating" among turning points, the absolute size of these changes has not been considered: one might have preferred to consider as turning points only those changes above some absolute value.

Consider again the plots in Figures 3.1 and 3.2. Two facts seem worth emphasizing:

(a) Both the expectations of wholesale and consumer price changes are timely and catch consistently the major changes which occurred in the rate of inflation. This is true not only for the increase in price changes of the early sixties and the reduction experienced in the mid-sixties but also for the three major fluctuations in the rate of inflation experienced in more recent years.[19]

(b) The success in correctly anticipating the waves of the actual inflation rates of the seventies has been accompanied by a clear underestimation of the changes which actually took place. This is particularly so for the wholesale price index. Yet, for consumer prices also, anticipation errors have tended to be generally positive (they are defined by the difference between actual and expected rates). This underestimation has not been proportionally constant; rather, it tended to disappear when the inflation rates came down from exceptionally high levels to levels more similar, even if somewhat higher on average, to those which occurred in the years preceding the first oil crisis.

On one side, then, it seems that the respondents to the surveys of *Mondo Economico* were aware of the factors which led to the sometimes dramatic changes in the rate of inflation. On the other side, when these changes were

---

[19]Four, if the experience of the 1968–70 period is included, when the changes which occurred were however very moderate if judged by the standards of the inflation rates of the seventies.

very large they tended to underestimate them, probably because similar increases had never occurred in the past, because anticipation of return to normality did play a role, and because events such as the Yom Kippur war and the first oil crisis (1973–74), the devaluation of 1976, the Iran Revolution (1979), and the second oil crisis (1979–80) were truly exceptional and unforeseeable.

Table 3.8 gives an analysis of the errors implicitly made by the interviewees in anticipating turning points with respect to the rate of change of prices. It should be noted that this is the case of interest in that only a very few reductions in the price levels (especially of consumer prices) have taken place in Italy over the past thirty years.

TABLE 3.8

ANALYSIS OF ERRORS IN FORECASTING TURNING POINTS IN THE
RATE OF CHANGE OF PRICES - MONDO ECONOMICO OPINION POLL

		PREDICTED TURNING POINTS				OCCURRED TURNING POINTS			
		occurred	not occurred	total predicted	ϕ_1	predicted	not predicted	total occurred	ϕ_2
WHOLESALE									
TOTAL	lower	11	1	12	.08	11	5	16	.31
	upper	10	3	13	.23	10	7	17	.41
	total	21	4	25	.16	21	12	33	.36
PRODUCTION	lower	11	2	13	.15	11	5	16	.31
	upper	10	3	13	.23	10	7	17	.41
	total	21	5	26	.19	21	12	33	.36
OTHER	lower	10	1	11	.09	10	6	16	.38
	upper	10	3	13	.23	10	7	17	.41
	total	20	4	24	.17	20	13	33	.39
CONSUMER									
TOTAL	lower	5	4	9	.44	5	7	12	.58
	upper	9	2	11	.18	9	3	12	.25
	total	14	6	20	.30	14	10	24	.42
PRODUCTION	lower	6	5	11	.45	6	6	12	.50
	upper	9	1	10	.10	9	3	12	.25
	total	15	6	21	.29	15	9	24	.38
OTHER	lower	5	3	8	.38	5	7	12	.58
	upper	8	2	10	.20	8	4	12	.33
	total	13	5	18	.28	13	11	24	.46

Note

ϕ_1 = Predicted but not occurred turning points as a ratio of total predicted turning points.
ϕ_2 = Occurred but not predicted turning points as a ratio of total occurred turning points.

MIX estimates of the expected rates of change.

Period: 2nd semester 1952-2nd semester 1980 for wholesale prices;
        2nd semester 1956-2nd semester 1980 for consumer prices.

As for forecasts of turning points, it is clear that there are four possible situations: (a) the forecast of a turning point (*FTP*) which occurred (*OTP*); (b) the forecast of a turning point (*FTP*) which did not occur (*NTP*); (c) the forecast of no turning point (*FNTP*) when one occurred (*OTP*); (d) the forecast of no turning point (*FNTP*) when none occurred (*NTP*). Cases (b) and (c) represent the two possible types of error. Synthetic measures of these errors proposed by Theil[20] are

$$\phi_1 = (FTP, NTP)/[(FTP, OTP)+(FTP, NTP)],$$
$$\phi_2 = (FNTP, OTP)/[(FTP, OTP)+(FNTP, OTP)],$$

where ϕ_1 is the ratio of the number of turning points predicted but which did not occur to the total number of turning points predicted (both those that occurred and those that did not), while ϕ_2 is the ratio of the number of turning points which occurred but which were not predicted to the total number of turning points which occurred (both those that were predicted and those that were not). Obviously if these measures are determinate (that is, the denominator is not zero), $0 \leq (\phi_1, \phi_2) \leq 1$, and small values of these indices correspond to a successful forecasting of the turning points.

The total of turning points have further been divided into lower and upper according to the sign of the change in the rate of inflation that was forecast or that did occur. Lower turning points are therefore those indicating a rise in the rate of change of prices after a period in which it had fallen and the upper ones are those indicating a fall after a period of increase.

On the whole, the results of Table 3.8 seem to be relatively satisfactory. It appears that the interviewees were more successful in anticipating turning points in wholesale rather than in consumer prices. The higher errors they made in forecasting changes in the former are consequently somewhat compensated by their better performance in forecasting turning points: this confirms the fact that it was more difficult – given the characteristics of the variables – to forecast the absolute changes of the wholesale price index than their direction. It also appears that errors of the first kind are more limited than those of the second: thus $\phi_1 = 0.16$ and $\phi_2 = 0.36$ for wholesale prices (total respondents) and $\phi_1 = 0.30$ and $\phi_2 = 0.42$ for consumer prices.[21] A further interesting result is that while for wholesale prices there have been fewer errors in predicting upper turns in the rate of inflation, the opposite is true for consumer prices: the interviewees seem to be more successful in anticipating sudden increases in the rate of change of the wholesale price

---

[20] See Theil (1961, p. 29).

[21] Practically identical results have been obtained using the *PUM* estimates instead of the *MIX* ones.

index and reductions in that of consumer prices. Finally, of the two groups of respondents, even if not many differences are self-evident, it seems that while the "production" group made the same or slightly higher percentage of errors of the first kind, it had a better performance than the "other" group in predicting turning points which did actually occur (that is, they committed less errors of the second kind).

3.6. Summary of the Results

In this chapter the estimates of inflation expectations obtained in Chapter 2 have been compared with the actual price changes and their forecasting accuracy has been evaluated. Although any attempt at accuracy evaluation can only be based on relative comparisons and since it does not seem possible to establish a criterion to assess the "absolute" performance of a set of forecasts, various aspects of the worth of these inflation expectations in predicting the actual rates have been examined. The most interesting findings can be summarized as follows:

(1) Over the entire sample period the expectations formed by the respondents to *Mondo Economico* surveys were consistently superior to "naive" predictions such as zero or equal change with respect to the previous semester; however, they were biased and serial correlation was present in the series of anticipation errors.

(2) For the sub-periods preceding the first oil crisis (1973–74), no bias and no serial correlation in the errors have been found, according to a mean square error decomposition and the von Neumann's ratio test against first-order serial correlation; in the more recent period, the latter seems also to be absent but large underestimation of the actual rates of inflation – chiefly for the wholesale price index – has occurred. This underestimation is not proportional to the actual rates of inflation; it is rather that only the extreme (or exceptionally) high rates experienced by the Italian economy have been substantially understated. Return to normality considerations, in the presence of substantial international shocks, can probably explain a large part of this underestimation. It is obvious that since the number of observations for the most recent past is quite small, these results – particularly those on the absence of serial correlation in the anticipation errors – should be considered as tentative: serially correlated errors over the whole sample period could be due to the large bias of the after 1974 forecasts.

(3) Overall, expected rates are highly positively correlated with the realizations. Even if accuracy measures such as mean absolute and mean square errors are much larger for the most recent period than for the non-inflationary years which preceded the first oil crisis, they are substan-

tially smaller when divided by the average actual rates of change of prices over the two sub-periods. This might seem to indicate that the more recent expectations – even if biased – were *proportionally* more accurate than those for the fifties and sixties. This does not imply that they were "better" since the pattern of inflation has changed. It might well be that over the first period the time series characteristics of the actual price changes were such to make it impossible to predict with smaller proportional error variance than that which could be achieved by "optimal" forecasts over the second period. It seems reasonable to conjecture that when high inflation is more persistent, past trends are easier to extrapolate. Some indications which seem to confirm this interpretation of the facts will be found in the next chapter where the expected rates will be compared with alternative predictors.

(4) The predictive performances of the "production" and the "other" respondents seem to be very similar, with perhaps only a slightly overall higher accuracy of the predictions from the former group.

(5) In general, the expectations of changes in consumer prices were superior to those of wholesale prices; the latter have been more volatile than the former and more exposed to international shocks, so that such a result does not seem surprising.

(6) The forecasting performance of the inflation expectations of the *Mondo Economico* respondents is very similar – in terms only of a general mean square error criterion – to that of those of other surveys on inflation expectations. Given that probably the inflation pattern, over the periods considered for these comparisons, has been for Italy more complex and more difficult to predict, the results could possibly show a superiority of the *Mondo Economico* panel in forecasting short-term price changes with respect to the respondents in the other surveys which have been considered, mainly so for the expectations on consumer price changes.

(7) Both the expectations of wholesale and consumer price changes are timely and catch consistently the major changes that occurred in the rate of inflation. It appears that the interviewees were more successful in anticipating turning points in wholesale rather than in consumer price changes. It also appears that in general the respondents incurred a more limited number of errors of the first kind (forecast of a turning point which did not occur) than of the second kind (forecast of no turning point when one occurred) and that while for wholesale prices there has been much less error in anticipating upper turns in the rate of inflation, the opposite is true for consumer prices. The "production" group has, finally, had a slightly better performance than the "other" respondents in predicting the turning points which did actually occur.

Before closing this chapter and passing to consider the performance of the expectations of the *Mondo Economico* panel with respect to that of alternative predictors of price changes, it should be re-emphasized that the *average* expected rates of inflation over the respondents to the surveys is the focus of study here. Over the whole sample, however, only about half of the answers lay in the right intervals, that is, those which contained the actual rates of change of prices, with a standard deviation of about one-fifth.

The dispersion of individual expectations is therefore quite high, a finding very similar to that obtained for other surveys on price change expectations. This might imply that either the respondents were not exposed to the same information set, or that, more likely, they did not make the same use of this information. In any case, it probably reflects high levels of uncertainty present in the society – even among informed persons – on the behavior of prices. This study is mainly concerned with the analysis of inflation expectations at the aggregate level; the previous finding cannot, however, be easily disposed of. When possible, use will be made of the additional evidence that a large and varying dispersion of individual expectations, particularly for what concerns the formation of such expectations, can provide.

CHAPTER 4

EVALUATION OF INFLATION EXPECTATIONS, 2: COMPARISON WITH ALTERNATIVE PREDICTORS

4.1. The Predictors of Wholesale and Consumer Price Changes Chosen for Comparison

In this chapter the predictive accuracy of the inflation expectations of the respondents to *Mondo Economico* surveys will be evaluated by means of comparisons with that of alternative predictors of price changes. An implicit comparison with "naive" predictors ("no change" or "equal change" of prices with respect to the previous semester) has already been performed, when Theil's inequality coefficients were computed in the last chapter. The inflation expectations proved then to be superior to these naive anticipations of the inflation rate; in this chapter the "equal change" predictors (labeled as Naive in what follows) will again be used, this time explicitly, as a possible yardstick for comparison. Concentration will be, however, on a number of alternative predictors which exploit the autocorrelation structure of actual price changes. If p_t were defined as the actual rate of change of prices in period t with respect to $t-1$, the autoregressive predictors of p_t would be obtained by estimating the parameters of

$$p_t = \beta_0 + \sum_{i=1}^{n} \beta_i p_{t-i} + u_t, \qquad (4.1)$$

where n will be determined in an "appropriate" way and u_t is a residual term. If p_t were a stationary stochastic process, it is well known that it would have a moving average representation,[1] and for general invertibility conditions this would imply also an autoregressive representation of possibly infinite order. Obviously, if other "exogenous" variables influenced p_t, the assumption would then have to be that they too were stationary stochastic processes and that the parameters of the structural model explaining p_t *jointly* with the other endogenous variables of the system would remain constant over time. As Nelson (1975) showed, the optimal prediction of p_t would then depend not only on past price changes but also on the past

---

[1] By the well known decomposition theorem of Wold (1953).

history of the exogenous inputs. That is, while by Wold's decomposition theorem, if the exogenous inputs are stationary and independent random processes, p_t will still have a moving average representation, the predictors obtained from the inversion of this representation (that is, an equation such as (4.1)) will be inefficient (under a mean square error criterion) with respect to those which could be generated by exploiting the information that p_t depends on these exogenous inputs and that these are random processes characterized by some constant (possibly unknown) parameters.[2] This would be obviously true even if instead of (4.1) predictors obtained by means of the so-called Box and Jenkins technique were used.[3] Indeed, as (4.1) could be obtained from the inversion of a moving average representation, the same would be true for an ARMA process of the kind used by Box and Jenkins. Not only, then, (4.1) should in principle produce inferior forecasts to those generated by a (well-specified, both in terms of the behavioral relations and of the dynamic characteristics) structural model, but uni-variate ARMA models would also produce relatively inefficient predictions.

If one considered, however, the possibly high costs of using information besides that contained in the past history of price changes, to forecast the future inflation rate,[4] it seems natural to compare the inflation expectations of individuals such as the respondents to *Mondo Economico* surveys with the predictions generated by an estimated autoregressive process such as (4.1), possibly investigating whether u_t could be represented by a moving average process (so that (4.1) would constitute a univariate ARMA model of p_t). Yet it does not seem completely appropriate to use the predictions generated by the estimation of (4.1) over the same sample period for which the estimates of the (average) inflation expectations have been considered in the past two chapters. When those expectations were formed, the respondents had only the information on price changes up to the date when the surveys were taken. Equation (4.1) should therefore be estimated using for each semester t only the price changes which occurred until $t-1$.

In more detail, the following steps have been taken:

(1) Monthly price changes have been considered for the period January 1953 through December 1980.[5] Substantial increases in both the means and

---

[2] See Nelson (1975); see also Zellner and Palm (1974), Palm (1977) and Wallis (1980).

[3] After Box and Jenkins (1970); see also Rose (1977).

[4] See Feige and Pearce (1976) and Darby (1976).

[5] The consumer price index has been published, on a monthly basis, only since 1954; the series has been extended backwards by means of the changes in the cost of living index.

the variances of the percentage rates of change are observed however, for both the price indices examined in this study, starting with 1973 when the first oil crisis took place, after a short period of internal upward pressures. No clear departures from stationarity can however be (visually) identified if one gives a separate look at the two sub-samples, from January 1953 to December 1972 and from January 1973 to December 1980, respectively. In Table 4.1 the autocorrelation and partial autocorrelation functions of the monthly changes of both the wholesale and the consumer price indices in these two sub-periods, are presented. Looking for simple models which would approximate the series under examination at an adequate level of accuracy for the purposes of this study, one can conclude that an AR(1) model would probably suffice for the consumer price changes in both

TABLE 4.1

MEANS, STANDARD DEVIATIONS AND AUTOCORRELATION FUNCTIONS
OF MONTHLY PRICE CHANGES

	WHOLESALE				CONSUMER			
	5301-7212		7301-8012		5301-7212		7301-8012	
M	.153		1.453		.280		1.311	
S	.415		1.281		.342		.608	
T	240		96		240		96	
Lag	Autocorre-lation Function	Partial Autocorre-lation Function	Autocorre-lation Function	Partial Autocorre-lation Function	Autocorre-lation Function	Partial Autocorre-lation Function	Autocorre-lation Function	Partial Autocorre-lation Function
1	.55	.55	.77	.77	.42	.42	.50	.50
2	.30	.00	.47	-.30	.24	.07	.23	-.03
3	.19	.03	.25	.02	.06	-.08	.08	-.03
4	.12	.01	.13	.04	.11	.12	.05	.03
5	.04	-.05	.13	.13	.11	.05	.04	.01
6	.06	.07	.14	-.01	.07	-.03	.12	.12
7	.10	.07	.16	.04	.08	.06	.07	-.05
8	.12	.03	.08	-.18	.15	.11	-.02	-.08
9	.15	.08	-.06	-.14	.15	.04	-.11	-.09
10	.22	.13	-.15	.07	.13	.02	-.09	.03
11	.22	.03	-.20	-.12	.10	.03	-.10	-.06
12	.21	.07	-.21	-.03	.04	-.04	-.06	-.00
13	.12	-.08	-.25	-.19	.05	.02	-.25	-.29
14	.03	-.06	-.30	-.07	.01	-.04	-.34	-.14
15	.03	.04	-.32	-.02	.04	.02	-.27	.03
16	.03	-.01	-.30	.04	.02	-.01	-.19	-.05
17	.01	-.02	-.26	-.05	.10	.09	-.11	.02
18	-.04	-.10	-.19	.03	.09	.01	-.01	.01
19	-.02	.00	-.15	-.06	.14	.08	-.04	-.03
20	.03	.03	-.12	.02	.10	.01	-.07	.02
21	.03	-.01	-.10	.04	.08	.01	-.14	-.11
22	.06	.02	-.09	-.07	.05	.00	-.09	-.04
23	.15	.13	-.02	.13	.13	.12	.06	.14
24	.18	.08	.12	.19	.10	-.00	.15	.04

Note

M = mean.
S = standard deviation.
T = number of observations.

sub-periods and for the wholesale price changes in the first but not in the second. For the latter, at least an AR(2) model should be used. An automatic identification procedure proposed by Akaike (1976) for ARMA models leads to the same results.[6] Thus, in what follows, only autoregressive models such as (4.1) have been considered, with $n = 1$ for consumer and $n = 2$ for wholesale prices, and with u_t assumed to be a white noise process.

(2) Equation (4.1) has then been estimated by ordinary least squares, starting with the period January 1953 to December 1957 (60 observations) and ending with the period January 1953 to June 1980 (330 observations);[7] from the estimates of the coefficients of (4.1) and the past changes in p_t, *semiannual* changes in prices have been generated for the semester of interest (from the first semester of 1958 to the second semester of 1980), obtaining a series of predicted rates of change of the wholesale price index and one for the consumer price index. As is well known, this amounts to using a Kalman filter to revise each period, when more information becomes available, the β coefficients of (4.1).[8] Actually, starting with the estimates of the first sample period, those for the next periods could be easily recursively updated without the need of further matrix inversions. Defining $\beta = (\beta_0, \beta_1, \ldots, \beta_n)'$, $z_t = (1, p_{t-1}, \ldots, p_{t-n})'$, $Z_T = (z_1, z_2, \ldots, z_T)'$, $y_T = (p_1, p_2, \ldots, p_T)'$, $v_T = (u_1, u_2, \ldots, u_T)'$, it is easy to show[9] that

$$\hat{\beta}_T - \hat{\beta}_{T-1} = \lambda_T (p_T - \hat{p}_{T,T-1}), \tag{4.2}$$

where

$$\hat{\beta}_{T-1} = \left(Z'_{T-1} Z_{T-1} \right)^{-1} Z'_{T-1} y_{T-1}, \tag{4.3}$$

$$\lambda_T = \left(Z'_T Z_T \right)^{-1} z_T, \tag{4.4}$$

and (4.1) has been written as

$$y_T = Z_T \beta_T + v_T, \tag{4.5}$$

so that

$$\hat{p}_{T,T-1} = z'_T \hat{\beta}_{T-1}. \tag{4.6}$$

---

[6] This procedure makes use of the state space representation of an ARMA model and of canonical correlation analysis to determine the order of the *MA* component, once the order of the *AR* component has been identified on the basis of the minimum *AIC* criterion (see Akaike (1969)) applied to the usual Yule–Walker equations. The analysis has been conducted with the Speakeasy linkule CANCML made available by Sergio Calliari of Banca Commerciale Italiana.

[7] Two observations for wholesale prices and one for consumer prices have been lost to account for the number of lags of the autoregressive processes.

[8] Kalman (1960); applications of the Kalman filter in econometrics are discussed in Chow (1981, ch. 6).

[9] For further details, see Riddell (1975) and Brown, Durbin and Evans (1975).

Equation (4.2) gives a rule to update the estimates of the βs each time a new observation becomes available and shows that this version follows an adaptive scheme: the parameter estimates change with the anticipation error $(p - \hat{p})$ and also the adaptation coefficient λ changes over time.[10] If the true parameters were actually constant (i.e., $\beta_T = \beta_{T-1} = \cdots = \beta$), such estimation procedure would simply imply a gain in asymptotic efficiency as more observations are used. If the βs were actually changing over time, the accuracy of the procedure would depend on these changes actually following an (approximately) adaptive process. Furthermore, there is no need for the matrix inversion of (4.4) since one can prove that

$$
\left(Z_T'Z_T\right)^{-1} = \left(Z_{T-1}'Z_{T-1}\right)^{-1}\left[I - \frac{z_T z_T'\left(Z_{T-1}'Z_{T-1}\right)^{-1}}{1 + z_T'\left(Z_{T-1}'Z_{T-1}\right)^{-1}z_T}\right], \qquad (4.7)
$$

which can be used recursively to obtain all successive inverses of the moment matrix starting with that for the first sample of $T-1$ observations.

The estimates of the βs have been obtained, as already observed, on the basis of monthly observations for periods ending, respectively, with the months of June and December. Monthly forecasts of the *rate of change* of prices one to six months ahead have then been computed which, applied to the last month price *level*, produced a forecast for the next semester *level*, and therefore, given the level for the last semester, for the next semester *rate of change*. The predictions of the inflation rates obtained by means of this procedure have been labeled *ARC* (*autoregressive* with *cumulating* observations). As one can see from Table 4.2 – which reports the estimates of the βs for the sample ending with the last month of each semester, those actually used to generate the semiannual predictions – for both price indices the process has been substantially stable until the end of 1972 and has then gradually changed over the more recent years, with a substantial increase in the response of actual to past price changes (without violating, however, the stationarity condition).[11]

(3) One might think that, as time passes by, persons will pay more attention to the more recent information rather than to that more distant in

---

[10] For a Bayesian interpretation of the learning process provided by the Kalman filter, see Anderson and Moore (1979, ch. 10); for details on the error learning that characterizes expectations which optimally exploit newly arriving information, see Friedman (1979b).

[11] Changes in the autoregressive structure of the rate of inflation might be due either to changes in the behavior of economic agents (i.e., in the coefficients of the "structural" system) or to changes in the processes generating the exogenous inputs, or both.

TABLE 4.2

ARC ESTIMATES FOR ALTERNATIVE PREDICTORS
OF PRICE CHANGES

SEM	WHOLESALE			CONSUMER	
	$\hat{\beta}_0$	$\hat{\beta}_1$	$\hat{\beta}_2$	$\hat{\beta}_0$	$\hat{\beta}_1$
5801	.054	.420	-.106	.167	.196
5802	.037	.428	-.133	.173	.207
5901	.003	.482	-.105	.129	.267
5902	-.004	.482	-.056	.114	.278
6001	.009	.498	-.072	.123	.294
6002	.001	.494	-.076	.116	.295
6101	.006	.478	-.068	.119	.286
6102	.003	.469	-.060	.119	.281
6201	.011	.485	-.070	.125	.283
6202	.020	.503	-.066	.134	.294
6301	.033	.501	-.035	.144	.330
6302	.039	.511	-.033	.143	.376
6401	.048	.530	-.044	.150	.386
6402	.045	.526	-.039	.156	.387
6501	.051	.527	-.046	.160	.392
6502	.049	.514	-.039	.159	.392
6601	.056	.514	-.057	.162	.387
6602	.052	.512	-.059	.157	.388
6701	.050	.505	-.055	.157	.394
6702	.047	.505	-.053	.157	.394
6801	.051	.491	-.058	.155	.390
6802	.047	.497	-.062	.150	.393
6901	.049	.495	-.054	.146	.400
6902	.054	.506	-.047	.148	.400
7001	.059	.532	-.022	.150	.400
7002	.059	.542	-.008	.152	.403
7101	.063	.542	-.013	.155	.403
7102	.064	.537	-.009	.157	.401
7201	.065	.536	-.008	.160	.401
7202	.067	.535	-.005	.164	.399
7301	.073	.562	.006	.163	.425
7302	.064	.645	.080	.158	.485
7401	.060	.683	.150	.156	.517
7402	.071	.933	-.126	.134	.628
7501	.070	.944	-.141	.118	.701
7502	.068	.937	-.134	.127	.687
7601	.074	.939	-.137	.129	.690
7602	.084	.979	-.174	.127	.712
7701	.087	.987	-.183	.127	.732
7702	.088	.978	-.172	.128	.737
7801	.089	.977	-.173	.129	.739
7802	.090	.976	-.172	.131	.741
7901	.093	.973	-.169	.134	.736
7902	.095	.976	-.170	.138	.739
8001	.099	.962	-.150	.139	.749
8002	.103	.956	-.148	.144	.746

Note

The semesters are those for which predictions are
formed on the basis of the reported estimates, obtained over samples ending with the last months of
the preceding semester.

time. A simple way to account for this idea is to assume that each time one
more observation is added to the information set, the forecaster drops the
first observation from the set he actually uses for prediction. This amounts
to not making use of the information contained in that first observation; it
does not, in general, appear to be an efficient way to make forecasts. If,
however, one believed that the structure of the model changes over time, one

might think of this procedure as a way to approximate these changes considering only the most recent experience, making use of a sufficiently large sample (the one that the forecaster considers the smallest possible one to produce reliable estimates of the parameters): the forecaster then gives zero weight to all the observations outside this sample and equal weight to those contained in it.[12]

Keeping the sample size always equal, say, to N, and defining $Z_s(N) = (z_{s-N+1}, z_{s-N+2}, \ldots, z_s)'$, $y_s(N) = (p_{s-N+1}, p_{s-N+2}, \ldots, p_s)'$, the estimates at time s of the vector of parameters β of (4.1) would now be

$$\tilde{\beta}_s = \left[Z_s(N)' Z_s(N) \right]^{-1} Z_s(N)' y_s(N). \tag{4.8}$$

Also in this case of *moving* regressions $\tilde{\beta}_s$ can be shown to follow an adaptive process, even if slightly more elaborate than in (4.2); furthermore, the repeated matrix inversion of (4.8) can again be avoided. Starting with the normal equations and making use of the orthogonality property of least-squares residuals, it is straightforward to show that:[13]

$$\tilde{\beta}_s - \tilde{\beta}_{s-1} = \lambda_s (p_s - \hat{p}_{s,s-1}) - \lambda_{s-N}(p_{s-N} - \hat{p}_{s-N,s-1}), \tag{4.9}$$

where

$$\lambda_s = \left[Z_s(N)' Z_s(N) \right]^{-1} z_s, \quad \lambda_{s-N} = \left[Z_s(N)' Z_s(N) \right]^{-1} z_{s-N}, \tag{4.10}$$

$$\hat{p}_{s,s-1} = z_s' \tilde{\beta}_{s-1}, \quad \hat{p}_{s-N,s-1} = z_{s-N}' \tilde{\beta}_{s-1}, \tag{4.11}$$

---

[12] This shows how arbitrary this assumption is; it can be found in Friedman (1979b) who justifies it on the basis of: (a) incomplete specification of the original model (omission of variables: the misspecified model approximates the "true" one only over finite ranges of the omitted variables); (b) use of a linear structure to approximate a complex relation; (c) changes in the data collection (old observations are inferior, or otherwise not comparable, to more recent ones); and (d) finite and imperfect memories of the economic agents. A more satisfactory assumption, also considered by Friedman (1979b, p. 36), would allow economic agents to "learn and form their expectations according to a weighted estimation procedure which exponentially discounts older observations".

[13] The estimates of the coefficients of regressions on moving samples of constant size have been derived recursively in terms of the initial estimates. Brown, Durbin and Evans (1975) also discuss the moving regression case but derive the parameter estimates from the Kalman filter ones (*ARC* in the present work, i.e., those obtained by updating the estimates when new information arrives, *without* discarding the old observations).

and the inverses of the moment matrix can be derived recursively from

$$
\begin{aligned}
&\left[Z_s(N)'Z_s(N)\right]^{-1} \\
&= \left[Z_{s-1}(N-1)'Z_{s-1}(N-1)\right]^{-1} \\
&\quad \times \left\{ I - \frac{z_s z_s' \left[Z_{s-1}(N-1)'Z_{s-1}(N-1)\right]^{-1}}{1 + z_s'\left[Z_{s-1}(N-1)'Z_{s-1}(N-1)\right]^{-1}z_s} \right\},
\end{aligned}
\tag{4.12}
$$

$$
\begin{aligned}
&\left[Z_{s-1}(N-1)'Z_{s-1}(N-1)\right]^{-1} \\
&= \left[Z_{s-1}(N)'Z_{s-1}(N)\right]^{-1} \\
&\quad \times \left\{ I + \frac{z_{s-N} z_{s-N}' \left[Z_{s-1}(N)'Z_{s-1}(N)\right]^{-1}}{1 - z_{s-N}'\left[Z_{s-1}(N)'Z_{s-1}(N)\right]^{-1}z_{s-N}} \right\}.
\end{aligned}
\tag{4.13}
$$

As it was the case for the *ARC* estimates, again the first sample that has been considered is the one between January 1953 and December 1957; thus, $N = 60$. From the monthly predictions (for each of the months of a semester, given the 60 observations ending with the last month of the preceding semester), semiannual predicted changes for the two price indices have been obtained and have been labeled as *ARM* (*autoregressive* with *moving observations*). In this case, as can be seen from Table 4.3, the parameter estimates are slightly more erratic – as one might have expected – than the *ARC* ones. An increase can still be noticed in the response of actual to past price changes for the semesters after 1972. However, the *ARM* estimates seem to differ from the *ARC* ones mainly for the substantial increase in the means of the autoregressive processes for both the price indices considered in this study, following the first oil crisis.

(4) For the *ARC* and *ARM* estimates of the parameters of the autoregressive processes out of which predictions have been generated to be compared in the next sections with the expectations of the respondents to *Mondo Economico* surveys, AR(2) and AR(1) models – respectively for wholesale and consumer price changes – have been considered. As it has been observed, these models have been identified considering separately the periods before and after January 1973, and over these sub-periods they appear to be adequate representations within the class not only of AR but also of ARMA models. Perhaps for consumer prices one could have identified, from the partial autocorrelation function of Table 4.1, a light presence of seasonality over the second sub-period, which has been ignored

TABLE 4.3

ARM ESTIMATES FOR ALTERNATIVE PREDICTORS
OF PRICE CHANGES

SEM	WHOLESALE			CONSUMER	
	$\hat{\beta}_0$	$\hat{\beta}_1$	$\hat{\beta}_2$	$\hat{\beta}_0$	$\hat{\beta}_1$
5801	.054	.420	-.106	.167	.196
5802	.032	.587	-.264	.185	.226
5901	-.006	.661	-.234	.099	.385
5902	-.013	.640	-.158	.078	.439
6001	-.004	.664	-.195	.084	.448
6002	-.016	.661	-.187	.084	.458
6101	-.027	.635	-.190	.080	.450
6102	-.024	.613	-.152	.074	.427
6201	-.017	.498	.005	.078	.436
6202	-.002	.576	-.033	.104	.446
6301	.037	.544	.040	.114	.515
6302	.055	.542	.054	.115	.549
6401	.118	.532	-.066	.178	.473
6402	.116	.575	-.120	.236	.402
6501	.120	.534	-.069	.213	.437
6502	.130	.499	-.071	.234	.414
6601	.160	.496	-.135	.251	.392
6602	.178	.470	-.164	.241	.408
6701	.132	.479	-.103	.229	.441
6702	.107	.490	-.071	.197	.478
6801	.106	.361	-.147	.185	.413
6802	.074	.524	-.191	.165	.443
6901	.056	.367	-.124	.127	.450
6902	.085	.434	-.101	.113	.489
7001	.081	.548	.043	.117	.451
7002	.065	.606	.070	.116	.489
7101	.071	.592	.091	.118	.536
7102	.082	.549	.129	.143	.493
7201	.093	.555	.112	.157	.449
7202	.093	.603	.077	.184	.417
7301	.103	.670	.107	.168	.552
7302	.066	.732	.245	.193	.623
7401	.069	.722	.298	.206	.650
7402	.247	1.158	-.364	.169	.772
7501	.242	1.161	-.374	.182	.793
7502	.221	1.154	-.358	.267	.716
7601	.267	1.155	-.373	.283	.707
7602	.367	1.137	-.390	.370	.662
7701	.451	1.133	-.417	.466	.624
7702	.481	1.110	-.406	.560	.570
7801	.442	1.131	-.417	.554	.571
7802	.403	1.144	-.416	.554	.575
7901	.385	.976	-.336	.559	.555
7902	.302	1.033	-.320	.572	.525
8001	.370	.936	-.231	.635	.476
8002	.503	.891	-.263	.659	.489

Note

The semesters are those for which predictions are formed on the basis of the reported estimates, obtained over samples ending with the last months of the preceding semester.

in order not to lose degrees of freedom in estimation (especially in the case of the moving sample estimates).[14] Apart from this matter, one might

[14]A sample of 60 monthly observations seems to be the minimum one out of which reliable estimates could be derived. The observations before 1953 have been intentionally ignored, because of the very high variability which has characterized the years which have followed the Second World War, especially the very high inflation of 1946–47 and the prolonged deflation which has followed the substantial monetary restraint of 1947–48.

question the choice of the above models, identified over two separate sub-periods, when the inflation process has shifted rather significantly over a short period of time. One could have alternatively proceeded by identifying a simple process making use of "intervention" analysis, as in a situation such as the one which time-series analysts would call an "interrupted time-series experiment".[15] It has been preferred to consider in this study the models more adequate for the two sub-periods under examination, letting the parameters change but not the models, on the grounds that the forecasts generated by their estimates should be compared with the expectations of survey respondents. On one side, it seems very likely that these persons could not have responded very quickly to the change in the inflation process (rapidly revising, for instance, their estimates of the mean of this process); on the other side, it would have been very arbitrary to fix a given period from which to start the intervention, that is the allowance of a deterministic shift in the mean and/or in the variance of the process, in order to consider only the residuals from this mean (possibly corrected for the change in variance) for the identification of a simple model over the whole period examined in this study. Anyway, the joint consideration of the ARC and ARM predictions is likely to help, since in both cases – and in the latter more rapidly than in the former – the weight of the observations for the years before 1973 decreases as the forecasts for the more recent years are generated.

The possibility that one could have reacted with a lag to the changes in the autoregressive structure, which can be seen from the estimates of Tables 4.2 and 4.3 for the years following 1972, does not concern only the model but also its parameters. If one were using a model such as (4.1), with constant parameters, to forecast into the near future, one would have probably taken time before changing his estimates, at least the time necessary to understand if the shocks that caused the changes were of a temporary or of a permanent nature. A further set of predictions has therefore been considered for the whole sample period under investigation, that is,

$$ARCI(i) = \begin{cases} ARC(i) & \text{for } i = 5801,\ldots,7202, \\ ARC(7202) & \text{for } i = 7301,\ldots,8002. \end{cases} \qquad (4.14)$$

Under this assumption, the alternative predictors used for comparison with the expected rate of inflation will be those obtained by the sequential estimates of model (4.1), under the hypothesis on the use of the available information considered in (2), until the second semester of 1972; after that

---

[15]A careful analysis of the subject is conducted by Gottman (1981, ch. 26).

date the predictions will be considered as generated by the parameter structure estimated immediately before the first oil crisis and the other large shocks that have characterized the second half of the seventies.

Also the forecasts generated under the assumption of a constant *ARM* structure after the second semester of 1972 have been considered. Since they are very similar to the *ARC1* predictions, only the latter will be discussed in the next sections.

(5) The predictions obtained from *ARC* and *ARM* estimates of the parameters of (4.1) have two not necessarily independent characteristics: (a) they make use only of the information available until the moment in which the forecasts are made; and (b) they allow for changes in parameters which, for the *ARC* case, can be shown to follow a process $\beta_T = M\beta_{T-1} + v$. In this latter case, if the parameters were actually constant (so that $M = I$ and $v = 0$), at each stage one would obtain consistent estimates and increases in efficiency as more observations are used. In the next sections the expectations of the respondents to *Mondo Economico* surveys will also be compared with the predictions obtained by estimating (4.1) over the whole period of comparison, which obviously makes uses of information which was unavailable to the respondents but which might suffer from the assumption of a constant autoregressive structure. Since the comparisons will be generally made for the period from the first semester of 1958 to the second semester of 1980 and for that from the first semester of 1958 to the second semester of 1972 for wholesale prices and to the first semester of 1974 for consumer prices – in accordance with the analysis of Chapter 3 – only the predictions of price changes obtained for these sub-periods (labeled as *AR*) will be examined, in order to deal with samples of "homogeneous" observations.

It is interesting to observe, before comparing the performance of the alternative predictors of inflation considered in this section with the expectations of the respondents to *Mondo Economico* surveys, that Pearce (1979) has compared the forecast errors of Livingston's data on experts' expectations of the U.S. consumer price index (*CPI*) with those from predictions generated by a first-order moving average process of the second difference of the *CPI*. He estimated this process on monthly data starting with the sample January 1947 to April 1959 and then reestimated it every six months, with six more observations, in the same spirit, as what has been done here in the *ARC* case. He found that these forecasts dominated those from Livingston's panel, and went on to comment about the rationality of the latter, a topic that will be considered in the next chapter. Also predictors of the *ARC* type have been used by Kennedy and Lynch (1979) to generate series of "statistically rational inflation expectations" for Canada. They considered an autoregressive model such as (4.1) and chose the order of the autoregression by a sequential *F*-test for successively increasing the number of lagged variables. This order varied from 3 to 6, and they used first and fourth differences of the logarithms of quarterly levels. The first sample considered was that comprised of the thirty quarters between the third of 1955 and the fourth of 1962. The spirit of the *ARM* estimates was instead followed by Riddell and Smith (1982), who used a proxy of inflation expectations in an econometric analysis of wage changes in Canada. The proxy they used was an ARIMA model, whose parameters were re-estimated repeatedly over a moving sample of 384 observations, the first sample going from January 1921 to December 1952.

4.2. Preliminary Comparison of Expected Rates of Price Changes and Alternative Predictors of Inflation

In Table 4.4 the means and the standard deviations of the expected price changes, of the forecasts generated by the alternative predictors discussed in Section 4.1 and of the actual price changes, for both the wholesale and the consumer price indices, are presented. They have been computed for the total sample over which the alternative forecasts were generated (first semester 1958 to second semester 1980) and for the sub-periods ending with the second semester of 1972 (wholesale prices) and the first semester of 1974 (consumer prices).[16] Without commenting in detail on each figure of Table 4.4, it is worth noting that, with the possible exception of the *ARCl* predictions for consumer price changes, over the whole sample – but mainly reflecting the more recent experience – the expected rates of inflation show a smaller variability than the alternative predictors. It is also interesting to observe that over the first sub-periods for both price indices the means of the actual changes are larger than those of the alternative predictors and smaller than those of the expected rates; over the whole sample they are larger also of the latter. Always larger are also the standard deviations of the actual price changes.

Figures 4.1 and 4.2 provide a graphical display of the actual and expected rates of inflation and the *ARC* and *ARCl* predictions, for the wholesale and consumer price indices, respectively. The plots of the anticipation errors are also presented.[17] While the *ARC* predictions are, if anything, more erratic

---

[16] For the choice of the periods see the discussion in Section 3.4.

[17] The forecast errors of the Naive predictions, even if not reported, have also been examined. The poor performance of these predictions which was clearly established by the results of Section 3.4 is mainly due to the very large anticipation errors which occur in the more recent years. In particular, these predictions tend to overestimate the actual changes when the expectations underestimated them. During these years the frequent and substantial swings that have characterized the rate of inflation make forecasts, based on the assumption that prices will increase in the next semester at the same rate as in the present semester, simply systematically wrong.

than the expected rates until the first oil crisis and do not present evident signs of a better performance during this period, they appear to be slightly better than the expectations in anticipating the upsurge of the first semester of 1974 for the wholesale price index and worse than the expectations for what concerns the consumer price index (for the second semester of the same year, given the lag which characterizes this index). In the more recent years, again for wholesale prices, the *ARC* forecasts do better than the expectations of the respondents to *Mondo Economico* surveys. In the case of consumer prices, they underestimate on average the actual changes more than the expected rates. In general, the predictions based on these autoregressive estimates – which are in effect updated as a Kalman filter – anticipate, as well as the expected rates, but with much smaller errors in the case of wholesale prices and slightly larger errors for consumer prices, all

TABLE 4.4

MEANS AND STANDARD DEVIATIONS OF EXPECTED CHANGES,
ALTERNATIVE PREDICTORS AND ACTUAL CHANGES OF PRICES

| | 5801-7202 | | | | 5801-8002 | | |
	Mean (A)	Stand.dev. (B)	(B)/(A)		Mean (A)	Stand.dev. (B)	(B)/(A)
WHOLESALE							
MIX	1.24	1.07	.86		2.49	2.34	.94
NAIVE.	.92	1.55	1.67		3.70	5.35	1.45
ARC	.78	1.00	1.28		2.81	3.89	1.39
ARM	.94	1.08	1.14		3.68	4.97	1.35
AR	1.02	1.07	1.04		-	-	-
ARC1	-	-	-		2.32	2.59	1.12
WPCS	1.04	1.58	1.51		3.84	5.33	1.39

| | 5801-7401 | | | | 5801-8002 | | |
	Mean (A)	Stand.dev. (B)	(B)/(A)		Mean (A)	Stand.dev. (B)	(B)/(A)
CONSUMER							
MIX	2.64	1.57	.59		3.72	2.36	.63
NAIVE	2.05	1.48	.72		3.81	3.31	.87
ARC	1.87	1.04	.56		2.92	2.07	.71
ARM	2.04	1.28	.63		3.47	2.62	.76
AR	2.24	1.11	.53		-	-	-
ARC1	-	-	-		2.52	1.46	.58
CPCS	2.30	1.96	.85		3.98	3.37	.85

Note

The MIX estimates of the expected rates of change refer to the total of respondents to the Mondo Economico opinion poll. See text, Section 4.1, for definitions of the alternative predictors. WPCS and CPCS are, respectively, the actual semi-annual rates of change of the wholesale and of the consumer price index.

Ignazio Visco

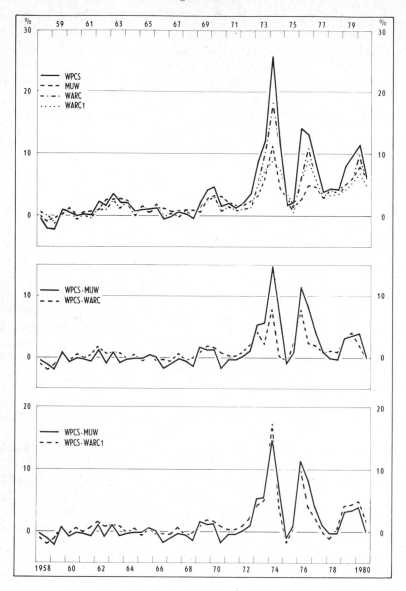

FIGURE 4.1

ACTUAL, EXPECTED AND ALTERNATIVE (ARC, ARC1) FORECASTS
OF THE RATE OF CHANGE OF WHOLESALE PRICES

Note: WPCS is the actual semiannual rate of change of the wholesale price
index; MUW is the average rate of change of wholesale prices expected by the
total of respondents to the Mondo Economico opinion poll (MIX estimates);
WARC and WARC1 are the forecasts of wholesale price changes generated by
the ARC and ARC1 alternative predictors.

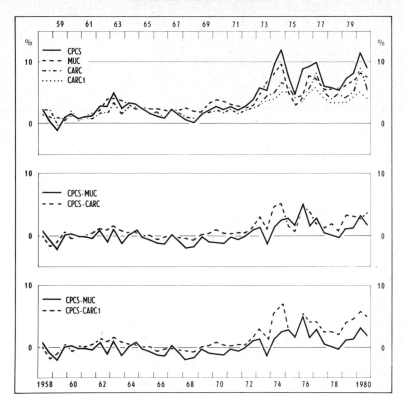

FIGURE 4.2
ACTUAL, EXPECTED AND ALTERNATIVE (ARC, ARC1) FORECASTS
OF THE RATE OF CHANGE OF CONSUMER PRICES

Note: CPCS is the total semiannual rate of change of the consumer price
index; MUC is the average rate of change of consumer prices expected by the
total of respondents to the Mondo Economico opinion poll (MIX estimates);
CARC and CARC1 are the forecasts of consumer price changes generated by
the ARC and ARC1 alternative predictors.

the major turns in the rates of price changes. This is somewhat surprising
since they are autoregressive predictors, but one should remember that the
forecasts are semiannual, based on the monthly history of price changes. It
appears that the use of information at a monthly frequency to produce
six-month predictions is rather successful when combined with an updating
of the estimates of the autoregressive structure *à la* Kalman.

It does not seem, therefore, that for wholesale prices the expectations
which are here considered have exploited completely the changes in the
autoregressive structure of the inflation rates (either coming from changes in

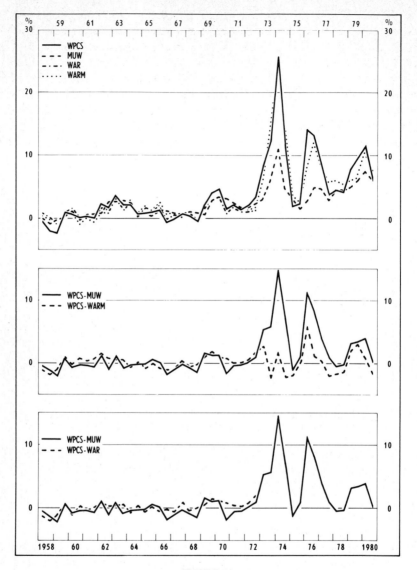

FIGURE 4.3
ACTUAL, EXPECTED AND ALTERNATIVE (AR, ARM) FORECASTS
OF THE RATE OF CHANGE OF WHOLESALE PRICES

Note: WPCS is the actual semiannual rate of change of the wholesale price
index; MUW is the average rate of change of wholesale prices expected by
the total of respondents to the Mondo Economico opinion poll (MIX
estimates); WAR and WARM are the forecasts of wholesale price changes
generated by the AR and ARM alternative predictors.

the behavior of the economic agents or in the processes generating the exogenous inputs to the process that generates the actual price changes). And indeed, if the *ARC1* forecasts – which are equal to the *ARC* ones until 1972 and are then generated by the estimates for the last month of that year – are considered, it is evident immediately that they are very similar to the expected rates of inflation, as clearly shown by the plots of the forecast errors in Figure 4.1. For consumer prices, instead, with the exception of 1975 when the errors practically coincide, the *ARC1* predictions underestimate the actual price changes considerably more than the expectations do (Figure 4.2).

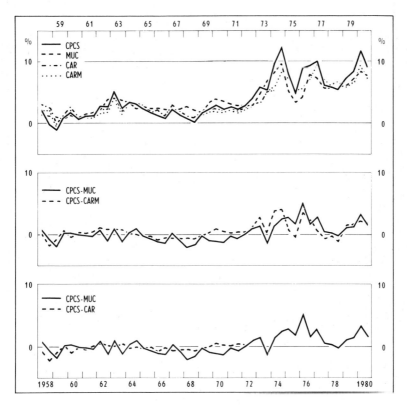

FIGURE 4.4

ACTUAL, EXPECTED AND ALTERNATIVE (AR, ARM) FORECASTS
OF THE RATE OF CHANGE OF CONSUMER PRICES

Note: CPCS is the actual semiannual rate of change of the wholesale price index; MUC is the average rate of change of consumer prices expected by the total of respondents to the Mondo Economico opinion poll (MIX estimates); CAR and CARM are the forecasts of consumer price changes generated by the AR and ARM alternative predictors.

Figures 4.3 and 4.4 present the plots of the actual and expected rates of price changes and of the forecasts generated by the *AR* and *ARM* predictors. While these plots again do not provide clear evidence to discriminate between the expectations and the alternative predictions for the period preceding the first oil crisis (which is also the only one considered for the *AR* predictions), they do, however, show that the autoregressive estimates obtained from moving samples do very well in the more recent periods in the prediction of wholesale price changes. The plots of the *ARM* forecast errors show that these forecasts are certainly also superior to the *ARC* ones, after the first oil crisis, while being very similar before that occasion. Also in the case of consumer prices the *ARM* forecasts are better than the *ARC*

TABLE 4.5

CORRELATIONS BETWEEN EXPECTED CHANGES, ALTERNATIVE PREDICTORS
AND ACTUAL CHANGES OF PRICES

WHOLESALE

	MIX	NAIVE	ARC	ARM	AR	ARC1	WPCS	
MIX	1	.716	.898	.900	–	.870	.884	
NAIVE	.859	1	.787	.774	–	.842	.679	
ARC	.723	.549	1	.988	–	.946	.962	
ARM	.731	.574	.975	1	–	.932	.957	5801-8002
AR	.692	.500	.991	.948	1	–	–	
ARC1	–	–	–	–	–	1	.902	
WPCS	.801	.602	.862	.830	.865	–	1	

5801-7202

CONSUMER

	MIX	NAIVE	ARC	ARM	AR	ARC1	CPCS	
MIX	1	.852	.893	.906	–	.879	.934	
NAIVE	.836	1	.888	.909	–	.881	.858	
ARC	.823	.759	1	.985	–	.978	.947	
ARM	.826	.756	.989	1	–	.966	.945	5801-8002
AR	.753	.693	.983	.968	1	–	–	
ARC1	–	–	–	–	–	1	.933	
CPCS	.882	.739	.905	.893	.880	–	1	

5801-7401

Note

The MIX estimates of the expected rates of change refer to the total of respondents to the Mondo Economico opinion poll. See text, Section 4.1, for definitions of the alternative predictors. WPCS and CPCS are, respectively, the actual semi-annual rates of change of the wholesale and of the consumer price index.

ones, and with the exception of 1974 they are also superior on average to the expected rates.

At this point, it might be of interest to consider the results of Table 4.5, which contains the sample correlation coefficients between the actual rates of inflation, the expected ones, and the alternative predictions. It can be seen that the coefficients relative to the consumer price index are generally higher than those for the wholesale index. They are all quite large with exceptions mainly connected with the Naive forecasts which are also in general more correlated with the expected rates than with the other predictions. With respect to the actual rates, fairly large correlations are present, again, with the possible exception of the Naive forecasts. It can also be noticed that the correlations are generally lower over the whole sample period than over the periods which exclude the more recent experience.

4.3. Comparison in Terms of Predictive Accuracy of Inflation Expectations and Alternative Predictors

In this section the prediction performance of the expectations of the respondents to *Mondo Economico* surveys will be compared to that of the alternative predictors described in Section 4.1 and considered in Section 4.2. The analysis will be based on the same accuracy measures – and related statistics – considered in Section 3.4 and defined in Table 3.4. The results for wholesale prices will be examined first, and then those for the consumer ones.

4.3.1. Wholesale Prices

If one considers the entire sample period (first semester 1958 to second semester 1980), both mean absolute and root mean square error statistics (Table 4.6) point to a greater accuracy in forecasting the actual price changes on the part of the *ARC* and particularly of the *ARM* predictions with respect to the estimates of (average) expected rates of change. The latter do better than the Naive predictions, and are marginally inferior to the *ARC1* forecasts generated, after 1972, from the autoregressive model estimated until the end of that year. The same result holds for the comparison of Theil's inequality coefficients (obviously, $UTC2 = 1$ for the Naive forecasts) and also of the estimates of the correlation with the actual changes. As regards the decomposition of the mean square error of prediction, all the forecasts present evidence of bias with the clear exception of the *ARM* predictions, which dominate all the other forecasts both in terms of bias and accuracy. By these standards there are only marginal differences

TABLE 4.6

MEASURES OF THE ACCURACY OF FORECASTS   -   WHOLESALE PRICES
COMPARISON BETWEEN EXPECTED RATES AND ALTERNATIVE PREDICTORS

5801-7202	MIX	NAIVE	ARC	ARM	AR
AM	1.045	1.045	1.045	1.045	1.045
EM	1.240	.924	.784	.942	1.025
ME	- .195	.121	.261	.103	.020
MAE	.798	1.035	.748	.758	.670
RMSE	.971	1.378	.901	.902	.833
%MAE	.764	.990	.716	.726	.641
%RMSE	.930	1.319	.863	.863	.797
UTC1	.518	.736	.481	.481	.445
UTC2	.705	1.000	.654	.654	.604
VNR	2.097	2.392	1.001	.949	1.016
RHO	.801	.602	.862	.830	.865
PM	.374	.780	.308	.332	.287
UM	.040	.008	.084	.013	.000
UR	.041	.180	.154	.064	.124
UD	.919	.812	.762	.922	.875
T	30	30	30	30	30

5801-8002	MIX	NAIVE	ARC	ARM	ARC1
AM	3.838	3.838	3.838	3.838	3.838
EM	2.491	3.697	2.810	3.677	2.321
ME	1.348	.141	1.029	.161	1.517
MAE	2.056	2.478	1.366	1.160	1.905
RMSE	3.655	4.236	2.144	1.544	3.501
%MAE	.536	.646	.356	.302	.496
%RMSE	.952	1.104	.559	.402	.912
UTC1	.561	.650	.329	.237	.537
UTC2	.863	1.000	.506	.365	.827
VNR	.889	1.967	1.297	1.601	1.224
RHO	.884	.679	.962	.957	.902
PM	.416	.646	.128	.085	.359
UM	.136	.001	.230	.011	.188
UR	.409	.164	.324	.007	.392
UD	.456	.835	.446	.982	.421
T	46	46	46	46	46

Note

For the definitions see Table 3.4. The MIX estimates of the expected rates of
change refer to the total of respondents to the Mondo Economico opinion poll.
See text, Section 4.1, for definitions of the alternative predictors.

between the expected rates and the *ARC1* forecasts, and also the *ARC* ones
do not seem to be much better.

  For the period preceding the first oil crisis, the relative performance of the
expectations is observed to improve substantially. On one side, they are only
slightly inferior to the *ARC* and *ARM* predictions in terms of mean absolute
and root mean square errors. The autoregressive forecasts generated by both
the *ARC* and *ARM* predictors show, however, clear signs of positive serial
correlation of the errors of prediction (as judged by the *VNR* statistics),
and, also, the expected rates prove to be less affected by prediction bias than the *ARC* forecasts as can be gauged from the mean square
error decomposition. The proportion due to the random component is about
92 percent for the expected price changes and the *ARM* predictions while it
is equal to 76 and 87 percent, for the *ARC* and the *AR* ones, respectively.

The latter, however, are on average a little more accurate, but it should be remembered that they make use of a larger amount of information. Finally, despite the smaller values for the *MAE* and *RMSE* measures for this sub-period than for the whole period, when they are taken as ratios of the average actual price changes practically equal results are obtained for both periods for the expected rates and smaller values for the alternative predictors.

4.3.2. Consumer Prices

Over the whole period, only the *ARM* predictions appear to be slightly more accurate in anticipating the actual consumer price changes than the ex-

TABLE 4.7

MEASURES OF THE ACCURACY OF FORECASTS - CONSUMER PRICES
COMPARISON BETWEEN EXPECTED RATES AND ALTERNATIVE PREDICTORS

5801-7401	MIX	NAIVE	ARC	ARM	AR
AM	2.304	2.304	2.304	2.304	2.304
EM	2.640	2.050	1.867	2.042	2.236
ME	- .336	.254	.437	.262	.068
MAE	.815	1.025	.752	.731	.643
RMSE	.982	1.323	1.175	1.019	1.056
%MAE	.354	.445	.354	.317	.279
%RMSE	.426	.574	.510	.442	.458
UTC1	.327	.440	.391	.339	.351
UTC2	.742	1.000	.896	.778	.806
VNR	1.898	2.198	.802	.966	.868
RHO	.882	.739	.905	.893`	.880
PM	.229	.454	.320	.261	.299
UM	.117	.037	.139	.066	.004
UR	.025	.001	.377	.206	.243
UD	.857	.963	.485	.727	.753
T	33	33	33	33	33

5801-8002	MIX	NAIVE	ARC	ARM	ARC1
AM	3.980	3.980	3.980	3.980	3.980
EM	3.717	3.807	2.920	3.467	2.521
ME	.243	.173	1.061	.514	1.459
MAE	1.101	1.340	1.287	.960	1.686
RMSE	1.450	1.766	1.875	1.326	2.519
%MAE	.277	.337	.323	.241	.423
%RMSE	.364	.444	.471	.333	.633
UTC1	.279	.340	.361	.255	.485
UTC2	.821	1.000	1.065	.754	1.432
VNR	1.000	2.217	.695	1.050	.433
RHO	.934	.858	.947	.945	.933
PM	.183	.278	.215	.135	.379
UM	.033	.010	.320	.150	.336
UR	.288	.053	.352	.174	.437
UD	.679	.937	.328	.675	.227
T	46	46	46	46	46

Note

For the definitions see Table 3.4. The MIX estimates of the expected rates of change refer to the total of respondents to the Mondo Economico opinion poll. See text, Section 4.1, for definitions of the alternative predictors.

pected rates (Table 4.7). The latter have a better performance than the Naive and the *ARC* forecasts and they clearly dominate the *ARC1* predictions. For all series, the errors of prediction are positively serially correlated.

If the period which ends with the first semester of 1974 is considered, while the best results hold for the *AR* estimates when mean absolute errors are examined, in terms of *RMSE* the expectations perform better than the forecasts generated by all the alternative predictors, even if there are only moderate differences. Again the autoregressive predictions show signs of positive serial correlation, and there is substantial bias in the *ARC* forecasts, as evidenced by the *MSE* decomposition. Also in this case there are signs of improvements in the *RMSE* and *MAE* statistics, when viewed as ratios of the average actual inflation rate, if the period including the more recent years is considered. This confirms the conjecture advanced in sub-section 3.4.1 that over the period preceding the first oil crisis, *relatively* larger errors are due to inherent difficulties in further increasing the variance of the predicted series with respect to the actual ones, as the results obtained for the alternative predictors also show.

4.4. Tests of Relative Forecasting Performance

In the last section it was seen that the expectations of the panel of *Mondo Economico*, if not always more accurate – by the standards here considered – than the forecasts generated by alternative predictors of inflation, did not do manifestly worse than the latter. It is difficult, however, to give more substance to this statement. One might wish to compare alternative forecasts under a formal statistical test of significance on their relative performance. There are, however, obvious problems stemming from the fact that there is no reason to assume *a priori* that these forecasts are uncorrelated.

If the forecasts are unbiased, however, as Granger and Newbold (1977, p. 281) have observed, it would then be possible to test equality of expected squared forecast errors (provided that they are serially uncorrelated) on the basis of the sample correlation coefficient between the two series obtained by the sum and the difference of the anticipation errors respectively. In such a case, the expected value of the product of these two variables will in fact be equal to the difference between the two error variances and, given the assumption of unbiasedness, also of the two expected squared forecast errors. They will be equal if these variables are uncorrelated, so that a test on their correlation coefficient is equivalent to one on the equality of the forecasts under the mean square error criterion.

In the present case, however, some of the alternative predictors show signs of bias even in the sub-periods considered. Over the whole sample period, furthermore, the expected rates are also clearly biased. Linear correction of both the series of expected price changes and the forecasts generated by the alternative predictors has thus been the next step. The above test has been performed on the residuals of these linear corrections: more specifically, the actual changes have been regressed on a constant and the prediction series, and the residuals of this regression have been considered as anticipation errors. The correlations of the variables obtained, respectively, as sum and difference of these (linearly corrected) anticipation errors have been computed for the series of expected price changes and each

TABLE 4.8

TESTS OF RELATIVE FORECASTING SUCCESS OF LINEARLY
CORRECTED EXPECTATIONS AND ALTERNATIVE PREDICTORS

	WHOLESALE PRICES				CONSUMER PRICES			
	5801-7202				5801-7401			
	MSE	MSEC	LM	RHO	MSE	MSEC	LM	RHO
MIX	.943	.866	1.205	-	.964	.826	.036	-
NAIVE	1.899	1.542	.127	- .495 (3.013)	1.749	1.684	2.204	- 452 (2.820)
ARC	.813	.619	2.966	.179 (.964)	1.379	.669	2.992	.110 (.618)
ARM	.813	.750	6.426	.081 (.431)	1.038	.755	7.125	.268 (.790)
AR	.694	.607	5.244	.184 (.991)	1.114	.839	4.231	- .008 (.004)
	5801-8002				5801-8002			
	MSE	MSEC	LM	RHO	MSE	MSEC	LM	RHO
MIX	13.361	6.086	7.185	-	2.102	1.428	2.998	-
NAIVE	17.945	14.975	3.934	- .486 (3.689)	3.120	2.924	1.978	- .372 (2.656)
ARC	4.598	2.049	1.069	.538 (4.232)	3.514	1.152	3.837	.109 (.727)
ARM	2.385	2.342	3.118	.491 (3.737)	1.759	1.188	4.871	.096 (.640)
ARC1	12.259	5.155	4.004	.095 (.633)	6.346	1.442	1.669	- .005 (.033)

Note

MSE = Mean square error of original forecasts.
MSEC = Mean square error of linearly corrected forecasts.
LM   = Lagrange multiplier test against second order autocorrelation in the residuals of the
       regressions for the linear correction.
RHO = Correlation coefficient between the sum and the difference of the linearly corrected
       errors in forecasting actual price changes by the expectations series and the alter -
       native predictors.
t-ratios are reported in parentheses under the estimated correlation coefficients.
The MIX estimates of the expected rates of change refer to the total of respondents to the Mon
do Economico opinion poll. See text, Section 4.1, for definitions of alternative predictors.

of the alternative predictors considered in the previous sections. These correlation coefficients, together with the mean square errors of the original forecasts and of the residuals of the linear regressions are presented, for the wholesale and the consumer price indices, in Table 4.8.

It must be observed that the linear corrections produce changes in the ranking of the different predictors only in the case of consumer prices. That is, it happens that predictors with larger mean square errors to start with, present smaller sums of squares of residuals (which, after dividing for the number of observations, are equal to the mean square errors of the linearly corrected forecasts). As can be seen from Table 4.9, which presents a summary of the results of this test, the predictor that benefits most from the linear correction is the *ARC* one. It should also be noticed that among the errors of prediction of the linearly corrected alternative forecasts and

TABLE 4.9

RELATIVE FORECASTING SUCCESS OF EXPECTATIONS AND
ALTERNATIVE PREDICTORS : SUMMARY RESULTS

WHOLESALE PRICES

	5801-7202			5801-8002	
RANK	MSE	MSEC	RANK	MSE	MSEC
1	AR	AR	1	ARM	ARM$^+$
2	ARC	ARC	2	ARC	ARC$^+$
3	ARM	ARM	3	ARC1	ARC1
4	MIX	MIX	4	MIX	MIX
5	NAIVE	NAIVE$^+$	5	NAIVE	NAIVE$^+$

CONSUMER PRICES

	5801-7401			5801-8002	
RANK	MSE	MSEC	RANK	MSE	MSEC
1	MIX	ARC	1	ARM	ARC
2	ARM	ARM	2	MIX	ARM
3	AR	MIX	3	NAIVE	MIX
4	ARC	AR	4	ARC	ARC1
5	NAIVE	NAIVE$^+$	5	ARC1	NAIVE$^+$

Note

The MIX estimates of the expected rates of change refer to the total of respondents to the Mondo Economico opinion poll. See text, Section 4.1, for definitions of alternative predictors.
The predictors are ranked according to their square error forecasting success before (MSE) and after (MSEC) linear correction for bias.

$^+$MIX significantly superior or inferior to alternative predictors at the .01 level, under the assumption of absence of serial correlation in the errors of the linearly corrected forecasts.

survey-based expectations, only for the *ARM* predictions on both price indices (but only for the sub-periods considered) and for the expected wholesale price changes (over the whole sample), could the hypothesis of absence of serial correlation be rejected. In particular, this hypothesis is rejected on the basis of a Lagrange multiplier test for a second order autocorrelation process (Table 4.8), at a 5 percent significance level. In these cases, therefore, the results of the formal test of relative forecasting success presented in Tables 4.8 and 4.9 should be taken with care.

Table 4.9 confirms the relatively good performance of the series of expected rates in forecasting the actual price changes. In the case of consumer prices, no alternative forecasts are significantly superior to the expected changes. For the wholesale price index, between the first semester of 1958 and the second semester of 1980 the expectations are outperformed by both the *ARC* and the *ARM* forecasts (at a significance level above 1 percent.) Over the sub-period, however, they are not significantly inferior than the latter at any reasonable significance level.

4.5. Turning Point Analysis

The performance in anticipating turning points in the rates of price change by the series of expectations and of alternative predictions is compared in Table 4.10. It appears that the alternative predictions do better than the expected rates in anticipating the changes in the inflation rates, if the measures of turning point errors ϕ_1 and ϕ_2, discussed in Section 3.5, are considered. For the autoregressive *ARM*, *ARC* and *ARC1* predictors, overall estimates of ϕ_1 of 8, 9 and 8 percent respectively for wholesale prices, and 14, 14 and 15 percent for consumer prices are obtained. For ϕ_2 the figures are somewhat higher, that is, 15, 23 and 27 percent for the former, and 14, 14 and 23 percent for the latter. As regards the performance of the expectations, 12 and 28 percent of errors of the first kind for the two price indices, respectively, are found, and 42 and 41 percent of errors of the second kind. Therefore, the main defect of the expected rates is in not predicting turning points that actually occurred.

A closer examination of the results of Table 4.10 reveals, however, a very interesting feature. The expectations of the respondents to *Mondo Economico* surveys present in fact a better or equal performance than the alternative predictions in anticipating *upper* turning points (that is, reductions in the actual inflation rates), if the ϕ_1 measures are considered and only a slightly worse performance in the case of the measures of errors of the second kind. The overall poorer performance is therefore due mainly to a less accurate prediction of increases in the rate of inflation after a period of continuous

Ignazio Visco

TABLE 4.10

ANALYSIS OF ERRORS IN FORECASTING TURNING POINTS IN THE RATE
OF CHANGE OF PRICES—MONDO ECONOMICO VS ALTERNATIVE PREDICTORS

1st semester 1958 - 2nd semester 1980

		PREDICTED TURNING POINTS				OCCURRED TURNING POINTS			
		occurred	not occurred	total predicted	ϕ_1	predicted	not predicted	total occurred	ϕ_2
WHOLESALE									
	lower	8	1	9	.11	8	5	13	.38
MIX	upper	7	1	8	.13	7	6	13	.46
	total	15	2	17	.12	15	11	26	.42
	lower	11	0	11	.00	11	2	13	.15
ARC	upper	9	2	11	.18	9	4	13	.31
	total	20	2	22	.09	20	6	26	.23
	lower	12	0	12	.00	12	1	13	.08
ARM	upper	10	2	12	.17	10	3	13	.23
	total	22	2	24	.08	22	4	26	.15
	lower	10	0	10	.00	10	3	13	.23
ARC1	upper	9	2	11	.18	9	4	13	.31
	total	19	2	21	.10	19	7	26	.27
CONSUMER									
	lower	5	4	9	.44	5	6	11	.55
MIX	upper	8	1	9	.11	8	3	11	.27
	total	13	5	18	.28	13	9	22	.41
	lower	10	2	12	.17	10	1	11	.09
ARC	upper	9	1	10	.10	9	2	11	.18
	total	19	3	22	.14	19	3	22	.14
	lower	10	2	12	.17	10	1	11	.09
ARM	upper	9	1	10	.10	9	2	11	.18
	total	19	3	22	.14	19	3	22	.14
	lower	9	2	11	.18	9	2	11	.18
ARC1	upper	8	1	9	.11	8	3	11	.27
	total	17	3	20	.15	17	5	22	.23

Note

ϕ_1 = Predicted but not occurred turning points as a ratio of total predicted turning points.
ϕ_2 = Occurred but not predicted turning points as a ratio of total occurred turning points.

The MIX estimates of the expected rates of change refer to the total of respondents to the Mondo Economico opinion poll. See text, Section 4.1, for definitions of the alternative predictors.

reduction. This finding seems to highlight the presence of "return-to-normality" factors in the process of expectation formation.

4.6. Summary of the Results

In this chapter, the performance of the expectations of price changes formed by the respondents to *Mondo Economico* surveys has been evaluated by means of a comparison with the forecasts generated by a number of alternative predictors of inflation.

As has been seen in Section 4.1, besides a *Naive* ("equal change") predictor other predictors which exploit the autoregressive structure of price changes have been considered. While only univariate models have been investigated and simple autoregressive models have been finally chosen, two important features have been allowed: (1) only the information on price changes prior to the date of each survey has been considered in the estimation of the parameters of the monthly autoregressive models; and (2) the parameters have been reestimated each time new observations were available either by recursive OLS, that is, following a Kalman filter – so that *cumulating* observations have been considered (*ARC*) – or by running a new regression each time deleting the first observation, so as to keep the sample size constant and *moving* the sample over time (*ARM*). In both cases, it has been shown that the estimates of the coefficients could be easily obtained by updating those for the *initial* samples, without the need for actually reestimating the model each time a new observation was available given the adaptive nature of the updating rules. Also, the forecasts have been considered generated by the first of these two predictors, for the period following the first oil crisis, under the assumption of parameter estimates equal to those obtained for the period ending in 1972 (*ARC1*). For the sub-samples which exclude the observations after the second semester of 1972, for wholesale prices, and the first semester of 1974, for consumer prices, autoregressive models (*AR*) have also been estimated, making also use of information which was not available to the survey respondents when they formed their expectations for the same semesters for which forecasts from these models were generated.

The results of the comparison of the expected rates of price changes with the forecasts from the above alternative predictors can be summarized as follows:

(1) While the expectations clearly outperform the Naive predictions, they do not do manifestly worse than the alternative autoregressive predictions, examined in this chapter, in anticipating actual price changes. In the case of wholesale prices, however, they seem to suffer from larger anticipation errors than those generated by the *ARC* and particularly the *ARM* forecasts for the most recent years. The fact that predictions generated from estimates on moving samples do so well in tracking the actual movement in prices, and the observation that such estimates seem to suggest a significative change in the inflation process, are two factors in support of the following conclusion: in the case of wholesale prices, survey based expectations do not appear to catch adequately the significant changes which have been iden-

tified for the period following the first oil crisis, reflecting a possible unwillingness on the part of the survey respondents to modify the models and/or the parameters on which they have founded their expectations. This conclusion is strongly supported by the further observation that these expectations are very similar to the forecasts of wholesale price changes generated by the *ARC1* predictors, obtained by keeping, after 1972, the coefficient estimates equal to those obtained for the period ending with the last month of that year. This result does not hold for consumer price changes. In this case, in fact, the expected rates suffer in the more recent years from smaller errors in anticipating the actual rates of change than the *ARC1* and also the *ARC* predictions. With respect to the predictions based on estimates from moving samples, the survey based expectations are more accurate in the period just after the first oil crisis and slightly less satisfactory between 1975 and 1977.

(2) In general, with the exception of the Naive forecasts, the differences in the accuracy measures considered do not seem to be very large for the expected as well as the alternative predictions of the inflation rates. Rather, for the period preceding the first oil crisis the performance of the former is very close to that of the latter. For the whole sample of comparison (1958–80) – considering the formal tests on "linearly corrected" anticipation errors introduced in Section 4.4 – only for wholesale prices are the *ARM* and the *ARC* forecasts significantly superior to the expectations of the panel of *Mondo Economico*.

(3) When signs of bias of prediction are present in the expected inflation series, they are in general also present in the *ARM*, *ARC* and *ARC1* forecasts which similarly show clear signs of positive serial correlation, with the only major exception of the *ARM* predictions of wholesale changes over the whole sample. Also, for the alternative predictors, the finding pointed out in the last chapter with reference to the expectations is confirmed: both root mean square and mean absolute errors of prediction are much lower for the sub-periods (when the large inflation rates experienced in the more recent years are excluded) than for the whole sample. When taken as ratios of the average actual inflation rate, however, they are smaller in the latter case than in the former. Therefore, the result found in Chapter 3 for the expectations data was not due to a somewhat poorer performance of the respondents in forecasting price changes during the fifties and sixties as opposed to the seventies. Rather, it was due to what appears to be an irreducible, larger random component of the total variance of price changes *relative* to their average value over the more distant years.

(4) While the performance in anticipating turning points – as measured by Theil's ratios of errors of the "first" and "second" kind, ϕ_1 and ϕ_2 – is better for the autoregressive predictors than for the expectations, when we

consider all turning points (that is, those occurring both at the peaks and at the troughs of the inflation series), the latter outperform or do not do substantially worse than the alternative predictors in anticipating *upper* turning points. This means that they are less accurate in predicting positive changes and more accurate in anticipating reductions in the actual rate of inflation. This might suggest that the respondents to *Mondo Economico* surveys have been generally reluctant in forecasting changes in prices which could imply considerable positive departures from what they might have been considering the "normal" rate of inflation.

CHAPTER 5

UNBIASEDNESS AND RATIONALITY OF INFLATION EXPECTATIONS

5.1. The Issue of "Rational" Expectations

It has become very popular in the last decade to advance strong criticisms on the *ad hoc* nature of the hypotheses of formation of individual expectations implicitly or explicitly adopted by the existing macroeconometric models. It has been argued, in particular, that these hypotheses should be replaced by the so-called "rational" expectations assumption which implies that individual expectations are true mathematical expectations of the variables of interest conditional on whatever information is available to the economic agents.[1] This hypothesis was originally formulated, in a rather limited context, by Muth who stated that "expectations of firms (or, more generally, the subjective probability distribution of outcomes) tend to be distributed, for the same information set, about the prediction of the theory (or the 'objective' probability distribution of outcomes)".[2] A very large number of articles have been published in the recent years, considering theoretical models with the rational expectations assumption; as a consequence new estimation techniques and new methods of policy evaluation have been proposed.[3] Still, however, it seems paradoxical that all this has led to the substitution of an untested assumption on expectations formation for other untested assumptions; likely, the label of "rationality" associated with it is what has made it so popular.

By "untested" is meant an assumption which has not been tested *independently* from a given theoretical view of the way the economy works or the way certain behavioral relationships are assumed to be formed. Indeed rational expectations by their nature imply strong restrictions on

---

[1]See, for example, Lucas and Sargent (1978). The "rational" expectations assumption is often considered to be the main determinant of theories such as that of the natural rate (of output, unemployment and whatever) or of efficient markets, which is not. These theories depend on particular market organizations and on peculiar assumptions about price flexibility and market clearing (for important contributions on these two subjects, see Lucas (1972, 1973, 1975) and Fama (1970, 1975)). For stimulating criticism, see Tobin (1980), Hahn (1980) and Ando (1981b).

[2]Muth (1961, p. 316).

[3]The literature is too numerous to make it possible to give exhaustive references. See Shiller (1978) and Buiter (1981) for two different critical evaluations of some of the contributions.

economic models, and many tests have been proposed and performed on these restrictions *jointly with* the hypothesized economic structure.[4] It has been shown, however, that it is almost impossible to identify econometric models with rational expectations.[5] Many doubts then arise about the estimates of models of this kind. Furthermore, many scholars have expressed serious doubts on the soundness of such an assumption when human beings are clearly limited in their optimizing capabilities;[6] when information is costly to achieve;[7] and when one considers that persons can behave in a perfectly consistent Bayesian way without necessarily implying that their subjective expectations should coincide, or tend to coincide, with objective expectations such as the conditional mathematical expectations of the variables of interest.[8] Great difficulties arise in considering problems such as the way learning takes place when, as must be the case, economic agents *do not* know the "true" parameters of the economic structure, when many different theories have been advanced to explain empirically observed regularities, when radically different views are present in the various societies not only on the positive side (for example, on how the economy actually works) but also on the normative one (on how it should work, on how income should be distributed, on how much private enterprise should be regulated, and so on).

In any event, it does not seem unreasonable to assume that persons might try – when clear economic incentives are present – to make optimal use of the information they have (and which they are able to collect). In this

[4] Not only tests like those of Revankar (1980) and Hoffman and Schmidt (1981) belong to this category, but also all the empirical results obtained from joint estimation and testing of theoretical propositions *cum* rational expectations such as those, for example, of Fama (1975), Sargent (1976a, 1977, 1978, 1981), and Barro (1977, 1978). For the econometric implications of the rational expectations assumption, see also the recent contributions by Wallis (1980) and Hansen and Sargent (1980). A useful survey is that of McCallum (1979).

[5] Pesaran (1981) and Swamy, Barth and Tinsley (1982). Pesaran writes: "in the absence of *a priori* information concerning the order of lags in economic relations, the RE and the non-RE models cannot be distinguished on empirical grounds. This general under-identification of RE models clearly sheds serious doubts on the soundness of the recent attempts by Sargent (1976a), Barro (1977) and others which purport to provide empirical evidence favoring the proposition that monetary and fiscal policies are incapable of influencing the path of real output and employment, even in the short-run!" (p. 377, RE stands for "rational expectations"). See also Buiter's (1979) comments on Barro's work. It is somewhat paradoxical that one of the most active researchers in this field was already aware of similar problems (Sargent (1976b)). Sims (1980) is also skeptical on the possibility that rational expectations models could be identified. Even in simple distributed lag approximations to expected variables, one cannot count multiple occurrences of the same variable, with lags, in a single equation in order to weaken the order condition for identification. That this is generally the case, when no *a priori* information is available on the exact lag lengths, has been shown by Hatanaka (1975b).

[6] See Simon (1978, 1979) and Ando (1981a).

[7] See Darby (1976), Feige and Pearce (1976) and Grossman and Stiglitz (1980).

[8] See Swamy, Barth and Tinsley (1982).

respect, their expectations should be such that different ways of organizing this information should not produce better expectations than those they hold. But what does "better" mean in this context? It suggests that their expectations are those which come from the minimization of a given risk function, that is, the expected value of the loss they would incur in the case of large deviations from the actual outcomes. This is the reason why the definition of rational expectations as true mathematical expectations, conditional on the available information, has received wide popularity. If the loss is quadratic, in fact, persons will minimize

$$R = \mathrm{E}\{[X - \phi(Y)]^2\}, \tag{5.1}$$

where X is the variable of interest, $X^e = \phi(Y)$ is the economic agents' anticipation of X formed making use of the information set Y, and E is the mathematical expectation operator. As it is well known,[9] R will be a minimum, for given realization y of the variables Y, when

$$\phi(y) = \mathrm{E}[X|Y = y]. \tag{5.2}$$

In fact (5.1) can be rewritten as

$$R = \mathrm{E}[X^2|Y = y] - 2\phi(y)\mathrm{E}[X|Y = y] + \phi^2(y), \tag{5.3}$$

and by differentiating (5.3) with respect to $\phi(y)$ the first-order condition is obtained:

$$-2\mathrm{E}[X|Y = y] + 2\phi(y) = 0, \tag{5.4}$$

from which (5.2) results.

This is, however, a very limited case. One can easily think of perfectly reasonable loss functions which do not generate the previous result.

For instance, when the loss is assumed to be proportional to the absolute value of the error of prediction $|X - \phi(Y)|$, its expected value will be a minimum for $\phi(y)$ equal to the *median* of the distribution of X given the realization y of Y.[10] Even if the loss is quadratic one might still end up with a result different than (5.2). The peculiar characteristic of (5.1) is in fact its symmetry. Assume instead that, rather than (5.1), the function to be minimized is still quadratic but not symmetric, such as

$$R = \mathrm{E}\{c_0[X - \phi(Y)]^2 + c_1[\phi(Y)]^2\}, \qquad c_0 > 0, \quad c_1 > 0. \tag{5.5}$$

[9]See, for example, Breiman (1969, pp. 145–146).
[10]See, for example, De Groot (1970, pp. 231–233).

The loss function of (5.5) is perfectly reasonable if one considers, for example, the case of a firm which might incur large costs due to overproduction for inventory holdings when the expected rate of inflation turns out to be much larger than expected (that is, when the real rate of interest on which its inventory design is based is widely underestimated). In this case the first-order condition will be

$$2c_0\phi(y) - 2c_0 E[X|Y=y] + 2c_1\phi(y) = 0, \tag{5.6}$$

so that

$$\phi(y) = \beta E[X|Y=y] < E[X|Y=y], \tag{5.7}$$

since

$$\beta = c_0/(c_0 + c_1) < 1. \tag{5.8}$$

Incidentally, (5.7) indicates that in such a case, when the decision maker penalizes more the possibility of negative than positive anticipation errors (the differences between actual and expected outcomes), his expectations turn out to be downward biased. But the latter is a result commonly observed in periods of high inflation rates (see, for example, Chapter 3).

The preceding discussion has been advanced only to advise caution about an uncritical use of the concept of "rational" expectations. As a further step in the *evaluation* of inflation expectations one can, however, proceed to verify if there are evident signs of sub-optimal use of the available information according to a quadratic criterion such as (5.1). This is certainly not an unreasonable criterion to start with, while being at the same time particularly simple in order to derive feasible testing procedures. It should, however, be clear that expectations which would prove to be sub-optimal under a symmetric quadratic loss function could still be optimal predictions under a different criterion.

To this end survey data can be used to test various necessary conditions of the rational expectations assumption, without *necessarily* depending on a joint formulation of the formation mechanism and the behavioral relationships. In fact, a number of studies have been recently published which – with varying degrees of sophistication – test this assumption using survey data.[11] Different degrees of optimal use of available information (under a

---

[11]See Turnovsky (1970), De Menil (1974), Pesando (1975, 1976), Carlson (1977a), Fackler and Stanhouse (1977), Mullineaux (1978), Pearce (1979), Friedman (1980), Leonard (1982), McDonald and Woodfield (1980), Hafer and Resler (1980), Figlewsky and Wachtel (1981), Praet (1981), Brown and Maital (1981), Aiginger (1981), Horne (1981), Saunders (1981), Tompkinson and Common (1981), Papadia (1982), Smith (1982), Noble (1982), Noble and Fields (1982), Hafer and Resler (1982), Pesaran (1983). The results of these papers are

symmetric quadratic loss function) have been considered in the literature (differentiating between strong or full and weak or partial rationality), and use has been made of conditional expectations as well as optimal linear predictions. In the next section a systematic approach will be considered and the exact nature of these tests will be specified.

It is fair to conclude the present discussion with the observation that Muth's rational expectations hypothesis has represented an important addition to the set of ingenious *ad hoc* assumptions introduced over the years in the economic literature. Even if it might be considered as a limit hypothesis and even if a whole theory on how expectations might *become* rational in the above sense has still to be developed, to solve econometric models under this assumption – as well as alternative ones – on the formation of expectations would probably produce further insight. A similar consideration was already advanced in a survey on the treatment of expectations in econometric models (a survey which indeed never mentioned "rational" expectations) by Lawrence Klein when he wrote:

> A complication is due to arise on the issue of self fulfilling (or defeating) expectations. If the larger corporations whose decisions are of predominant importance for the functioning of the American Economy, act on the econometric results of a given model, the model is likely to have a great bearing on the outcome of the economy's performance. This bearing would be predictable if we could estimate the "feedback" effects of a model solution on business or public behavior. [...] It is now necessary to turn attention to the feedback problem to try to estimate relationships that explicitly show the effects of econometric predictions on economic behavior. It is logically possible to close the system this way; econometricians simply have not tried extensively.[12]

For estimation purposes, however, direct data on expectations should be used, when possible, in econometric models. Their performance and predictions should then be compared under the alternative hypotheses of "rationality" (that is, forcing the expectations to coincide with the predictions of

---

somewhat mixed, being obviously dependent also on the "quality" of the survey-based expectations which they considered. In the most favorable situations these data seem to pass tests of weak-form rationality, but it appears possible to find cases of non-optimal use of relevant available information. In some occasions these results have been referred to as not rejecting the rationality hypothesis, but as indicating that the survey-based expectations are not equal to the expectations of the market (*assumed* to be rational). While it is clearly possible that the survey data might not be accurate representations of the "true" expectations (due to inadequateness of surveys, arbitrariness of transformations, etc.), the previous statement seems to be quite arbitrary.

[12] Klein (1972, p. 190).

the model) and of other mechanisms of expectation formation[13] as suggested by the direct data themselves. In this light, survey-based expectations will fully prove their potential utility.

5.2. The Testing of Rational Expectations

If one considers a quadratic loss function such as (5.1) and if I_{t-1} is the complete information set at the end of $t-1$ available to form expectations for period t, it will then be the case that, if economic agents make an optimal use of a subset J_{t-1} of this information set (where J_{t-1} can be considered to be a vector of known realizations of a number of random variables), the rational inflation expectation will be given by

$$p_t^e(J_{t-1}) = \mathrm{E}[\, p_t | J_{t-1}], \tag{5.9}$$

where p_t^e is the rate of inflation anticipated by the economic agents to occur in period t, and p_t is the actual rate of inflation in period t.

If only optimal linear forecasts[14] (linear least squares projections of p_t on J_{t-1}) are considered, that is, if the quadratic function

$$R = \mathrm{E}\big\{ c[\, p_t - p_t^e(J_{t-1})]^2 \big\} \tag{5.10}$$

is minimized, with $p_t^e(J_{t-1})$ assumed to be a linear function of J_{t-1}, it follows (under the assumption that p_t and the random variables in J_{t-1} have finite population means and second moments) that

$$p_t^e(J_{t-1}) = J_{t-1}\beta, \tag{5.11}$$

$$\beta = \big[\mathrm{E}(J_{t-1}'J_{t-1})\big]^{-1}\mathrm{E}(J_{t-1}'p_t). \tag{5.12}$$

If the true structure is linear, that is, if one can think of p_t and J_{t-1} being jointly normally distributed, it will further be

$$p_t^e(J_{t-1}) = \mathrm{E}[\, p_t | J_{t-1}] = J_{t-1}\beta. \tag{5.13}$$

---

[13] It has to be stressed however that there is not necessarily a contradiction between the rational expectations assumption and other once more popular formation mechanisms. Indeed Muth (1960) and Sargent and Wallace (1973) provide examples of models in which rational expectations are adaptive, and an adaptive-regressive formation mechanism is shown to be rational in the framework considered by Mussa (1975).

[14] This is the case considered, for example, by Shiller (1972); see also Sargent (1979, ch. X).

Condition (5.9) implies that

$$E[p_t - p_t^e(J_{t-1})|J_{t-1}] = 0. \tag{5.14}$$

That is, one can write in this case

$$p_t - p_t^e(J_{t-1}) = u_t, \tag{5.15}$$

where u_t is a serially uncorrelated disturbance; in particular, $E[u_t|J_{t-1}] = 0$. Equation (5.15) shows that, under the "rational" expectations hypothesis (5.9), the anticipation errors should be serially uncorrelated. This is a first testable necessary condition for rational expectations. A second condition is that the expectations p^e should be unbiased. From (5.15) one immediately sees that a regression of p on p^e and a constant term should not yield estimates of the intercept and the slope coefficients significantly different from zero and one, respectively. Finally, if one writes

$$p_t - p_t^e(J_{t-1}) = J_{t-1}\gamma + u_t, \tag{5.16}$$

it follows, from (5.14), that

$$E[J_{t-1}\gamma + u_t|J_{t-1}] = J_{t-1}\gamma + E[u_t|J_{t-1}] = 0. \tag{5.17}$$

Under rational expectations $E[u_t|J_{t-1}] = 0$; one then sees from (5.17) that it must be $\gamma = 0$. This is, therefore, a third condition for rationality, that is, the anticipation error should be orthogonal to all the conditioning variables contained in J_{t-1}.

Thus, if the vector of anticipation errors $(p - p^e)$ is regressed on the information matrix J,[15] and an estimate of γ significantly different from zero is obtained, condition (5.9) will be rejected. Also the hypothesis of optimal linear predictions of p_t from any information vector S_{t-1} of which J_{t-1} is a proper sub-vector will then be rejected, as Shiller was the first to show.[16] Consider in fact:

$$p_t^e(S_{t-1}) = S_{t-1}\delta, \tag{5.18}$$

$$\delta = [E(S'_{t-1}S_{t-1})]^{-1}E(S'_{t-1}p_t). \tag{5.19}$$

---

[15] In what follows, J is a matrix of T sample observations on the vector J_{t-1}, as p and p^e are vectors of T observations on p_t and p_t^e. A similar notation applies further on to the matrices Z_1 and Z_2 and to the vector u in expressions (5.25) to (5.34).

[16] Shiller (1972, pp. 36–39).

It will then be the case that

$$p_t = S_{t-1}\delta + v_t,$$ (5.20)

with the orthogonality property that

$$E[v_t|S_{t-1}] = 0,$$ (5.21)

so that also

$$E[v_t|J_{t-1}] = 0,$$ (5.22)

and therefore

$$\text{plim}\,\hat{\gamma} = \text{plim}\big(J_{t-1}'J_{t-1}\big)^{-1}J_{t-1}'\big(p_t - p_t^e\big) = 0.$$ (5.23)

A rejection of $\gamma = 0$ will then imply that p_t^e is not the best linear predictor in J_{t-1} and therefore also in S_{t-1}.

What if $\gamma = 0$ will not be rejected? The hypothesis of rational expectations will not then be necessarily accepted. On one side, since also optimal linear predictions could pass this test, when $\gamma = 0$ is not rejected one might still have the result – unless the true structural model is linear – that expectations are not rational in the sense of them not being equal to the conditional mathematical expectations as given by (5.9). Even if the true structure was linear, the non-rejection of $\gamma = 0$ could come simply from the fact that the test could be biased in favor of the null hypothesis.[17] Assume, for example, that p_t is generated by the model

$$p_t = Z_{1t}\beta_1 + Z_{2t}\beta_2 + u_t,$$ (5.24)

and that Z_{1t} and Z_{2t} are known at the end of period $t-1$. A regression of $(p - p^e)$ on Z_1 would give

$$\hat{\gamma} = \big(Z_1'Z_1\big)^{-1}Z_1'(p - p^e).$$ (5.25)

Observe that, under rational expectations, one would have that in the equation

$$p_t^e = Z_{1t}\beta_1^* + Z_{2t}\beta_2^* + e_t,$$ (5.26)

$\beta_1^* = \beta_1$, $\beta_2^* = \beta_2$ and $e_t = 0$ for all t. Then, $\hat{\gamma}$ would be a consistent estimate of γ_1 in the equation

$$p - p^e = Z_1\gamma_1 + Z_2\gamma_2 + v,$$ (5.27)

[17]See also Abel and Mishkin (1983, sec. 2).

since, under rational expectations, $\gamma_2 = \beta_2 - \beta_2^* = 0$ and $v = u - e = u$. Furthermore, since

$$\hat{\gamma} = \gamma_1 + \left(Z_1'Z_1\right)^{-1}Z_1'(Z_2\gamma_2 + v), \tag{5.28}$$

the rationality hypothesis implies that $\gamma_1 = \gamma_2 = 0$, and

$$\text{plim}\,\hat{\gamma} = 0. \tag{5.29}$$

To test the hypothesis $\hat{\gamma} = 0$, the usual procedure would then be to apply a standard F-test (which, however, is strictly correct only for non-stochastic Z_1 and Z_2). Defining $y = p - p^e$, one would use the statistic

$$F = \frac{\hat{\gamma}'Z_1'Z_1\hat{\gamma}/K}{(y - Z_1\hat{\gamma})'(y - Z_1\hat{\gamma})/(T - K)}, \tag{5.30}$$

which, under $\gamma_1 = 0$ *and* $\gamma_2 = 0$, reduces to

$$F = \frac{v'Mv/K}{v'(I - M)v/(T - K)}, \tag{5.31}$$

where $M = Z_1(Z_1'Z_1)^{-1}Z_1'$ and K and T are, respectively, the number of columns of Z_1 and the sample size. The variable defined in (5.30) would then have a central F-distribution, under the null hypothesis, with K and $T - K$ degrees of freedom. What happens if γ_2 is actually different than zero, so that expectations are not rational, even if $\gamma_1 = 0$? It is easy to show that the quadratic form in the numerator of (5.30) would now be equal to

$$\hat{\gamma}'Z_1'Z_1\hat{\gamma} = \gamma_2'Z_2'MZ_2\gamma_2 + 2\gamma_2'Z_2'Mv + v'Mv, \tag{5.32}$$

and that in the denominator

$$(y - Z_1\hat{\gamma})'(y - Z_1\hat{\gamma}) = \gamma_2'Z_2'(I - M)Z_2\gamma_2$$
$$+ 2\gamma_2'Z_2'(I - M)v + v'(I - M)v. \tag{5.33}$$

As the sample size increases, the second terms in the right-hand side of (5.32) and (5.33) tend to their zero means. Ignoring them, these two expressions would then define two non-central chi-squares. But observe that, if Z_1 and Z_2 tend to be orthogonal (so that $Z_1'Z_2 = 0$), the F-statistic defined in (5.30) would tend to be equal to

$$F = \frac{v'Mv/K}{[\gamma_2'Z_2'Z_2\gamma_2 + v'(I - M)v]/(T - K)}. \tag{5.34}$$

Since $\gamma_2' Z_2' Z_2 \gamma_2 \geq 0$, then, there will be a bias towards the null in the test of the hypothesis $\gamma = 0$.

Finally, one can easily see that even for expectations inefficient with respect to optimal linear predictions, it could still be not possible in some cases to reject the previous hypothesis. Assume that, instead of (5.18), the following holds:

$$p_t^e(S_{t-1}) = S_{t-1}\delta + \varepsilon_t, \tag{5.35}$$

where ε_t is a possibly very large residual *uncorrelated* with S_{t-1}. It still would be the case that $\text{plim }\hat{\gamma} = 0$, but obviously p_t^e would in this case be inefficient with respect to the optimal linear predictor.

All the previous discussion has been intended to show that tests of this kind, based on the estimates of regressions of the anticipation error on whatever information is considered available when the expectations were formed, are more suited to give evidence against the rational expectations assumption rather than in its favor. It is also evident from the foregoing that, in the case of rejection of a weak rationality assumption, a strong rationality assumption will also be rejected. Since it is impossible to consider, in the testing process, the complete information set, when the hypothesis will not be rejected one might only conclude that there is no evidence of sub-optimal use of information with respect to the particular weak rationality assumption considered.

Even with these limitations, tests of this kind (or variants thereof) are practically the only ones one can find in the literature when use is made of direct evidence on expectations that have the purpose of verifying the rational expectations assumption, without specifying (and jointly testing) a detailed theoretical structure. These tests will then be performed with reference to the inflation expectations of the respondents to *Mondo Economico* surveys. First, the condition of absence of serial correlation in the anticipation errors will be examined; then tests of unbiasedness of the expectations will be performed; and finally the optimal use of relevant information will be verified in the following sections of this chapter.

5.3. *Statistical Analysis of Anticipation Errors and Tests of Unbiasedness*

In Table 5.1 the autocorrelation and the partial autocorrelation functions are represented for the anticipation errors of wholesale and consumer price changes, respectively. When only the semesters before 1973 for the former and before 1974 for the latter are considered,[18] no signs of serial correlation

---

[18] The sub-periods are the same considered in the last two chapters; more details on their choice have been given in Section 3.4.

TABLE 5.1

ANALYSIS OF THE ERRORS OF PREDICTION OF THE EXPECTATIONS OF PRICE CHANGES, 1

Lags	Autocorrelation Function		Partial Autocorrelation Function	
	WHOLESALE			
	5202-7202	5202-8002	5202-7202	5202-8002
1	.01	.58	.01	.58
2	.01	.21	.01	- .18
3	- .04	.16	- .04	.19
4	.07	.34	.07	.30
5	.02	.34	.01	- .03
6	- .17	.33	- .17	.23
7	.09	.18	.10	- .15
8	- .00	.09	- .01	- .03
9	- .13	.02	- .15	- .11
10	- .22	.06	- .19	- .03
11	- .06	.03	- .06	- .08
12	- .11	.04	- .16	.05
Standard Error	.16	.13	.16	.13
BP(12)	5.03	45.26		
T	41	57		
	CONSUMER			
	5602-7401	5602-8002	5602-7401	5602-8002
1	.08	.50	.08	.50
2	- .04	.39	- .04	.19
3	.08	.31	.09	.08
4	.26	.39	.24	.24
5	.03	.20	.01	- .15
6	- .11	.25	- .11	.12
7	- .15	.17	- .19	- .04
8	- .11	.23	- .18	.07
9	- .16	.11	- .18	- .05
10	- .10	.09	- .03	- .08
11	- .17	- .01	- .06	- .07
12	- .22	- .07	- .14	- .18
Standard Error	.17	.14	.17	.14
BP(12)	8.69	42.34		
T	36	49		

Note

MIX estimates for the expected rates of change (total of respondents to the Mondo Economico opinion poll).
T is the number of observations.
Significance limits for the Box-Pierce test for autocorrelation of the errors up to the 12th order, BP(12): $\chi^2_{.05}$ (12) = 21.03 , $\chi^2_{.01}$ (12) = 26.22.

in the anticipation errors are present. This result is confirmed by the low values of the Box–Pierce statistics[19] and gives statistical support to the general comments on the plots of the actual and expected price changes advanced in Section 3.2 (Figures 3.1, 3.2 and 3.3). Regarding the whole sample period, however, which includes the more recent years when large prediction errors have been experienced, the pattern of the autocorrelation

[19]Box and Pierce (1970): $BP(m) = m \sum r_i^2$ $(i = 1,...,m)$ – where r_i is the ith-order autocorrelation coefficient – is asymptotically distributed in the present case as a chi-square with m degrees of freedom.

functions changes dramatically with significantly non-zero coefficients at lags 1, 4, 5, and 6 for wholesale prices and at lags 1, 2, 3, and 4 for consumer prices. That anticipation errors became positively serially correlated in the second half of the seventies was also evident from Figures 3.1 and 3.2. One wonders if this is a spurious result due to the occurrence, in the recent experience, of shocks to the inflation process which may account for such large anticipation errors. Obviously, oil crises, wars, and dramatic and abrupt devaluations such as those experienced, could have not been predictable under normal circumstances: it is then interesting to consider how the autocorrelation functions would look, once the anticipation errors which might be reasonably attributed to such special events are deleted from the sample (Table 5.2).[20]

Consider first *wholesale* prices. If the large errors after 1973 are constrained to zero *with the exception* of the three for which it is easier to provide justification,[21] no signs of serial correlation emerge from the Box–Pierce statistics, even if a significant positive value is obtained for the autocorrelation coefficient at lag 4 (a finding which has no immediate interpretation). The errors constrained to zero concern six semesters, and for them, too, some justification could be provided (lagged effects of the first oil crisis, of the 1976 devaluation and of the Iran revolution). It is clear, however, that they cannot be considered as due to totally unpredictable (even if we can say so only *a posteriori*) circumstances. If only the three more readily justifiable errors are constrained to zero, signs of serial correlation are still present. Only when all nine of them are simultaneously put equal to zero can one reject the hypothesis of serial correlation. Obviously one could have experimented with various combinations at the likely expense, however, of largely weakening the statistical significance of the tests. One can conclude that probably the serial correlation in the series of fifty-seven anticipation errors on wholesale price changes is due in part to exceptional events, but also in part to a genuine understatement of the actual inflation process. This seems to be confirmed by the fact that when expectations are assumed to coincide with realizations in the five semesters when large errors[22] have been experienced for the *consumer* price index, a persistence of *positive* coefficients over the first eight lags (four years) is still

---

[20]Actually, instead of simply eliminating these errors from the sample, the stronger case in which they are kept in the sample with a value of zero (i.e., expectations are constrained to equal realizations) has been considered.

[21]So, in the first semester of 1974 the effects of the Yom Kippur war and of the first oil crisis should certainly have played a role, as those of the sudden exchange rate crisis of the first semester of 1976 and those of the second oil crisis for the first semester of 1980.

[22]"Large" errors were considered to be all those errors larger than *any one* of those occurred before the first oil crisis.

TABLE 5.2

ANALYSIS OF THE ERRORS OF PREDICTION OF THE EXPECTATIONS OF PRICE CHANGES, 2

Lags	Autocorrelation Function				Partial Autocorrelation Function			
			WHOLESALE, 5202-8002					
	WA	WB	WC	WD	WA	WB	WC	WD
1	.58	- .00	.25	.01	.58	- .00	.25	.01
2	.21	- .06	.22	.03	- .18	- .06	.17	.03
3	.16	.08	.06	.07	.19	.08	- .04	.07
4	.34	.41	.26	.09	.30	.41	.24	.09
5	.34	- .03	.20	- .01	- .03	- .01	.11	- .02
6	.33	.05	.25	- .08	.23	.10	.12	- .09
7	.18	- .00	.31	.16	- .25	- .08	.24	.15
8	.09	.13	.12	- .03	- .03	- .03	- .08	- .04
9	.02	.02	.13	- .03	- .11	.02	.01	- .02
10	.06	.12	.01	- .17	- .03	.09	- .10	.18
11	.03	- .12	.04	- .03	- .08	- .11	- .14	- .05
12	.04	.13	- .03	- .08	.05	.11	- .11	- .07
Standard Error	.13	.13	.13	.13	.13	.13	.13	.13
BP(12)	42.26	14.24	23.88	4.83				
T	57	57	57	57				

Lags			CONSUMER, 5602-8002					
		CA	CB				CA	CB
1		.50	.18				.50	.18
2		.39	.15				.19	.12
3		.31	.24				.08	.21
4		.39	.25				.24	.19
5		.20	.25				- .15	.17
6		.25	.05				.12	- .09
7		.17	.07				- .04	- .05
8		.23	.10				.07	- .03
9		.11	- .04				- .05	- .14
10		.09	.04				- .08	.02
11		- .01	- .08				- .07	- .10
12		- .07	- .17				- .18	- .17
Standard Error		.14	.14				.14	.14
BP(12)		42.34	14.60					
T		49	49					

Note

MIX estimates for the expected rates of change (total of respondents to the Mondo Economico opinion poll).
T is the number of observations.
WA = Actual forecasting error;
WB = WA with errors for 7301, 7302, 7402, 7602, 7701, 7902 equal to 0;
WC = WA with errors for 7401, 7601, 8001 equal to 0;
WD = WA with errors for 7301, 7302, 7401, 7402, 7601, 7602, 7701, 7902, 8001 equal to 0;
CA = Actual forecasting error;
CB = CA with errors for 7402, 7501, 7601, 7701, 8001 equal to 0.
Significance limits for the Box-Pierce test for autocorrelation of the errors up to the 12th order,
BP(12): $\chi^2_{.05}$ (12) = 21.03, $\chi^2_{.01}$ (12) = 26.22.

TABLE 5.3

DEFINITIONS OF VARIABLES FOR TABLES 5.4-5.22

WPCS   = actual semiannual rate of change of wholesale prices (source: Istat; see Table D.22).

CPCS   = actual semiannual rate of change of consumer prices (source: Istat; see Table D.25).

MUW   = expected semiannual rate of change of wholesale prices (source: MIX estimates from the answers of the respondents to Mondo Economico opinion poll; see Table D.22).

MUC   = expected semiannual rate of change of consumer prices (source: MIX estimates from the answers of the respondents to Mondo Economico opinion poll; see Table D.25).

SIW   = standard deviation of individual expected rates of change of wholesale prices (source: MIX estimates from the answers of the respondents to Mondo Economico opinion poll; see Table D.22).

SIC   = standard deviation of individual expected rates of change of consumer prices (source: MIX estimates from the answers of the respondents to Mondo Economico opinion poll; see Table D.25).

WPCQ   = actual quarterly rate of change of wholesale prices (source: Istat, Bol - lettino mensile di statistica, various issues).

CPCQ   = actual quarterly rate of change of consumer prices (before 1953 : cost of living index; source: Istat, Bollettino mensile di statistica, various issues).

UTCQ   = quarterly index of industrial capacity utilization (ratio of the index of industrial production to the weighted "peak to peak" interpolation of the same index; source: Bodo (1981)).

URQ   = quarterly rate of unemployment (ratio of the number of individuals unem - ployed or searching for a job to the total labor force: both figures obtained as averages of the observations for the first months of two contiguous quarters; source: Istat, Bollettino mensile di statistica, various issues, and Istat, "Una metodologia di raccordo delle serie statistiche sulle for ze di lavoro", Note e relazioni, n.56, luglio 1979).

URQA   = quarterly rate of unemployment, seasonally adjusted (each single compo - nent seasonally adjusted by means of the additive X11 procedure of the U.S. Bureau of the Census).

DURQ   = first difference of URQ.

DURQA = first difference of URQA.

DPRODQ = percentage rate of change of the quarterly average of the monthly index of industrial production (excluding construction) (source: Istat, Bollettino mensile di statistica, various issues).

DPRODQA = percentage rate of change of the quarterly average of the seasonally adjust ed monthly index of industrial production (excluding construction) (multi- plicative X11 procedure).

DWHQ   = percentage rate of change of quarterly wages per hour worked in industry (excluding construction) (source: Ministero del lavoro e della previdenza sociale, Statistiche del lavoro, various issues).

DWHQA = percentage rate of change of seasonally adjusted quarterly wages per hour worked in industry (multiplicative X11 procedure).

TABLE 5.3 (Continued)

DWDQ = percentage rate of change of quarterly wages per dependent worker in industry (excluding construction) (source: Ministero del lavoro e della previdenza sociale, Statistiche del lavoro, various issues).

DWDQA = percentage rate of change of seasonally adjusted quarterly wages per dependent worker in industry (multiplicative X11 procedure).

DWCQ = percentage rate of change of quarterly average of monthly contractual wage rates per worker in industry (before 1975: hourly contractual wage rates in industry; source: Istat, Bollettino mensile di statistica, various issues).

LRQ = quarterly short-term lending bank rate ("tasso sugli impieghi bancari"; source, since 1969: Banca d'Italia, Bollettino, various issues; before 1969, unpublished series reconstructed by Ufficio Mercato Monetario, Servizio Studi, Banca d'Italia).

BRQ = quarterly average of monthly medium-long term bond rates ("rendimento medio obbligazioni Istituti di Credito Mobiliare"; source: Banca d'Italia, Bollettino, various issues).

DM2Q = quarterly percentage rate of change of money supply (M2) (source, since 1963: Banca d'Italia, Bollettino, various issues; before 1963, series published in "Le attività e le passività finanziarie del pubblico", Banca di Italia, Bollettino, n.5, 1972).

DM2QA = quarterly percentage rate of change of seasonally adjusted money supply (M2) (multiplicative X11 procedure).

DEXLDQ = percentage rate of change of quarterly average of the exchange rate between the Italian lira and the U.S. dollar (source: Banca d'Italia, Bollettino, various issues).

Series available on request from the author.

detected. Indeed, at lags 3, 4, and 5 they are also significantly greater than zero at the 5 percent level (on the basis of one-sided tests for a normal distribution). This is the case even if the Box–Pierce statistic does not point to the presence of serial correlation and no autocorrelation coefficients larger than twice the (asymptotic) standard error, exist.

The results on the autoregressive pattern of the anticipation errors could be considered as an introduction to the more stringent tests of unbiasedness presented in Tables 5.4 and 5.5 (Table 5.3 contains a complete listing of all the variables considered for the tests of this chapter). Here actual price changes are regressed on a constant and on the expected rate of change of prices. If the rational expectations assumption holds, one should not be able to reject the hypothesis that the intercept and the slope coefficient of these regressions are respectively equal to zero and one (and the regression residuals should not be serially correlated). When the periods before the first oil crisis are considered, only in the case of consumer prices (for the "total" and the "other" but not for the "production" respondents) the unbiasedness hypothesis can be rejected (at the 5 percent level for the joint F-test, but not for the t-tests on the single coefficients). Furthermore, if the observation for the first semester of 1957 – when, as shown in Chapter 3, a large anticipa-

TABLE 5.4

WHOLESALE PRICES, TESTS OF UNBIASEDNESS

	α	β	F	R^2	DW	T
5202-7202						
TOTAL	-.108 (.529)	.917 (.626)	1.03	.55	1.82	41
PRODUCTION	.034 (.176)	.845 (1.249)	1.07	.54	1.86	41
OTHER	-.215 (.989)	.959 (.290)	1.51	.54	1.79	41
5202-8002						
TOTAL	-.830 (1.898)	1.893[+] (6.346)	25.47[+]	.77	1.21	57
PRODUCTION	-.673 (1.527)	1.886[+] (6.130)	24.64[+]	.76	1.33	57
OTHER	-.900* (2.069)	1.881[+] (6.401)	25.43[+]	.77	1.17	57

	α	β	F	R^2	DW	T
5801-7202						
TOTAL	-.428 (1.571)	1.188 (1.118)	1.24	.64	2.25	30
PRODUCTION	-.246 (.972)	1.103 (.659)	.47	.64	2.37	30
OTHER	-.531 (1.808)	1.218 (1.217)	1.69	.62	2.13	30
5801-8002						
TOTAL	-1.161* (2.128)	2.007[+] (6.282)	26.29[+]	.78	1.20	46
PRODUCTION	-1.080 (1.979)	2.030[+] (6.286)	26.88[+]	.78	1.35	46
OTHER	-1.140* (2.091)	1.968[+] (6.146)	25.06[+]	.78	1.15	46

OLS regression (for definitions, see Table 5.3):   WPCS = α + βMUW + u.

Note

Absolute values of t-statistics are reported under the estimated coefficients.
*Significant at the .05 level (two tails test for t-statistics).
+Significant at the .01 level (two tails test for t-statistics).
The t and F-tests are for the hypothesis $\alpha=0$, $\beta=1$; R^2 is the (unadjusted) determination coefficient; DW is the Durbin-Watson statistic; T is the number of observations.

TABLE 5.5

CONSUMER PRICES, TESTS OF UNBIASEDNESS

	α	β	F	R^2	DW	T
5602-7401						
TOTAL	-.624 (1.799)	1.066 (.572)	3.50*	.71	1.80	36
PRODUCTION	-.480 (1.387)	1.023 (.205)	2.80	.70	1.67	36
OTHER	-.697 (1.951)	1.083 (.706)	3.99*	.71	1.90	36
5602-8002						
TOTAL	-1.089 (3.131)+	1.339 (4.188)+	9.07+	.85	1.56	49
PRODUCTION	-.879 (2.506)*	1.289 (3.564)+	6.73+	.84	1.40	49
OTHER	-1.119 (3.088)+	1.335 (3.997)+	8.16+	.84	1.71	49

	α	β	F	R^2	DW	T
5801-7401						
TOTAL	-.604 (1.867)	1.101 (.958)	2.58	.78	1.95	33
PRODUCTION	-.447 (1.379)	1.053 (.505)	1.78	.76	1.78	33
OTHER	-.685 (2.093)*	1.121 (1.138)	3.14	.78	2.10	33
5801-8002						
TOTAL	-.976 (2.880)+	1.333 (4.318)+	10.39+	.87	1.57	46
PRODUCTION	-.760 (2.206)*	1.283 (3.621)+	7.70+	.86	1.38	46
OTHER	-1.006 (2.835)+	1.330 (4.104)+	9.19+	.86	1.76	46

OLS regression (for definitions, see Table 5.3): CPCS = α + βMUC + u.

Note

Absolute values for t-statistics are reported under the estimated coefficients.
*Significant at the .05 level (two tails test for t-statistics).
+Significant at the .01 level (two tails test for t-statistics).
The t and F-tests are for the hypothesis $\alpha=0$, $\beta=1$; R^2 is the (unadjusted) determination coefficient; DW is the Durbin-Watson statistic; T is the number of observations.

tion error did take place due to the expected but not realized effects of the Suez crisis – is excluded from the sample, the unbiasedness test is passed also by the expectations on consumer price changes for the "other", and thus also the "total", respondents.

Again, over the entire sample, expectations are instead clearly biased. One can conclude then that over a period of moderate oscillations in the rates of change of prices, expectations have been unbiased and there has been no evidence of serial correlation in the anticipation errors. However, when the few additional observations for the more recent years are added to the sample, these results are reversed. This can in part be explained by the fact that after the first oil crisis the inflation pattern has changed dramatically in Italy and that a number of shocks which were difficult to anticipate, not only by the public at large, have taken place. One would expect that if the inflation rate will come back to more usual ranges of variation, expectations would also come back to be unbiased. Nothing more can be added to this statement: it is the case that all the large anticipation errors have been concentrated in the last years of the sample and Italy is still experiencing very high and variable inflation rates.

5.4. *Tests of Rationality of Inflation Expectations*

In this section the results of the tests of the "rationality" of expectations – performed along the lines of the discussion advanced in Section 5.2 – will be discussed.[23] As observed, it is impossible to test the optimality of expectations with respect to the complete information set because total knowledge of it is not within grasp (and also because of obvious problems of degrees of freedom). Tests of weak rationality have been considered, examining if at least the information contained in the past history of inflation rates has been efficiently utilized. Alternative information, that is, the past history of other variables, has been examined considering one variable at a time. As shown in Section 5.2, in these tests omitted variables may play an important role, resulting in the non-rejection of the hypothesis of rationality only because of a downward bias in the tests performed. Here the main interest is in examining if, over the period for which the expectations series pass the tests of unbiasedness and of absence of serial correlation in the anticipation errors, they would also pass the strong tests of optimal use of relevant information. An extensive search over many variables which *a priori* could

---

[23] To minimize the computation burden only total answers have been considered. As it has been repeatedly stressed and as the results of Section 2.5 (as well as the unbiasedness tests) show, very similar results should be obtained also for the "production" and the "other" respondents, when considered separately.

be considered as relevant determinants of the inflation process has thus been conducted. Finally, some of these variables have also been considered jointly, testing for an efficient use of composite information.

5.4.1. Past History of Price Changes

In Table 5.6 the results are presented of regressions of the difference between actual and expected price changes on the actual price changes that occurred in the four quarters preceding the survey date. Also regressions on

TABLE 5.6

RATIONALITY TESTS, 1 (WHOLESALE AND CONSUMER PRICES)

4 Quarterly Lags on Past History of Variable to be Forecast ("Efficiency")

Dependent Variable	Regressors	Period	T	$F_{(4, T-5)}$	DW	BP(4)	BP(8)
WPCS-MUW							
	WPCQ	5202-7202	41	.65	1.95	.84	2.50
	WPCQL	5202-7202	41	.48	1.93	.47	2.30
	WPCQ	5202-8002	57	11.97	1.83	7.49	9.34
	WPCQL	5202-8002	57	5.64	1.62	8.73	14.01
CPCS-MUC							
	CPCQ	5602-7401	36	2.40	2.05	1.80	1.91
	CPCQL	5602-7401	36	.28	1.84	3.88	5.19
	CPCQ	5602-8002	49	11.17	1.99	1.92	4.45
	CPCQL	5602-8002	49	6.87	1.82	2.26	3.71

Significance Limits:

	.05	.01
$F_{(4,52)}$	2.56	3.71
$F_{(4,44)}$	2.58	3.78
$F_{(4,36)}$	2.63	3.87
$F_{(4,31}$	2.68	3.99
$\chi^2(4)$	9.49	13.28
$\chi^2(8)$	15.51	20.09

Note

For definitions see Table 5.3. All regressions include a constant.
The F-test is for the hypothesis that the coefficients of the regressors are equal to 0; DW is the Durbin-Watson statistic; BP(k) is the Box-Pierce statistic for autocorrelation of the residuals up to the kth order; T is the number of observations.
WPCQ and CPCQ define the 4 quarterly percentage wholesale and consumer price changes starting backward from the second quarter of the semester at the end of which expectations are formed; WPCQL and CPCQL similarly define the 4 quarterly percentage changes backward from the first quarter of the same semester.

the four price changes, excluding that of the second quarter of the semester at the end of which expectations were formed, have been performed. While, as for the tests of the previous section, over the whole sample period the inflation expectations of the respondents to *Mondo Economico* surveys do not pass this rationality test, they do pass over the shorter periods (still, however, with 41 and 36 observations for wholesale and consumer prices, respectively) that exclude the years after the 1973 oil crisis. In particular, the *F*-statistics are well below the proper significance limits and the residuals are not serially correlated.

This test is probably the most popular among tests of the rational expectations hypothesis with survey data. It is known as a test of the "efficiency" requirement of rational expectations (that is, "efficient utilization of the information contained in realized rates of inflation to generate one-period forecasts")[24] as opposed to the "consistency" requirement which comes from the consistent application of the "chain rule of forecasting" in a multispan forecasting situation.[25] With the present data from the *Mondo Economico* surveys, the consistency of inflation expectations cannot yet be tested since, starting only with the first semester of 1978, expectations collected for one *and* two semesters ahead are available. As far as the efficiency requirement (with respect to the past history of inflation) is concerned, mixed results have been obtained in the literature on the basis of other survey data. It is interesting to observe that only when the inflation rate becomes much more volatile and much higher on average than for the previous quarter of a century it appears, in the case of *Mondo Economico* surveys, that some gains in efficiency could have been obtained by means of a better utilization of the information contained in the realized rates of change of prices.

5.4.2. *Past History of Other Single Variables*

As observed in the introduction to this chapter, the anticipation errors have been regressed on the past history (four quarterly lags) of a number of relevant variables. They are as follows: the rate of change of consumer prices for tests on wholesale prices and wholesale price changes for tests on consumer prices; a measure of utilized capacity (a Wharton-like index); the rate of unemployment, both seasonally adjusted and not, as well as its first difference; the rate of change of the index of industrial production (again, seasonally adjusted and not); a long-term bond interest rate and a short-term

---

[24] Pesando (1975, p. 851).
[25] See, for example, Shiller (1978) and Sargent (1979, ch. X).

TABLE 5.7

RATIONALITY TESTS, 2A (WHOLESALE PRICES)

4 Quarterly Lags on Alternative Information ("Orthogonality")

Dependent Variable	Regressors	Period	T	$F_{(4, T-5)}$	DW	BP(4)	BP(8)
WPCS-MUW							
	CPCQ	5202-7202	41	1.54	2.11	.45	2.37
	UTCQ	5401-7202	38	.87	2.04	.83	2.41
	URQ	6001-7202	26	1.23	1.90	1.96	3.37
	URQA	6001-7202	26	.44	2.14	1.50	2.12
	DURQ	6002-7202	25	1.23	1.82	2.57	3.62
	DURQA	6002-7202	25	.34	2.15	1.66	2.08
	LRQ	6301-7202	20	.54	1.59	1.30	2.07
	BRQ	5301-7202	40	.72	1.84	.84	2.93
	DM2Q	5902-7202	27	1.02	1.77	3.00	5.38
	DM2QA	5902-7202	27	.62	1.99	2.08	3.91
	DWHQ	5902-7202	27	.48	1.79	2.42	5.02
	DWHQA	5902-7202	27	.35	2.08	1.58	1.72
	DWDQ	5902-7202	27	.70	1.82	.46	2.61
	DWDQA	5902-7202	27	.91	1.80	.89	.94
	DWCQ	6002-7202	25	.82	1.85	.42	.56
	DPRODQ	5402-7202	37	1.35	1.83	.24	1.42
	DPRODQA	5402-7202	37	.96	1.85	.23	.75
	DEXLDQ	5802-7202	29	.40	2.11	1.34	3.70
Significance Limits:							
		.05	.01		.05	.01	
	$F_{(4,36)}$	2.63	3.89	$F_{(4.21)}$	2.84	4.37	
	$F_{(4,35)}$	2.65	3.91	$F_{(4,20)}$	2.86	4.43	
	$F_{(4,33)}$	2.66	3.95	$F_{(4,15)}$	3.06	4.89	
	$F_{(4,32)}$	2.67	3.97	$\chi^2_{(4)}$	9.49	13.28	
	$F_{(4,24)}$	2.78	4.22	$\chi^2_{(8)}$	15.51	20.09	
	$F_{(4,22)}$	2.82	4.31				

Note

For definitions see Table 5.3. All regressions include a constant.
The F-test is for the hypothesis that the coefficients of the regressors are equal to O; DW is the
Durbin-Watson statistic; BP(k) is the Box-Pierce statistic for autocorrelation of the residuals up to
the kth order; T is the number of observations.

lending rate; the rate of change of the exchange rate between the Italian lira
and the U.S. dollar; and, finally, the percentage changes of money supply
(*M2*), hourly and per worker actual wages (industry excluding construction),
as well as the contractual wage rate (all the last four variables both
seasonally adjusted and not).[26]

An extensive search has therefore been conducted since, as it has been
observed in Section 5.2, there are chances that the test statistics would be
biased in favor of the rationality hypothesis. Furthermore, one might not be

[26]All tests have been performed considering as regressors the four lagged quarterly values of
these variables starting both with the second and the first quarter of the semester at the end of
which the survey took place. The results obtained are qualitatively similar and only those
relating to the former are presented. Obviously, for different variables it has been necessary to
consider different sample periods depending on the date when statistical data became available
on each of these variables.

rejecting this hypothesis simply because the information considered here was not relevant in the determination of the inflation process (and was rightly considered to be so in forming the appropriate expectations).

The results of these tests are presented in Tables 5.7 and 5.8 for wholesale, and in Tables 5.9 and 5.10 for consumer price changes. As usual, over the entire sample both wholesale and consumer price expectations fail to pass this test ("orthogonality" with respect to possibly relevant alternative information). It is very impressive, however, that of all the above mentioned variables, none turns out to be significant in explaining, over the sub-periods preceding the first oil crisis, the anticipation errors in the rates of change of the two price indices considered in this study, with the sole exception of the change in the exchange rate on the rate of change of consumer prices (but at the 5 percent, not the 1 percent significance level).

TABLE 5.8

RATIONALITY TESTS, 2B (WHOLESALE PRICES)

4 Quarterly Lags on Alternative Information ("Orthogonality")

Dependent Variable	Regressors	Period	T	$F_{(4, T-5)}$	DW	BP(4)	BP(8)
WPCS-MUW							
	CPCQ	5202–8002	57	5.35	1.51	9.63	10.46
	UTCQ	5401–8002	54	3.15	.90	41.00	52.27
	URQ	6001–8002	42	4.77	1.48	5.12	8.05
	URQA	6001–8002	42	4.93	1.00	11.32	15.87
	DURQ	6002–8002	41	6.01	1.26	10.65	12.28
	DURQA	6002–8002	41	3.78	.90	17.98	26.21
	LRQ	6301–8002	36	1.73	1.25	8.05	10.50
	BRQ	5301–8002	56	3.44	1.30	11.66	14.38
	DM2Q	5902–8002	43	7.31	1.05	12.85	14.37
	DM2QA	5902–8002	43	7.49	1.06	12.95	14.17
	DWHQ	5902–8002	43	2.26	1.10	11.20	14.87
	DWHQA	5902–8002	43	1.93	1.28	7.80	10.94
	DWDQ	5902–8002	43	4.12	1.30	8.99	14.87
	DWDQA	5902–8002	43	3.51	1.44	5.74	10.21
	DWCQ	6002–8002	41	3.36	1.18	6.47	8.87
	DPRODQ	5402–8002	53	7.86	1.16	10.60	12.71
	DPRODQA	5402–8002	53	2.69	.92	31.39	49.46
	DEXLDQ	5802–8002	45	4.14	1.35	18.99	21.41

Significance Limits:

		.05	.01		.05	.01
	$F_{(4,52)}$	2.56	3.71	$F_{(4,37)}$	2.63	3.87
	$F_{(4,51)}$	2.56	3.72	$F_{(4,36)}$	2.63	3.89
	$F_{(4,49)}$	2.56	3.73	$F_{(4,25)}$	2.76	4.18
	$F_{(4,48)}$	2.56	3.74	$\chi^2(4)$	9.49	13.28
	$F_{(4,40)}$	2.61	3.83	$\chi^2(8)$	15.51	20.09
	$F_{(4,38)}$	2.62	3.86			

Note

For definitions see Table 5.3. All regressions include a constant.
The F-test is for the hypothesis that the coefficients of the regressors are equal to 0; DW is the Durbin-Watson statistic; BP(k) is the Box-Pierce statistic for autocorrelation of the residuals up to the kth order; T is the number of observations.

TABLE 5.9

RATIONALITY TESTS, 2A (CONSUMER PRICES)

4 Quarterly Lags on Alternative Information ("Orthogonality")

Dependent Variable	Regressors	Period	T	F(4, T-5)	DW	BP(4)	BP(8)
CPCS-MUC							
	WPCQ	5602-7401	36	.66	1.78	2.64	4.75
	UTCQ	5602-7401	36	.44	1.66	3.31	5.32
	URQ	6001-7401	29	.51	1.65	3.55	5.55
	UROA	6001-7401	29	.66	1.67	3.88	6.33
	DURQ	6002-7401	28	.47	1.64	2.53	4.88
	DURQA	6002-7401	28	.55	1.68	3.50	5.80
	LRQ	6301-7401	23	.73	1.72	2.36	3.76
	BRQ	5602-7401	36	.66	1.67	3.12	4.63
	DM2Q	5902-7401	30	2.40	1.99	.37	3.39
	DM2QA	5902-7401	30	1.27	2.21	1.36	2.70
	DWHQ	5902-7401	30	1.91	1.56	2.54	4.45
	DWHQA	5902-7401	30	.74	1.80	3.11	4.80
	DWDQ	5902-7401	30	1.32	1.56	2.46	4.72
	DWDQA	5902-7401	30	.88	1.65	3.29	4.43
	DWCQ	6002-7401	28	.97	1.98	.73	2.22
	DPRODQ	5602-7401	36	.78	1.62	2.96	5.72
	DPRODQA	5602-7401	36	.08	1.71	2.26	3.99
	DEXLDQ	5802-7401	32	3.67	1.99	1.78	3.76

Significance Limits:

	.05	.01
$F_{(4,31)}$	2.68	3.99
$F_{(4,27)}$	2.73	4.11
$F_{(4,25)}$	2.76	4.18
$F_{(4,24)}$	2.78	4.22
$F_{(4,23)}$	2.80	4.26
$F_{(4,18)}$	2.93	4.58
$\chi^2_{(4)}$	9.49	13.28
$\chi^2_{(8)}$	15.51	20.09

Note

For definitions see Table 5.3. All regressions include a constant.
The F-test is for the hypothesis that the coefficients of the regressors are equal to 0; DW is the Durbin-Watson statistic; BP(k) is the Box-Pierce statistic for autocorrelation of the residuals up to the kth order; T is the number of observations.

5.4.3. Composite Information

The previous results are totally confirmed when, instead of four quarterly lags of each single piece of information, one at a time, a composite of this information is considered. Experiments have been conducted with two lags in consumer and wholesale price percentage changes and in capacity utilization; the same plus two lags in the percentage change of *M2*; and the same plus two lags in the percentage change of actual hourly wages. The results are presented in Tables 5.11 and 5.12 for wholesale prices, and in Tables 5.13 and 5.14 for consumer prices.

TABLE 5.10

RATIONALITY TESTS, 2B (CONSUMER PRICES)

4 Quarterly Lags on Alternative Information ("Orthogonality")

Dependent Variable	Regressors	Period	T	$F(4, T-5)$	DW	BP(4)	BP(8)
CPCS-MUC							
	WPCQ	5602-8002	49	6.30	1.78	1.30	4.45
	UTCQ	5602-8002	49	.18	.98	29.53	36.89
	URQ	6001-8002	42	2.65	1.20	10.25	10.49
	URQA	6001-8002	42	1.30	1.08	20.78	21.25
	DURQ	6002-8002	41	3.56	1.18	6.87	7.66
	DURQA	6002-8002	41	.42	.96	31.84	40.67
	LRQ	6301-8002	36	4.14	1.59	3.49	6.78
	BRQ	5602-8002	49	5.83	1.71	3.51	5.60
	DM2Q	5902-8002	43	7.30	1.25	7.58	11.63
	DM2QA	5902-8002	43	5.63	1.52	4.75	10.76
	DWHQ	5902-8002	43	7.18	1.10	9.52	11.95
	DWHQA	5902-8002	43	3.27	1.32	6.35	8.39
	DWDQ	5902-8002	43	4.81	1.06	10.43	12.23
	DWDQA	5902-8002	43	3.11	1.31	6.85	9.80
	DWCQ	6002-8002	41	5.65	1.63	2.52	4.51
	DPRODQ	5602-8002	49	3.00	1.16	10.21	10.71
	DPRODQA	5602-8002	49	.41	1.11	21.07	26.02
	DEXLDQ	5802-8002	45	1.61	1.31	13.04	18.86

Significance Limits:

		.05	.01
	$F(4,45)$	2.58	3.77
	$F(4,40)$	2.61	3.83
	$F(4,38)$	2.62	3.86
	$F(4,37)$	2.63	3.87
	$F(4,36)$	2.63	3.89
	$F(4,25)$	2.76	4.18
	$\chi^2(4)$	9.49	13.28
	$\chi^2(8)$	15.51	20.09

Note

For definitions see Table 5.3. All regressions include a constant.
The F-test is for the hypothesis that the coefficients of the regressors are equal to O; DW is the Durbin-Watson statistic; BP(k) is the Box-Pierce statistic for autocorrelation of the residuals up to the kth order; T is the number of observations.

The reservations advanced on these tests notwithstanding, when the tests concluded in favor of the rationality hypothesis, it was not expected that the inflation expectations of the *Mondo Economico* respondents would pass these tests so convincingly – even if only for the periods of mild inflation between the second quarter of 1952 and the second quarter of 1972 for the wholesale and between the second quarter of 1956 and the first quarter of 1974 for the consumer price index. It is therefore appropriate to analyze if, by accounting for aggregation and measurement error problems, these results might be extended to the whole sample period. This matter will be examined in the next two sections. In Section 5.7, the question whether improvements on the inflation expectations were possible on the basis of the alternative predictors examined in Chapter 4, will be investigated.

TABLE 5.11

RATIONALITY TESTS, 3A (WHOLESALE PRICES)

2 Quarterly Lags on Composite Information

Dependent Variable	Regressors (m)	Period	T	$F(m, T-m-1)$	DW	BP(4)	BP(8)
WPCS-MUW							
WPCQ CPCQ UTCQ	(6)	5302–7202	39	.60	2.11	.98	2.50
WPCQ CPCQ UTCQ DM2Q	(8)	5901–7202	28	1.12	1.85	3.16	5.25
WPCQ CPCQ UTCQ DM2Q DWHQ	(10)	5901–7202	28	1.61	1.79	5.94	7.20

Significance Limits:

	.05	.01
$F(6,32)$	2.40	3.42
$F(8,19)$	2.48	3.63
$F(10,17)$	2.45	3.59
$\chi^2(4)$	9.49	13.28
$\chi^2(8)$	15.51	20.09

Note

For definitions see Table 5.3. All regressions include a constant.
The F-test is for the hypothesis that the coefficients of the regressors are equal to 0; DW is the Durbin-Watson statistic; BP(k) is the Box-Pierce statistic for autocorrelation of the residuals up to the kth order; T is the number of observations.

5.5. Aggregation Problems and Tests of Unbiasedness and Rationality

The tests of Sections 5.3 and 5.4 have been performed using as the expectation variable the percentage price change expected *on average* by the respondents to *Mondo Economico* surveys. A possible source of bias could, however, come from the fact that the average expected rate has been utilized. Consider, for example, the rationality tests of the last section (a similar argument applies also to the unbiasedness tests of Section 5.3). Ordinary least squares regressions have been estimated of the kind

$$p_t - \gamma p_t^e = X_t \beta + u_t, \qquad (5.36)$$

where p_t is the rate of change of prices, p_t^e is its average survey-based expectation, X_t is a given information set, and γ has been forced to be equal

TABLE 5.12

RATIONALITY TESTS, 3B (WHOLESALE PRICES)

2 Quarterly Lags on Composite Information

Dependent Variable	Regressors (m)		Period	T	F(m. T-m-1)	DW	BP(4)	BP(8)
WPCS-MUW								
	WPCQ CPCQ UTCQ	(6)	5302-8002	55	9.34	2.21	7.36	9.58
	WPCQ CPCQ UTCQ DM2Q	(8)	5901-8002	44	8.37	2.26	3.11	6.54
	WPCQ CPCQ UTCQ DM2Q DWHQ	(10)	5901-8002	44	8.83	1.64	3.01	5.72

Significance Limits:

	.05	.01
$\bar{F}(6,48)$	2.30	3.20
$F(8,35)$	2.22	3.06
$F(10,33)$	2.13	2.92
$\chi^2(4)$	9.49	13.28
$\chi^2(8)$	15.51	20.09

Note

For definitions see Table 5.3. All regressions include a constant.
The F-test is for the hypothesis that the coefficients of the regressors are equal to 0; DW is the Durbin-Watson statistic; BP(k) is the Box-Pierce statistic for autocorrelation of the residuals up to the kth order; T is the number of observations.

to one by the unbiasedness condition. The test has been then carried out by verifying the difference from zero of the estimate of β. But consider (5.36) at the individual level; one would have

$$p_t - \gamma_i p_{ti}^e = X_t \beta_i + u_{ti}, \qquad i = 1, \ldots, n. \tag{5.37}$$

Aggregating over the n respondents to the surveys, one obtains

$$p_t - \gamma p_t^e = X_t \beta + v_t, \tag{5.38}$$

where

$$p_t^e = \frac{1}{n} \sum p_{ti}^e, \qquad \beta = \frac{1}{n} \sum \beta_i, \qquad \gamma = \frac{1}{n} \sum \gamma_i,$$

$$v_t = u_t + \frac{1}{n} \sum \gamma_i d_{it}, \qquad u_t = \frac{1}{n} \sum u_{ti}, \qquad d_{it} = p_{ti}^e - p_t^e,$$

with all the sums for i going from 1 to n.

TABLE 5.13

RATIONALITY TESTS, 3A (CONSUMER PRICES)

2 Quarterly Lags on Composite Information

Dependent Variable	Regressors (m)		Period	T	F(m, T-m-1)	DW	BP(4)	BP(8)
CPCS-MUC								
	CPCQ WPCQ UTCQ	(6)	5602-7401	36	1.98	2.04	2.57	3.31
	CPCQ WPCQ UTCO DM2Q	(8)	5901-7401	31	2.24	2.06	2.47	4.11
	CPCQ WPCQ UTCQ DM2Q DWHQ	(10)	5901-7401	31	3.05	2.11	1.92	3.14

Significance Limits:

	.05	.01
F(6,29)	2.43	3.50
F(8,22)	2.40	3.45
F(10,20)	2.35	3.37
$\chi^2_{(4)}$	9.49	13.28
$\chi^2_{(3)}$	15.51	20.09

Note

For definitions see Table 5.3. All regressions include a constant.
The F-test is for the hypothesis that the coefficients of the regressors are equal to 0; DW is the Durbin-Watson statistic; BP(k) is the Box-Pierce statistic for autocorrelation of the residuals up to the kth order; T is the number of observations.

Even if the unbiasedness condition is imposed which could be done since the stronger "efficiency" and "orthogonality" conditions are being verified, still one has a residual v_t which consists of two terms: one which might be white noise with constant variance, u_t, and another for which there is no reason to accept this assumption. As a matter of fact, there is strong evidence that the variance of this second term could be not constant (because it is a weighted average of the differences between individual and average expectations – knowing from Chapter 2 that these expectations do not have, over the entire sample period, a constant variance).

A moderately reasonable assumption could instead be the following:

$$d_{it} = \lambda_i \sigma_t + e_{it}, \tag{5.39}$$

where σ_t is the square root of the variance of the individual expectations and

TABLE 5.14

RATIONALITY TESTS, 3B (CONSUMER PRICES)

2 Quarterly Lags on Composite Information

Dependent Variable	Regressors (m)	Period	T	F(m, T-m-1)	DW	BP(4)	BP(8)
CPCS-MUC							
WPCQ UTCQ	( )	5602	49	8.28	2.01	1.35	5.33
CPCQ WPCQ UTCO DM2Q	(8)	5901-8002	44	6.19	1.80	1.96	7.30
CPCQ WPCQ UTCO DM2Q DWHQ	(10)	5901-8002	44	5.77	1.67	2.34	6.24

Significance Limits:

	.05	.01
F(6,42)	2.32	3.26
F(8,35)	2.22	3.06
F(10,33)	2.13	2.92
$\chi^2(4)$	9.49	13.28
$\chi^2(8)$	15.51	20.09

Note

For definitions see Table 5.3. All regressions include a constant.
The F-test is for the hypothesis that the coefficients of the regressors are equal to 0; DW is the Durbin-Watson statistic; BP(k) is the Box-Pierce statistic for autocorrelation of the residuals up to the kth order; T is the number of observations.

e_{it} is an individual-specific white noise element. One would then have

$$v_t = \delta\sigma_t + \varepsilon_t, \tag{5.40}$$

where

$$\varepsilon_t = u_t + e_t, \qquad e_t = \frac{1}{n}\sum \gamma_i e_{it}, \qquad \delta = \frac{1}{n}\sum \gamma_i \lambda_i.$$

Imposing the unbiasedness condition on the average of the individual expectations (that is, $\gamma = 1$), one obtains

$$p_t - p_t^e = X_t\beta + \delta\sigma_t + \varepsilon_t, \tag{5.41}$$

which differs from the equations considered in Section 5.4 for the presence of the σ_t variable among the regressors.

Similarly, for the unbiasedness tests,

$$p_t = \beta_0 + \gamma p_t^e + \delta\sigma_t + \varepsilon_t. \tag{5.42}$$

The same tests of Sections 5.3 and 5.4 could then be repeated – still testing for $\beta = 0$ for each information set in (5.41) and for $\beta_0 = 0$, $\gamma = 1$ in (5.42) – estimating the latter two equations with the inclusion among the regressors of the standard deviation of the inflation expectations as it results from the estimates obtained in Chapter 2.

5.5.1. Tests of Unbiasedness

In Table 5.15 the results of the regressions given by (5.42) are reported. The inclusion among the regressors of the standard deviation of individual expectations leads to a generally sizable reduction in the F-statistics. Although the result is that one cannot anymore reject the unbiasedness assumption both for the total and the "other" respondents over the second semester 1956 through first semester 1974 period (for which it was rejected in Section 5.3 at the 5 percent significance level for consumer prices), it still is rejected over the entire sample period.

5.5.2. Tests of Rationality

Regressions of the kind given by (5.41) have been performed over the entire sample period considering, as alternative information sets, the past history (four quarterly lags) of the percentage changes in the two price indices (Table 5.16). After the unbiasedness hypothesis has been rejected, it is no surprise that also these stronger tests still reject the rationality assumption. It should be noticed, however, that if the most recent (possibly not completely known) quarterly price changes are excluded, the F-statistics do not indicate a sub-optimal use of this information. In the case of wholesale prices, however, there are signs of serial correlation among the residuals (even if, for the presence of lagged dependent variables, at least in the case of past history of the same wholesale price changes, the Durbin–Watson and Box–Pierce statistics do not provide proper tests against serial correlation): the F-tests must therefore be considered, in this occasion, with some care.

TABLE 5.15

WHOLESALE AND CONSUMER PRICES, TESTS OF UNBIASEDNESS AND AGGREGATION

	$F(2,T-3)$	Significance limits		DW
		.05	.01	
WHOLESALE				
5202-7202 (T=41)				
Total	.26 (1.03)	3.30	5.22	1.82 (1.82)
Production	.83 (1.07)	3.30	5.22	1.86 (1.86)
Other	.10 (1.51)	3.30	5.22	1.79 (1.79)
5801-7202 (T=30)				
Total	.54 (1.24)	3.36	5.50	2.25 (2.25)
Production	.20 (.47)	3.36	5.50	2.36 (2.37)
Other	.65 (1.69)	3.36	5.50	2.12 (2.13)
5202-8002 (T=57)				
Total	18.82 (25.47)	3.17	5.03	1.32 (1.21)
Production	18.95 (24.64)	3.17	5.03	1.42 (1.33)
Other	18.15 (25.43)	3.17	5.03	1.28 (1.17)
5801-8002 (T=46)				
Total	14.35 (26.29)	3.21	5.14	1.29 (1.20)
Production	15.24 (26.88)	3.21	5.14	1.41 (1.35)
Other	13.11 (25.06)	3.21	5.14	1.26 (1.15)
CONSUMER				
5602-7401 (T=36)				
Total	1.36 (3.50)	3.29	5.33	1.81 (1.80)
Production	2.23 (2.80)	3.29	5.33	1.69 (1.67)
Other	1.08 (3.99)	3.29	5.33	1.90 (1.90)
5801-7401 (T=33)				
Total	1.23 (2.58)	3.32	5.39	1.99 (1.95)
Production	1.66 (1.74)	3.32	5.39	1.86 (1.78)
Other	1.24 (3.14)	3.32	5.39	2.11 (2.10)
5602-8002 (T=49)				
Total	7.81 (9.07)	3.20	5.11	1.68 (1.56)
Production	4.93 (6.73)	3.20	5.11	1.46 (1.40)
Other	7.33 (8.16)	3.20	5.11	1.84 (1.71)
5801-8002 (T=46)				
Total	7.02 (10.49)	3.21	5.14	1.71 (1.57)
Production	4.34 (7.70)	3.21	5.14	1.44 (1.38)
Other	6.51 (9.19)	3.21	5.14	1.90 (1.76)

OLS regressions (for definitions, see Table 5.3): $WPCS = \alpha + \beta MUW + \gamma SIW + u$,
$CPCS = \alpha + \beta MUC + \gamma SIW + u$.

Note

The F-test is for the joint hypothesis $\alpha=0$, $\beta=1$; DW is the Durbin-Watson statistic; T is the number of observations. The numbers in parentheses are, respectively, the values of the F and DW statistics for the constrained estimates with $\gamma=0$ (see Tables 5.4 and 5.5).

TABLE 5.16

WHOLESALE AND CONSUMER PRICES, TESTS OF RATIONALITY AND AGGREGATION

4 Quarterly Lags on Past History of Price Changes

Dependent Variable	Regressors	Period	T	$F(4, T-6)$	DW	BP(4)	BP(8)
WPCS-MUW							
	WPCQ	5202-8002	57	8.52 (11.97)	1.77 (1.83)	5.66 (7.49)	10.93 (9.34)
	WPCQL	5202-8002	57	2.15 (5.64)	1.34 (1.62)	7.29 (8.73)	18.03 (14.01)
	CPCQ	5202-8002	57	3.40 (5.35)	1.47 (1.51)	6.40 (9.63)	14.82 (10.46)
	CPCQL	5202-8002	57	.99 (3.04)	1.08 (1.16)	12.79 (13.73)	27.31 (20.89)
CPCS-MUC							
	CPCQ	5602-8002	49	5.02 (11.17)	1.98 (1.99)	1.83 (1.92)	4.39 (4.45)
	CPCQL	5602-8002	49	2.58 (6.87)	1.82 (1.82)	2.42 (2.26)	4.05 (3.71)
	WPCQ	5602-8002	49	1.74 (6.30)	1.81 (1.78)	1.36 (1.30)	4.98 (4.45)
	WPCQL	5602-8002	49	1.18 (5.12)	1.64 (1.58)	2.66 (2.90)	8.37 (8.28)

Significance Limits:

	.05	.01
$F(4,51)$	2.56	3.72
$F(4,43)$	2.58	3.79
$\chi^2(4)$	9.49	13.28
$\chi^2(8)$	15.51	20.09

Note

For definitions, see Table 5.3. All regressions include a constant and the standard deviation of the inflation expectations (SIW and SIC, respectively). The F-test is for the hypothesis that the coefficients of the regressors are equal to 0; DW is the Durbin-Watson statistic; BP(k) is the Box-Pierce statistic for autocorrelation of the residuals up to the kth order; T is the number of observations. WPCQ and CPCQ define the 4 quarterly percentage wholesale and consumer price changes starting backward from the second quarter of the semester at the end of which expectations are formed; WPCQL and CPCQL similarly de-fire the 4 quarterly percentage changes starting backward from the first quarter of the same semester. The numbers in parentheses are, respectively, the values of the F, DW and BP statistics for the estimates of the regressions without SIW and SIC (i.e., with their coefficients constrained to be equal to 0; these are the estimates presented in Tables 5.6, 5.8 and 5.10).

5.5.3. *Tests of Unbiasedness without "Irregular" Observations*

In Tables 5.17 and 5.18 some further experiments are presented. In particular, tests of unbiasedness have been performed, on the one hand, eliminating from the sample a number of "irregular" observations (that is, large anticipation errors), and, on the other, including among the regressors dummy variables to account for the largest errors (first semesters of 1974 and 1976 for wholesale, and first semester of 1976 for consumer price changes). In the latter cases, the regressions have been run for all the with and without the standard deviation of the individual expectations as a regressor. As it can be seen, only when a large number of recent observa-

TABLE 5.17

WHOLESALE PRICES, TESTS OF UNBIASEDNESS WITHOUT "IRREGULAR" OBSERVATIONS

		F(2,T-K)	Significance limits		DW
			.05	.01	
5202-8002					
Total					
A	(T=53, K=2)	11.57	3.18	5.05	1.66
B	(T=47, K=2)	.70	3.20	5.12	1.95
C	(T=57, K=4)	15.40	3.17	5.04	1.71
D	(T=57, K=5)	11.60	3.17	5.04	1.71
Production					
A	(T=53, K=2)	11.50	3.18	5.05	1.76
B	(T=47, K=2)	.33	3.20	5.12	2.00
Other					
A	(T=53, K=2)	11.11	3.18	5.05	1.59
B	(T=47, K=2)	1.19	3.20	5.12	1.88
5801-8002					
Total					
A	(T=42, K=2)	15.37	3.23	5.18	1.76
B	(T=36, K=2)	.94	3.28	5.31	2.30
C	(T=46, K=4)	17.91	3.22	5.16	1.77
D	(T=46, K=5)	10.99	3.22	5.17	1.76
Production					
A	(T=42, K=2)	17.20	3.23	5.18	1.97
B	(T=36, K=2)	.47	3.28	5.31	2.48
Other					
A	(T=42, K=2)	13.34	3.23	5.18	1.63
B	(T=36, K=2)	1.20	3.28	5.31	2.09

OLS regressions (for definitions, see Table 5.3): WPCS = α + βMUW + u.

Note

The F-test is for the joint hypothesis $\alpha=0$, $\beta=1$; DW is the Durbin-Watson statistic; T and K are, respectively, the number of observations and the number of regressors.

A : observations for 7401, 7402, 7601, 7602 eliminated from the sample;
B : observations for 7301, 7302, 7401, 7402, 7601, 7602, 7701, 7901, 7902, 8001 eliminated from the sample;
C : dummies for 7401 and 7601 included among the regressors;
D : dummies for 7401 and 7601 and standard deviation of the expected inflation included among the regressors.

TABLE 5.18

CONSUMER PRICES, TESTS OF UNBIASEDNESS WITHOUT "IRREGULAR" OBSERVATIONS

		$F(2,T-K)$	Significance limits .05	.01	DW
5602-8002					
Total					
A	(T=44, K=2)	4.59	3.22	5.16	1.72
B	(T=49, K=3)	11.29	3.20	5.11	1.66
C	(T=49, K=4)	11.71	3.20	5.12	1.74
Production					
A	(T=44, K=2)	3.65	3.22	5.16	1.55
Other					
A	(T=44, K=2)	4.61	3.22	5.16	1.86
5801-8002					
Total					
A	(T=41, K=2)	4.85	3.24	5.20	1.80
B	(T=46, K=3)	13.37	3.21	5.14	1.67
C	(T=46, K=4)	11.19	3.22	5.16	1.81
Production					
A	(T=41, K=2)	3.93	3.24	5.20	1.56
Other					
A	(T=41, K=2)	4.54	3.24	5.20	2.00

OLS regressions (for definitions, see Table 5.3): CPCS = α + βMUC + u.

Note

The F-test is for the joint hypothesis $\alpha=0$, $\beta=1$; DW is the Durbin-Watson statistic; T and K are, respectively, the number of observations and the number of regressors.
A : observations for 7401, 7501, 7601, 7701, 8001 eliminated from the sample;
B : dummy for 7601 included among the regressors;
C : dummy for 7601 and standard deviation of the expected inflation included among the regressors.

tions is eliminated from the sample, the unbiasedness assumption is not rejected. This result is equivalent to the one obtained in testing for absence of serial correlation among the anticipation errors (Section 5.3, Table 5.2), and there is no need to repeat what has been said on that occasion.

5.6. Error of Measurement Problems: Some Tentative Results

As shown in Chapter 1, between 1974 and 1976 while the rate of inflation in Italy passed to double-digit figures even on a semiannual basis, the questionnaire of *Mondo Economico* surveys remained unchanged and the pre-set intervals became inadequate in their coverage of the possible spectrum of inflation rates. This fact led to the introduction in Chapter 2 of a somewhat arbitrary procedure to fix the upper limit of the open-ended interval for the piecewise uniform distribution estimates. This section will consider the question whether a possible measurement error, still present after that correction, might account for the bias in the expected inflation that has been found for the more recent expectations. If one assumes, then, that inflation expectations are measured with error, one can write

$$p_t^e = p_t^{e*} + e_t, \qquad (5.43)$$

where p_t^{e*} is the "true" inflation expectation, and one might think that

$$e_t = \begin{cases} f(X_t) + \varepsilon_t & \text{if } \quad \phi_t \subset \Phi_t, \\ \varepsilon_t & \text{otherwise,} \end{cases} \qquad (5.44)$$

where ε_t is a white noise residual and X_t is the percentage of answers which fell in the upper open-ended interval. Therefore, a measurement error $f(X_t)$ corresponds to X_t only if the event $\phi_t \in \Phi_t$ takes place. Assume that $\phi_t = X_t$ and $\Phi_t = (X_t > X_0)$, where X_0 is a given percentage number of answers (call it *WO* for wholesale and *CO* for consumer prices). Assume also that $f(X_t)$ is a linear function of X_t. One can then estimate the following relation:

$$p_t = \alpha + \beta p_t^e + \gamma_1 y_t + \gamma_2 w_t + \gamma_3 z_t + \varepsilon_t, \qquad (5.45)$$

where

$$f(X_t) = \gamma_2 w_t + \gamma_3 z_t. \qquad (5.46)$$

In particular, $w_t = 1$ and $z_t = X_t$ when $X_t > X_0$, and y_t is a dummy variable which is equal to zero until the second semester of 1972 (the first semester of 1974 for consumer prices) and equal to one afterwards. The parameters of (5.45) can be estimated scanning for the value of X_0 that minimizes the standard error of the regressions. The joint hypothesis $\alpha = 0$, $\beta = 1$ can then be tested, as it has been done in Section 5.3, and so can the further hypothesis $\gamma_1 = 0$. In the case that both hypotheses are not rejected, one might conclude that expectations have indeed been unbiased over the entire sample period; if only the first is verified, a constant bias of the size of the estimate of γ_1 – independent, then, from the size of the actual inflation – has been experienced; if only the second hypothesis is not rejected even with this correction for a possible measurement error of the kind considered in this section, one has to return to the conclusions of Section 5.3, that is, that expectations have been biased and this bias has not been constant with respect to the various levels of the rate of inflation which have been experienced.

In Tables 5.19 and 5.20 the estimates of (5.45) – and variants with constraints $\gamma_2 = 0$, $\gamma_1 = 0$, $\gamma_1 = \gamma_2 = 0$ – are reported.[27] For wholesale prices

[27] The reported estimates are those which minimized, for different values of *WO* and *CO*, the standard error of the regression. *WO* and *CO* have been allowed to change between 0 and 40 percent at steps of 5 percentage points each.

TABLE 5.19

WHOLESALE PRICES, TESTS OF UNBIASEDNESS AND MEASUREMENT ERROR

	α	β	Y_1	Y_2	Y_3	WO	R^2	DW	F	SER	T
TOTAL											
a	-.216 (.451)	1.017 (.069)	3.055 (2.887)+	-12.022 (3.213)+	27.089 (4.110)+	.30	.87	1.87	.14	2.033	46
b	-.571 (1.188)	1.303 (1.331)	1.744 (1.784)	-----	8.234 (4.047)+	.35	.85	2.03	1.01	2.130	46
c	-.480 (.949)	1.571 (3.095)+	-----	-5.064 (2.732)+	15.568 (3.843)+	.20	.84	1.90	6.25+	2.196	46
d	-.620 (1.262)	1.565 (3.175)+	-----	-----	8.275 (3.968)+	.35	.84	1.93	6.15+	2.183	46
PRODUCTION											
a	-.234 (.479)	1.093 (.360)	2.852 (2.594)*	-12.986 (3.115)+	27.964 (3.863)+	.35	.86	1.90	.12	2.115	46
b	-.519 (1.064)	1.335 (1.395)	1.648 (1.615)	-----	8.069 (3.882)+	.40	.84	2.14	1.02	2.183	46
c	-.506 (.987)	1.567 (2.967)+	-----	-2.982 (.539)	12.840 (1.409)	.40	.83	2.00	5.90+	2.242	46
d	-.568 (1.146)	1.509 (3.227)+	-----	-----	8.071 (3.812)+	.40	.83	2.05	6.59+	2.223	46
OTHER											
a	-.188 (.398)	.953 (.204)	3.304 (3.272)+	-10.725 (3.153)+	25.276 (4.164)+	.25	.87	1.89	.26	1.991	46
b	-.561 (1.190)	1.241 (1.131)	2.019 (2.174)*	-----	8.236 (4.088)+	.30	.86	1.98	.85	2.094	46
c	-.438 (.861)	1.515 (2.828)+	-----	-4.481 (2.518)*	15.002 (3.784)*	.20	.84	1.83	5.69+	2.197	46
d	-.587 (1.194)	1.526 (2.993)+	-----	-----	8.360 (3.983)+	.30	.84	1.86	5.45+	2.183	46

See text for explanation of regressions performed.

Note

Absolute values of t-statistics are reported under each coefficient estimate.
* significant at the .05 level (two tails test for t-statistics);
+ significant at the .01 level (two tails test for t-statistics).
The t-tests are for the hypotheses: $\alpha=0$, $\beta=1$, $Y_1=0$, $Y_2=0$, $Y_3=0$; the F-tests for the joint hypothesis: $\alpha=0$, $\beta=1$; R^2 is the (un-adjusted) coefficient of determination; DW is the Durbin-Watson statistic; SER is the standard error of the regression; T is the number of observations; for WO see text; estimation period: 1st semester 1958-2nd semester 1980.

TABLE 5.20

CONSUMER PRICES, TESTS OF UNBIASEDNESS AND MEASUREMENT ERROR

	α	β	Y_1	Y_2	Y_3	CO	R^2	DW	F	SER	T
TOTAL											
a	-.751 (1.865)	1.145 (.927)	.970 (1.303)	6.204 (2.558)*	-8.187 (2.249)*	.40	.91	1.64	2.89	1.041	46
b	-.227 (.607)	.903 (.682)	2.064+ (3.140)	-----	1.015 (1.265)	.35	.90	1.76	2.62	1.102	46
c	-1.071+ (3.337)	1.315+ (3.582)	-----	7.885+ (3.809)	10.489+ (3.268)	.40	.91	1.54	6.58+	1.050	46
d	-.783* (2.183)	1.238* (2.428)	-----	-----	1.368 (1.531)	.40	.98	1.58	2.98	1.204	46
PRODUCTION											
a	-.198 (.515)	.905 (.659)	2.249+ (3.418)	1.781 (.858)	-2.350 (.709)	.40	.90	1.59	2.20	1.126	46
b	-.067 (.187)	.846 (1.105)	2.437+ (3.858)	-----	.484 (.598)	.30	.90	1.64	2.37	1.121	46
c	-.833* (2.204)	1.278* (2.645)	-----	3.544 (1.574)	-4.795 (1.323)	.40	.87	1.32	3.50*	1.261	46
d	-.664 (1.802)	1.232* (2.259)	-----	-----	.720 (.761)	.40	.86	1.36	2.56	1.282	46
OTHER											
a	-.570 (1.434)	1.021 (.139)	1.523* (2.238)	4.225* (2.563)	-5.154 (1.936)	.40	.91	1.62	3.55*	1.067	46
b	-.185 (.472)	.876 (.847)	2.051+ (2.972)	-----	1.366 (1.641)	.40	.89	1.84	2.88	1.135	46
c	-1.074+ (3.134)	1.288+ (3.103)	-----	5.343+ (3.249)	-6.669 (2.475)	.40	.90	1.43	5.27+	1.116	46
d	-.781* (2.137)	1.215* (2.163)	-----	-----	1.678 (1.869)	.40	.87	1.74	2.52	1.234	46

See text for explanation of regressions performed.

Note

Absolute values of t-statistics are reported under each coefficient estimate.
* significant at the .05 level (two tails test for t-statistics);
+ significant at the .01 level (two tails test for t-statistics).
The t-tests are for the hypotheses: $\alpha=0$, $\beta=1$, $Y=0$, $Y=0$, $Y=0$; the F-tests for the joint hypothesis: $\alpha=0$, $\beta=1$; R^2 is the (un-adjusted) coefficient of determination; DW is the Durbin-Watson statistic; SER is the standard error of the regression; T is the number of observations; for CO see text; estimation period: 1st semester 1958-2nd semester 1980.

it is immediately evident that the second case, that of a constant bias (but a slope coefficient not significantly different from one), is not rejected. The size of this bias is approximately 3 percent (which amounts to about one-third of the average inflation rate). In the case of consumer prices there is less clear-cut evidence. If one considers separately the "production" and the "other" respondents, one obtains results similar to those for wholesale prices (with a constant bias of about 1.5 to 2 percent, approximately ·one-fifth to one-fourth the average actual inflation rate). This is also the case for the total of respondents if γ_2 is constrained to be equal to zero, but the best equation without this constraint gives γ_2 significantly different from zero at the 5 percent level and does not reject the hypotheses $\alpha = 0$, $\beta = 1$ and $\gamma_1 = 0$. It is likely, however, that this is a spurious result stemming from the aggregation of the "production" and the "other" respondents.

It must be understood that this test is only of a tentative nature since there are high chances that the estimates of γ_2 and γ_3 turn out to be significantly different from zero only because of spurious correlation between p_t on one hand and w_t and z_t on the other (that is, when the inflation rate is "high" many answers fall in the upper open-ended interval). While it might be concluded, however, that there is evidence against the unbiasedness assumption, it seems that the bias, present only in the period which has followed the first oil crisis, might have been constant, independent of the size of the actual inflation rates.

5.7. Comparison with the Alternative Predictors

The results obtained so far are interesting and surprising. They are interesting in that they suggest that when the inflation rates oscillate moderately around a low ("equilibrium"?) average rate, informed persons have not only unbiased expectations but also expectations that do not contrast with the hypothesis of optimal use of available information, even if many alternative and composite information sets are considered. The results are surprising in that most of the studies on survey-based expectations seem to indicate at least an incomplete (if not inefficient) use of relevant readily available information.[28] Also noteworthy are the findings that the rejection of ration-

---

[28] Consider, for example, Brown and Maital (1981) which is probably the more comprehensive and careful analysis of the rationality of the experts' expectations (on a number of different variables) collected twice a year by J.A. Livingston. They conclude that "we cannot, therefore, reject the possibility that in formulating their expectations, experts did make efficient use of incomplete information" (p. 492).

ality conditions over the entire sample period might in part be due to exceptional shocks to the inflation process in Italy in more recent years (during a transition to a new "rational expectations equilibrium"?), and that over these years expectations seem to have suffered a constant downward bias. It might also be that this bias, while contradicting the rationality requirement that individual expectations are equal to the mathematical expectations of the variables of interest conditional on the information set, could be justified on the basis of arguments similar to those advanced in Section 5.1, when asymmetric loss functions were considered.

As a final step of the analysis the performance of the expectations of the *Mondo Economico* respondents will again be compared with that of the alternative predictors considered in Chapter 4. A comparison in terms of mean square errors only, such as the one conducted in that chapter, cannot be considered as a sufficient test of rationality. One can reject this assumption only if there is strong evidence of significantly inferior mean square errors for the alternative predictors, as it seems to be the case for the University of Michigan SRC surveys considered by Pearce (1979). The possibility of information in these alternative predictors that has yet not been utilized in formulating the inflation expectations object of this study will therefore be investigated. Before that, it is of interest to determine if the alternative predictors pass the same tests applied to the expectations series.

5.7.1. Are the Alternative Predictors "Rational"?

The alternative predictors considered in this paragraph are those discussed in Chapter 4.

When the period preceding the first oil crisis is considered, for both wholesale and consumer prices, the weak rationality assumption of orthogonality with respect to the history of the variable to be forecast cannot be rejected for any of the alternative predictors. Furthermore, in the case of wholesale prices for the *AR* and *ARC* predictors one can reject, at the 5 percent significance level, the orthogonality assumption only with respect to the largest composite information set encompassing past price changes, utilized capacity and percentage changes of money supply and wages; not even in this case can the orthogonality condition be rejected for the *ARM* predictions of wholesale price changes which already outperformed the others in terms of forecasting accuracy. In the case of consumer prices, instead, the above condition can be rejected for the *AR* and the *ARC* predictors at the 1 percent level with respect to all the variables considered but the bond rate, the level of industrial production and the level (not the first difference) of the unemployment rate. The *ARM* forecasts are orthogonal not only to these variables, but also to the percentage changes of past consumer prices and contractual wages as well as to the difference in the rate of unemployment.

One can observe, then, that over the sub-periods which exclude the more recent years the survey-based expectations seem to make a better use, on the whole, of the available information than the forecasts from the alternative predictors. This is a logical result if one considers that the latter only exploit the autoregressive structure of the two series of price changes considered in this study. One should notice, however, the good performance of the autoregressive predictors, particularly of the *ARM* forecasts, in the case of wholesale prices. Over the entire sample period, as it was the case with the expectations data, for both price indices the forecasts generated from the alternative predictors do not result to be orthogonal to a very large number of information sets, with the very interesting exception of the moving autoregressive predictions (*ARM*) of wholesale price changes which again pass widely all the rationality tests considered in this study.

5.7.2. *Conditional Efficiency as a Test of Rational Expectations*

If the expectations made optimal use of all the available information, they should be conditionally efficient also with respect to the alternative predictors. That is, running the tests of the kind proposed by Nelson and Granger and Newbold,[29] one should not be able to reject the hypothesis that the information content of the expectations series is at least not inferior to that of the alternative predictors. This implies that in a regression of the kind

$$p_t = \alpha + \beta_1 p_t^e + \beta_2 AP_t + u_t, \qquad (5.47)$$

where AP_t is the alternative predictor, one should find β_1 not significantly different from one and β_2 from zero. In an effort to avoid collinearity problems, also the constrained regressions have been estimated:

$$p_t - AP_t = \alpha + \beta(p_t^e - AP_t) + u_t, \qquad (5.48)$$

where the test of conditional efficiency consists in verifying if β is significantly different from one. However, results very similar to those of regression (5.47) have been obtained, so that only the tests of the latter are reported in Table 5.21 for both wholesale and consumer price changes. The standard deviation of the individual expectations has also been added to the

[29] Nelson (1972) and Granger and Newbold (1977, p. 283).

TABLE 5.21

WHOLESALE AND CONSUMER PRICES: TESTS OF CONDITIONAL EFFICIENCY

WHOLESALE PRICES

5801-7202	Regression		5801-8002	Regression	
(T=30)	(1)	(2)	(T=46)	(1)	(2)
Alternative Predictor	$F(2,T-3)$	$F(2,T-4)$	Alternative Predictor	$F(2,T-3)$	$F(2,T-4)$
NAIVE	1.82	1.72	NAIVE	20.10	3.92
ARC	13.06	14.10	ARC	102.97	50.55
ARM	8.53	9.13	ARM	87.92	51.12
AR	15.74	16.56	ARC1	39.76	16.21
ARC*	3.83	3.59	ARC*	22.84	7.04
ARM*	1.86	1.64	ARM*	20.13	4.38
AR*	5.28	5.02	ARC1*	23.12	7.15

CONSUMER PRICES

5801-7401	Regression		5801-8002	Regression	
(T=33)	(1)	(2)	(T=46)	(1)	(2)
Alternative Predictor	$F(2,T-3)$	$F(2,T-4)$	Alternative Predictor	$F(2,T-3)$	$F(2,T-4)$
NAIVE	.44	.10	NAIVE	12.98	3.63
ARC	13.13	12.01	ARC	38.74	22.06
ARM	9.94	8.83	ARM	31.95	17.00
AR	14.84	13.83	ARC1	32.41	17.80
ARC*	2.83	2.40	ARC*	19.70	8.45
ARM*	1.63	1.12	ARM*	17.94	7.17
AR*	6.57	5.91	ARC1*	20.81	9.44

Significance Limits:	.05	.01
$F(2,43)$	3.21	5.14
$F(2,42)$	3.22	5.15
$F(2,30)$	3.32	5.39
$F(2,29)$	3.33	5.42
$F(2,27)$	3.35	5.49
$F(2,26)$	3.37	5.53

(1) OLS regressions: $WPCS = \alpha + \beta_1 MUW + \beta_2 AP + u$;
$\qquad\qquad\qquad\quad CPCS = \alpha + \beta_1 MUC + \beta_2 AP + u$.
(2) OLS regressions: $WPCS = \alpha + \beta_1 MUW + \beta_2 AP + \beta_3 SIW + u$;
$\qquad\qquad\qquad\quad CPCS = \alpha + \beta_1 MUC + \beta_2 AP + \beta_3 SIC + u$.

Note

For definitions, see Table 5.3, and see text, Section 4.1, for the alternative predictors (AP). The stars identify forecasts generated from alternative predictors without making use of the most recent monthly observation (both in estimation and in prediction). The F-tests are for the joint hypothesis $\beta_1=1$, $\beta_2=0$. T is the number of observations.

regressors of (5.47), along the lines of the discussion of Section 5.5. All the alternative predictors examined in Chapter 4 have been considered.

The result is that over the entire sample period the information contained in the alternative predictors has not been efficiently used by the respondents to *Mondo Economico* surveys in formulating their inflation expectations. But consider the evidence for the sub-periods which exclude the more recent observations. There is no evidence of sub-optimal use of the information contained in the Naive predictions. There is evidence, however, that the expectations could have been improved by a more efficient utilization of the information contained in the ARC, the ARM and the AR predictions, for which the hypothesis $\beta_1 = 1$, $\beta_2 = 0$ can be rejected at the 1 percent level for both price indices (with and without the standard deviation of the expectations included among the regressors).

Even if these results are rather strong, care should be exercised in their evaluation. One should consider, in fact, that the AR predictions are based on a model which is estimated over the whole period of comparison. Information is used in this case which was unavailable to the respondents. It has been noticed in Chapter 4 that this assumption might be balanced to some extent by the hypothesis of a constant autoregressive structure over the whole sample period. Still, however, it is likely that there is a built-in bias in favor of the AR predictions when they are compared with the expectations of the respondents to *Mondo Economico* surveys. A similar advantage has been given to the ARC and ARM forecasts. In estimating the autoregressive models used to generate predictions, say, for semester j, the observation for the last month of semester $j - 1$ has in fact been used. Estimates for this observation, however, usually start to come out at least two weeks *after* the end of each survey. Therefore, it might be more reasonable to compare the survey-based expectations with the predictions generated from the same models estimated over periods which do not contain the observation for the last month of the semester preceding the survey. This has been done and the forecasts have been labeled ARC^* and ARM^*. For consistency reasons, also the predictions based on models estimated over the whole periods of comparison have been obtained out of estimates which exclude the last months of these periods (respectively, December 1972, for wholesale, and June 1974, for consumer prices), and they have been labeled AR^*. The same has been done in the case of the $ARC1^*$ estimates.

In Table 5.22 the root mean square errors for this set of predictions are reported and they are compared with those of the predictions generated from the same models estimated on samples inclusive of the last observation, as well as with those of the expectations of the survey respondents.

TABLE 5.22

ROOT MEAN SQUARE ERRORS OF FORECASTS: COMPARISON BETWEEN
EXPECTED RATES AND ALTERNATIVE PREDICTORS OF PRICE CHANGES

Alternative Predictor	WHOLESALE		CONSUMER	
	5801-7202 (T=30)	5801-8002 (T=46)	5801-7401 (T=33)	5801-8002 (T=46)
NAIVE	1.378	4.236	1.323	1.766
ARC	.901	2.144	1.175	1.875
ARM	.902	1.544	1.019	1.326
AR	.833	-	1.056	-
ARC1	-	3.501	-	2.519
ARC*	1.177	3.947	1.471	1.965
ARM*	1.165	3.506	1.312	1.586
AR*	1.121	-	1.346	-
ARC1*	-	4.689	-	2.822
MIX	.971	3.655	.982	1.450

Note

See text, Section 4.1, for definitions of the alternative predictors. The stars identify forecasts generated from alternative predictors without making use of the most recent monthly observation (both in estimation and in prediction). The MIX estimates of the expected rates of change refer to the total of respondents to the Mondo Economico opinion poll. T is the number of observations.

Two facts are worth noticing in the examination of the figures of Table 5.22: (1) the forecasts generated from the estimates which ignore the last sample observation are evidently inferior to the corresponding forecasts from the estimates obtained on the assumption of knowledge of this observation; and (2) the expectations of the *Mondo Economico* respondents, which were already very satisfactory when compared with the latter as shown in Chapter 4, perform even better with respect to the former. In the case of wholesale prices, they appear to be even better forecasts than these predictions, with the single (slight) exception of the $ARM*$ ones over the whole sample period (through the second semester of 1980).

What is most interesting, coming back to the tests of conditional efficiency reported in Table 5.21 one observes a dramatic reduction in the relevant F-statistics when this set of forecasts is considered. Over the whole sample period, however, the hypothesis of an efficient utilization of the information contained in the $ARC*$, $ARM*$ and $ARC1*$ predictions is still rejected. Paradoxically, it is only in the case of the $ARM*$ forecasts for wholesale prices that this rejection takes place at the 5 and not the 1 percent level of significance. The results for the sub-periods which exclude the years following the first oil crisis are the more relevant ones. In fact, in the case of the ARC^* and ARM^* forecasts, the hypothesis of conditional efficiency of the survey-based expectations cannot be anymore easily rejected. Even in the case of the AR^* predictions, for wholesale prices the hypothesis cannot be rejected at the 1 percent significance level.

5.8. Summary of the Results

In this chapter the evaluation of the inflation expectations formulated by the respondents to *Mondo Economico* surveys has been completed. The statistical characteristics of the anticipation errors have been considered. Formal tests of the unbiasedness assumption have then been performed, and further necessary conditions of the so-called "rational expectations" hypothesis have been verified, such as the "efficiency" with which expectations utilize the information contained in the past history of the variables to be predicted, and the "orthogonality" of the anticipation errors with respect to different pieces of information.

As noticed at the outset of this chapter, a strict version of "rationality" is difficult to accept on *a priori* grounds for a number of reasons. Expectations could be optimal, in the sense of minimizing a given loss function with respect to a function of the available information set, even if they are not equal to the mathematical expectation of the variable of interest conditional on that information set. Only when the loss is a symmetric quadratic function would that condition be satisfied, but certainly there are possible situations for different (for example, asymmetric) loss functions. Furthermore, it may be that persons could act as consistent Bayesian statisticians and still find that their subjective probability distributions do not coincide with the objective (frequentist) probability distribution, as Swamy, Barth and Tinsley (1982) have recently argued forcefully. In any case, learning takes times, the economic scene changes continuously, on one hand information is costly, and on the other not all persons have equal opportunities for access to the same information set. Last, but likely not least, different persons have different views of the world, and the ultimate, definitive theory on the working of any given economy (and if "theory" is considered to be an hazardous term, *the* ultimate, definitive interpretation) has still to be proposed and accepted.

It seems, however, that from the rationality assumption descend a number of interesting, sensible, and testable propositions. First, there is no reason to disregard a symmetric quadratic loss function (on which, as a matter of fact, a large part of our statistical and estimation "baggage" still heavily depends for a number of different applications). Even if the hypothesis of "rational" expectations could not be the best explanation on how actual expectations are truly formed, still, at the same time, it has been shown that even the old fashioned *ad hoc* formation hypotheses could be rational in not terribly unrealistic economic frameworks.[30] Also, one might be justified in considering with suspicion direct data on expectations when they do not pass – even in periods of moderate variability and regular trends of the variable under investigation – such elementary requirements as the absence of a large bias of prediction.

In Section 5.2 a systematic analysis of the testing procedures utilized with survey-based expectations has been provided, in an effort to point out the reliability of these procedures and the conclusions that could be drawn from the results of the tests. In the remaining sections of the chapter, then, the absence of serial correlation in the anticipation errors, the unbiasedness of the expectations, and the efficient use of alternative and composite information sets have been investigated.

It has been found that the inflation expectations which are the object of this work have been, on average, unbiased over the twenty and more years on which observations are available, prior to the 1973 oil crisis. During the same period, no serial correlation has been found in the anticipation errors and – what might be more surprising – no alternative or composite information set has been found which could adequately reject the assumption of an optimal use of the relevant available information. However, when the information content of the survey-based expectations was compared with that of the two alternative predictors obtained from the estimation of an autoregressive model over a cumulating and a moving sample (*ARC* and *ARM*), even in this period it appears that the expectations might have been improved had they taken account of the changes in structure (whether due to parameter changes or changes in the pattern of exogenous factors) which the predictors were approximating. This result is however significantly weakened if one considers that the information content of the *ARC* and *ARM* predictions is necessarily superior to that which could be possibly contained in the survey-based expectations. The models out of which those predictions were generated have in fact been estimated on samples which include one observation unavailable at the time when the surveys were taken. Reestimating these models excluding such observation conducts to predictions (*ARC** and *ARM**) with respect to which it is not anymore possible to reject the hypothesis of conditional efficiency of the expectations of the respondents to the *Mondo Economico* opinion polls.

Over the entire sample period, including also the more recent years, the expectations series do not pass any of the above tests. This finding might be

---

[30] See Footnote 13.

justified on the grounds that unpredictable shocks have conditioned, during these years, the inflation process in Italy (shocks mainly due to international events). The data set is, however, too limited to allow one to advance, with great confidence, reasons for these results. After all, during a transition period there is no reason to exclude, *a priori*, possible serial correlation of the anticipation errors. It should, however, be noticed that it does not appear that aggregation problems account for the rejection of the rationality assumption over this period. Similarly, on the basis of some tentative tests, it does not seem that this result depends on a possible measurement error for the years over which a somewhat arbitrary procedure was adopted to approximate the upper limit of the open-ended interval in obtaining estimates of the average expected rates of change of prices from a piecewise uniform interpolation of the individual answers (see Chapter 2 for the details). On the basis of these tests, however, there is some evidence of a constant downward bias of the expectations, after the oil crisis, a bias that is independent of the size of the actual rates of inflation. This finding – which could be rationalized even in a framework of optimal use of the available information, provided enough care in specifying the appropriate loss function were exercised – seems however too tentative to be worthy of further attention. It is instead preferable to close this chapter by emphasizing again the surprising level of optimality that these survey-based expectations seem to possess (or not to reject) over the long period of mild but variable (even if only moderately) inflationary conditions which occurred in Italy during the fifties, the sixties, and the early seventies.

CHAPTER 6

THE FORMATION OF INFLATION EXPECTATIONS

6.1. Hypotheses of Expectations Formation

Various hypotheses have been advanced in the economic literature to approximate *realistically* the mechanisms generating individual expectations. Even if most of the time it has been recognized that expectations might be affected by many other variables, most of the attention has been devoted to models in which only the history of the variable to be predicted matters, so that the expectations could be reduced, in one way or another, to distributed lags of observed values of that variable (its history).[1] The idea implicit in these models has been that, even if other variables should in principle explain individual expectations, these variables could on average be lumped together in a residual, approximately random and possibly small.[2] Of course, with the recent popularity of the "rational expectations" hypothesis, economists have become aware of the importance of other variables in explaining the formation of expectations, even if it is by now understood that the "time-honored" formation hypotheses may also produce expectations with various degrees of "rationality".[3] It is in some instances not unreasonable to assume that most of the information on a future value of a given variable is almost completely contained in its present value (depending on the lags existing in real life); it can also be the case that changes in expectations may not be attributed to any measurable factor or that they may depend on events not experienced in the past.

One should, however, try to investigate whether expectations could be explained satisfactorily in terms of observed data and/or could be related

[1] See, for a "pre-rational" expectations survey, Klein (1972).

[2] This is not to say that there was no criticism of this approach. Katona has, for example, always been skeptical of distributed lag representations, which he called the "proxy theory" (see Katona (1951)) and which he considered to be quite incomplete, even if "while not acceptable as proxy variables for expectations, past experience with income and prices must be considered as a factor contributing to these expectations" (Katona (1972, p. 552)). With reference to the influence of other variables, consider the following statement by Duesenberry (1958, p. 77): "Short-term expectations will also be influenced by movements in the financial markets, and the rise and fall of speculative activity in particular industries."

[3] Adaptive expectations are rational in Muth's (1960,1961) examples as well as in Sargent and Wallace's (1973); the rationality of the adaptive-regressive expectations is considered by Mussa (1975); Modigliani and Shiller (1973) obtained evidence that an extrapolative-regressive model might also be consistent with (linearly) optimal expectations.

to events that actually took place. Furthermore, if direct data are available, both the strong restrictions of the rational expectations hypothesis as well as the *ad hoc* nature of distributed lag representations can be avoided; by means of proper regression analysis the factors which most likely had a relevant influence on the survey-based expectations might be identified. As seen in the last chapter, even if the expectations of *Mondo Economico* respondents might have been near to optimal before the first oil crisis, they have proved not to be as successful (by this criterion) during the later experience; it might be the case that these respondents have been learning from the new events and that this learning process could take an indefinite amount of time before becoming restored to near optimal expectations. However, this does not necessarily imply that a stable relationship does not exist between the expectations and other variables over the whole period under investigation.

Before a discussion of the lines followed in the estimation of a model of expectations formation – which will be presented in the next section – a short review of some of the suggestions in the literature may prove worthwhile. Some of the hypotheses advanced in the past might actually represent reasonable approximations to the way expectations are actually formed. Also some of the recent empirical work, where use has been made of survey evidence to verify these approximations, will be briefly considered.

6.1.1. The Hypotheses

Popular expectations-generating mechanisms can probably be divided into two categories: extrapolative and adaptive. As will be seen, however, they have much in common. A simple extrapolative model could take the following form:

$$x_t^e = x_{t-1} + \alpha(x_{t-1} - x_{t-2}), \tag{6.1}$$

where x_t^e is the expectation of x_t formed at time $t-1$. A model of this kind is generally attributed to Hicks and Metzler, in the context of what they called, the "elasticity" and the "coefficient" of expectation.[4] It is denominated an "extrapolative" model because if α is positive, x_t^e will result in the extrapolation of x_{t-1} adjusted, in the same direction, for the most recent change in the variable of interest. For $\alpha = 0$ there is the case of "naive" expectations ($x_t^e = x_{t-1}$) which was once a common way of closing

---

[4] See Hicks (1939) and Metzler (1941). This is also the mechanism considered by Goodwin (1947) and, later, by Hahn (1952) and by Enthoven and Arrow (1956).

cobweb-type models.[5] For α negative, there is instead a model of "regressive" expectations of which Keynes was one of the first proponents.[6] If for x_{t-2} in (6.1) something is substituted which could be called the "normal" level of x – say a moving average or, in general, a long-term function of relevant variables – with $\alpha < 0$, a "return-to-normality" model is the result. This model states simply that persons, rather than anticipating a continuation of the recent trend, do expect that the variable of interest will return (regress) towards this normal level. Return to normality can be found often in the literature, mainly on interest rates and their term structure. For a relatively recent contribution see, for example, Malkiel's analysis.[7]

The adaptive expectations hypothesis is also well known, even if it was proposed somewhat later. It has become so popular that many chapters of econometric textbooks have been devoted to the analysis and estimation problems stemming from the model it generates.[8] It can be formulated as

$$x_t^e = x_{t-1}^e + \beta(x_{t-1} - x_{t-1}^e),\qquad(6.2)$$

and was first proposed by Cagan and Nerlove.[9] Muth, and Nerlove and Wage were the first to give the conditions under which (6.2) could be considered an optimal (under a mean square error criterion) forecast of x_t.[10] In particular, x_t should be – in the terminology of Box and Jenkins – an ARIMA (0,1,1) model (stationary in its first difference) with the moving average coefficient equal to $1 - \beta$.[11] Indeed, optimal linear forecasts can always be put in the form of an "error-learning" mechanism of which the adaptive expectations hypothesis (6.2) is just a special case. The error-learning principle was first introduced by Meiselman in the context of the term

[5]Such as that of Ezekiel (1938).

[6]Reference is generally made to Keynes (1936, pp. 201–204). The concept however is already present in Keynes (1923, pp. 40–41).

[7]Malkiel (1966).

[8]See, for one, the monograph on distributed lags by Dhrymes (1971).

[9]See Cagan (1956) and Nerlove (1958a,1958b); see also the contribution to the analysis of the dynamic stability of competitive markets by Arrow and Nerlove (1958) (which is a sequel, with a different expectation formation hypothesis, of the article by Enthoven and Arrow, quoted in Footnote 4).

[10]Muth (1960) and Nerlove and Wage (1964).

[11]As Rose (1972) has observed, the usual restriction $0 < \beta < 1$, which implies an exponentially decaying structure to the distributed lag representation of (6.2) in terms of the past history of x, might be overly restrictive. For an ARIMA (0,1,1) model with MA coefficient $\Theta = 1 - \beta$ the stability condition is $|\Theta| < 1$, that is $-1 < \Theta < 1$, so that $0 < \beta < 2$. Thus, if Θ is in reality negative "even where adaptive expectations is optimal in structure the usual restriction may destroy this" (Rose (1972, p. 19)).

structure of interest rates, and its optimality has been proved by Mincer and Diller.[12] It can be written, in the simplest case, as

$$x^e_{t,t-1} = x^e_{t,t-2} + \gamma(x_{t-1} - x^e_{t-1,t-2}), \tag{6.3}$$

where $x^e_{k,j}$ is the expectation of x formulated at time j for time k. Equation (6.3) is in a form for updating forecasts formed at *different* points in the past for the *same* point in the future. It can be rewritten in various ways; the one nearest to the spirit of the adaptive expectations hypothesis having been proposed by Rose,[13]

$$x^e_t = x^e_{t-1} + \sum_{i=1}^{\infty} \delta_i(x_{t-i} - x^e_{t-i}), \tag{6.4}$$

where all expectations have been considered, in this case, to be formed one period before. Only when $\delta_i = \beta$ for $i = 1$ and $\delta_i = 0$ for $i \neq 1$, (6.4) reduces to the special case of the adaptive formulation (6.2).

The generality of the "error-learning" principle for optimal linear forecasts of a given variable (in terms of its past only) is such that it accounts also for mixed models of expectations formation such as the extrapolative-regressive model considered, for example, by DeLeeuw, Kane, Modigliani and Sutch, and Modigliani and Shiller.[14] It also encompasses the adaptive-regressive formulation of Frenkel.[15] It must, however, be clear that these mixed models in which expectations are assumed to be composed of both a term which stands for a regression towards a previous (or normal) level and a term which accounts for the extrapolation of recent trends – in a blend of long- and short-term components – even if they can be considered as special cases of an optimal expectation model, could very well be far from the true optimal linear forecast of the given variable. Indeed, they might simply come from the aggregation of different individual expectation mechanisms.[16]

At an elementary level then, three possible components of the "expectation function" have been suggested by the above hypotheses: (1) past

---

[12] See Meiselman (1962), Mincer (1969) and Diller (1969).

[13] Rose (1972); this paper also contains an interesting analysis of "special" cases. Equation (6.4) defines the optimal forecast of x_t if it is an ARIMA process; alternatively, it is its optimal linear forecast. For the relations between the δ_i coefficients of (6.4) and those of the optimal forecast (in its moving average form), see again Rose's paper (p. 18).

[14] See De Leeuw (1965), Kane (1970), Modigliani and Sutch (1967), Modigliani and Shiller (1973) and, for an early suggestion, Duesenberry (1958, p. 318).

[15] Frenkel (1975); see also a recent extension by Auernheimer (1979).

[16] See, for example, Bierwag and Grove (1966) who consider the aggregation of Koyck functions (such as the one behind the adaptive hypothesis (6.2)).

forecasting errors, (2) past actual trends, and (3) the difference between a previous level and a "normal" one. All these are models in which expectations could be eventually represented as distributed lags of the past history of the variable to be predicted by the economic agents. Several studies therefore have simply utilized unrestricted forms of these distributed lags as the "proxy" for "unobservable" expectations and have estimated them in connection with other hypotheses.[17] The problems with the testing of "joint" hypotheses are well known, and the proper interpretations of the estimates are very difficult. Direct data can, therefore, be very useful in breaking these joint hypotheses; it would also be useful to attempt to identify the presence of the three above-mentioned components as separate factors explaining the formation of expectations.

Aside from the strong version of the rational expectations hypothesis which calls for the presence in the expectation function of *all* the variables which actually have an effect on the variable to be predicted, other variables besides the history of the latter have often been considered as relevant for the formation of expectations. These variables usually are those which researchers also consider to be those most likely to have a direct effect on the variable of interest; they therefore vary from case to case. Also the possibility of changes in the adaptation and adjustment coefficients of the various hypotheses illustrated above has been considered by some authors.[18] This will be further examined with reference to the empirical work which will now be discussed briefly.

6.1.2. The Evidence on Inflation Expectations

The first estimates of models of inflation expectations which are based on survey data are from the work of Turnovsky (1970).[19] He made use of Livingston's data and considered a number of alternative hypotheses, the most successful being the extrapolative one (with also regressive compo-

---

[17]Possibly the first attempt was that by Fisher (1930) for the relation between the nominal rate of interest and a (linear) distributed lag of price changes, if we accept the interpretation advanced by many that this distributed lag was intended to be a proxy for expected inflation. A linear distributed lag proxy has also been considered by Vanderkamp (1972).

[18]See for example, in the context of adaptive expectations, Turnovsky (1969). Mueller (1959, p. 261) has indeed observed that "perceptions of price changes and attitudes towards prices are subject to change", which might both imply the presence of other variables besides the past history of that to be predicted and changing coefficients for the simple hypotheses illustrated in the text (or, in general, the simultaneous presence of the various extrapolative, return-to-normality and adaptive components).

[19]Turnovsky and Wachter (1972) also considered Livingston's data but with reference to wage expectations.

nents). The same data, variously revised, have later been used by Severn (1973), De Milner (1975), Lahiri (1976,1977), McGuire (1976a,1976b), Holden and Peel (1977), Resler (1980), Jacobs and Jones (1980), Mullineaux (1980a) and Figlewsky and Wachtel (1981). The results differ widely, support being given to extrapolative, regressive, and adaptive formulations depending on the periods investigated, the data revisions, the horizon of the expectations, and the aggregation level. In particular, Lahiri, Holden and Peel, and Resler found evidence in favor of Frenkel's adaptive-regressive hypothesis. The remaining studies did not consider mixed hypotheses. Some evidence was found for effects of other variables such as the unemployment rate or its change (Severn, Holden and Peel) and changes in money supply (Resler, Mullineaux). A "multilevel" adaptive expectations hypothesis (both in the price level and its change) was estimated by Jacobs and Jones. Adaptive coefficients of different size for high and low anticipation errors were considered by De Milner, and coefficients increasing with the inflation rate, and with inflation uncertainty (measured by the dispersion of individual answers), by Figlewsky and Wachtel. McGuire estimated instead a model determining simultaneously inflation expectations and other endogenous variables.

Other U.S. data (plant and equipment surveys conducted by the Bureau of Economic Analysis) have been used by De Leeuw and McKelvey (1981), who have found some support for the adaptive model augmented to capture the effects of other variables such as capacity utilization and money supply changes, and by De Menil (1974), who used the SRC data to compare the estimates of a model of actual price change determination with those of a model explaining expected inflation in terms of the same determinants of the actual rate of change of consumer prices. A cross-section analysis has been carried out by Curtin (1982) on a subsample of the regular quarterly SRC surveys, for answers collected in 1978 and 1979, giving support to an interpretation of inflation expectations in terms of error-learning and return-to-normality. British data also tend to support the adaptive expectations hypothesis (in general, the error-learning principle), as can be seen from the works of Carlson and Parkin (1975), Holden and Peel (1977), where the adaptive-regressive model performs best, Hudson (1978), with adaptive coefficients different for different ranges of inflation rate changes, and Smith (1978,1982), even if a recent paper by Severn (1983) questions the validity of the error-learning model estimated by Carlson and Parkin, supporting, as an alternative, an extrapolative-regressive specification. Other variables, out of many possible candidates, have also been found at times to be significant, among which a devaluation dummy appears to be the most important.

Many studies have also been conducted with Australian data. While the first by Jonson and Mahoney (1973) appeared to favor a model in which expectations were influenced by a number of variables different from the inflation history, more "traditional" models were successfully estimated by Danes (1975), Valentine (1977), Defris and Williams (1979b), Saunders (1980) and Mills (1981). It was clear, however, that the estimated functions generally suffered from parameter instability and some other variables, introduced to catch changes in money supply and in the indexation system, also appeared to have an effect on expectations.

A static expectations model and an error-learning model were considered to be successful in explaining expectations in two industrial sectors in New Zealand (Hall and King (1978)); for Germany, Knöbl (1974) obtained better results with an extrapolative model (with capacity utilization effects); Praet (1981) also found a similar model to be adequate in explaining expectations obtained from surveys of EEC firms.

Utilizing data obtained from Israeli capital markets (by means of a comparison of indexed and non-indexed bonds), Cukierman (1977) was able to give support to the adaptive-regressive hypothesis. With similar data for Finland, Paunio and Suvanto (1977) obtained best results with an adaptive model (and devaluation dummies). Return-to-normality elements were instead found to be most important in a cross-section study by Kane and Malkiel (1976), who used panel data collected in 1969, 1970, and 1972. Finally, experimental data were generated by Schmalensee (1976), who estimated an adaptive expectations model with speed of adjustment falling at turning points.

If one should then indicate the "mode" of the evidence summarized in the above cursory review, probably the adaptive error-learning hypothesis, with some regressive or return-to-normality elements, would stand as a good candidate. Much of the data utilized in these studies was, however, of mediocre quality for the reasons advanced in Chapter 2 and for the particular features and/or the limited size of the samples from which expectations were collected. Furthermore, with the exception only of Valentine's study, that tried to estimate general models out of which the various hypotheses could be obtained as special cases by a proper use of restrictions, this evidence has been obtained by a comparison of many alternative estimates, with generally weak power for satisfactory tests of the competing hypotheses. Finally, in a number of cases, a considerable amount of data mining has accompanied the search for significant variables besides the history of inflation and autoregressive expectational terms; this, too, makes the obtained results somewhat weak. It is with these considerations in mind and with the general feeling that the results of these studies have provided

that an attempt is made here to estimate a model of inflation expectations from the answers to *Mondo Economico* surveys. The general lines of the estimation strategy will be given in the next section and then the estimates will be presented and evaluated in the remainder of this chapter.

6.2. The Estimation Strategy

Models for the formation of inflation expectations in Italy between the second semester of 1953[20] and the second semester of 1980 will be presented in the remainder of this chapter. Attention will be limited to the *wholesale price changes* expected, on average, by the respondents to *Mondo Economico* surveys. On the basis of the experience accumulated in the previous studies on the formation of inflation expectations, which have been briefly surveyed in Section 6.1, the estimation strategy has proceeded according to the lines summarized as follows:

(1) Only a limited number of experiments have been performed in order to identify the general relations between expected rates, (past) actual rates of inflation, and some other relevant variables. First, unrestricted estimates have been obtained, and then restrictions have been applied.

(2) In particular, the restrictions have aimed at identifying separate effects on expectations of error learning and return-to-normality terms and at verifying if the adjustment coefficients could be dependent on uncertainty elements and on the discrepancy between the actual rate of capacity utilization and its "normal" level.[21]

(3) Dummies have been used to take account of only two main factors: (a) the Suez crisis when, as suggested by the respondents' answers, an increase in the rate of inflation was anticipated (but did not occur), and (b) a possible inflation bias in the forecasts for the second semester of 1969, when the social climate was such that a general structural change – mainly in industrial relations – might have been anticipated (which actually did occur, even if the inflation rate reached its peak only during 1970). Other dummies for other exceptional periods have not been experimented with,[22]

---

[20] Two observations are lost for the presence of two lagged dependent variables among the regressors.

[21] Variables (or transformations thereof) purported to measure the cyclical conditions of the economy have been found to have significant (but generally small) influence on expected inflation by Severn (1973, unemployment), Knöbl (1974, industrial capacity utilization), Holden and Peel (1977, unemployment), Praet (1981, assessments of the actual to normal ratio of orders in industry), De Leeuw and McKelvey (1981, capacity utilization). Uncertainty effects, suggested by Turnovsky (1969), have been investigated by Smith (1978) and Figlewsky and Wachtel (1981), with fruitful results obtained in the last study.

[22] See, however, Section 6.3.3 where a dummy for the second semester of 1976 and a seasonal dummy are introduced as a result of further investigation.

on one hand, because too many *ad hoc* explanations of particular phases of the expectations process would have to be relied on, and, on the other hand, because – as can be seen from the plots of Section 3.2 – it is not immediately evident that on other occasions the respondents anticipated changes in the rate of inflation which could not be attributed to observed factors (instead, as examined in the last chapter, there are instances in the recent years when available information has not been properly used).

(4) All restricted equations have been estimated with the previous rate of inflation unrestricted; in this way the constraint that the coefficients of the distributed lag representation of expected rates of inflation would sum to unity has not been imposed *a priori*.[23]

(5) The expected rate of inflation considered in this work is the *average* of the individual expected rates. If p_{it}^e stands for the rate expected for semester t by the i-th individual, the equations to be estimated result from the aggregation of *elementary* equations such as[24]

$$p_{it}^e = \sum_j \psi_{ij} x_{jt} + u_{it}, \qquad i = 1, \ldots, n_t, \tag{6.5}$$

where the variables x_j are commonly observed by all the n_t respondents and u_i is a purely random component. Averaging, one obtains

$$p_t^e = \sum_j \psi_j x_{jt} + u_t, \tag{6.6}$$

where

$$p_t^e = \frac{1}{n_t} \sum p_{it}^e, \qquad \psi_j = \frac{1}{n_t} \sum \psi_{ij}, \qquad u_t = \frac{1}{n_t} \sum u_{it},$$

all sums for $i = 1, \ldots, n_t$. Assuming independence of the u_i random components, the variance of the residual u_t will then be equal to

$$\mathrm{E}(u_t^2) = \mathrm{E}\left[\left(\frac{1}{n_t} \sum u_{it}\right)^2\right] = \mathrm{E}\left\{\left[\frac{1}{n_t} \sum (p_{it}^e - \mathrm{E}p_{it}^e)\right]^2\right\} = \frac{1}{n_t} \mathrm{var}(p_{it}^e), \tag{6.7}$$

where $\mathrm{var}(p_{it}^e)$ is the *population* variance of the individual expectations. Then a clear problem of heteroscedasticity results. As seen in Chapter 2, the

---

[23]A similar approach has been proposed by Valentine (1977).

[24]"Heteroscedasticity also naturally arises [...] when the observations are based on average data" (Judge, Griffiths, Hill and Lee (1980, p. 125)).

sample estimate of var(p_{it}^e) is *not* constant over time. The number of respondents n_t has instead presented only a limited variability. On these grounds the regression estimates presented in the next sections have been generally obtained by means of *weighted least squares* (WLS), that is, ordinary least squares (OLS) have been applied to the observations weighted by the inverse of the standard deviation of the individual expectations estimated in Chapter 2.[25] Observe, however, that in (6.5) the assumption has been made that the variables x_j are commonly observed by all the respondents. If $h < j$ of these variables are instead individual-specific, one should introduce in (6.6) a further residual term, $v_t = \sum\sum \psi_{ih} x_{iht}/n_t$, where the double sum is taken over i and h, and where x_{iht} could also be the deviation from one of the other $j - h$ commonly observed variables. This residual term could very well have, at times, a non-zero (and therefore non-constant) mean and could be heteroscedastic and serially correlated. Had it a negligible variance, the standard error of the WLS regression should be approximately equal to the inverse of the square root of the average number of respondents (about 6 percent), which should therefore be considered as a lower bound. There is not much that can be done in case v_t had at times a non-zero mean, except perhaps a cautious and accurate examination of the single estimated residuals. If v_t were homoscedastic with a large variance relative to u_t, the WLS could potentially introduce a serious specification error; it is reasonable, however, to assume v_t not to have a constant variance and it is likely that the weights chosen here would be appropriate also for this component of the error term. Finally, the serial correlation problem is very likely the most difficult to consider. One would expect that the omitted individual-specific variables (or their deviations from an average aggregate term) could be positively serially correlated. The likely presence, however, in an equation as (6.6) of lagged dependent variables could cause, due to measurement error, negative serial correlation in the u_t component of the residual, as will be shown in Section 6.4.2. It is felt that this negative serial correlation (actually in a moving average form) could dominate over that which could be attributed to the v_t component, even if there is the possibility that a simple process could not be a reasonable approximation at the aggregate level. In any case, OLS estimates have also been computed on the basis of the unweighted observations, which ignore all the problems in the error term considered above. They will be compared, in some occasions,

---

[25] Some of the regressions considered in the text have also been estimated using as weights the ratios $\sqrt{n_t}/\sigma_t$ (where n_t is the total number of respondents for each survey and σ_t is the standard deviation of individual expectations), obtaining results very similar to those presented in the next section. Indeed, over the whole sample period the ratio between the standard deviation and the mean of σ_t has been equal to 31 percent against a value of only 7 percent for $\sqrt{n_t}$.

with the WLS ones (and for both standard tests for the presence of residual serial correlation will be performed).

(6) Many studies, as has been seen, have tried to identify other factors influencing the expected rate of inflation, besides past actual and expected rates. This has, however, been generally done by simply augmenting standard adaptive and extrapolative models with the variables assumed to have an effect on expectations. By means of a more or less substantial amount of "data mining", a number of "significant" variables has been found. The pursuit of this approach has been decided against; only the effects that departures of capacity utilization rates and of uncertainty from their "normal" levels could have on the expected inflation have been considered. In particular, attempts have been made at verifying if changes in the adjustment coefficients could be linked to these departures, so that a simple augmentation of standard schemes of expectations formation could be avoided. In the estimates that follow, the normal rate of capacity utilization has been assumed to be constant over the regression period. As a measure of the difference between the actual and the "normal" state of uncertainty, the difference between the standard deviation of the individual expectations for period $t-1$ and a moving average of this standard deviation has been considered. Obviously this is only a proxy of the effects that uncertainty at the *individual* level can have on the *average* expected rate of inflation. The dispersion of the individual expectations, however, cannot be ignored in attempts to explain the formation process. A statement such as the following one by Figlewsky and Wachtel seems, in particular, very reasonable: "In periods of high uncertainty it is hypothesized that information from the relatively distant past is less important than recent experience".[26] It is important to try to give a quantitative assessment of this proposition – for which there is some theoretical justification for predictions obtained by using a Bayesian sampling procedure, as shown by Turnovsky (1969). A proxy based on the variance of individual expectations is then probably the most that can be derived from survey data, *unless* answers were also available on the odds that the individual respondents would give to their predictions. In particular, under the assumption that an adaptive element existed in the explanation of expected inflation, the hypothesis has been investigated whether the adjustment coefficient could be an increasing function of such a proxy of the average state of uncertainty. Similarly, it is quite reasonable to assume that, say, in a return-to-normality model, when the actual inflation rate exceeded the level considered to be normal by the respondents, the adjustment process would be delayed if demand pressures were such that utilized capacity would be kept at very high levels. This has

[26] Figlewsky and Wachtel (1981, p. 9).

therefore been the focus of the interest in examining if this variable had significant explanatory power with respect to the *Mondo Economico* data.

(7) As has been seen, "normal" levels might play important roles in the estimation process. The approach here, in the absence of other more direct information, was to use simple approximations. As already mentioned, "normal" utilized capacity has been assumed to be constant and the "normal" dispersion of individual expectations has been obtained as a moving average of previous standard deviations. Similarly, the "normal" (long-run) inflation rate has been obtained as a moving average of past inflation rates over the years preceding each survey. Obviously other assumptions might have also been reasonable. The choice, however, has been made not to ask too much from the data, keeping the possible experimentation to a minimum. On the basis of the obtained results, future work in this direction might, however, prove fruitful.

(8) In the same spirit, other variables could conceivably help to explain the formation of inflation expectations, both directly or in affecting, say, "normal" levels or adjustment coefficients. Still, however, the choice was made against running too many regressions. Therefore, all that was considered was the afterthought, if – on the basis of what would be the closest approximation to the "true" formation model – there would still be some role to be played by factors such as changes in money supply, wages, and the exchange rate. This analysis led to highlighting a problem in the estimates obtained so far, which were then accordingly revised.

(9) Finally, three points deserved special investigation: first, the analysis of the stability properties of the model which has been estimated (stability in prediction, as suggested by Hendry (1980)); second, the existence of possible measurement error in the series of expected inflation here constructed; and third, the consideration of a possible aggregation bias. Each of these points has been examined with reference to the estimates obtained. These will be discussed in Section 6.4 following the presentation of the estimation results.

6.3. The Estimation Results

The search for an appropriate model of formation of inflation expectations has been started by relating expectations with two past values of the actual inflation rate, a "normal" rate, two autoregressive components (that is, one and two semesters lagged expected rates), uncertainty and capacity utilization variables, and dummies to correct for the anticipated, but not occurred, effects of the Suez crisis and to further account for the possibility that the events anticipated for the second semester of 1969 could not be caught by the explanatory variables considered in the regressions. It is useful to start with a description of the variables involved:

p_t^e = percentage rate of change of wholesale prices expected at the end of semester $t-1$ for semester t (total respondents, *MIX* estimates; see Table D.22);

p_{t-i} = actual percentage rate of change of wholesale prices between semester $t-i-1$ and semester $t-i$ ($i=1,2$; see Table D.22);

σ_{t-1}^e = standard deviation of individual expected wholesale price changes for semester $t-1$ (total respondents, *MIX* estimates; see Table D.22);

p_{t-1}^{NP} = "normal" rate of inflation for semester $t-1$ ($= \sum_{i=1}^{NP} p_{t-i}/NP$);

σ_{t-1}^{NS} = "normal" standard deviation of expectations for semester $t-1$ ($= \sum_{i=1}^{NS} \sigma_{t-i}/NS$);

UTC_{t-1} = index of industrial capacity utilization (ratio of utilized to potential capacity, obtained by peak to peak interpolation, *à la* Wharton index; see Table 5.3) in the second quarter of semester $t-1$;

$UTCI_{t-1}$ = $UTC_{t-1}(p_{t-1} - p_{t-1}^{NP})$;

UNC_{t-1} = $\sigma_{t-1} - \sigma_{t-1}^{NS}$;

$UNCI_{t-1}$ = $(\sigma_{t-1} - \sigma_{t-1}^{NS})(p_{t-1}^e - p_{t-1})$;

$DU5701$ = dummy variable for the 1st semester of 1957 ($=1$ in 5701; $=0$ elsewhere);

$DU5702$ = dummy variable for the 2nd semester of 1957 ($=1$ in 5702; $=0$ elsewhere);

$DU5801$ = dummy variable for the 1st semester of 1958 ($=1$ in 5801; $=0$ elsewhere);

$DU6902$ = dummy variable for the 2nd semester of 1969 ($=1$ in 6902; $=0$ elsewhere);

$DU7001$ = dummy variable for the 1st semester of 1970 ($=1$ in 7001; $=0$ elsewhere);

DU7002   = dummy variable for the 2nd semester of 1970 (=1 in 7002;
            = 0 elsewhere).

6.3.1. Specification Problems

A general unrestricted equation such as

$$p_t^e = \alpha + \beta_1 p_{t-1} + \beta_2 p_{t-2} + \gamma p_{t-1}^{NP} + \delta_1 p_{t-1}^e + \delta_2 p_{t-2}^e + \varepsilon_1 UTC_{t-1}$$
$$+ \varepsilon_2 UTCl_{t-1} + \zeta_1 UNC_{t-1} + \zeta_2 UNCl_{t-1} + \eta_1 DU5701 + \eta_2 DU5702$$
$$+ \eta_3 DU5801 + \theta_1 DU6902 + \theta_2 DU7001 + \theta_3 DU7002 + u_t, \quad (6.8)$$

has therefore been the starting point of the specification search. Before going in the details of the selection of the regressors, the following points should be made:

(a) As observed in Section 6.2, "normal" levels might play important roles in the estimation process. In particular, moving averages of past price changes, of order NP, and of past standard deviations of expected inflation, of order NS, have been considered. Values for NP between 6 and 16 (3 to 8 years) and for NS between 2 and 6 (1 to 3 years) have been tried, and the selection of the "preferred" values has been conducted jointly with that of the appropriate regressors.

(b) With respect to the dummies for 1957 and 1969, the possibility has been investigated that the respondents could have anticipated increases in the first and second semesters of these two years, respectively, and then could have reacted in the following semesters by bringing back their expectations to lower levels. On the occasion of the Suez crisis, for example, once they observed that no inflationary pressures were actually generated, the respondents discontinued their expectations of a high rate of inflation. Given the presence of lagged dependent variables in (6.8), the implication is that one should consider having dummy variables also for the semesters immediately following the first of 1957. If the actual changes in wholesale prices in 1969 and 1970 (Table D.22) are observed, inflation is seen to increase substantially during 1969 but actually to peak in the first semester of 1970. Expectations did follow the same pattern, although they were one percentage point short of the actual rates in the second semester of 1969 *and* in the following one. They remained, however, on a level quite higher than that of the actual price changes for the following year and a half. There are no signs, then, on this occasion, of immediate return to the previous levels. Also in this case, however, the possibility of lagged reactions has been investigated by means of dummies for the two semesters following the second of 1969.

(c) If (6.8) were to be rewritten as

$$p_t^e = \alpha + \beta p_{t-1} - \gamma (p_{t-1} - p_{t-1}^{NP}) + \delta_1 (p_{t-1}^e - p_{t-1})$$
$$+ \delta_2 (p_{t-2}^e - p_{t-2}) + \varepsilon_1 UTC_{t-1} + \varepsilon_2 UTCl_{t-1}$$
$$+ \zeta_1 UNC_{t-1} + \zeta_2 UNCl_{t-2} + \text{dummies} + u_t, \qquad (6.9)$$

an equation would be obtained which contains two "error-learning" terms, a "return-to-normality" component and which does not impose any constraint on the "long-run" sum of coefficients of the implicit distributed lag in terms of past rates of inflation. This equation is derived from (6.8) by simply imposing the restriction $\delta_2 = -\beta_2$ and defining $\beta = \beta_1 + \gamma + \delta_1$. The adaptive and regressive schemes briefly illustrated in Section 6.1 are obviously special cases of (6.9) which is near in spirit to the mixed model proposed by Frenkel (1975). Furthermore, one can see how uncertainty and capacity effects are treated in this analysis. Apart from the dummies and the residual, and defining $K \equiv UTC$, (6.9) could in fact be rewritten as

$$p_t^e = \alpha' + \beta p_{t-1} + \gamma_t (p_{t-1} - p_{t-1}^{NP}) + \delta_{1t} (p_{t-1}^e - p_{t-1})$$
$$+ \delta_2 (p_{t-2}^e - p_{t-2}) + \varepsilon_1 (K_{t-1} - K^N) + \zeta_1 (\sigma_{t-1} - \sigma_{t-1}^{NS}), \qquad (6.10)$$

where

$$\gamma_t = -\gamma' + \varepsilon_2 (K_{t-1} - K^N), \qquad (6.11)$$

$$\gamma' = \gamma - \varepsilon_2 K^N, \qquad (6.12)$$

$$\delta_{1t} = \delta_1 + \zeta_2 (\sigma_{t-1} - \sigma_{t-1}^{NS}), \qquad (6.13)$$

$$\alpha' = \alpha + \varepsilon_1 K^N, \qquad (6.14)$$

and K^N is the "normal" (constant) rate of capacity utilization. It is clear, however, that there is no way to separately identify K^N. In particular, (6.10) – or for that matter (6.9) and (6.8) – could be estimated for any value of K^N, always obtaining the same fitted values. One would not expect, however, K^N to differ sensibly from the average value of K over the sample period, so that taking this value and the estimates of α, γ, ε_1 and ε_2 in (6.8) and (6.9) one could probably obtain sensible estimates of α' and γ' from the definitions (6.12) and (6.14).

(d) The presence of capacity and uncertainty effects have therefore been related in this work to the variability of the adjustment coefficients. In the absence of these relations one might expect a constant negative "return-to-normality" effect (that is, $\gamma_t \equiv -\gamma < 0$) and constant positive adaptive coefficients (that is, $\delta_{1t} \equiv \delta_1 > 0$, $\delta_2 > 0$, and $\delta_1 + \delta_2 < 1$ for stability reasons).[27] There are obvious reasons, however, to hypothesize variable coefficients. Consider, for example, a situation when the inflation rate has just been well above its normal level. A constant adjustment coefficient would then imply that persons will expect inflation to come down at the same rate both in a situation in which there still are conditions of demand substantially above what one might call potential output and in the case when, instead, resources are largely under-utilized. It might be more reasonable to assume, instead, that this adjustment coefficient changes over time under a scheme such as (6.11), with $\varepsilon_2 > 0$. Similarly, it is reasonable to hypothesize that the uncertainty variable has a positive effect on the adaptive coefficient, as suggested by Turnovsky (1969) and found by Figlewsky and Wachtel (1981). This coefficient should then be an increasing function of uncertainty under the assumption that when persons are less confident in their views about the future they tend to consider more heavily the recent experience rather than rely on their memories of what has occurred in the more distant past, so that $\zeta_2 > 0$. If these were the only reasons for the presence of capacity and uncertainty factors in the explanation of inflation expectations one would anticipate $\varepsilon_1 = 0$ and $\zeta_1 = 0$ in (6.8) and (6.9). Separate positive effects from the utilized capacity and negative effects from the uncertainty variable cannot however be discarded *a priori* given the intuitive and widespread beliefs that when the business cycle moves upwards inflation tends to be high, and vice versa, and that higher uncertainty generally leads to more conservative forecasts.

(e) When utilized capacity and uncertainty are fixed at their normal levels, (6.9) can be rewritten as[28]

$$p_t^e = \alpha'' + A(L)p_{t-1} + b(L)u_t, \tag{6.15}$$

where

$$\alpha'' = \alpha'/(1 - \delta_1 - \delta_2), \tag{6.16}$$

$$b(L) = 1/(1 - \delta_1 L - \delta_2 L^2), \tag{6.17}$$

$$A(L) = \left(\beta - \gamma - \delta_1 + \frac{1}{NP}\gamma \sum_{i=0}^{NP-1} L^i - \delta_2 L \right) \Big/ (1 - \delta_1 L - \delta_2 L^2), \tag{6.18}$$

L being the lag operator ($L^n x_t = x_{t-n}$).

---

[27] Some experiments have also been performed to investigate whether also δ_2 could be treated as a variable coefficient, with negative results. Other lags in the level of utilized capacity have also been considered, again with best results obtained when only that for the second quarter of the semesters at the end of which the surveys were taken was included among the regressors.

[28] The same could obviously be done also with (6.8).

It is straightforward that (6.15) evaluated at $L = 1$ produces the "steady state" (long-run or total multiplier, in other definitions) effect of a change in the actual rate of inflation on the expected one. In particular,

$$A(1) = (\beta - \delta_1 - \delta_2)/(1 - \delta_1 - \delta_2).$$ (6.19)

For $\delta_1 + \delta_2 \neq 1$, one then has $A(1) = 1$ only when the restriction $\beta = 1$ is imposed. It has been considered quite logical in the late sixties and early seventies to impose this condition on distributed lag proxies of expected inflation, on the grounds that this was a necessary condition to have coincident "steady state" values for actual and expected inflation. On this condition interpretations of joint estimates of the formation process of inflation expectations *and* of their effects on the percentage change of nominal wages (the so-called "augmented Phillips curve")[29] and on the nominal interest rates (the "Fisher effect")[30] have also heavily depended. As Sargent has convincingly argued in his comment to this interpretation of the joint estimates,[31] however, there is no reason to consider the condition $A(1) = 1$ necessary for the steady state equality of p^e and p. The easiest way to see why this is so is perhaps simply to observe that in the steady state $p^e = \alpha'' + A(1)p$. If the actual rate of inflation converges to $p = 0$, for *any* possible value of $A(1)$, $p^e = p$ if and only if $\alpha'' = 0$ (and therefore $\alpha' = 0$). If the actual rate of inflation converges to $p > 0$, $p^e = p$ if and only if $A(1) = 1 - \alpha''/p$. Only in the special case, then, that $\alpha'' = 0$ should $A(1)$ be equal to unity, when p_t converges to $p > 0$; if $\alpha'' > 0$, $A(1)$ should be strictly less than one to have coincident actual and expected inflation in the steady state.

To conclude, there is no reason to impose *a priori* a restriction such as $A(1) = 1$, while it seems convenient to test for it, by means of a test of the hypothesis $\beta = 1$ in (6.9) (which would correspond to $\beta_1 + \gamma + \delta_1 = 1$ in (6.8)).

6.3.2. *Preliminary Investigation*

Equation (6.8) has been the starting point of a preliminary search, with the aim of obtaining a general unrestricted regression which excluded irrelevant variables. To this end the (actual, expected and "normal") inflation terms have always been included in the regression and the dummies have been

[29]See, for example, the discussion in Tobin (1972).
[30]See, among others, Yohe and Karnosky (1969).
[31]Sargent (1971).

TABLE 6.1

FORMATION OF EXPECTATIONS OF WHOLESALE PRICE CHANGES: UNRESTRICTED ESTIMATES

(Dependent Variable = p^e_t; WLS estimates; Estimation period: 2nd Semester 1953 – 2nd Semester 1980)

	Regressions			
	A1	A2	A3	A4
Constant	-10.355 (3.185)	-11.806 (3.944)	.411 (2.080)	.572 (2.674)
p_{t-1}	-3.657 (4.090)	-4.104 (5.110)	.099 (1.380)	.171 (2.281)
p_{t-2}	-.076 (1.424)	-.050 (1.032)	-.126 (1.882)	-.148 (2.002)
NP_{t-1}	3.855 (4.382)	4.293 (5.426)	.221 (2.872)	.217 (2.529)
p^e_{t-1}	.551 (3.707)	.463 (3.654)	.574 (3.301)	.344 (1.948)
p^e_{t-2}	.176 (1.523)	.223 (2.065)	.038 (.252)	.150 (.926)
UTC_{t-1}	.119 (3.245)	.136 (4.027)		
$UTC1_{t-1}$	.042 (4.239)	.047 (5.228)		
$UNC1_{t-1}$	.086 (1.125)			
DU5701	2.292 (3.993)	2.243 (3.908)	2.233 (2.698)	
DU5702	-1.709 (2.169)	-1.495 (1.950)	-2.348 (2.214)	

DU6902	2.696 (4.589)	2.850 (4.973)	1.442 (1.900)	
R^2	.905	.909	.665	.622
SER	.312	.313	.452	.504
DW	2.189	2.149	1.970	1.883
LM	4.223	3.311	.328	2.848
T	55	55	55	55

Legend

p_t^e = rate of change of wholesale prices between semester t-1 and semester t, expected at the end of semester t-1 (MIX, total respondents);

p_{t-i} = actual rate of change of wholesale prices between semester t-i-1 and semester t-i;

$p_{t-.}^{NP}$ = $\Sigma p_{t-i}/14$ (i=1,..., 14);

UTC_{t-1} = index of industrial capacity utilization (average for the second quarter of semester t-1);

UTC_{t-1}^- = $UTC_{t-1}(p_{t-1} - p_{t-1}^{NP})$;

$UNCI_{t-1}$ = $(\sigma_{t-1} - \sigma_{t-1}^{NS})(p_{t-1}^e - p_{t-1})$, where σ_{t-1} is the standard deviation of the individual expectations of wholesale price changes at the end of semester t-2 for semester t-1 (MIX, total respondents) and $\sigma_{t-1}^{NS} = \Sigma\sigma_{t-i}/2$ (i = 1, 2);

DU5701 = dummy variable for the 1st semester of 1957 (= 1 in 5701; = 0 elsewhere);

DU5702 = dummy variable for the 2nd semester of 1957 (= 1 in 5702; = 0 elsewhere);

DU6902 = dummy variable for the 2nd semester of 1969 (= 1 in 6902; = 0 elsewhere);

WLS estimates computed as OLS regressions on variables scaled by σ_t; R^2 is the (unadjusted) coefficient of determination computed with respect to the original dependent variable, p_t^e; SER is the standard error of the regression (it refers to the dependent variable p_t^e/σ_t); DW is the Durbin-Watson statistic; LM is the Lagrange multiplier test against joint first and second order autocorrelation or moving average in the residuals; T is the number of observations; absolute values of t-statistics are reported in parentheses below the coefficient estimates.

considered in nests, going from the general specification with three dummies, for each one of the two episodes for which they have been introduced, to the specification restricted to those which came out significant in these sequences of three. The main purpose of the analysis has been that of finding out the relevant capacity utilization and uncertainty effects, if any, as well as the proper values for *NP* and *NS*, that is, the orders of the moving averages for the proxies of the "normal" levels of the rate of inflation and of the standard deviation of individual expectations discussed in the previous section. As mentioned, values for *NP* between 6 and 16 and for *NS* between 2 and 6 have been considered. The search has been conducted on the basis of a predictive criterion (*PC*) proposed by Amemiya (1980) which might be preferred to the estimated standard error of the regression (corrected for the degrees of freedom, *SER*) since it takes care of the possible loss due to the choice of an incorrect model. In practice, $PC = (SER)^2(1 + K/T)$, where K is the number of regressors and T the number of observations.[32] WLS have always been used during this search process. Care has been taken to look also at the values of the *t*-ratios of each single regressor and at the absolute magnitudes of the estimated coefficients, and to check for residual serial correlation.

The results of this preliminary analysis, which has led to the estimates presented in column A1 of Table 6.1,[33] have generally been rather clear cut. In particular, only in the case of the Suez crisis, as anticipated in the previous section, there has been a quick reaction of expectations, in the following semester, to the wrong anticipation of a large rise in inflation. *DU5801, DU7001* and *DU7002* always came out insignificant and of small magnitude. While, therefore, the large increase in the expected inflation rate that followed the Suez crisis has been rapidly offset, an increase of more than 2.5 percentage points *above* that predicted by the explanatory variables considered in Regression A1 of Table 6.1 has been only slowly (via the stable estimated autoregressive structure) cut down after the second semester of 1969. Very high *t*-ratios have always been associated to the estimates of the coefficients of the two terms catching direct and indirect effects of utilized capacity on expected inflation. Values of *NP* between 12 and 14 (6 and 7 years) have given the best performance, with a slight preference for

[32]Amemiya (1980) has shown that the *PC* criterion leads to results very similar to those obtained by means of Akaike's *AIC* criterion which has been used in Chapter 4 (see Footnote 6). See also, for a general discussion, Judge, Griffiths, Hill and Lee (1980, ch. 11).

[33]Serial correlation has been tested by means of a Lagrange multiplier test against second-order autocorrelation *or* moving average in the residuals; see also, for further details, Section 6.4.2. This test has been independently proposed by Breusch (1978) and Godfrey (1978a, 1978b); for an excellent discussion of Lagrange multipliers and model specification in econometrics, see Breusch and Pagan (1980). Observe also that the R^2 statistics have always been computed with respect to the original dependent variable, p^e.

the latter so that the proxy for the "normal" inflation rate utilized in this work is given by the moving average of actual inflation over the seven years preceding each survey. Finally, with respect to the uncertainty effects, the following are the most relevant conclusions: (1) the best results have been obtained for low values (2 or 3) of *NS*, with a preference for a moving average over the two semesters which preceded each survey; (2) the two uncertainty terms considered here have never turned out "significant" when introduced together in the regressions; (3) even when introduced one at a time they have resulted in only moderate reductions in the estimated *SER* (but with equal or slightly higher *PC*), with a preference for the *UNC1* variable (included in Regression A1 of Table 6.1); and (4) the signs of the estimated coefficients of the *UNC* and *UNC1* variables have been, respectively, negative and positive.

The latter result is in accordance with the interpretation that the presence of an uncertainty effect in models of formation of inflation expectations should be mainly linked to the importance of more recent relative to more distant events, rather than to a general tendency of people to be more conservative (with lower expectations) when they are more uncertain about the future. Consider again, in fact, (6.10). If the only role for "uncertainty" was that via its positive effect on the adaptation coefficient expressed by (6.13), so that $\zeta_2 > 0$ and $\zeta_1 = 0$, the adaptive element in the explanation of expected inflation could be approximated by the following Taylor expansion around the averages of $y \equiv (\sigma_{t-1} - \sigma_{t-1}^{NS}) \equiv UNC$ and $x \equiv (p_{t-1}^e - p_{t-1})$, respectively $\bar{y}$ and $\bar{x}$:

$$\delta_{1t}x = \delta_1 x + \zeta_2 yx \approx \delta_1 x + \phi_0 + \phi_1 y + \phi_2 x. \tag{6.20}$$

Over the whole sample, however, $\bar{y}$ is practically zero, so that $\phi_0 = \zeta_2 \bar{x}\bar{y} = 0$ and $\phi_2 = \zeta_2 \bar{y} = 0$, and $\bar{x}$ is negative, with the result that $\phi_1 = \zeta_2 \bar{x} < 0$. It is clear then that in a regression on x and y ($\equiv UNC$) – apart from other variables – one would obtain a negative coefficient for y if this was only an approximation of the ("true") regression on x and xy ($\equiv UNC1$) with a positive coefficient for xy.

As can be seen from Table 6.1, considering the inflation terms, high *t*-ratios have been obtained for the coefficients of p_{t-1}, p_{t-1}^e and p_{t-1}^{NP}, while small and not highly significant have been the estimates of the coefficients of p_{t-2} and p_{t-2}^e. In Table 6.1 the regression estimates obtained excluding from A1, respectively, only the uncertainty term (A2), this term and the two utilized capacity variables (A3), and these three regressors and the dummies (A4), have also been reported. One can then appreciate the importance of utilized capacity in explaining expected inflation, with a value of the *SER* for A2 more than 30 percent lower than that for A3. The numerical values

Ignazio Visco

TABLE 6.2

FORMATION OF EXPECTATIONS OF WHOLESALE PRICE CHANGES: RESTRICTED ESTIMATES, 1
(Dependent variable = P_t^e; WLS and OLS estimates; Estimation period: 2nd Semester 1953 – 2nd Semester 1980)

	Regressions			
	B1	B2	B3	B4
Constant	- 8.802 (3.226)	- 7.593 (2.786)	-11.367 (3.551)	- 9.948 (3.150)
P_{t-1}	.852 (10.799)	1.	.861 (10.591)	1.
$P_{t-1} - P_{t-1}^{NP}$	- 3.595 (4.346)	- 3.672 (4.324)	- 4.592 (7.065)	- 4.658 (7.030)
$P_{t-1}^e - P_{t-1}$	.641 (5.928)	.805 (12.153)	.724 (6.016)	.892 (12.541)
$P_{t-2}^e - P_{t-2}$	.085 (1.626)	.133 (2.860)	.035 (.662)	.081 (1.746)
UTC$_{t-1}$	.102 (3.292)	.086 (2.810)	.130 (3.590)	.112 (3.163)
UTC1$_{t-1}$	.039 (4.202)	.040 (4.169)	.051 (6.996)	.052 (6.975)

	B1	B2	B3	B4
$UNC1_{t-1}$	.125 (2.005)	.161 (2.658)	.104 (1.888)	.145 (2.886)
DU5701	2.340 (4.105)	2.421 (4.145)	2.352 (3.094)	2.440 (3.152)
DU5702	- 1.974 (2.715)	- 2.334 (3.237)	- 2.072 (2.557)	- 2.436 (3.049)
DU6902	2.579 (4.517)	2.580 (4.396)	2.975 (3.682)	2.972 (3.601)
R^2	.898	.892	.911	.905
SER	.312	.320	.750	.766
DW	2.299	2.384	2.349	2.406
LM	5.007	9.052	7.690	10.812
T	55	55	55	55

Legend

See Table 6.1.

WLS estimates for regressions B1 and B2 (SER refers to dependent variable p_t^e/σ_t);

OLS estimates for regressions B3 and B4 (SER refers to dependent variable p_t^e).

of the coefficients of p_{t-1}, p_{t-1}^{NP} and of the intercept are conditioned by the fact that the "normal" level of capacity utilization has been let free to take any constant value. When it is constrained to be equal to the average level of utilized capacity over the whole sample period ($\bar{K} = 89.193$), so that $UTC_{t-1} = K_{t-1} - \bar{K}$ and $UTC1_{t-1} = (K_{t-1} - \bar{K})(p_{t-1} - p_{t-1}^{NP})$, one obtains the following estimates for Regression A1 (*t*-ratios in parentheses): 0.263(1.839) for the intercept, 0.092(1.783) for p_{t-1}, and 0.106(1.908) for p_{t-1}^{NP}.

In Table 6.2 the results are reported (Regression B1) for the restricted equation (6.9) – with $\zeta_1 = 0$ and only three dummies as resulted from the preliminary search – obtained by imposing the restriction $\delta_2 = -\beta_2$ on (6.8) (estimated by A1 in Table 6.1), and rewriting the latter so that $\beta = \beta_1 + \gamma + \delta_1$. As observed, this restricted equation contains two "error-learning" terms and a "return-to-normality" component. In Regression B2 the further constraint that the long-run sum of coefficients of the implicit distributed lag on actual inflation be equal to one (that is, $\beta = 1$) has been imposed. Regressions B3 and B4 correspond exactly to B1 and B2 with the estimates obtained by means of OLS rather than WLS.

One should first of all notice the similarity between the WLS and the OLS estimates. Furthermore, with respect to Regression A1, B1 results to satisfy easily the *F*-test on the restriction.[34] The test on the coefficient of p_{t-1} is not as conclusive since the *t*-ratio for the hypothesis $\beta = 1$ is only equal to 1.880 in the case of the WLS estimate, not enough to reject it at a 5 percent significance level. In passing from Regression B1 to B2 one observes, however, a deterioration in the *LM* statistic for serial correlation. The return-to-normality term appears to be significant with the right sign (-0.117 for $K^N = \bar{K}$ in Regression B1, with a *t*-ratio of 2.150) and so does the first of the two error-learning components, the second term being small and significant, in Regression B1, at about only the 10 percent level. The capacity utilization effects are practically equal to those of Regression A1 while the uncertainty variable has a larger coefficient estimate with a considerably higher *t*-ratio. Also similar to that of A1 is the estimate for the intercept which is equal, for $K^N = \bar{K}$, to 0.263. On the whole the fit appears to be rather satisfactory,[35] even if the *LM* statistics are somewhat high to

---

[34] In particular, for Regression B1, $F(1,43) = 0.782$. It should be remembered that, due to the presence of lagged dependent variables, this test is only approximately valid. The same holds, obviously, for the discussion of significance based on the *t*-statistics.

[35] As observed in the discussion following expression (6.7) a lower bound for the standard error of the *WLS* regression should be approximately equal to 0.06 (the inverse of the square root of the average number of respondents to *Mondo Economico* surveys). For Regression B1 one obtains an estimate of 0.31 which points to the fact that omitted individual-specific terms do not have a negligible variance.

conclude forcefully against the hypothesis of absence of serial correlation in the error term (or, under a more general criterion, against the hypothesis of absence of misspecification).[36]

6.3.3. The Final Results

The results presented in Table 6.2, and particularly Regression B1, are a good starting point for an improvement of the specification considered so far. The choice has been made, however, to keep the possible experimentation to a minimum and to investigate how well simple and reasonable extensions of standard models of inflation expectations would describe the *aggregate* and highly variable survey observations examined in this work. The estimates of Tables 6.1 and 6.2 appear to be quite adequate to this end, pointing at a number of interesting effects on inflation expectations from past errors, discrepancies between actual and normal rates, utilized capacity and the state of uncertainty. It seems, however, worthwhile to undertake a brief, further examination of these estimates, investigating, on one side, the scope for other, possibly omitted, determinants of inflation expectations, and then, what will be done in Section 6.4, a number of important issues such as the stability of the estimates, errors of measurement and aggregation problems. These issues will however be treated within the framework considered so far, leaving for a future research the analysis of some further interesting points which will be briefly highlighted in Section 6.5.

With respect to other possible determinants of inflation expectations it seems that one should not rely, at this point, on an extensive search for *any* other "significant" variable. Moreover, there are substantial differences depending on whether one tries to discover the effects of other variables via, for example, their influence on the "normal" rate of inflation by changing the specification of such a variable, or looks for the possible influence of a given factor in a number of special occasions.

To offer an idea on how things would develop, Regression B1 of Table 6.2 has been reestimated by adding to the list of regressors, respectively, the lagged percentage change of money supply, of wages per dependent worker in industry and of the Italian lira/US dollar exchange rate. Since these series are not available for the whole period on which Regression B1 has

---

[36] Observe that if one used the so called modified Lagrange multiplier test, which is described in Harvey (1980, p. 277) and which is shown to be preferable to the standard *LM* test by Kiviet (1981), one would obtain in the case of Regression B1 a value of 2.149 which would not reject at the 5 percent level of significance (on the basis of an *F*-distribution with 2 and 42 degrees of freedom) the hypothesis of *absence* of second-order autocorrelation or moving average in the residuals.

TABLE 6.3

FORMATION OF EXPECTATIONS OF WHOLESALE PRICE CHANGES: REGRESSIONS AUGMENTED FOR
PERCENTAGE CHANGES OF MONEY SUPPLY, INDUSTRIAL WAGES AND EXCHANGE RATE
(Dependent variable = p_t^e; WLS estimates; Estimation period: 1st Semester 1959 – 2nd Semester 1980)

	Regressions			
	C1	C2	C3	C4
Constant	- 7.655 (2.248)	- 7.670 (2.207)	- 6.770 (2.184)	- 7.025 (2.393)
P_{t-1}	.834 (8.833)	.833 (8.533)	.840 (9.813)	.758 (9.030)
$P_{t-1} - P_{t-1}^{NP}$	- 3.504 (3.992)	- 3.495 (3.795)	- 3.580 (4.499)	- 3.632 (4.803)
$P_{t-1}^{e} - P_{t-1}$	.598 (4.670)	.600 (4.491)	.591 (5.087)	.314 (2.329)
$P_{t-2}^{e} - P_{t-2}$	.097 (1.648)	.097 (1.603)	.138 (2.495)	.136 (2.621)
UTC_{t-1}	.090 (2.317)	.090 (2.282)	.078 (2.220)	.084 (2.518)
$UTCl_{t-1}$	.038 (3.831)	.038 (3.677)	.039 (4.332)	.039 (4.587)
$UNCl_{t-1}$	.122 (1.836)	.122 (1.770)	.125 (2.080)	.126 (2.200)

	(1)	(2)	(3)	(4)
DU6902	2.387 (3.903)	2.390 (3.825)	2.528 (4.545)	1.921 (3.546)
$DM2_{t-1}$		.003 (.040)		
DWD_{t-1}			.019 (2.936)	
DEX_{t-1}				- .152 (3.640)
R^2	.883	.883	.910	.921
SER	.322	.326	.292	.277
DW	2.263	2.274	1.917	2.715
LM	6.125	6.575	1.696	9.985
T	44	44	44	44

Legend

See Table 6.1. Furthermore:

$DM2_{t-1}$ = percentage change of money supply (M2) between semester t-2 and semester t-1 (see Table 5.3);

DWD_{t-1} = percentage change of wages in industry (excluding construction) per dependent worker between semester t-2 and semester t-1 (see Table 5.3);

DEX_{t-1} = percentage change of the exchange rate between the Italian lira and the U.S. dollar between semester t-2 and semester t-1 (see Table 5.3).

been estimated, it too has been reestimated so that all regressions would refer to the same period (second semester 1959 to 2nd semester 1980), obtaining very similar results (Regression C1). The estimates are presented in Table 6.3.

While simply adding the change in money supply (Regression C2) does not produce significant overall differences in the estimates, with an extremely low t-ratio for such an additional variable, changes in wages and in the exchange rate appear to have coefficients "significantly" different from zero. Consider the exchange rate first (Regression C4). Quite strangely, it comes out with a negative sign, which might lead one to think of its effect as a signal of a further element of a regressive component. The coefficient estimates of the other variables are also somewhat modified. Most important, there is a large deterioration in the statistic for the test of serial correlation, which somehow contrasts with the sensible improvement of the overall fit. This fact strongly suggests that, before looking for any economic reason of a possible negative relationship between exchange rate changes and inflation expectations, one should investigate whether the above result might be a consequence of spurious correlation. Since the exchange rate has been constant over a large portion of the sample period, it might be the case that the highly significant negative relation between the dependent variable and the change in the exchange rate is at least in part due to the accidental coincidence of large values of the latter variable and large regression errors, of an opposite sign, during the more recent experience. Looking at the estimated residuals it is indeed evident that in one single occasion, in the second semester of 1976, when the lira/dollar exchange rate went up by an exceptional 21 percent, the estimate of the expected rate of inflation from Regression B1 was short of the actual value for about 3 percentage points.

In the case of the change in wages (Regression C3), one observes again a sensible improvement of the fit. However, even if significant, the coefficient estimate for this variable is very small, and the estimates of the coefficients of the other variables are much less modified than in the case of the exchange rate. Also, there is a very substantial reduction in the LM statistic, which does not point anymore at the presence of serial correlation or at a possibly misspecified structure. In this case too the possibility of spurious correlation should be investigated first. One observes, then, immediately, that the percentage change in industrial wages per dependent worker is a variable with a very large seasonal component, due to the Italian wage system where a double monthly wage is generally paid in December of each year. Indeed, reestimating Regression C3 substituting DWD with the change in seasonally adjusted wages does not produce anymore a significant coefficient estimate.

On the basis of these observations, the four regressions of Table 6.3 have been reestimated with the addition, among the regressors, of a dummy for the second semester of 1976 and a seasonal dummy. The presence of the former variable could be justified on the grounds that, following the crisis in the exchange rate market and the rapid surge in the rate of inflation, the survey respondents shared the belief that strong monetary restrictions, to be taken (or already in course), could have a quick effect on inflation, the high rate of capacity utilization notwithstanding. It might also be the case that the specification of the "normal" rate of inflation considered in the present work gives too much weight to large, unexpected, and probably temporary, rises of the price level or that there is a difference between actual and perceived price changes, particularly when sudden changes in the rate of inflation take place. In such a case a dummy like the one for the second semester of 1976 might be partially compensating for the difference between the actual change of prices occurred in the previous semester and the perceived one.[37] The presence of the seasonal dummy could account instead for some residual seasonality of inflation expectations still present in the estimates of Table 6.2. The estimates obtained adding these two dummies to the regressors of Table 6.3 are clear cut: the coefficient estimate of the change of money supply remains insignificant at the 5 percent level as are, in the present case, the estimates of the coefficients of changes in wages and in the exchange rate. Furthermore there is a very large reduction in the *LM* statistics for serial correlation.

Table 6.4 contains the results, for the whole sample period, obtained adding to the regressors of Regressions B1 and B3 (WLS and OLS estimates, respectively) the two dummies under discussion (Regressions D1 and D3). It is immediately evident the improvement in the overall fit, in the significance of the coefficient estimates and in the *LM* statistics. The most interesting results are the rise in the coefficient estimate of the uncertainty term and the fall in that of the first error-learning component only partially compensated by the increase for the second. This increase (and the large

---

[37]One should observe, however, that the possible difference between actual and perceived inflation in the first semester of 1976 cannot account for the whole difference between the expected inflation for the second semester of 1976 and its "static" prediction obtained from the regression estimates. On the basis of the results of Table 6.4 (Regression D1) to be discussed, one obtains in fact a total derivative of p_t^e with respect to p_{t-1} equal to 0.563 (for $K^N = \bar{K}$) and a coefficient for the dummy for the second semester of 1976 equal to -3.862. In the first semester of 1976 the actual change of wholesale prices was equal to 14.1 percent, so that in order to have the dummy variable to account only for the difference between actual and perceived inflation one should be prepared to accept the latter to have been equal to about one half of the value actually observed (since one would have $-3.862 = 0.563(x - 14.1)$ so that $x = 7.2$, where x would be the perceived price change for the first semester of 1976).

TABLE 6.4

FORMATION OF EXPECTATIONS OF WHOLESALE PRICE CHANGES: RESTRICTED ESTIMATES, 2

(Dependent variable = p_t^e; WLS and OLS estimates; Estimation period: 2nd Semester 1953 - 2nd Semester 1980)

	Regressions			
	D1	D2	D3	D4
Constant	- 8.069 (3.803)	- 8.133 (3.608)	- 9.402 (3.997)	- 9.622 (3.754)
P_{t-1}	.839 (13.621)	.842 (12.408)	.832 (13.802)	.825 (12.529)
$P_{t-1} - P_{t-1}^{NP}$	- 4.807 (6.935)	- 4.810 (6.692)	- 5.353 (10.728)	- 5.331 (10.258)
$P_{t-1}^e - P_{t-1}$	.441 (4.583)	.438 (4.358)	.443 (4.209)	.435 (3.936)
$P_{t-2}^e - P_{t-2}$	.178 (4.031)	.161 (3.152)	.160 (3.642)	.149 (2.697)
$P_{t-3}^e - P_{t-3}$		.022 (.545)		.008 (.191)
UTC_{t-1}	.091 (3.780)	.092 (3.584)	.105 (3.938)	.108 (3.695)
$UTC1_{t-1}$	.052 (6.763)	.052 (6.522)	.059 (10.613)	.058 (10.156)
$UNC1_{t-1}$	.180 (3.611)	.170 (3.206)	.166 (3.955)	.159 (3.271)
DU5701	2.091 (4.680)	2.081 (4.576)	2.042 (3.662)	2.034 (3.567)

DU5702	- 1.278 (2.213)	- 1.306 (2.196)	- 1.173 (1.935)	- 1.172 (1.869)
DU6902	2.428 (5.364)	2.429 (5.272)	2.645 (4.400)	2.650 (4.310)
DU7602	- 3.862 (4.231)	- 3.835 (4.125)	- 4.120 (4.723)	- 4.100 (4.573)
DUSEAS	.508 (3.660)	.473 (3.170)	.630 (4.014)	.607 (3.558)
R^2	.951	.950	.955	.954
SER	.242	.246	.545	.557
DW	2.115	1.996	2.009	1.926
LM	1.606	1.501	1.625	1.560
T	55	54	55	54

Legend

See Table 6.1. Furthermore:

DU7601 = dummy variable for the 2nd semester of 1976 (= 1 in 7602; = 0 elsewhere);

DUSEAS = dummy variable for seasonality (= 1 in the first semester of each year; = 0 in the second semester).

WLS estimates for regressions D1 and D2 (SER refers to dependent variable p_t^e / σ_{p_t});

OLS estimates for regressions D3 and D4 (SER refers to dependent variable p_t^e).

The sample period for the estimates of regressions D2 and D4 starts with the 1st Semester 1954.

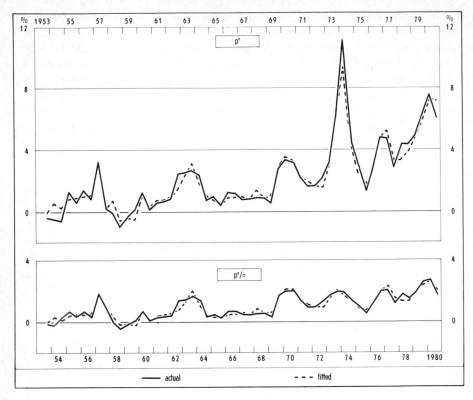

FIGURE 6.1
FORMATION OF INFLATION EXPECTATIONS:
ACTUAL AND FITTED VALUES OF REGRESSION D1

t-ratio associated to the coefficient of such component) has suggested to investigate whether the introduction of the new dummies could have modified the dynamic structure of the equation identified by the results of the preliminary investigation. As one can see from the results of Regressions D2 and D4 of Table 6.4, which contain a third error-learning component, this is not the case.[38]

Consider in more detail Regression D1 (the same conclusions apply to the OLS estimates of Regression D3 which are remarkably similar, suggesting a low degree of heteroscedasticity, if any). First of all, one should observe the extremely good fit of this regression estimates (and chiefly so, recalling that the dependent variable is the expected *rate of change* of wholesale prices). A

---

[38]The same conclusion is obtained when instead of introducing a third error-learning component as in Regression D2, one introduces p^e_{t-3} and p_{t-3} as separate regressors.

second interesting consideration concerns the large t-ratios associated with all the coefficient estimates and the absence of serial correlation in the estimated residuals suggested by the very low value of the LM statistic (asymptotically distributed as a chi-square with two degrees of freedom). Third, under the assumption that $K^N = \overline{K}$, one obtains a coefficient of -0.125 for the return-to-normality term, with a t-ratio of 2.956, and a very small and highly insignificant intercept (0.029 with t-ratio of 0.218).[39] Finally, one can reject at about the 1 percent significance level the hypothesis $\beta = 1$ of (6.9), so that the coefficients of the implicit distributed lag in terms of past actual price changes sum to less than one (about 60 percent, obtained using expression (6.19)).

On the whole, the model of formation of inflation expectations estimated by Regression D1 of Table 6.4 seems to be quite satisfactory both in terms of the coefficient estimates and of the analysis of the residuals. The plot of the actual and fitted values of this "preferred" regression is given in Figure 6.1.[40] It is rather impressive how well such a simple model approximates the inflation expectations of the panel of respondents to *Mondo Economico* surveys.

6.4. Further Evaluation

Three topics deserve further investigation before one can conclude with a favorable evaluation of the model of inflation expectations estimated in Section 6.3. These topics concern the analysis of the stability of the estimates, the consideration of a potential measurement error problem and the possibility of aggregation bias. These will be considered in order.

6.4.1. Stability of the Estimates

"Stability" is defined here with Hendry, as the condition related to "the constancy over time of the estimated parameters in an equation and not to the latent roots of the dynamics of a model being such to yield convergence to equilibrium or steady-state".[41] With respect to the latter the characteristic roots of the autoregressive structure of Regression D1 of Table 6.4 are such

[39] Observe that the intercept being practically zero does not imply that the regression has no constant, this being given by one half of the coefficient of the seasonal dummy, that is about 0.25.

[40] Notice that the plots in the lower part of Figure 6.1 refer to the actual and fitted values of the dependent variable of Regression D1 which has been estimated applying least squares to the original variables weighted by $1/\sigma_t$; multiplying back the fitted values of Regression D1 by σ_t, the fitted values plotted in the upper part of Figure 6.1 have been obtained.

[41] Hendry (1980, p. 217).

that the model is intrinsically stable.[42] What is of interest in this context is the possibility of "predictive failure" of the model of inflation expectations which has been estimated. To assess this possibility, one should consider post-sample predictions generated from the model. What is generally done is to reserve a number of observations at the end of the sample, say N, and estimate the model with $T - N$ observations; then predictions are generated for the remaining N observations out of the estimated model and a test is applied to gauge the performance of these predictions. The ratio of $T - N - K$ times the sum of squares of the errors of prediction over those N observations to the sum of squares of the estimated residuals (from the model estimated with $T - N$ observations) is asymptotically distributed as a chi-square with N degrees of freedom and is generally the test most used to this end.[43] Hendry also suggests the computation of one of the tests proposed by Chow (1960), which for a classical linear regression model is distributed as an F with N and $T - K$ (K = number of regressors) degrees of freedom. This test consists of comparing the residual sum of squares of the model estimated with $T - N$ observations with that of the model estimated with all T data points, respectively S^2_{T-N} and S^2_T, by means of the statistic $F(N, T - K) = (T - N - K)(S^2_T - S^2_{T-N})/NS^2_{T-N}$.[44]

The suggestion of leaving N observations for prediction testing, without using them in the estimation process is a controversial one. The consequence could be that some information which could instead be very useful in obtaining better model estimates would not be used. In the present case, all the available data points (fifty-five out of fifty-seven observations, two being lost for lagged dependent variables) have been used to account properly for the more disturbed period which has followed the first oil crisis. As a check of the estimates obtained over the entire sample period, however, the Regression D1 of Table 6.4 has been reestimated by deleting the last eight observations (that is, from the second semester of 1953 to the second semester of 1976). The estimates of this regression are reported in Table 6.5 (where those of Regression D1 are again presented for comparison).

It turns out that, despite the absence of eight observations over a most crucial historical experience, the overall estimates obtained with the smaller sample are not widely different from those for the whole period. There is a reduction in the coefficient of p_{t-1}, from 0.839 to 0.739, as well as in the coefficients of the two error-learning components. The basic message of

---

[42] The roots being equal to 0.697 and -0.256.

[43] See Hendry (1980, p. 222) and Harvey (1981, pp. 180–181).

[44] Due to the presence of lagged dependent variables, and in general of stochastic regressors, this statistic is only approximately distributed as F.

TABLE 6.5

FORMATION OF EXPECTATIONS OF WHOLESALE PRICE CHANGES: COMPARISON BETWEEN THE ESTIMATES FOR THE PERIOD
2ND SEMESTER 1953 – 2ND SEMESTER 1980 AND THE PERIOD 2ND SEMESTER 1953 – 2ND SEMESTER 1976
(Dependent variable = p_t^e; WLS estimates)

	Regressions	
	E1 = D1 5301–8002	E2 5301–7602
Constant	− 8.069 (3.803)	− 7.821 (3.697)
P_{t-1}	.839 (13.621)	.739 (7.460)
$P_{t-1} - P_{t-1}^{NP}$	− 4.807 (6.935)	− 4.965 (6.962)
$P_{t-1}^e - P_{t-1}$	.441 (4.583)	.378 (3.596)
$P_{t-2}^e - P_{t-2}$	.178 (4.031)	.122 (2.191)
UTC_{t-1}	.091 (3.780)	.089 (3.726)
$UTC1_{t-1}$	.052 (6.763)	.055 (6.976)
$UNC1_{t-1}$	.180 (3.611)	.173 (3.357)
DU5701	2.091 (4.680)	2.101 (4.864)
DU5702	− 1.278 (2.213)	− 1.129 (1.971)
DU6902	2.428 (5.364)	2.443 (5.546)
DU7602	− 3.862 (4.231)	− 3.946 (4.008)
DUSEAS	.508 (3.660)	.479 (3.407)
R^2	.951	.955
SER	.242	.233
DW	2.115	2.293
LM	1.606	2.590
T	55	47

Legend

See Table 6.4.

these estimates is, however, identical to that of the regression estimated for the whole sample period: there is a significant autoregressive component in the formation of expectations with a strong cyclical effect approximated by the deviation of capacity from a constant "normal" level; return-to-normality elements are also present and there are signs that the adaptive coefficient is a positive function of uncertainty on future inflation; the sum of coefficients of past rates of inflation in the distributed lag implicit in the regression estimates is significantly smaller than one (0.48 for Regression E2 to be compared to 0.58 for Regression E1 (= D1)).

The two statistics proposed by Hendry have also been computed, obtaining values of 1.39 for the "Chow-test" and of 25.43 for the asymptotic chi-square test. In the former case the statistic does not reject the stability hypothesis (the critical value of the F-distribution at the 5 percent level being equal to 2.17). This hypothesis is instead rejected in the latter case (with a critical value of the chi-square distribution equal to 15.51 at the same significance level). This second testing procedure appears to be less reliable, however, than the "Chow-test", particularly in small samples, as recently shown by Kiviet (1981). On this basis, there does not seem to be sufficient evidence of "prediction-failure" that would suggest that the regressions estimated in Table 6.5 were inadequate. Furthermore, excluding the seasonal dummy from the regressors of Table 6.5 one would obtain a much lower chi-square statistic (equal to 15.61) and still a very small F-statistic (1.33), with practically no changes in the coefficient estimates. This result might point to a possible, even if light, modification in the seasonality of inflation expectations which might have taken place in the more recent years. Finally, it must be understood that these tests are *not* exactly in the same spirit as the ones suggested by Hendry, since the test here is for possible "prediction-failure" of the "best" model obtained with the first $T - N = 47$ observations, and not of that obtained with all the (55) sample observations which have been used in the specification search of Section 6.3.

6.4.2. Measurement Error

It is obvious that expectations are measured with error (when they are measured!). This does not only refer to the possibility of error in the transformations of the raw answers in expected rates of inflation – a case which has been considered for the rationality tests of Chapter 5, but which will be put aside in this discussion. It mainly refers to the fact that survey data have been used and to draw inferences about the expectations of the "population" calls for the consideration of sampling errors. However, not only are *Mondo Economico* surveys conducted on a panel and are therefore not at all random surveys, but also one has not even the faintest idea of the possible characteristics of those errors. Assume, however, that what is "observed", p^e, is related the "true" expected rate of change of prices, p^{*e}, by

$$p_t^e = p_t^{*e} + e_t, \tag{6.21}$$

with the model of formation being equal to

$$p_t^{*e} = Y_t \phi + \delta_1 p_{t-1}^{*e} + \delta_2 p_{t-2}^{*e} + u_t, \tag{6.22}$$

where Y_t are variables other than the two past expected rates of inflation, and

$$Eu_t = Ee_t = 0, \quad Eu_t^2 = \sigma_u^2, \quad \forall t, \quad Eu_t u_{t'} = 0, \quad \forall t \neq t',$$

$$Ee_t^2 = \sigma_e^2, \quad \forall t, \quad Ee_t e_{t'} = 0, \quad \forall t \neq t', \quad Ee_t u_s = 0, \quad \forall t, s.$$

Therefore, by substituting (6.21) in (6.22) and solving for p_t^e, one obtains

$$p_t^e = Y_t \phi + \delta_1 p_{t-1}^e + \delta_2 p_{t-2}^e + v_t, \tag{6.23}$$

where

$$v_t = u_t + e_t - \delta_1 e_{t-1} - \delta_2 e_{t-2}, \tag{6.24}$$

so that v_t is a second-order moving average with

$$Ev_t v_{t'} = \begin{cases} \left(\lambda + 1 + \delta_1^2 + \delta_2^2\right)\sigma_e^2 & \text{for} \quad t = t', \lambda = \sigma_u^2/\sigma_e^2, \\ -\delta_1 \sigma_e^2 & \text{for} \quad |t - t'| = 1, \\ -\delta_2 \sigma_e^2 & \text{for} \quad |t - t'| = 2, \\ 0 & \text{otherwise.} \end{cases}$$

Equation (6.23) could then be estimated by appropriately taking into account the moving average in the residual component and, possibly, the restrictions between its parameters and the coefficients of the lagged dependent variables. If, however, σ_e^2 is small, this measurement error could well be only a minor problem. This is why the Lagrange multipliers have been computed for the residuals of the regressions of Section 6.3 against the hypothesis of a second order autocorrelation *or* moving average in the residuals. This is a valid test also when lagged dependent variables are present in the regression. In this case, it can be simply computed as TR^2, where T is the number of observations and R^2 is the determination coefficient (computed about zero in the case of *WLS* estimates since no constant is included in the least squares estimates on the weighted observations) of the regressions of the estimated residuals $\hat{u}_t$ on Y_t, p^e_{t-1}, p^e_{t-2} and $\hat{u}_{t-1}$, $\hat{u}_{t-2}$ (respectively augmented by one and two zero values for the initial missing observations).[45] As it has already been mentioned, this statistic is asymptotically distributed as a chi-square with two degrees of freedom. It can then be observed from the results of Table 6.4 that there is no evidence of a possible measurement error, in expected inflation, of the kind considered in this section.

6.4.3. Aggregation Bias

As has been seen in Chapter 5, Section 5.5, the estimates here might suffer from aggregation problems. That is, not only is this a clear situation of possible heteroscedasticity, as shown in Section 6.2, which has led to consider the use of weighted least squares, but also the possibility of aggregation bias exists. Under the assumption of Section 6.2 and following the discussion of Section 5.5, the proper specification might then be

$$p^e_t = X_t\psi + \lambda_1\sigma_{t-1} + \lambda_2\sigma_{t-2} + \eta_t, \tag{6.25}$$

instead of

$$p^e_t = X_t\psi + u_t, \tag{6.26}$$

where X_t stands for the explanatory variables of the regressions of Section 6.3 and η_t has a form similar to ε_t in (5.40). The presence of the two lagged values of the standard deviation of individual inflation expectations is clearly related to the presence of two lagged dependent variables in the regressions of Section 6.3. As has been observed in Section 6.2 (point 5), however, there is an obvious possibility that besides the term u_t, with zero mean and variance equal to var(p^e_{it})/n_t, the regression residuals might include also a term v_t, reflecting omitted individual-specific components, possibly with a non-zero and non-constant mean. Under the assumptions of Section 5.5, this fact might call for the presence of a further regressor in (6.25), given by – following (5.39) – the current standard deviation σ_t.

Regressions D1 and D3 of Table 6.4 have therefore been reestimated adding to the regressors, respectively, a constant and the variables σ_{t-1}/σ_t,

---

[45] Obviously, in the case of Regressions D1 and D2, Y_t, p^e_{t-1} and p^e_{t-2} are all divided by σ_t.

σ_{t-2}/σ_t for the former (estimated by means of least squares on the weighted observations), and the variables σ_t, σ_{t-1}, σ_{t-2} for the latter (least squares on the original observations). Very low F-statistics for the hypothesis that the coefficients of these regressors were equal to zero have been obtained, equal, respectively, to 0.271 and 1.242, so that the hypothesis is rejected. This does not necessarily imply that there is no aggregation bias in the coefficient estimates of Table 6.4. It might simply be that the conditions under which an equation such as (6.25) is derived are not correct. While this subject might deserve further investigation, no further search for a possible aggregation bias will be made, concluding that, on the basis of the simple test just reported there is not, so far, supporting evidence.

6.5. General Remarks

The model of formation of inflation expectations estimated in Section 6.3.3 has a number of interesting features. The level of capacity utilization and the "state" of uncertainty appear to have a significant impact on the expectations of *Mondo Economico* survey respondents. It is also noteworthy that the model allows for variable adjustment coefficients and that this is the only way through which uncertainty appears to affect inflation expectations. One might also investigate, in a future research, possible feedback effects such as those revealed in the experimental study by Schmalensee (1976), who found an inverse relation between the confidence with which expectations are held and past forecasting performance. Also probably worthwhile would be an investigation of possible differences in the adaptive and return-to-normality coefficients at turning points, at different levels of the inflation rate, and for different ranges (and signs) of past anticipation errors and deviations of actual and normal inflation rates, as it has been suggested in the literature on expectations.

On the basis of the estimates of Regression D1 of Table 6.4, a 5 percentage points deviation of the rate of capacity utilization from its (constant) normal level, in the last quarter of the semester at the end of which expectations are formed, would produce a variation of the rate of inflation expected for the next semester of slightly less than half a percentage point (on a semiannual basis), with a total change of 2.4 percent – over one half of which taking place in less than twelve months. One should add to this effect that due to the interaction between such a deviation of the rate of capacity utilization from its normal value and the deviation of actual from normal inflation. For every percentage point in the latter, a 5 percent deviation of the former would have an impact effect on inflation expectations of about a quarter of a percent and a total effect near to 0.7 percent.

Also the effect of a deviation in the uncertainty term from its normal level could have a potentially relevant impact on expectations. In particular, for a given forecasting error of 5 percent, an increase of the uncertainty term one percentage point above its normal value would produce a 0.9 percent change in the semiannual rate of inflation expected for the next semester and a total change of slightly less than 2.5 percent. Of course, this would be a rather extreme situation since the standard deviation of the uncertainty proxy utilized in this work is less than two thirds of one percent.

6.5.1. The Implicit Lag Structure on Expected Inflation

The question of the impact and total effects on inflation expectations of actual past changes in prices, which has been discussed at length in Section 6.3.1, is also a relevant one. An examination of the lag structure implicitly embedded in the regression estimates is therefore of interest.

From (6.18) one can obtain all the partial effects of a change in actual on expected inflation from a given semester forward in time (with utilized capacity and uncertainty fixed at their normal levels). In Table 6.6 the distributed lag coefficients for selected regressions of Section 6.3 have been computed, for 20 lags, from the rational lag operator $A(L)$ described in (6.18); as it is well known one can, in fact, obtain

$$p_t^e = A(L)p_{t-1} = \sum_{i=1}^{\infty} a_i p_{t-i}, \tag{6.27}$$

where the a_i $(i = 1, \ldots, 20)$ are the coefficients presented in Table 6.6. Not only the estimates of the "preferred" regression (D1) have been considered, but also those of Regressions B1 and B2. There is no question that the latter two regressions are significantly inferior to the former. In particular, B1 does not allow for the seasonal dummy and for the correction for the second semester of 1976; and B2 has the further characteristic that it has been obtained under the constraint that the sum of the coefficients of the distributed lag was equal to one, that is $A(1) = 1$. As has already been observed, this restriction does not appear to be well founded, nor does it receive any statistical support from the results obtained. It is of interest, however, to examine the difference that imposing such a constraint would make on the structure of the distributed lag.

The pattern of lags of Regressions D1 and B1 is quite similar. The main difference lies in the impact coefficient, equal to 0.10 for B1 and 0.28 for D1, with a total effect of past actual price changes on the expected ones equal, respectively, to 0.46 and 0.58 (in both cases much less than one). If one considers Regression B2, where $A(1) = 1$ by constraint, even if, eventually, a once and for all change in actual inflation raises the expected rate by an equal percentage, this effect is distributed over a long period of time. Indeed, for Regressions D1 and B1 the median lag is equal to three and ten semesters, while for B2 it is equal to twenty-seven semesters! Furthermore, in the constrained case the cumulative sum of coefficients is still lower than for the unconstrained regressions after more than twenty semesters (as can be easily derived from the figures of Table 6.6).

TABLE 6.6

THE IMPLICIT DISTRIBUTED LAG OF THE EXPECTED RATE OF CHANGE OF WHOLESALE PRICES IN TERMS OF PAST ACTUAL RATES, FROM SELECTED REGRESSIONS OF EXPECTATIONS FORMATION

	Regressions		
Lag	D1	B1	B2
1	.282	.102	.076
2	− .045	− .012	− .063
3	.040	.009	− .031
4	.018	.013	− .025
5	.024	.017	− .015
6	.023	.020	− .006
7	.023	.022	.002
8	.023	.024	.010
9	.023	.025	.017
10	.024	.026	.024
11	.024	.027	.031
12	.024	.028	.037
13	.024	.028	.043
14	.024	.028	.048
15	.015	.020	.045
16	.011	.016	.042
17	.007	.012	.040
18	.005	.009	.038
19	.004	.007	.036
20	.002	.005	.034
...			
∞ (total effect)	.578	.460	1.000
Median lag	3	10	27

Note

The entries are the first 20 coefficients of the distributed lag of past rates of change of wholesale prices, obtained from the regression estimates, setting utilized capacity and the uncertainty term at their normal values and solving for the expected rate of price changes. The median lag is the number of semesters containing fifty percent of the total effect of actual on expected price changes.

The form of the distributed lags of the above regressions is obviously that which stems from an adaptive-regressive (in general, an extrapolative-regressive) model of expectations formation with a dip at the beginning of the lag process due to the regressive component. It can be immediately observed that all the estimated lag structures present a fall after the fourteenth lag; this is due to the fact that, as a result of the preliminary investigation of Section 6.3.2, the "normal" inflation rate has been approximated by a moving average of the past fourteen semiannual inflation rates. Although other proxies have been intentionally not experimented with here,[46] such experimentation might be done in the future; possible interesting approximations might be suggested by studies on the term structure of interest rates.[47]

6.5.2. The Role of the Dummy Variables and the Rationality Issue

The inflation expectations of the panel of respondents to *Mondo Economico* surveys seem to be explained to a rather satisfactory degree by the factors considered in Section 6.3. It should not be neglected that it has been necessary to introduce a few dummies in order to take account of a number of events which, at times, had a strong influence on expectations but were not considered by a specification which only included lagged actual and expected rates of inflation, the rate of capacity utilization and the uncertainty term. Apart from the seasonal dummy, which corrects for a moderate amount of (constant) seasonality present in the answers on inflation expectations, zero–one dummy variables have been introduced on three occasions: the first semester of 1957, when expectations were highly influenced by the Suez crisis (which did not produce, however, an increase in the rate of inflation, a fact acknowledged by the survey respondents and which has called for the introduction of a second dummy for the next semester); the second semester of 1969, when the effects of a structural change in industrial

---

[46]Lahiri (1976,1977) has used as the rate of inflation towards which short-term inflation expectations could regress, the twelve months ahead expectations of Livingston's surveys (to explain the formation of the six months ahead ones); similarly, Kane and Malkiel (1976) have considered the inflation rate expected on average over the next ten years. Multispan forecasts cannot obviously be used in the present case since only with the survey for the first semester of 1978 are expectations two semesters ahead being collected. Valentine (1977) has assumed the normal rate to follow a Koyck process (in terms of actual inflation), with the coefficient estimated jointly with those of all the other components of the formation equation. Resler (1980) has instead approximated the normal rate of inflation with a twenty quarter moving average of past *M1* growth, and Figlewsky and Wachtel (1981) have assumed it to be equal to the mean rate of price increase over the five year period prior to the survey.

[47]See, for example, Shiller (1979).

relations were anticipated; and the second semester of 1976, following a rather dramatic crisis in the exchange rate market.

Two observations are worth making: (1) On the first two occasions, the dummies were introduced *a priori*, before starting the specification search, after having examined the data on expected and actual price changes and the evolution of the Italian economic and social conditions over the period considered in this study; on the third occasion, however, the inclusion of a dummy has been forced by further examination of the estimation results and has been justified *ex post*, in Section 6.3.3. (2) No experiments with other dummies have been intentionally performed for other exceptional periods since it was not clear beforehand that the anticipated changes in the rate of inflation could not be explained by the observed factors included in the regressions.

There are instances, then, when occasional factors occur which generate a climate among the economic agents leading to (right or wrong, does not matter) anticipations which cannot be explained on the basis of a given model of formation. This is certainly not a novel remark and should not be confused, in the author's opinion, with the criticism associated with Lucas (1976), that one should allow for changes in expectations due to changes in the policy process; probably, it might be better related to some of Keynes' (1936, 1937) observations about the "animal spirits" of businessmen[48] and "the fact that our knowledge of the future is fluctuating, vague and uncertain".[49] In the above mentioned instances, the predictions about what inflation expectations will be, at a given date, still appear to be the best one can do *on the basis of the data at hand*; one should however be prepared not only to observe possibly large errors between expectations and realizations, but also between the expectations themselves and their predictions generated by regression estimates such as those of Table 6.4.

This discussion leads to a further remark. To assume expectations to be rational, in the sense of fully exploiting the available information, is probably at time a convenient and useful device. It has been observed, however, that the inflation expectations considered in this work do not reject the rationality assumption only over the period of mild even if variable inflation which occurred in Italy during the fifties and sixties, and the early seventies up to the first oil crisis. Afterwards, large anticipation errors have been observed, which on average do not compensate each other, large rises of the inflation rate being generally underestimated. It might then be dangerous to *estimate* a relationship containing an expectational term on the assumption that the latter was "rational", since this hypothesis would

---

[48] Keynes (1936, ch. 12).

[49] Keynes (1937, p. 213).

imply a random zero–mean difference between such a term and its realization. It is instead interesting to observe that the estimates presented in Section 6.3 refer to the *whole* sample period, inclusive of the more recent experience, and that they show that a satisfactory approximation of the survey expectations considered in this study can be obtained in terms of past actual and expected inflation (possibly with an interpretation in terms of error-learning and return-to-normality), cyclical conditions of real activity and the general state of uncertainty. Apart from the latter term, this is a quite standard and simple model of expectations formation. The fitted values of this model have been subjected to exactly the same tests of rationality applied in Chapter 5 to the actual series of expected inflation. It is remarkable that very similar results have been obtained: these fitted values *do not reject* the rationality assumption over the period up to the first oil crisis, clearly rejecting it afterwards.

With respect to the rationality issue, one can then assert that either the tests of rationality usually conducted are not powerful enough (and there might be some truth in this statement), or that all the available and relevant information necessary to form rational expectations is contained in a specification such as the one considered in Section 6.3. If the second interpretation is correct, since this specification proves to be satisfactory all over the sample period – inclusive of the last eight years when large, asymmetric and serially correlated anticipation errors have been observed – it is possible to conclude that while an adaptive-regressive (in general, extrapolative-regressive) framework is not *per se* in contradiction with an assumption of rational expectations, it might prove to be more general and capable to provide a better interpretation of the actual process of formation of inflation expectations. Such an assessment, of course, relies on the experiments conducted on the limited set of directly observed data on expectations utilized in this work.

6.6. *Summary of the Results*

This chapter has considered the estimation of a model of formation of the inflation expectations of the respondents to *Mondo Economico* surveys. After a brief summary of the relevant literature and an outline of the estimation approach, results for the expectations of wholesale price changes have been presented – those for consumer price changes being an obvious candidate for future analysis. These results can be summarized as follows:

(1) On the basis of the estimates of Section 6.3 – obtained by means of ordinary and weighted least squares, the weights being equal to the inverse of the estimated standard deviations of the individual expectations – the

most successful model has proved to be a version of the adaptive-regressive hypothesis.

(2) The regressive component, represented by the deviation of the past inflation rate from a moving average ("normal") term, has been shown to be a function of capacity utilization, so that when a positive deviation of inflation from the "normal" rate is the case, the regression towards normality is slowed down by the presence of a positive difference of capacity utilization from its "normal" rate (and vice versa). The effects of the latter on inflation expectations are not, however, completely accounted for by this variation in the return-to-normality coefficient.

(3) Error-learning up to the second order is also present; the coefficient for the error that has just occurred is a positive function of uncertainty (proxied by the dispersion of individual expectations in the most recent survey); a separate effect of this uncertainty term does not appear to be present.

(4) The distributed lag on past inflation rates, obtained by setting utilized capacity and uncertainty at their "normal" levels, has the standard regressive-extrapolative pattern, but the sum of its coefficients appears to be smaller than one and not much larger than one half. Furthermore, the reaction of expected to actual inflation appears to be rapid enough, with fifty percent of the total effect taking place in less than one and a half years.

(5) No evidence has been found of significant aggregation bias and measurement error in the expectations series. With respect to the former, however, the test performed is conditional on a simplifying assumption which has not been separately tested.

(6) Tests on the stability of the (parameter estimates of the) model of inflation expectations have been performed, comparing the estimates over the whole sample period with those from the sample with the last eight observations deleted. While a "Chow-test" on the equality of the two sets of estimates has not rejected the stability hypothesis, a prediction (chi-square) test has given the opposite result. This result might, however, depend on a possible change in seasonality over the more recent years. Furthermore, it has been recently shown that the results of the first test are more reliable than those of the second.

As seen in the last chapter, inflation expectations *have not* been "rational" over the entire sample period, but they have not been clearly sub-optimal over the period preceding the first oil crisis. The model which has been estimated here is not *per se* in contrast with the rationality assumption. As a matter of fact the fitted values of the regressions reported in Table 6.4 *do not* reject this assumption over the same period over which the same result is obtained with the actual survey-based inflation expectations. At the same time the estimated model is in the same tradition of other proposed hypotheses of formation of inflation expectations, for which it accounts in a general mixed form (with also uncertainty and cyclical components appearing to be contributing factors). It is not easy to account in a reasonable way for the effect of other variables, and the rationality hypothesis seems indeed to be too restrictive if assumed to hold under all circumstances. On the whole, the model estimated here seems to summarize effectively the main components of the formation process. However, on the basis of the results of this chapter, one might gain both in terms of stability of the estimates and improved understanding of this process, by allowing for different adjustment coefficients in different ranges (and absolute size, as well as signs) of past anticipation errors and deviations of actual inflation from its trend. In particular, the evidence presented in Chapter 3 seems to indicate that when inflation is substantially higher than the recent average, expectations tend to be more moderate with return-to-normality considerations probably playing a larger role than on other occasions.

CHAPTER 7

CONCLUSIONS

A few years ago, in a survey on inflation Laidler and Parkin[1] wrote:

> In view of the central importance of inflation expectations, it is not surprising that this topic has generated a large literature in its own right. Three questions arise in connection with expectations. First, what precisely is the expected rate of inflation, is this a unique variable or may several measures of it coexist? And if they do, what consequences flow from differences between expectations? Secondly, how may expectations be measured (or proxied)? Third, how are expectations formed?

This study has dealt with these three questions, taking into account previous work and examining in depth the evidence provided by the surveys conducted in Italy twice a year by the economic magazine *Mondo Economico*. It has been shown that these surveys have many interesting features. They date back to 1952 and are not qualitative surveys; the interviewee can provide an appropriate answer, not being asked for an exact estimate but having only to choose from among a number of pre-selected intervals that which he expects will contain the rate of price change for the next semester. The respondents are "qualified" and "informed" businessmen in production, commerce, the banking and financial world, and economic experts. The structure of the surveys – which also ask for expectations on other relevant economic variables – has been updated over the years, with revisions of the questionnaire, of the panel of participants, of the horizon and, recently, of the frequency. Continuity, however, has been preserved, never reducing the amount of information collected in the surveys and introducing appropriate changes which could effectively deal with the modifications occurring in the economic environment. A detailed analysis of the surveys has been conducted in Chapter 1.

On the basis of the individual answers it has been possible to construct, in Chapter 2, estimates of the expected rate of inflation. The problems of qualitative surveys have been briefly reviewed and it has been shown that *Mondo Economico* surveys, by placing numerical limits on a sufficient number of intervals of possible answers, do not share the same problems. It

---

[1] Laidler and Parkin (1975, p. 770).

has also been argued that the fact that the interviewees are not asked for an exact answer does not appear to be a disadvantage. Individual expectations are in fact of a probabilistic nature, and likely it is easier for the respondents to choose a possible *quantitative* interval rather than come out with a precise forecast. On the basis of alternative distributions of individual expectations, taking care also of the problems present when many answers lie in the upper open-ended interval (a serious occurrence only for the first series of surveys, between 1974 and 1976), measures of *average* expected rate of change of prices and of the *standard deviation* across the respondents have been obtained. The horizon of these expectations – as well as the frequency – is equal to a semester; both the consumer and the wholesale price indices have been considered; and measures have been constructed for the "production" group and the "other" (finance, commerce, and experts) respondents considered as a unit, as well as for the total.

It has been shown that the expectations of the "production" respondents do not differ significantly over the entire sample, both in mean and standard deviation, from those of the "other". This is an interesting finding since the two groups do not overlap and might be exposed to different information. It justifies the consideration of the whole panel of respondents as a unit. However, similarly to what has been found in other surveys on inflation expectations, the dispersion of the answers is not negligible. Furthermore, while the variance of the individual inflation expectations across the respondents has been roughly constant until 1973, it has followed in the more recent years the same pattern of the average expected rate. In this period Italy has experienced difficult economic conditions, characterized by high, variable inflation and low, also variable, real growth. It is likely that considerable uncertainty has accompanied this situation; this fact probably helps to explain why only over the more recent years a positive correlation has been observed between the average expected rate of inflation and its standard deviation across persons. Using these measures in econometric analysis, one cannot therefore ignore the heteroscedasticity and the aggregation problems which naturally arise under these conditions. One can furthermore fruitfully utilize the variance of inflation expectations across the survey respondents as a proxy of uncertainty at the individual level, a device which has been followed in many recent contributions.

In Chapters 3 and 4 the predictive accuracy of the estimates of inflation expectations obtained in Chapter 2 has been evaluated. The analysis conducted in Chapter 3 has shown that over the entire sample period expectations were biased and serial correlation was present in the anticipation errors. For the period preceding the first oil crisis (1973–74), however, these two results were not found. Overall, the expected rates are highly and positively correlated with the realizations. Expectations of consumer price changes have been generally more accurate than those of wholesale prices. Underestimation of the actual inflation rates has, however, occurred in the years following the 1973 oil crisis; this is particularly evident for expectations on wholesale prices. Even if accuracy measures such as mean absolute and mean square errors are much larger for the more recent period than for the non-inflationary years which have preceded the first oil crisis, they are substantially smaller when divided by the average actual rates of inflation which have been observed over the two sub-periods. This indicates that the more recent expectations – even if biased – were *proportionally* more accurate than those for the fifties and sixties. This result is probably due to the fact that when inflation is persistent, it is easier to extrapolate than during a period of variable but small inflation rates. Both the expectations of wholesale and consumer price changes were timely and did catch all the major changes observed in the actual rates of inflation. Interviewees were more successful in anticipating turning points in wholesale than in consumer price changes. It has also been shown that the forecasting performance of the inflation expectations of the *Mondo Economico* respondents has been at least as good as that of those of other surveys on inflation expectations for different countries. This is noteworthy since the inflation pattern, over the periods considered for these comparisons, has probably been for Italy more complex and more difficult to predict.

The expectations of the respondents to *Mondo Economico* surveys have been compared in Chapter 4 with the forecasts generated by alternative predictors of the inflation process. It has been found that inflation expectations have dominated "naive" predictors of inflation, with mixed results when compared to autoregressive predictors estimated over a cumulating sample (that is, essentially using a Kalman filter to update the model estimates) and over a moving sample of fixed size. However, the differences in the accuracy measures considered for the comparison have not been very large. In particular, this is so for the period preceding the first oil crisis, when the performance of the expected rates has been very similar to that of the alternative autoregressive predictors. Afterwards, the expected rates have had a pattern similar (but with generally smaller anticipation errors, especially in the case of consumer prices) to that of the forecasts generated by estimates of autoregressive models based only on the information accumulated until 1973, before the large shocks to the inflation process in Italy took place. In anticipating turning points, expectations have proved to be slightly less successful than the autoregressive predictors if all turning points are considered, that is those occurring both at the peaks and at the troughs of the inflation process. For both price indices, however, the expected rates performed better, or not substantially worse, than the alternative predictors in anticipating upper turns of the inflation process, and they were less successful in predicting positive changes. This might suggest that expectations depend to some extent on a "normal" rate of inflation, positive departures from which have tended to be reluctantly anticipated by the respondents to the surveys.

Chapter 5 has presented an investigation of the "rationality" of inflation expectations. Even if this hypothesis has gained considerable popularity in recent years, it appears to be a very restrictive assumption of expectations formation which has been criticized on many grounds, briefly considered in Section 5.1. It is, however, a hypothesis certainly worth verifying. It has sensible implications such as the unbiasedness of expectations, the absence of serial correlation of the anticipation errors and their orthogonality with respect to information which was available at the time expectations were formed by the participants to the surveys. These conditions have been verified, taking care also of possible aggregation problems and measurement errors caused by the particular assumption used in Chapter 2 to solve the upper open-ended interval problem. Over the entire sample period these conditions were decisively rejected. When one excluded, however, the observations for the more recent years, characterized – as observed – by many, possibly unpredictable, shocks to the inflation process, a different story resulted. Not only did expectations not show signs of bias and serial correlation in the anticipation errors, but also the orthogonality condition was impossible to reject, even if many alternative and composite information sets were considered. This was a result not expected beforehand and was somewhat surprising. The inflation expectations of the respondents to *Mondo Economico* surveys appear then to possess a considerable level of optimality over the long period of mild but variable inflationary conditions which occurred in Italy during the fifties and sixties, and the early seventies. One has to be careful, however, before strongly concluding in favor of the rationality assumption. On one hand, there is in fact a tendency for the tests on rationality conducted in Chapter 5 (and in the entire literature on survey-based inflation expectations) to favor the null hypothesis. Indeed, it has been shown that these tests are also passed, over the period preceding the first oil crisis, by some of the forecasts generated by the simple autoregressive model estimated, for the same period, in Chapter 4. On the other hand, it has been possible to show that the survey-based expectations might have been improved in their forecasting ability if they were combined with the forecasts generated by the autoregressive models estimated on the basis of the new information which becomes available at the end of each semester (either considering cumulating or moving samples). Strictly rational expectations should instead have completely exploited all the information available at the time when they were formulated, inclusive of that contained in the above forecasts. This result is, however, significantly weakened if possible information lags are taken into consideration.

Chapter 6 has been devoted to the estimation of a model of formation of inflation expectations, in particular those on wholesale prices. The estimates have been obtained using ordinary and weighted least squares (with weights equal to the inverse of the standard deviations associated to the individual expectations) to account for possible heteroscedasticity in the average expected rate of price changes measured in Chapter 2. The most successful model of formation has proved to be a mixed adaptive-regressive model, with two "error-learning" terms and a "return-to-normality" component. In this model expected inflation is also influenced by the rate of capacity utilization (better, its deviation from a normal rate, assumed to be constant) and by an uncertainty term proxied by the difference between the previous semester standard deviation of the individual expectations and a moving average of two previous standard deviations. In particular, the uncertainty component affects the adaptive coefficient (so that the higher uncertainty, the larger is the weight given to the more recent experience). Capacity utilization influences, instead, return to normality (with the "normal" inflation level equal to a moving average of past inflation rates over seven years): when there is a positive departure of inflation from its normal level, regression towards normality is slowed down if capacity is utilized above normal (and vice versa). A separate, direct effect of capacity utilization on the expected rate of inflation has, however, also been discovered, besides its influence through the channel just described. No restriction has been imposed on the total sum of the implicit representation of the expected rate of inflation as a distributed lag of past actual rates. As a matter of fact, it has been found that such a restriction is rejected by the data. As a result, an estimate of this sum lower than sixty percent has been obtained. No evidence has been found of bias coming from a possible measurement error in the series of expected inflation: this would have induced a second-order moving average in the residuals which has been rejected on the basis of a proper test. Similarly, significant aggregation bias – investigated on the basis of an untested simplifying hypothesis – has not been discovered. While on the basis of a Chow-test which has compared the estimates over the entire sample period with those for the period exclusive of the last eight observations, the hypothesis of stability has not been rejected, an asymptotically equivalent test proposed by Hendry gave the opposite result. This result might, however, partly depend on a change in the seasonal pattern of inflation expectations occurring over the more recent years. It has also been recently shown that the former testing procedure is likely to be more reliable than the latter. There is space, however, for further improvement of the estimated model, even if the results obtained so far are very encouraging. In particular, one might gain by allowing for different adjustment coefficients (for the return-to-normality and the error-learning terms) in different ranges – and absolute size, as well as signs – of the past anticipation errors and deviations of actual inflation from its trend.

In the analysis of the formation of inflation expectations one should also further investigate if other variables could still play a role besides those considered in Chapter 6 (lagged changes of money supply, wages and the exchange rate, which either did not appear to be significant, or appeared to be substituting for the other neglected factors). Anyhow, a remarkable result has been obtained when the fitted values of the model of expectations formation estimated in Section 6.3 have been subjected to exactly the same tests of rationality applied in Chapter 5 to the inflation expectations actually observed. As was the case for the actual values, also the fitted ones did not reject the rationality assumption over the period preceding the first oil crisis. The hypothesis of rational expectations, however, does not seem to be a sensible substitute for a model of formation such as the one estimated in Chapter 6, as does not a simple extrapolative or adaptive model, or even an unrestricted distributed lag of past inflation rates. The main implication of the present study is indeed that one cannot assume *a priori* a model of formation, substitute it to the expectation variable (assumed to be "unobservable") in given relations between other economic variables and expected inflation, and estimate these relations without separate information on the mechanism which actually generates the inflation expectations. In fact, distributed lags might confuse expectation and adjustment components and without prior knowledge of their length, lags do not help in identifying these relations. Rational expectations, furthermore, constitute too restrictive an hypothesis, the implications of which have been shown to be rejected, at least when large shocks affect the inflation process. Also, as Sims has observed, "rational expectations is more deeply subversive of identification than has yet been recognized".[2] Instead of resorting to the estimation of reduced forms as it has been argued by Sims, it appears that one can make profitable use of survey-based expectations.

It is therefore the conclusion of this study that surveys can clearly help in obtaining measures of expectations, in this instance of expected inflation rates, which can be used to model both the formation mechanisms and the effects expectations have on other economic magnitudes. One has to exercise some care in considering appropriate surveys and obtaining sensible estimates from the individual answers. The surveys considered in the present effort appear to be adequately designed and contain relevant information.

[2] Sims (1980, p. 7).

There is space for many other direct inquiries on expectations which might only produce more, very useful and needed information on these once considered to be unobservable variables.

Obviously the decisive verdict on the validity of the series of expected inflation in approximating the expected rates on which economic agents actually base their decisions can only come from studies which fruitfully make use of these series. Future research on the effects of expected inflation on variables such as wages, inventory, and production decisions, consumption demand, demand for financial assets, etc., is therefore the next objective to be pursued on the basis of the estimates of expected rates of price changes constructed and utilized in the present study. Preliminary successful attempts on the basis of the estimates contained in a previous paper[3] represent an encouraging first step in this direction, one that only demands that it be carried on.

[3] Visco (1976). See, for example, the study on a measure for the short-term real rate of interest by Carosio and Visco (1977), which has been utilized by Conti and Filosa (1980) and, with revisions, by Conti and Visco (1982), in the analysis of the determinants of production and inventory decisions by industrial enterprises. Measures of expected inflation contained in Visco (1976), and substantially equal to the *PUM* estimates of Chapter 2, have been also used by Padoa Schioppa (1979), in a study on the variability of inflation; by Cotula and Masera (1980), in a study on private savings, public deficits and the inflation tax; by Cesarano (1980), in an investigation on the demand of long-term bonds; by Spinelli (1980), in a test of the wage-push hypothesis for Italy; and by Tullio (1981), in a small model of the Italian economy.

BIBLIOGRAPHY

Abel, A.B. and F.S. Mishkin, 1983, An integrated view of tests of rationality, market efficiency and the short-run neutrality of monetary policy, Journal of Monetary Economics, Jan.

Adams, F.G., 1964, Consumer attitudes, buying plans and purchases of durable goods, Review of Economics and Statistics, Nov.

Adams, F.G. and V.G. Duggal, 1974, Anticipations variables in an econometric model: Performance of the anticipations version of Wharton Mark III, International Economic Review, June.

Adams, F.G. and E.W. Green, 1965, Explaining and predicting consumer attitudes, International Economic Review, Sept.

Adams, F.G. and L.R. Klein, 1972, Anticipations variables in macro-econometric models, in: B. Strumpel, J.N. Morgan and E. Zahn, eds., Human Behavior in Economic Affairs (Jossey-Bass, San Francisco, CA).

Akaike, H., 1969, Fitting autoregressive models for prediction, Annals of the Institute of Statistical Mathematics.

Akaike, H., 1976, Canonical correlation analysis of time series and the use of an information criterion, in: R.K. Mehra and D.G. Lainiotis, eds., System Identification, Advances and Case Studies (Academic Press, New York).

Aiginger, K., 1981, Empirical evidence on the rational expectations hypothesis using reported expectations, Empirica, No. 1.

Amemiya, T., 1980, Selection of regressors, International Economic Review, June.

Amihud, Y., 1981, Price level uncertainty, indexation and employment, Southern Economic Journal, Jan.

Anderson, B.D.O. and J.B. Moore, 1979, Optimal Filtering (Prentice-Hall, Engelwood Cliffs, NJ).

Anderson, O., Jr., 1952, The business test of the IFO Institute for Economic Research, Munich, and its theoretical model, Revue de l'Institut International de Statistique, No. 1.

Anderson, O., Jr., R.K. Bauer and E. Fels, 1954, On the accuracy of short-term entrepreneurial expectations, in: Proceedings of the Business and Economic Statistics Section (American Statistical Association, Washington, DC).

Ando, A.K., 1981a, On a theoretical and empirical basis of macroeconometric models, in: J. Kmenta and J.B. Ramsey, eds., Large-Scale Macroeconometric Models: Theory and Practice (North-Holland, Amsterdam).

Ando, A.K., 1981b, Equilibrium business cycle models: An appraisal, in: Festschrift in Honor of Lawrence R. Klein, forthcoming.

Arrow, K.J. and M. Nerlove, 1958, A note on expectations and stability, Econometrica, April.

Auernheimer, L., 1979, Adaptive-regressive expectations and the price level, Journal of Monetary Economics, Jan.

Barnea, A., A. Dotan and J. Lakonishok, 1979, The effect of price level uncertainty on the determination of nominal interest rates: Some empirical evidence, Southern Economic Journal, Oct.

Barro, R.J., 1977, Unanticipated monetary growth and unemployment in the United States, American Economic Review, March.

Barro, R.J., 1978, Unanticipated money, output, and the price level in the United States, Journal of Political Economy, Aug.

Batchelor, R.A., 1981, Aggregate expectations under the stable laws, Journal of Econometrics, June.

Batchelor, R.A., 1982, Expectations, output and inflation: The European experience, European Economic Review, Jan.

Batchelor, R.A. and T.D. Sheriff, 1980, Unemployment and unanticipated inflation in postwar Britain, Economica, May.

Bierwag, G.O. and M.A. Grove, 1966, Aggregate Koyck functions, Econometrica, Oct.

Bodo, G., 1981, Misura e analisi della capacità produttiva, Bollettino della Banca d'Italia, Jan.–Dec.

Bomberger, W.A. and W.J. Frazer, 1981, Interest rates, uncertainty and the Livingston data, Journal of Finance, June.

Bossons, J. and F. Modigliani, 1960, The source of regressiveness in businessmen's short-run expectations, in: Universities – National Bureau Committee for Economic Research, ed., The Quality and Economic Significance of Anticipations Data (Princeton University Press, Princeton, NJ).

Box, G.E.P. and G.M. Jenkins, 1970, Time Series Analysis: Forecasting and Control (Holden-Day, San Francisco, CA).

Box, G.E.P. and D.A. Pierce, 1970, Distribution of residual autocorrelation in autoregressive-integrated moving average time series models, Journal of the American Statistical Association, Dec.

Breiman, L., 1969, Probability and Stochastic Processes: With a View toward Applications (Houghton-Mifflin, Boston, MA).

Breusch, T.S., 1978, Testing for autocorrelation in dynamic linear models, Australian Economic Papers, Dec.

Breusch, T.S. and A.R. Pagan, 1980, The Lagrange multiplier test and its applications to model specification in econometrics, Review of Economic Studies, Jan.

Brinner, R.E., 1977, The death of the Phillips curve reconsidered, Quarterly Journal of Economics, Aug.

Brown, B.W. and S. Maital, 1981, What do economists know? An empirical study of experts' expectations, Econometrica, March.

Brown, R.L., J. Durbin and J.M. Evans, 1975, Techniques for testing the constancy of regression relationships over time, Journal of Royal Statistical Society B, No. 2.

Buiter, W.H., 1979, Some problems of estimation and hypothesis testing in rational expectations models: A simple example, Unpublished paper, Nov.

Buiter, W.H., 1981, The role of economic policy after the new classical macroeconomics, in: D. Currie, R. Nobay and D.A. Peel, eds., Macroeconomic Analysis: Essays in Macroeconomics and Econometrics (Croom Helm, London).

Cagan, P., 1956, The monetary dynamics of hyperinflation, in: M. Friedman, ed., Studies in the Quantity Theory of Money (Chicago University Press, Chicago, IL).

Cargill, T.F., 1976, Anticipated price changes and nominal interest rates in the 1950's, Review of Economics and Statistics, Aug.

Cargill, T.F., 1977, Direct evidence of the Darby hypothesis for the United States, Economic Inquiry, Jan.

Carlson, J.A., 1967, Forecasting errors and business cycles, American Economic Review, June.

Carlson, J.A., 1975, Are price expectations normally distributed?, Journal of the American Statistical Association, Dec.

Carlson, J.A., 1977a, A study of price forecasts, Annals of Economic and Social Measurement, No. 1.

Carlson, J.A., 1977b, Short-term interest rates as predictors of inflation: Comment, American Economic Review, June.

Carlson, J.A., 1979, Expected inflation and interest rates, Economic Inquiry, Oct.

Carlson, J.A., 1980, Systematic errors in inflation forecasts, in: W.H. Striegel, ed., Business Cycle Analysis (CIRET – Gower, Farnborough).

Carlson, J.A. and M. Parkin, 1975, Inflation expectations, Economica, May.

Carlson, J.A. and H.E. Ryder, 1973, Quantitative expectations from qualitative surveys: A maximum likelihood approach, Unpublished paper, Oct.

Carlucci, F., 1982, La costruzione di una serie mensile di aspettative di inflazione, Note Economiche, No. 2.

Carosio, G. and I. Visco, 1977, Nota sulla costruzione di un tasso d'interesse reale, Bollettino della Banca d'Italia, Oct.–Dec.

Cesarano, F., 1980, La domanda di titoli a lungo termine da parte del pubblico, Note Economiche, No. 4.

Chan-Lee, J.H., 1980, A review of recent work in the area of inflationary expectations, Weltwirtschaftliches Archiv, No. 1.

Chow, G.C., 1960, Tests of equality between sets of coefficients in two linear regressions, Econometrica, July.

Chow, G.C., 1981, Econometric Analysis by Control Methods (Wiley, New York).

Cohen, M., 1960, The national industrial conference board survey of capital appropriations, in: Universities – National Bureau Committee for Economic Research, ed., The Quality and Significance of Anticipations Data (Princeton University Press, Princeton, NJ).

Conti, V., 1975, Produzione e domanda in un modello di disequilibrio, Contributi alla Ricerca Economica della Banca d'Italia, No. 5. English translation: 1977, Production and demand in a disequilibrium model, Economic Papers of the Bank of Italy, No. 1.

Conti, V. and R. Filosa, 1980, Offerta interna, importazioni di manufatti e scorte in un modello di disequilibrio, Giornale degli Economisti e Annali di Economia, Jan.–Feb.

Conti, V. and I. Visco, 1978, Che cosa dicono gli indici sintetici, Mondo Economico, 9 Sept.

Conti, V. and I. Visco, 1982, The determinants of 'normal' inventories of finished goods in the Italian manufacturing sector, Unpublished paper presented to the Second International Symposium on Inventories, Budapest, Aug.

Cotula, F. and R. Masera, 1980, Private savings, public deficits and the inflation tax, Review of Economic Conditions in Italy, Oct.

Cukierman, A., 1977, A test of expectations processes using information from the capital markets: The Israeli case, International Economic Review, Oct.

Cukierman, A. and P. Wachtel, 1979, Differential inflationary expectations and the variability of the rate of inflation: Theory and evidence, American Economic Review, Sept.

Cukierman, A. and P. Wachtel, 1982, Inflationary expectations: Reply and further thoughts on inflation uncertainty, American Economic Review, June.

Curtin, R.T., 1982, Determinants of price expectations: Evidence from a panel study, in: H. Laumer and M. Ziegler, eds., International Research on Business Cycle Surveys (CIRET – Gower, Aldershot).

Danes, M., 1975, The measurement and explanation of inflationary expectations in Australia, Australian Economic Papers, June.

Darby, M.R., 1976, Rational expectations under conditions of costly information, Journal of Finance, June.

De Groot, M.H., 1970, Optimal Statistical Decisions (McGraw-Hill, New York).

De Leeuw, F., 1965, A model of financial behavior, 1965, in: J. Duesenberry, G. Fromm, L.R. Klein and E. Kuh, eds., Brookings Quarterly Econometric Model of the United States Economy (Rand-McNally, Chicago, IL).

De Leeuw, F. and M.J. McKelvey, 1981, Price expectations of business firms, Brookings Papers on Economic Activity, No. 1.

De Menil, G., 1974, The rationality of popular price expectations, Unpublished paper, Dec. (Princeton University, Princeton, NJ).

De Menil, G. and S.S. Bhalla, 1975, Direct measurement of popular price expectations, American Economic Review, March.

De Milner, L.E., 1975, Nonlinearities in the formation and influence of price expectations, Unpublished paper presented to the Third World Congress of the Econometric Society, Toronto, Aug.

Defris, L.V. and R.A. Williams, 1979a, Quantitative versus qualitative measures of price expectations, Economics Letters, No. 2.

Defris, L.V. and R.A. Williams, 1979b, The formation of consumer inflation expectations in Australia, Economic Record, June.

Dhrymes, P.J., 1971, Distributed lags: Problems of estimation and formation (Holden-Day, San Francisco, CA).

Di Fenizio, F., 1961, Le Leggi dell'Economia (ISCO, Roma).

Diller, S., 1969, Expectations in the term structure of interest rates, in: J. Mincer, ed., Economic Forecasts and Expectations (N.B.E.R. – Columbia University Press, New York).

Dramais, A. and E. Waelbroeck, 1979, A probabilistic approach to the quantification of business survey data, Unpublished paper presented to the European Meetings of the Econometric Society, Athens, Sept.

Duesenberry, J., 1958, Business Cycles and Economic Growth (McGraw-Hill, New York).

Eisner, R., 1956, Determinants of Capital Expenditures: An Interview Study, Studies in Business Expectations and Planning, No. 2 (Bureau of Economic and Business Research – University of Illinois, Urbana, IL).

Eisner, R., 1958, Expectations, plans, and capital expenditures: A synthesis of ex post and ex ante data, in: M.J. Bowman, ed., Expectations, Uncertainty and Business Behavior (Social Science Research Council, New York).

Eisner, R., 1965, Realization of investment anticipations, in: J. Duesenberry, G. Fromm, L.R. Klein and E. Kuh, eds., Brookings Quarterly Econometric Model of the United States Economy (Rand-McNally, Chicago, IL).

Enthoven, A.C. and K.J. Arrow, 1956, A theorem on expectations and stability of equilibrium, Econometrica, April.

Evans, M.K. and E.W. Green, 1966, The relative efficacy of investment anticipations, Journal of the American Statistical Association, March.

Ezekiel, M., 1938, The Cobweb theorem, Quarterly Journal of Economics, Feb.

Fackler, J. and B. Stanhouse, 1977, Rationality of the Michigan price expectations data, Journal of Money, Credit and Banking, Nov.

Fama, E.F., 1970, Efficient capital markets: A review of theory and empirical work, Journal of Finance, May.

Fama, E.F., 1975, Short-term interest rates as predictors of inflation, American Economic Review, June.

Feige, E.L. and D.K. Pearce, 1976, Economically rational expectations: Are innovations in the rate of inflation independent of innovations in measures of monetary and fiscal policy?, Journal of Political Economy, June.

Ferber, R., 1953, The Railroad Shippers' Forecasts, Studies in Business Expectations and Planning, No. 1 (Bureau of Economic and Business Research – University of Illinois, Urbana, IL).

Ferber, R., 1958, The accuracy and structure of industry expectations in relation to those of individual firms, Journal of the American Statistical Association, June.

Ferber, R., 1960, The Railroad Shippers' forecasts and the Illinois employers' labor force anticipations, in: Universities – National Bureau Committee for Economic Research, ed., The Quality and Economic Significance of Anticipations Data (Princeton University Press, Princeton, NJ).

Fields, T.W. and N.R. Noble, 1981, Testing the Friedman–Phelps natural rate hypothesis using survey data, Journal of Monetary Economics, March.

Figlewsky, S., 1983, Optimal price forecasting using survey data, Review of Economics and Statistics, Feb.

Figlewsky, S. and P. Wachtel, 1981, The formation of inflation expectations, Review of Economics and Statistics, Feb.

Fishe, R.P.H. and K. Lahiri, On the estimation of inflationary expectations from qualitative responses, Journal of Econometrics, May.

Fischer, S. and J. Huizinga, 1982, Inflation, unemployment, and public opinion polls, Journal of Money, Credit and Banking, Feb.

Fisher, I., 1930, The Theory of Interest (Macmillan, New York).

Foss, M.F. and V. Natrella, 1960, The structure and realization of business investment anticipations, in: Universities – National Bureau Committee for Economic Research, ed., The Quality and Economic Significance of Anticipations Data (Princeton University Press, Princeton, NJ).

Foster, J., 1977, Tests of the simple Fisher hypothesis utilizing observed inflationary expectations: Some further evidence, Scottish Journal of Economics, Nov.

Foster, J., 1979, Interest rates and inflation expectations: The British experience, Oxford Bulletin of Economics and Statistics, May.

Foster, J. and M. Gregory, 1977, Inflation expectations: The use of qualitative survey data, Applied Economics, Dec.

Frenkel, J.A., 1975, Inflation and the formation of expectations, Journal of Monetary Economics, Oct.

Friedman, B.M., 1979a, Interest rate expectations vs. forward rates: Evidence from an expectations survey, Journal of Finance, Sept.

Friedman, B.M., 1979b, Optimal expectations and the extreme information assumption of rational expectations macro models, Journal of Monetary Economics, Jan.

Friedman, B.M., 1980, Survey evidence on the 'rationality' of interest rate expectations, Journal of Monetary Economics, Oct.

Friend, I., 1958, Critical evaluation of surveys of expectations, plans and investment behavior, in: M.J. Bowman, ed., Expectations, Uncertainty and Business Behavior (Social Science Research Council, New York).

Friend, I. and F.G. Adams, 1970, The predictive ability of consumer attitudes, stock prices and nonattitudinal variables, Journal of the American Statistical Association, June.

Friend, I. and J. Bronfenbrenner, 1955, Plant and equipment programs and their realization, in: Short-Term Economic Forecasting, Studies in Income and Wealth, Vol. 17 (N.B.E.R. – Princeton University Press, Princeton, NJ).

Friend, I. and W.C. Thomas, 1970, A reevaluation of the predictive ability of plant and employment anticipations, Journal of the American Statistical Association, June.

Gibson, W., 1972, Interest rates and inflationary expectations: New evidence, American Economic Review, Dec.

Godfrey, L.G., 1978a, Testing against general autoregressive and moving average models when the regressors include lagged dependent variables, Econometrica, Nov.

Godfrey, L.G., 1978b, Testing for higher order serial correlation in regression equations when the regressions include lagged dependent variables, Econometrica, Nov.

Goodwin, R.M., 1947, Dynamical coupling with especial reference to markets having production lags, Econometrica, July.

Gordon, R.J., 1971, Inflation in recession and recovery, Brookings Papers on Economic Activity, No. 1.

Gottman, J.M., 1981, Time-Series Analysis (Cambridge University Press, Cambridge).

Granger, C.W.J. and P. Newbold, 1973, Some comments on the evaluation of economic forecasts, Applied Economics, March.

Granger, C.W.J. and P. Newbold, 1977, Applied Economic Forecasting (Academic Press, New York).

Grossman, S.J. and J.E. Stiglitz, 1980, On the impossibility of informationally efficient markets, American Economic Review, June.

Grunberg, E. and F. Modigliani, 1954, The predictability of social events, Journal of Political Economy, Dec.

Hafer, R.W. and D.H. Resler, 1980, The 'rationality' of survey-based inflation forecasts, Review of the Federal Reserve Bank of St. Louis, Nov.

Hafer, R.W. and D.H. Resler, 1982, On the rationality of inflation forecasts: A new look at the Livingston data, Southern Economic Journal, April.

Hahn, F.H., 1952, Expectations and equilibrium, Economic Journal, Dec.

Hahn, F.H., 1980, Monetarism and economic theory, Economica, Feb.

Hall, V.B., 1980, Excess demand and expectations influences on price changes in Australian manufacturing industry, Economic Record, March.

Hall, V.B. and M.L. King, 1976, Inflationary expectations in New Zealand: A preliminary study, New Zealand Economic Papers.

Hansen, L.P. and T.J. Sargent, 1980, Formulating and estimating dynamic linear rational expectations models, Journal of Economic Dynamics and Control, Feb.

Hart, A.G., 1960, Quantitative evidence from the interwar period of the course of business expectations: A reevaluation of the Railroad Shipper's forecasts, in: Universities – National Bureau Committee for Economic Research, ed., The Quality and Economic Significance of Anticipations Data (Princeton University Press, Princeton, NJ).

Hart, B.I., 1942, Significance levels for the ratio of the mean square difference to the variance, Annals of Mathematical Statistics, Dec.

Harvey, A.C., 1981, The Econometric Analysis of Time Series (Philip Allan, Oxford).

Hastay, M., 1954, The Dun and Bradstreet surveys of businessmen expectations, in: Proceedings of the Business and Economic Statistics Section (American Statistical Association,

Washington, DC).

Hastay, M., 1960, The formation of business expectations about operating variables, in: Universities – National Bureau Economic Committee for Economic Research, ed., The Quality and Economic Significance of Anticipations Data (Princeton University Press, Princeton, NJ).

Hatanaka, M., 1975a, The underestimation of variation in the forecast series: A note, International Economic Review, Feb.

Hatanaka, M., 1975b, On the global identification of the dynamic simultaneous equation model with stationary disturbances, International Economic Review, Oct.

Hendry, D.F., 1980, Predictive failure and econometric modelling in macro-economics: The transactions demand for money, in: P. Ormerod, ed., Economic Modelling (Heinemann, London).

Hicks, J.R., 1939, Value and Capital (Oxford University Press, London).

Hirsch, A.A. and M.C. Lovell, 1969, Sales Anticipations and Inventory Behavior (Wiley, New York).

Hoffman, D.L. and P. Schmidt, 1981, Testing the restrictions implied by the rational expectations hypothesis, Journal of Econometrics, Feb.

Holden, K. and D.A. Peel, 1977, An empirical investigation of inflationary expectations, Oxford Bulletin of Economics and Statistics, Nov.

Holden, K. and D.A. Peel, 1978, Price expectations: Workers vs. capitalists, Applied Economics, Sept.

Holmes, A.B. and M.L. Kwast, 1979, Interest rates and inflationary expectations: Tests for structural change 1952–1976, Journal of Finance, June.

Horne, J., 1981, Rational expectations and the Defris–Williams inflationary expectations series, Economic Record, Sept.

Hudson, J., 1978, Expectations of wage inflation and their formation, Applied Economics, Sept.

Hymans, S.H., 1970, Consumer durable spending: Explanation and prediction, Brookings Papers on Economic Activity, No. 2.

Jacobs, D.P. and R.A. Jones, 1980, Price expectations in the United States: 1947–75, American Economic Review, June.

Jonson, P.D. and D.M. Mahoney, 1973, Price expectations in Australia, Economic Record, March.

Jorgenson, D. and J.A. Stephenson, 1969, Anticipations and investment behavior in U.S. manufacturing, 1947–1960, Journal of the American Statistical Association, March.

Judge, G.G., W.E. Griffiths, R.C. Hill and T.C. Lee, 1980, The Theory and Practice of Econometrics (Wiley, New York).

Juster, F.T., 1959, Consumer expectations, plans, and purchases: A progress report, Occasional Paper No. 70 (N.B.E.R., New York).

Juster, F.T., 1960, The predictive value of consumer union spending intentions data, in: Universities – National Bureau Economic Committee for Economic Research, ed., The Quality and Economic Significance of Anticipations Data (Princeton University Press, Princeton, NJ).

Juster, F.T., 1969, Consumer anticipations and models of durable goods demand: the time-series cross-section paradox re-examined, in: J. Mincer, ed., Economic Forecasts and Expectations (N.B.E.R. – Columbia University Press, New York).

Juster, F.T., 1974, Savings behavior, uncertainty and price expectations, in: The Economic Outlook for 1974 (University of Michigan, Ann Arbor, MI).

Juster, F.T. and R. Comment, 1978, A note on the measurement of price expectations, Unpublished paper.

Juster, F.T. and J.B. Taylor, 1979, Personal savings in the postwar world: Implications for the theory of economic behavior, American Economic Review, May.

Juster, F.T. and P. Wachtel, 1972a, Uncertainty, expectations and durable goods demand models, in: B. Strumpel, J.N. Morgan and E. Zahn, eds., Human Behavior in Economic Affairs (Jossey-Bass, San Francisco, CA).

Juster, F.T. and P. Wachtel, 1972b, Inflation and the consumer, Brookings Papers on Economic Activity, No. 1.

Juster, F.T. and P. Wachtel, 1972c, A note on inflation and the savings rate, Brookings Papers on Economic Activity, No. 3.

Kalman, R.E., 1960, A new approach to linear filtering and prediction problems, Journal of Basic Engineering, Transactions of the ASME D, No. 1.

Kane, E.J., 1970, The term structure of interest rates: An attempt to reconcile teaching with practice, Journal of Finance, May.

Kane, E.J. and B.G. Malkiel, 1976, Autoregressive and non-autoregressive elements in cross-section forecasts of inflation, Econometrica, Jan.

Katona, G., 1951, Psychological Analysis of Economic Behavior (McGraw-Hill, New York).

Katona, G., 1958, Business expectations in the framework of psychological economics (towards a theory of expectations), in: M.J. Bowman, ed., Expectations, Uncertainty and Business Behavior (Social Science Research Council, New York).

Katona, G., 1959, On the predictive value of consumer intentions and attitudes: A comment, Review of Economics and Statistics, Aug.

Katona, G., 1960, Changes in consumer expectations and their origin, in: Universities – National Bureau Committee for Economic Research, ed., The Quality and Economic Significance of Anticipations Data (Princeton University Press, Princeton, NJ).

Katona, G., 1972, Theory of expectations, in: D. Strumpel, J.N. Morgan and E. Zahn, eds., Human Behavior in Economic Affairs (Jossey-Bass, San Francisco, CA).

Katona, G. and E. Mueller, 1953, Consumer Expectations (Survey Research Center, Ann Arbor, MI).

Keen, H., Jr., 1981, Who forecasts best? Some evidence for the Livingston survey, Business Economics, Sept.

Kennedy, M. and K. Lynch, 1979, The modelling of inflation expectations, Bank of Canada unpublished paper, Aug.

Keynes, J.M., 1923, A Tract of Monetary Reform (Macmillan, London).

Keynes, J.M., 1936, The General Theory of Employment, Interest and Money (Macmillan, London).

Keynes, J.M., 1937, The general theory of employment, Quarterly Journal of Economics, Feb.

Kiviet, J.F., 1981, On the rigour of some specification tests for modelling dynamic relationships, Unpublished paper, May.

Klein, L.R., 1954, Applications of survey methods and data to the analysis of economic fluctuations, in: L.R. Klein, ed., Contributions of Survey Methods to Economic Fluctuations (Columbia University Press, New York).

Klein, L.R., 1955, Statistical testing of business cycle theory: The econometric method, in: E. Lundberg, ed., The Business Cycle in the Postwar World (Macmillan, London).

Klein, L.R., 1971, An Essay in the Theory of Economic Prediction (Markham, Chicago, IL).

Klein, L.R., 1972, The treatment of expectations in econometrics, in: C.F. Carter and J.L. Ford, eds., Uncertainty and Expectations in Economics (Basil Blackwell, Oxford).

Klein, L.R. and J.R. Lansing, 1955, Decisions to purchase consumer durable goods, Journal of Marketing, Oct.

Knight, F.H., 1921, Risk Uncertainty and Profit (Houghton-Mifflin, New York).

Knöbl, A., 1974, Price expectations and actual price behavior in Germany, IMF Staff Papers, March.

Koenig, H., M. Nerlove and G. Oudiz, 1981, On the formation of price expectations: An analysis of business test data by log-linear probability models, European Economic Review, May.

Lahiri, K., 1976, Inflationary expectations: Their formation and interest rates effects, American Economic Review, March.

Lahiri, K., 1977, A joint study of expectations formation and the shifting Phillips curve, Journal of Monetary Economics, July

Lahiri, K., 1980, Rational expectations and the short-run Phillips curve: Reply and further results, Journal of Macroeconomics, Spring.

Lahiri, K., 1981, The Econometrics of Inflationary Expectations (North-Holland, Amsterdam).

Lahiri, K. and J.S. Lee, 1979a, Rational expectations and the short-run Phillips curves, Journal of Macroeconomics, Spring.

Lahiri, K. and J.S. Lee, 1979b, Tests of rational expectations and Fisher effect, Southern Economic Journal, Oct.

Lahiri, K. and J.S. Lee, 1981a, On the constancy of real interest rates and the Mundell effect, Journal of Banking and Finance, Dec.

Lahiri, K. and J.S. Lee, 1981b, Inflationary expectations and the wage–price dynamics: An econometric analysis, in: E.G. Charatsis, ed., Proceedings of the Econometric Society European Meeting, 1979 (North-Holland, Amsterdam).

Lahiri, K. and Y. Lee, 1981, An empirical study on the econometric implications of the rational expectations hypothesis, Empirical Economics, No. 6.

Lakonishok, J., 1980, Stock market return expectations: Some general properties, Journal of Finance, Sept.

Laidler, D.E.W. and M. Parkin, 1975, Inflation: A survey, Economic Journal, Dec.

Lansing, J.B. and S.B. Whitney, 1955, Consumer anticipations: Their use in forecasting consumer behavior, in: Short-Term Economic Forecasting, Studies in Income and Wealth, Vol. 17 (N.B.E.R. – Princeton University Press, Princeton, NJ).

Leonard, J.S., 1982, Wage expectations in the labor market: Survey evidence on rationality, Review of Economics and Statistics, Feb.

Levi, M.D. and J.H. Makin, 1979, Fisher, Friedman, Phillips and the measured impact of inflation on interest, Journal of Finance, March.

Levi, M.D. and J.H. Makin, 1980, Inflation uncertainty and the Phillips curve: Some empirical evidence, American Economic Review, Dec.

Levi, M.D. and J.H. Makin, 1981, Fisher, Phillips, Friedman and the measured impact of inflation on interest: A reply, Journal of Finance, Sept.

Levine, R.A., 1960, Capital expenditures forecasts by individual firms, in: Universities – National Bureau Committee for Economic Research, ed., The Quality and Economic Significance of Anticipation Data (Princeton University Press, Princeton, NJ).

Lovell, M.C., 1967, Sales anticipations, planned inventory investment, and realizations, in: R. Ferber, ed., Determinants of Investment Behavior (Columbia University Press, New York).

Lucas, R.E., Jr., 1972, Expectations and the neutrality of money, Journal of Economic Theory, April.

Lucas, R.E., Jr., 1973, Some international evidence on output – inflation tradeoffs, American Economic Review, June.

Lucas, R.E., Jr., 1975, An equilibrium model of the business cycle, Journal of Political Economy, Dec.

Lucas, R.E., Jr., 1976, Econometric policy evaluation: A critique, in: K. Brunner and A.H. Meltzer, eds., The Phillips Curve and Labor Markets, Carnegie-Rochester Series on Public Policy, No. 1 (North-Holland, Amsterdam).

Lucas, R.E., Jr. and T. J. Sargent, 1978, After Keynesian macroeconomics, in: After the Phillips Curve, Federal Reserve Bank of Boston Conference Series, No. 19.

Maital, S., 1979, Inflation expectations in the monetarist box, American Economic Review, June.

Malkiel, B.G., 1966, The Term Structure of Interest Rates: Expectations and Behavior Patterns (Princeton University Press, Princeton, NJ).

McCallum, B.T., 1979, Topics concerning the formation, estimation, and use of macroeconometric models with rational expectations, in: Proceedings of the Business and Economic Statistics Section (American Statistical Association, Washington, DC).

McDonald, J. and A. Woodfield, 1980, A comparison of the Carlson–Parkin inflation expectations: Measures and optimal time series forecasts of inflation, New Zealand Economic Papers.

McGuire, T.W., 1976a, Price change expectations and the Phillips curve, in: K. Brunner and A.H. Meltzer, eds., The Econometrics of Price and Wage Controls, Carnegie-Rochester Series on Public Policy, No. 2 (North-Holland, Amsterdam).

McGuire, T.W., 1976b, On estimating the effects of controls, in: K. Brunner and A.H. Meltzer, eds., The Econometrics of Price and Wage Controls, Carnegie-Rochester Series on Public Policy, No. 2 (North-Holland, Amsterdam).

Meiselman, D., 1962, The Term Structure of Interest Rates (Prentice Hall, Englewood Cliffs, NJ).

Metzler, L.A., 1941, The nature and stability of inventory cycles, Review of Economics and Statistics, Aug.

Mills, T.C., 1981, Modelling the formation of Australian inflation expectations, Australian Economic Papers, June.

Mincer, J., 1969, Models of adaptive forecasting, in: J. Mincer, ed., Economic Forecasts and Expectations (N.B.E.R. – Columbia University Press, New York).

Mincer, J. and V. Zarnovitz, 1969, The evaluation of economic forecasts, in: J. Mincer, ed., Economic Forecasts and Expectations (N.B.E.R. – Columbia University Press, New York).

Mitchell, D.W., 1981, Determinants of inflation uncertainty, Eastern Economic Journal, April.

Mitchell, D.W. and H.E. Taylor, 1982, Inflationary expectations: A comment, American Economic Review, June.

Modigliani, F. and K.J. Cohen, 1958, The significance and uses of ex ante data, in: M.J. Bowman, ed., Expectations, Uncertainty and Business Behavior (Social Science Research Council, New York).

Modigliani, F. and K.J. Cohen, 1961, The Role of Anticipations and Plans in Economic Behavior and their Use in Economic Analysis and Forecasting (Bureau of Economic and Business Research, University of Illinois, Urbana, IL).

Modigliani, F. and O.H. Sauerlender, 1955, Economic expectations and plans of firms in relation to short-term forecasting, in: Short-Term Economic Forecasting, Studies in Income and Wealth, Vol. 17 (N.B.E.R. – Princeton University Press, Princeton, NJ).

Modigliani, F. and R.J. Shiller, 1973, Inflation, rational expectations and the term structure of interest rates, Economica, Feb.

Modigliani, F. and R. Sutch 1967, Debt management and the term structure of interest rates: An empirical analysis of recent experience, Journal of Political Economy, Aug.

Modigliani, F. and H.M. Weingartner, 1958, Forecasting uses of anticipatory data on investment and sales, Quarterly Journal of Economics, Feb.

Mueller, E., 1957, The effects of consumer attitudes on purchases, American Economic Review, Dec.

Mueller, E., 1959, Consumer reactions to inflation, Quarterly Journal of Economics, May.

Mueller, E., 1960, Consumer attitudes: Their influence and forecasting value, in: Universities – National Bureau Committee for Economic Research, ed., The Quality and Economic Significance of Anticipations Data (Princeton University Press, Princeton, NJ).

Mullineaux, D.J., 1977, Inflation expectations in the U.S.: A brief anatomy, Business Review of the Federal Reserve Bank of Philadelphia, July/Aug.

Mullineaux, D.J., 1978, On testing for rationality: Another look at the Livingston price expectations data, Journal of Political Economy, April.

Mullineaux, D.J., 1980a, Inflation expectations and money growth in the United States, American Economic Review, March.

Mullineaux, D.J., 1980b, Unemployment industrial production, and inflation uncertainty in the United States, Review of Economics and Statistics, May.

Mussa, M. 1975, Adaptive and regressive expectations in a rational model of the inflationary process, Journal of Monetary Economics, Oct.

Muth, J.F., 1960, Optimal properties of exponentially weighted forecasts, Journal of the American Statistical Association, June.

Muth, J.F., 1961, Rational expectations and the theory of price movements, Econometrica, July.

Nelson, C.R., 1971, The prediction performance of the FRB-MIT-PENN model of the U.S. economy, American Economic Review, Dec.

Nelson, C.R., 1973, Applied Time Series Analysis (Holden-Day, San Francisco, CA).

Nelson, C.R., 1975, Rational expectations and the predictive efficiency of economic models, Journal of Business, July.

Nerlove, M., 1958a, Adaptive expectations and Cobweb phenomena, Quarterly Journal of Economics, May.

Nerlove, M., 1958b, The Dynamics of Supply: Estimation of Farmers' Response to Price

(Johns Hopkins Press, Baltimore, MD).

Nerlove, M. and S. Wage, 1964, On the optimality of adaptive forecasting, Management Science, Jan.

Noble, N.R., 1982, Granger causality and expectations rationality, Journal of Money, Credit and Banking, Nov., Part 1.

Noble, N.R. and T.W. Fields, 1982, Testing the rationality of inflation expectations derived from survey data: A structure based approach, Southern Economic Journal, Oct.

Okun, A.M., 1960, The value of anticipation data in forecasting national product, in: Universities – National Bureau Committee for Economic Research, ed., The Quality and Economic Significance of Anticipations Data (Princeton University Press, Princeton, NJ).

Osgood, C.E., 1953, Method and theory in experimental psychology (Oxford University Press, New York).

Ozga, S.A., 1965, Expectations in Economic Theory (Weidenfeld and Nicolson, London).

Padoa Schioppa, F., 1979, Inflazione e prezzi relativi, Moneta e Credito, Dec.

Palm, F., 1972, On univariate time series methods and simultaneous equation econometric models, Journal of Econometrics, May.

Papadia, F., 1982, Rationality of inflationary expectations in the European Economic Communities countries, Unpublished paper, March.

Papadia, F. and V. Basano, 1981, Survey based inflationary expectations for the EEC countries, EEC-DG II, Economic Paper No. 1, May.

Parkin, M., M. Sumner and R. Ward, 1976, The effects of excess demand, generalized inflation and wage price controls on wage inflation in the UK: 1956–71, in: K. Brunner and A.H. Meltzer, eds., The Economics of Price and Wage Controls, Carnegie-Rochester Conference Series on Public Policy, No. 2 (North-Holland, Amsterdam).

Pashigian, B.P., 1964, The accuracy of the commerce–S.E.C. sales anticipations, Review of Economics and Statistics, Nov.

Pashigian, B.P., 1965, The relevance of sales anticipatory data in explaining inventory investment, International Economic Review, Jan.

Paunio, J.J. and A. Suvanto, 1977, Changes in price expectations: Some tests using data on indexed and non-indexed bonds, Economica, Feb.

Pearce, D.K., 1979, Comparing survey and rational measures of expected inflation: Forecast performance and interest rate effects, Journal of Money, Credit and Banking, Nov.

Pesando, J.E., 1975, A note on the rationality of the Livingston price expectations, Journal of Political Economy, Aug.

Pesando, J.E., 1976, Rational expectations and distributed lag proxies, Journal of the American Statistical Association, March.

Pesaran, M.H., 1981, Identification of rational expectation models, Journal of Econometrics, Aug.

Pesaran, M.H., 1983, Expectations formation and macroeconometric modelling, Unpublished paper, Jan.

Poole, W., 1976, Rational expectations in the macro-model, Brookings Papers on Economic Activity, No. 2.

Praet, P., 1981, A comparative approach to the measurement of expected inflation, Cahiers Economiques de Bruxelles, 2nd quarter.

Pyle, D.H., 1982, Observed price expectations and interest rates, Review of Economics and Statistics, Aug.

Resler, D.H., 1980, The formation of inflation expectations, Review of the Federal Reserve Bank of St. Louis, April.

Revankar, N.S., 1980, Testing of the rational expectations hypothesis, Econometrica, Sept.

Riddell, W.C., 1975, Recursive estimation algorithms for economic research, Annals of Economic and Social Measurement, No. 3.

Riddell, W.C. and P.M. Smith, 1982, Expected inflation and wage changes in Canada, 1967 – 81, Canadian Journal of Economics, Aug.

Rose, D., 1972, A general error-learning model of expectations formation, Unpublished paper presented to the European Meetings of the Econometric Society, Budapest, Sept.

Rose, D., 1977, Forecasting aggregates of independent ARIMA processes, Journal of Econometrics, May.

Samuelson, P.A., 1976, Optimality of sluggish predictors under ergodic probabilities, International Economic Review, Feb.

Sargent, T.J., 1971, A note on the accelerationist controversy, Journal of Money, Credit and Banking, Aug.

Sargent, T.J., 1976a, A classical macroeconomic model for the United States, Journal of Political Economy, April.

Sargent, T.J., 1976b, Observational equivalence of natural and unnatural rate theories of macroeconomics, Journal of Political Economy, June.

Sargent, T.J., 1977, The demand for money during hyperinflations under rational expectations I, International Economic Review, Feb.

Sargent, T.J., 1978, Estimation of dynamic labor demand schedules under rational expectations, Journal of Political Economy, Dec.

Sargent, T.J., 1979, Macroeconomic Theory (Academic Press, New York).

Sargent, T.J., 1981, Interpreting economic time series, Journal of Political Economy, April.

Sargent, T.J. and N. Wallace, 1973, Rational expectations and the dynamics of hyperinflation, International Economic Review, June.

Saunders, A., 1978, Expected inflation, unexpected inflation and the return on UK shares, 1961–1973, Journal of Business, Finance and Accounting, No. 3.

Saunders, P., 1980, Price and cost expectations in Australian manufacturing firms, Australian Economic Papers, June.

Saunders, P., 1981, The formation of producers' price expectations in Australia, Economic Record, Dec.

Schmalensee, R., 1976, An experimental study of expectation formation, Econometrica, Jan.

Schweiger, I., 1955, The contribution of consumer anticipations in forecasting consumer demand, in: Short-Term Economic Forecasting, Studies in Income and Wealth, Vol. 17 (N.B.E.R. – Princeton University Press, Princeton, NJ).

Severn, A.K., 1973, Further evidence in the formation of price expectations, Quarterly Review of Economics and Business, Winter.

Severn, A.K., 1983, Formation of inflation expectations in the U.K., European Economic Review, Jan.

Shackle, G.L.S., 1952, Expectations in Economics (Cambridge University Press, Cambridge).

Shackle, G.L.S., 1955, Uncertainty in Economics (Cambridge University Press, Cambridge).

Sheffrin, S.M., 1978, Comparative evidence on price expectations, Quarterly Review of Economics and Business, Autumn.

Shiller, R.J., 1972, Rational expectations and the structure of interest rates, Ph.D. Dissertation (Massachusetts Institute of Technology, Cambridge, MA).

Shiller, R.J., 1978, Rational expectations and the dynamic structure of macroeconomic models, Journal of Monetary Economics, Jan.

Shiller, R.J., 1979, The volatility of long-term interest rates and expectations models of the term structure, Journal of Political Economy, Dec.

Shuford, H., 1970, Subjective variables in economic analysis: A study of consumers' expectations, Ph.D. Dissertation (Yale University, New Haven, CT).

Simon, H.A., 1978, Rationality as process and as product of thought, American Economic Review, May.

Simon, H.A., 1979, Rational decision making in business organizations, American Economic Review, Sept.

Sims, C.A., 1980, Macroeconomics and reality, Econometrica, Jan.

Smith, G.W., 1978, Producers' price and cost expectations, in: M. Parkin and M.T. Sumner, eds., Inflation in the U.K. (Manchester University Press, Manchester).

Smith, G.W., 1982, Inflation expectations: Direct observations and their determinants, in: M.J. Artis, C.J. Green, D. Leslie and G.W. Smith, eds., Demand Management, Supply Constraints and Inflation (Manchester University Press, Manchester).

Spinelli, F., 1980, The wage push hypothesis: The Italian case, Journal of Monetary Economics, Oct.

Su, V., 1978, An error analysis of econometric and noneconometric forecasts, American

Economic Review, May.

Su, V., and J. Su, 1975, An evaluation of ASA/NBER business outlook survey forecasts, Explorations in Economic Research, Fall.

Swamy, P.A.V.B., J.R. Barth and P.A. Tinsley, 1982, The rational expectations approach to economic modelling, Journal of Economic Dynamics and Control, May.

Tanzi, V., 1980, Inflationary expectations, economic activity, taxes, and interest rates, American Economic Review, March.

Tanzi, V., 1982, Inflationary expectations, taxes and the demand for money in the United States, IMF Staff Papers, June.

Taylor, L., 1974, Price expectations and households' demand for financial assets, Explorations in Economic Research, Fall.

Taylor, H., 1981, Fisher, Phillips, Friedman and the measured impact of inflation on interest: A comment, Journal of Finance, Sept.

Theil, H., 1952, On the time shape of economic microvariables and the Munich business test, Revue de l'Institut International de Statistique, No. 2-3.

Theil, H., 1955, Recent experiences with the Munich business test, Econometrica, April.

Theil, H., 1961, Economic Forecasts and Policy, 2nd ed. (North-Holland, Amsterdam).

Theil, H., 1966, Applied Economic Forecasting (North-Holland, Amsterdam).

Tobin, J., 1959, On the predictive value of consumer intentions and attitudes, Review of Economics and Statistics, Feb.

Tobin, J., 1972, The wage–price mechanism: Overview of the conference, in: O. Eckstein, ed., The Econometrics of Price Determination (Board of Governors of the Federal Reserve System, Washington, DC).

Tobin, J., 1980, Asset Accumulations and Economic Theory: Reflections on Contemporary Macroeconomics, Yrjo Johnsson Lectures (University of Chicago Press, Chicago, IL).

Tompkinson, P. and M. Common, 1981, Evidence on the rationality of expectations in the British manufacturing sector, Unpublished paper, July.

Tullio, G., 1981, Demand management and exchange rate policy: The Italian experience, IMF Staff Papers, March.

Turnovsky, S.J., 1969, A Bayesian approach to the theory of expectations, Journal of Economic Theory, Aug.

Turnovsky, S.J., 1970, Empirical evidence on the formation of price expectations, Journal of the American Statistical Association, Dec.

Turnovsky, S.J., 1972, The expectations hypothesis and the aggregate wage equation: Some empirical evidence for Canada, Economica, Feb.

Turnovsky, S.J. and M.L. Wachter, 1972, A test of the expectations hypothesis using directly observed wage and price expectations, Review of Economics and Statistics, Feb.

Valentine, T.J., 1977, Price expectations in Australia: An alternative analysis, Economic Record, Sept.

Van Duyne, C., 1980, Food prices, expectations, and inflation, Institute for International Studies unpublished seminar paper, No. 140 (University of Stockholm, Stockholm).

Vanderkamp, J., 1972, Wage adjustment, productivity and price change expectations, Review of Economic Studies, Jan.

Vining, D.R. and T.C. Elvertowksy, 1977, The relationship between relative prices and the general price level, American Economic Review, Sept.

Visco, I., 1976, Misura ed analisi delle aspettative inflazionistiche: L'esperienza italiana, Contributi alla Ricerca Economica della Banca d'Italia, No. 6. English translation: 1979, The measurement and analysis of inflation expectations: The case of Italy, Economic Papers of the Bank of Italy, No. 2.

Von Neumann, J., 1941, Distribution of the ratio of the mean square successive difference to the variance, Annals of Mathematical Statistics, Dec.

Wachtel, P., 1977a, Survey measures of expected inflation and their potential usefulness, in: J. Popkin, ed., Analysis of Inflation: 1965–1974, Studies in Income and Wealth, Vol. 42 (N.B.E.R. – Ballinger, Cambridge, MA).

Wachtel, P., 1977b, Inflation uncertainty and saving behavior since the mid-1950s, Explorations in Economic Research, Fall.

Wallis, K.F., 1980, Econometric implications of the rational expectations hypothesis, Econometrica, Jan.

Wecker, W.E., 1979, Predicting turning points of a time series, Journal of Business, Jan.

Williams, R.A. and L.V. Defris, 1980, Australian inflationary expectations and their influence on consumption and saving, in: W.H. Strigel, ed., Business Cycle Analysis (CIRET – Gower, Farnborough).

Wold, H., 1953, A Study in the Analysis of Stationary Time Series, 2nd ed. (Almqvist and Wicksell, Stockholm).

Yohe, W. and D. Karnosky, 1969, Interest rates and price level changes, 1952–69, Review of the Federal Reserve Bank of St. Louis, Dec.

Zarnovitz, V., 1969, The new ASA-NBER survey of forecasts by economic statisticians, The American Statistician, Feb.

Zarnovitz, V., 1972, Forecasting economic conditions: The record and the prospect, in: V. Zarnovitz, ed., The Business Cycle Today (National Bureau of Economic Research, New York).

Zarnovitz, V., 1978, On the accuracy and properties of recent macroeconomic forecasts, American Economic Review, May.

Zarnovitz, V., 1979, An analysis of annual and multiperiod quarterly forecasts of aggregate income, output and the price level, Journal of Business, Jan.

Zarnovitz, V., 1982, An analysis of predictions from business outlook surveys, in: H. Laumer and M. Ziegler, eds., International Research on Business Cycle Surveys (CIRET – Gower, Aldershot).

Zellner, A. and F. Palm, 1974, Time series analysis and simultaneous equation econometric models, Journal of Econometrics, May.

Other Publications

Banca d'Italia, Bollettino, Rome, various issues.

Banca d'Italia, Relazione Annuale per il 1980, Rome, 1981.

Istat, Bollettino Mensile di Statistica, Rome, various issues.

Istat, Una metodologia di raccordo delle serie statistiche sulle forze di lavoro, Note e Relazioni, No. 56, Rome, 1979.

Ministero del Lavoro e della Previdenza Sociale, Statistiche del lavoro, Rome, various issues.

Mondo Economico, Milano, various issues.

DATA APPENDIX

TABLE D.1

MONDO ECONOMICO ISSUES REPORTING THE RESULTS OF THE SEMI-ANNUAL SURVEYS

Survey	Semester	Issue	Survey	Semester	Issue
1	2nd 1952	N.22, May 31 1952	30	1st 1967	N. 4, Jan. 28 1967
2	1st 1953	N. 1, Jan. 3 1953	31	2nd 1967	N.31-32, Aug. 5-12 1967
3	2nd 1953	N.28, July 11 1953	32	1st 1968	N. 5, Feb. 3 1968
4	1st 1954	N. 1, Jan. 2 1954	33	2nd 1968	N.30-31, July 27-Aug. 3 1968
5	2nd 1954	N.28, July 10 1954	34	1st 1969	N. 4, Feb. 1 1969
6	1st 1955	N. 4, Jan. 22 1955	35	2nd 1969	N.30-32, Aug. 2-9-16 1969
7	2nd 1955	N.28, July 9 1955	36	1st 1970	N. 5, Feb. 7 1970
8	1st 1956	N. 4, Jan. 28 1956	37	2nd 1970	N.31-32, Aug. 8-15 1970
9	2nd 1956	N.31, Aug. 4 1956	38	1st 1971	N. 6-7, Feb. 13-20 1971
10	1st 1957	N. 2, Jan. 12 1957	39	2nd 1971	N.31-32, Aug. 7-14 1971
11	2nd 1957	N.30, July 27 1957	40	1st 1972	N. 5, Feb. 7 1972
12	1st 1958	N. 4, Jan. 25 1958	41	2nd 1972	N.31-32, Aug. 5-12 1972
13	2nd 1958	N.29, July 19 1958	42	1st 1973	N. 5, Feb. 10 1973
14	1st 1959	N. 4, Jan. 24 1959	43	2nd 1973	N.30-31, Aug. 4-18 1973
15	2nd 1959	N.30, July 25 1959	44	1st 1974	N. 4, Feb. 2 1974
16	1st 1960	N. 5, Jan. 30 1960	45	2nd 1974	N.29-30, July 27-Aug. 3 1974
17	2nd 1960	N.31, July 30 1960	46	1st 1975	N. 3, Jan. 25 1975
18	1st 1961	N. 4, Jan. 28 1961	47	2nd 1975	N.29-30, July 26-Aug. 2 1975
19	2nd 1961	N.30, July 29 1961	48	1st 1976	N. 7, Feb. 21 1976
20	1st 1962	N. 4, Jan. 27 1962	49	2nd 1976	N.33, Sept. 4 1976
21	2nd 1962	N.30-31, July 28-Aug. 4 1962	50	1st 1977	N. 5, Feb. 12 1977
22	1st 1963	N. 4, Jan. 26 1963	51	2nd 1977	N.32-33, Aug. 27-Sept. 3 1977
23	2nd 1963	N.30-31, July 27-Aug. 3 1963	52(*)	1st 1978	N. 8, Feb. 25 1978
24	1st 1964	N. 5, Feb. 1 1964	53	2nd 1978	N.35, Sept. 9 1978
25	2nd 1964	N.31, Aug. 1 1964	54	1st 1979	N. 4, Jan. 27 1979
26	1st 1965	N. 4, Jan. 30 1965	55	2nd 1979	N.30, July 28 1979
27	2nd 1965	N.29-30, July 24-31 1965	56	1st 1980	N. 4, Jan. 26 1980
28	1st 1966	N. 4, Jan. 29 1966	57	2nd 1980	N.30, July 26 1980
29	2nd 1966	N.29-30, July 23-30 1966			

(*) Second series of surveys begins.

TABLE D.2

		DISPATCHED QUESTIONNAIRES (PERCENTAGES)				PERCENTAGE OF RETURNED OVER DISPATCHED QUESTIONNAIRES				
SEM	TOT	PRO	FIN	COM	EXP	PRO	FIN	COM	EXP	TOT
5402	784	47.7	17.3	25.3	9.7	31.0	33.1	33.8	27.6	31.8
5501	773	48.4	16.9	25.0	9.7	30.2	31.3	35.2	34.7	32.1
5502	734	46.6	17.6	26.2	9.7	33.9	32.6	45.3	39.4	37.2
5601	817	45.8	17.4	24.6	12.2	30.5	30.3	43.3	36.0	34.3
5602	805	46.1	17.6	24.7	11.6	33.2	32.4	37.7	30.1	33.8
5701	1018	44.9	22.2	22.1	10.8	32.4	30.1	36.9	34.5	33.1
5702	993	44.5	22.3	22.6	10.7	29.6	31.2	36.2	34.9	32.0
5801	981	44.1	22.4	22.7	10.7	30.5	36.4	40.4	34.3	34.5
5802	976	43.9	21.9	23.5	10.8	34.1	32.2	36.2	35.2	34.3
5901	961	44.0	22.0	23.1	10.9	32.4	30.3	37.8	37.1	33.7
5902	943	43.9	22.0	22.9	11.2	32.4	25.6	32.9	33.0	31.1
6001	941	43.4	21.6	23.9	11.2	31.1	28.6	39.1	34.3	32.8
6002	905	43.5	21.5	24.0	10.9	29.9	27.2	31.3	34.3	30.2
6101	902	43.0	21.6	24.4	11.0	29.1	29.2	31.4	36.4	30.5
6102	881	43.4	21.7	24.9	10.1	27.2	30.4	29.2	34.8	29.2
6201	880	43.6	21.0	25.2	10.1	30.5	25.9	33.3	32.6	30.5
6202	880	43.4	20.7	26.0	9.9	33.5	24.7	34.5	32.2	31.8
6301	866	44.2	20.4	25.5	9.8	29.2	26.0	32.6	30.6	29.6
6302	900	44.0	20.2	25.1	10.7	30.1	18.7	30.1	30.2	27.8
6401	888	43.6	20.0	25.2	11.1	26.1	24.7	32.1	29.3	27.7
6402	988	41.6	19.9	22.8	15.7	28.2	22.3	36.9	23.9	28.3
6501	974	41.7	20.3	22.7	15.3	30.8	28.3	37.6	19.5	30.1
6502	944	41.8	20.3	22.5	15.4	30.9	23.4	38.7	19.3	29.3
6601	935	42.2	20.3	22.8	14.7	31.6	23.2	38.5	24.8	30.5
6602	909	41.9	21.1	21.3	15.6	33.9	29.7	41.2	19.0	32.2
6701	902	42.2	21.1	21.2	15.5	27.6	27.9	35.6	21.4	28.4
6702	928	44.2	20.4	20.5	15.0	31.2	27.5	34.7	25.2	30.3
6801	903	43.3	20.7	20.8	15.2	34.0	25.7	40.4	24.1	32.1
6802	899	43.0	21.1	20.9	14.9	32.0	22.6	32.4	23.1	28.8
6901	898	42.8	21.4	20.9	14.9	33.9	24.5	35.1	22.4	30.4
6902	880	43.0	21.6	20.7	14.8	26.5	22.1	33.0	20.8	26.0
7001	881	43.7	21.2	20.7	14.4	24.9	21.9	32.4	22.8	25.5
7002	881	44.0	21.7	20.5	13.7	26.5	26.2	33.1	22.3	27.2
7101	883	42.7	23.2	20.3	13.8	28.4	22.0	35.2	23.8	27.6
7102	1348	49.3	22.4	19.8	8.5	27.1	21.5	27.3	24.3	25.7
7201	1367	50.3	21.9	19.6	8.3	23.6	21.4	31.0	30.1	25.1
7202	1368	50.7	22.1	19.2	8.0	24.5	27.5	27.8	22.9	25.7
7301	1492	46.8	20.6	17.6	15.0	27.5	25.1	33.6	22.8	27.3
7302	1450	47.2	20.3	17.8	14.6	18.4	21.4	19.4	19.3	19.3
7401	1423	46.9	20.4	17.9	14.8	18.0	19.0	24.3	9.0	18.0
7402	1416	46.8	20.5	17.9	14.8	16.9	16.6	20.2	14.8	17.1
7501	1392	46.6	20.7	18.0	14.7	17.4	18.4	24.3	6.9	17.3
7502	1367	46.5	20.6	18.1	14.7	23.1	23.8	25.8	14.4	22.5
7601	1301	48.0	21.7	19.1	11.2	23.2	21.3	31.0	21.2	24.1
7602	1289	48.3	21.9	18.9	11.0	23.3	20.6	27.2	19.7	23.0
7701	1316	47.7	21.3	18.5	12.5	23.7	22.9	27.5	17.7	23.5
7702	1303	47.6	21.1	18.9	12.4	22.4	20.4	24.0	14.2	21.3
7801	1648	58.8	16.4	14.9	9.9	14.8	13.7	25.7	14.7	16.2
7802	1882	53.8	18.5	14.2	13.4	16.8	16.9	20.5	18.6	17.6
7901	1942	52.9	18.1	13.8	15.2	16.3	16.5	19.4	19.9	17.3
7902	1922	53.0	18.0	13.6	15.4	16.1	12.4	21.4	17.2	16.3
8001	1922	53.1	18.0	13.5	15.3	12.7	12.4	18.5	18.6	14.4
8002	1877	53.9	16.2	13.5	16.3	14.0	16.7	16.9	18.0	15.5

TABLE D.3

	MONDO ECONOMICO OPINION POLL RETURNED QUESTIONNAIRES BY CLASS OF RESPONDENTS (2ND SEMESTER 1952 - 2ND SEMESTER 1980)								
	NUMBER OF RETURNED QUESTIONNAIRES					PERCENTAGE OF RETURNED QUESTIONNAIRES			
SEM	PRO	FIN	COM	EXP	T	PRO	FIN	COM	EXP
5202	105	42	55		202	52.0	20.8	27.2	
5301	106	42	55	30	233	45.5	18.0	23.6	12.9
5302	97	38	55	22	212	45.8	17.9	25.9	10.4
5401	75	30	47	21	173	43.4	17.3	27.2	12.1
5402	116	45	67	21	249	46.6	18.1	26.9	8.4
5501	113	41	68	26	248	45.6	16.5	27.4	10.5
5502	116	42	87	28	273	42.5	15.4	31.9	10.3
5601	114	43	87	36	280	40.7	15.4	31.1	12.9
5602	123	46	75	28	272	45.2	16.9	27.6	10.3
5701	148	68	83	38	337	43.9	20.2	24.6	11.3
5702	131	69	81	37	318	41.2	21.7	25.5	11.6
5801	132	80	90	36	338	39.1	23.7	26.6	10.7
5802	146	69	83	37	335	43.6	20.6	24.8	11.0
5901	137	64	84	39	324	42.3	19.8	25.9	12.0
5902	134	53	71	35	293	45.7	18.1	24.2	11.9
6001	127	58	88	36	309	41.1	18.8	28.5	11.7
6002	118	53	68	34	273	43.2	19.4	24.9	12.5
6101	113	57	69	36	275	41.1	20.7	25.1	13.1
6102	104	58	64	31	257	40.5	22.6	24.9	12.1
6201	117	48	74	29	268	43.7	17.9	27.6	10.8
6202	128	45	79	28	280	45.7	16.1	28.2	10.0
6301	112	46	72	26	256	43.8	18.0	28.1	10.2
6302	119	34	68	29	250	47.6	13.6	27.2	11.6
6401	101	44	72	29	246	41.1	17.9	29.3	11.8
6402	116	44	83	37	280	41.4	15.7	29.6	13.2
6501	125	56	83	29	293	42.7	19.1	28.3	9.9
6502	122	45	82	28	277	44.0	16.2	29.6	10.1
6601	125	44	82	34	285	43.9	15.4	28.8	11.9
6602	129	57	80	27	293	44.0	19.5	27.3	9.2
6701	105	53	68	30	256	41.0	20.7	26.6	11.7
6702	128	52	66	35	281	45.6	18.5	23.5	12.5
6801	133	48	76	33	290	45.9	16.6	26.2	11.4
6802	124	43	61	31	259	47.9	16.6	23.6	12.0
6901	130	47	66	30	273	47.6	17.2	24.2	11.0
6902	100	42	60	27	229	43.7	18.3	26.2	11.8
7001	96	41	59	29	225	42.7	18.2	26.2	12.9
7002	103	50	60	27	240	42.9	20.8	25.0	11.3
7101	107	45	63	29	244	43.9	18.4	25.8	11.9
7102	180	65	73	28	346	52.0	18.8	21.1	8.1
7201	162	64	83	34	343	47.2	18.7	24.2	9.9
7202	170	83	73	25	351	48.4	23.6	20.8	7.1
7301	192	77	88	51	408	47.1	18.9	21.6	12.5
7302	126	63	50	41	280	45.0	22.5	17.9	14.6
7401	120	55	62	19	256	46.9	21.5	24.2	7.4
7402	112	48	51	31	242	46.3	19.8	21.1	12.8
7501	113	53	61	14	241	46.9	22.0	25.3	5.8
7502	147	67	64	29	307	47.9	21.8	20.8	9.4
7601	145	60	77	31	313	46.3	19.2	24.6	9.9
7602	145	58	66	28	297	48.8	19.5	22.2	9.4
7701	149	64	67	29	309	48.2	20.7	21.7	9.4
7702	139	56	59	23	277	50.2	20.2	21.3	8.3
7801	143	37	63	24	267	53.6	13.9	23.6	9.0
7802	170	59	55	47	331	51.4	17.8	16.6	14.2
7901	167	58	52	59	336	49.7	17.3	15.5	17.6
7902	164	43	56	51	314	52.2	13.7	17.8	16.2
8001	130	43	48	55	276	47.1	15.6	17.4	19.9
8002	142	51	43	55	291	48.8	17.5	14.8	18.9

TABLE D.4

				MONDO ECONOMICO OPINION POLL - WHOLESALE PRICES BREAKDOWN OF ANSWERS - TOTAL (1) 2ND SEMESTER 1952 - 2ND SEMESTER 1977 (2)				
				NUMBER OF ANSWERS				
SEM1	N1	N2	N3	N4	N5	ND	NT
5202	0	18	48	100	0	36	202
5301	4	43	111	48	9	18	233
5302	5	27	105	49	5	21	212
5401	0	20	101	44	2	6	173
5402	4	73	124	30	1	17	249
5501	7	99	114	11	0	17	248
5502	1	70	163	19	1	19	273
5601	10	128	119	18	0	5	280
5602	6	93	133	30	1	9	272
5701	90	198	33	2	1	13	337
5702	1	72	175	50	2	18	318
5801	4	56	182	67	2	27	338
5802	2	25	164	111	6	27	335
5901	0	35	191	64	3	31	324
5902	1	42	200	28	1	21	293
6001	4	129	162	11	0	3	309
6002	1	42	193	32	0	5	273
6101	3	62	191	12	2	5	275
6102	3	56	188	6	0	4	257
6201	10	69	176	12	0	1	268
6202	31	183	58	3	1	4	280
6301	27	170	49	4	0	6	256
6302	23	182	42	1	0	2	250
6401	14	168	61	1	0	2	246
6402	7	83	154	24	3	9	280
6501	2	116	151	20	2	2	293
6502	1	58	195	19	1	3	277
6601	3	117	159	4	0	2	285
6602	2	109	175	2	1	4	293
6701	4	61	184	4	0	3	256
6702	1	79	191	7	1	2	281
6801	2	89	189	5	0	5	290
6802	2	71	182	0	0	4	259
6901	0	62	200	7	2	2	273
6902	30	158	39	0	0	2	229
7001	58	155	8	3	1	0	225
7002	53	159	22	1	0	5	240
7101	11	163	66	2	0	2	244
7102	5	180	150	6	0	5	346
7201	9	178	151	5	0	0	343
7202	16	231	101	1	0	2	351
7301	72	293	37	5	0	1	408
7302	190	80	8	2	0	0	280
7401	210	38	2	1	0	5	256
7402	124	73	30	10	1	4	242
7501	78	99	43	14	4	3	241
7502	24	127	117	34	1	4	307
7601	53	182	67	8	0	3	313
7602	160	115	18	1	0	3	297
7701	164	129	10	4	0	2	309
7702	56	153	60	7	0	1	277

(1) THE ANSWERS REFER TO THE FOLLOWING CLASSES:
N1: 'UP A LOT'   (5% OR MORE)
N2: 'UP A LITTLE'   (BETWEEN 2% AND 4%)
N3: 'NO CHANGE'   (BETWEEN -1% AND 1%)
N4: 'DOWN A LITTLE' (BETWEEN -4% AND -2%)
N5: 'DOWN A LOT'   (-5% OR LESS)
ND: 'DON'T KNOW'
NT IS THE TOTAL NUMBER OF ANSWERS
(2) THE SEMESTERS ARE THOSE FOR WHICH EXPECTATIONS
ARE FORMED AT THE END OF THE PREVIOUS SEMESTER

TABLE D.5

```
+------------------------------------------------------------------+
I     MONDO ECONOMICO OPINION POLL - WHOLESALE PRICES              I
I        BREAKDOWN OF ANSWERS - PRODUCTION (1)                     I
I        2ND SEMESTER 1952 - 2ND SEMESTER 1977 (2)                 I
+-------+----------------------------------------------------------+
I       I                 NUMBER OF ANSWERS                        I
+-------+------+------+------+------+------+------+------+
I SEM1  I  N1  I  N2  I  N3  I  N4  I  N5  I  ND  I  NT  I
+-------+------+------+------+------+------+------+------+
I 5202  I   0  I   8  I  24  I  56  I   0  I  17  I 105  I
I 5301  I   3  I  13  I  49  I  29  I   6  I   6  I 106  I
I 5302  I   2  I  12  I  44  I  27  I   1  I  11  I  97  I
I 5401  I   0  I   8  I  40  I  25  I   0  I   2  I  75  I
I 5402  I   2  I  34  I  55  I  16  I   0  I   9  I 116  I
I 5501  I   1  I  38  I  57  I   6  I   0  I  11  I 113  I
I 5502  I   0  I  28  I  69  I   8  I   1  I  10  I 116  I
I 5601  I   4  I  54  I  45  I   8  I   0  I   3  I 114  I
I 5602  I   3  I  42  I  56  I  18  I   1  I   3  I 123  I
I 5701  I  45  I  85  I  11  I   1  I   0  I   6  I 148  I
I 5702  I   0  I  28  I  76  I  18  I   1  I   8  I 131  I
I 5801  I   1  I  17  I  66  I  32  I   0  I  16  I 132  I
I 5802  I   0  I   5  I  62  I  57  I   4  I  18  I 146  I
I 5901  I   0  I  15  I  74  I  30  I   0  I  18  I 137  I
I 5902  I   0  I  11  I  96  I  14  I   1  I  12  I 134  I
I 6001  I   2  I  60  I  60  I   4  I   0  I   1  I 127  I
I 6002  I   0  I  11  I  80  I  24  I   0  I   3  I 118  I
I 6101  I   0  I  33  I  68  I   7  I   2  I   3  I 113  I
I 6102  I   0  I  26  I  72  I   4  I   0  I   2  I 104  I
I 6201  I   6  I  29  I  72  I  10  I   0  I   0  I 117  I
I 6202  I  14  I  73  I  35  I   2  I   1  I   3  I 128  I
I 6301  I  12  I  66  I  29  I   3  I   0  I   2  I 112  I
I 6302  I  10  I  85  I  23  I   0  I   0  I   1  I 119  I
I 6401  I   6  I  63  I  31  I   0  I   0  I   1  I 101  I
I 6402  I   4  I  33  I  61  I  10  I   2  I   6  I 116  I
I 6501  I   2  I  53  I  58  I  11  I   0  I   1  I 125  I
I 6502  I   0  I  19  I  93  I  10  I   0  I   0  I 122  I
I 6601  I   1  I  51  I  69  I   2  I   0  I   2  I 125  I
I 6602  I   0  I  48  I  76  I   2  I   1  I   2  I 129  I
I 6701  I   1  I  28  I  71  I   2  I   0  I   3  I 105  I
I 6702  I   0  I  31  I  88  I   6  I   1  I   2  I 128  I
I 6801  I   2  I  40  I  86  I   4  I   0  I   1  I 133  I
I 6802  I   2  I  32  I  90  I   0  I   0  I   0  I 124  I
I 6901  I   0  I  34  I  88  I   4  I   2  I   2  I 130  I
I 6902  I  15  I  70  I  14  I   0  I   0  I   1  I 100  I
I 7001  I  30  I  63  I   2  I   1  I   0  I   0  I  96  I
I 7002  I  24  I  65  I  12  I   1  I   0  I   1  I 103  I
I 7101  I   8  I  67  I  29  I   1  I   0  I   2  I 107  I
I 7102  I   3  I  92  I  78  I   3  I   0  I   4  I 180  I
I 7201  I   6  I  84  I  70  I   2  I   0  I   0  I 162  I
I 7202  I   9  I 109  I  50  I   0  I   0  I   2  I 170  I
I 7301  I  43  I 134  I  13  I   1  I   0  I   1  I 192  I
I 7302  I  89  I  35  I   1  I   1  I   0  I   0  I 126  I
I 7401  I  96  I  19  I   1  I   1  I   0  I   3  I 120  I
I 7402  I  59  I  34  I  15  I   3  I   0  I   1  I 112  I
I 7501  I  42  I  44  I  19  I   6  I   1  I   1  I 113  I
I 7502  I  12  I  61  I  56  I  15  I   0  I   3  I 147  I
I 7601  I  27  I  84  I  30  I   3  I   0  I   1  I 145  I
I 7602  I  74  I  59  I   8  I   1  I   0  I   3  I 145  I
I 7701  I  80  I  63  I   2  I   2  I   0  I   2  I 149  I
I 7702  I  26  I  74  I  34  I   4  I   0  I   1  I 139  I
+-------+------+------+------+------+------+------+------+
I (1) THE ANSWERS REFER TO THE FOLLOWING CLASSES:                  I
I N1: 'UP A LOT'        (5% OR MORE)                               I
I N2: 'UP A LITTLE'     (BETWEEN 2% AND 4%)                        I
I N3: 'NO CHANGE'       (BETWEEN -1% AND 1%)                       I
I N4: 'DOWN A LITTLE'   (BETWEEN -4% AND -2%)                      I
I N5: 'DOWN A LOT'      (-5% OR LESS)                              I
I ND: 'DON'T KNOW'                                                 I
I NT IS THE TOTAL NUMBER OF ANSWERS                                I
I (2) THE SEMESTERS ARE THOSE FOR WHICH EXPECTATIONS               I
I ARE FORMED AT THE END OF THE PREVIOUS SEMESTER                   I
+------------------------------------------------------------------+
```

TABLE D.6

MONDO ECONOMICO OPINION POLL - WHOLESALE PRICES BREAKDOWN OF ANSWERS - OTHER (1) 2ND SEMESTER 1952 - 2ND SEMESTER 1977 (2)							
NUMBER OF ANSWERS							
SEM1	N1	N2	N3	N4	N5	ND	NT
5202	0	10	24	44	0	19	97
5301	1	30	62	19	3	12	127
5302	3	15	61	22	4	10	115
5401	0	12	61	19	2	4	98
5402	2	39	69	14	1	8	133
5501	6	61	57	5	0	6	135
5502	1	42	94	11	0	9	157
5601	6	74	74	10	0	2	166
5602	3	51	77	12	0	6	149
5701	45	113	22	1	1	7	189
5702	1	44	99	32	1	10	187
5801	3	39	116	35	2	11	206
5802	2	20	102	54	2	9	189
5901	0	20	117	34	3	13	187
5902	1	31	104	14	0	9	159
6001	2	69	102	7	0	2	182
6002	1	31	113	8	0	2	155
6101	3	29	123	5	0	2	162
6102	3	30	116	2	0	2	153
6201	4	40	104	2	0	1	151
6202	17	110	23	1	0	1	152
6301	15	104	20	1	0	4	144
6302	13	97	19	1	0	1	131
6401	8	105	30	1	0	1	145
6402	3	50	93	14	1	3	164
6501	0	63	93	9	2	1	168
6502	1	39	102	9	1	3	155
6601	2	66	90	2	0	0	160
6602	2	61	99	0	0	2	164
6701	3	33	113	2	0	0	151
6702	1	48	103	1	0	0	153
6801	0	49	103	1	0	4	157
6802	0	39	92	0	0	4	135
6901	0	28	112	3	0	0	143
6902	15	88	25	0	0	1	129
7001	28	92	6	2	1	0	129
7002	29	94	10	0	0	4	137
7101	3	96	37	1	0	0	137
7102	2	88	72	3	0	1	166
7201	3	94	81	3	0	0	181
7202	7	122	51	1	0	0	181
7301	29	159	24	4	0	0	216
7302	101	45	7	1	0	0	154
7401	114	19	1	0	0	2	136
7402	65	39	15	7	1	3	130
7501	36	55	24	8	3	2	128
7502	12	66	61	19	1	1	160
7601	26	98	37	5	0	2	168
7602	86	56	10	0	0	0	152
7701	84	66	8	2	0	0	160
7702	30	79	26	3	0	0	138

(1) THE ANSWERS REFER TO THE FOLLOWING CLASSES:
N1: 'UP A LOT'   (5% OR MORE)
N2: 'UP A LITTLE'   (BETWEEN 2% AND 4%)
N3: 'NO CHANGE'   (BETWEEN -1% AND 1%)
N4: 'DOWN A LITTLE' (BETWEEN -4% AND -2%)
N5: 'DOWN A LOT'   (-5% OR LESS)
ND: 'DON'T KNOW'
NT IS THE TOTAL NUMBER OF ANSWERS
(2) THE SEMESTERS ARE THOSE FOR WHICH EXPECTATIONS
ARE FORMED AT THE END OF THE PREVIOUS SEMESTER

TABLE D.7

MONDO ECONOMICO OPINION POLL - CONSUMER PRICES
BREAKDOWN OF ANSWERS - TOTAL (1) (2)
2ND SEMESTER 1956 - 2ND SEMESTER 1977 (3)

	NUMBER OF ANSWERS						
SEM	N1	N2	N3	N4	N5	ND	NT
5602	13	173	66	6	0	14	272
5701	115	188	18	1	0	15	337
5702	8	138	129	11	0	32	318
5801	2	149	145	9	1	32	338
5802	4	111	167	15	0	38	335
5901	5	114	136	31	1	37	324
5902	2	71	180	14	0	26	293
6001	7	120	169	5	0	8	309
6002	0	82	164	15	0	12	273
6101	4	113	146	5	1	6	275
6102	9	118	123	3	0	4	257
6201	15	157	85	2	0	9	268
6202	97	162	11	0	0	10	280
6301	94	150	4	0	0	8	256
6302	79	145	18	0	0	8	250
6401	50	168	22	1	0	5	246
6402	26	158	79	3	0	14	280
6501	23	204	51	3	0	12	293
6502	8	186	67	2	0	14	277
6601	12	196	68	2	0	7	285
6602	9	185	89	0	1	9	293
6701	11	144	94	0	0	7	256
6702	8	178	84	2	0	9	281
6801	13	218	47	0	0	12	290
6802	6	141	97	0	0	15	259
6901	7	134	122	0	0	10	273
6902	50	147	24	0	0	8	229
7001	77	138	4	1	0	5	225
7002	64	154	8	1	0	13	240
7101	23	187	28	0	0	6	244
7102	29	257	47	3	0	10	346
7201	32	243	60	1	0	7	343
7202	30	276	30	0	0	15	351
7301	194	186	6	0	0	22	408
7302	192	77	0	0	1	10	280
7401	190	55	3	0	0	8	256
7402	182	39	8	1	0	12	242
7501	141	70	13	4	3	10	241
7502	83	154	51	6	1	12	307
7601	130	153	16	1	1	12	313
7602	214	64	7	0	0	12	297
7701	219	72	3	2	2	11	309
7702	62	177	36	1		1	277

(1) THE ANSWERS REFER TO THE FOLLOWING CLASSES:
N1: 'UP A LOT'   (5% OR MORE)
N2: 'UP A LITTLE'   (BETWEEN 2% AND 4%)
N3: 'NO CHANGE'   (BETWEEN -1% AND 1%)
N4: 'DOWN A LITTLE' (BETWEEN -4% AND -2%)
N5: 'DOWN A LOT'   (-5% OR LESS)
ND: 'DON'T KNOW'
NT IS THE TOTAL NUMBER OF ANSWERS
(2) FOR THE 2ND SEMESTER 1972 THE CLASSES ARE:
N1: 'UP A LOT'   (8% OR MORE)
N2: 'UP A LITTLE'   (BETWEEN 4% AND 7%)
N3: 'NO CHANGE'   (BETWEEN -1% AND 3%)
N4: 'DOWN A LITTLE' (-2% OR LESS)
(3) THE SEMESTERS ARE THOSE FOR WHICH EXPECTATIONS
ARE FORMED AT THE END OF THE PREVIOUS SEMESTER

Ignazio Visco

TABLE D.8

	NUMBER OF ANSWERS						
SEM	N1	N2	N3	N4	N5	ND	NT
5602	7	79	29	4	0	4	123
5701	48	89	6	1	0	4	148
5702	5	51	55	5	0	15	131
5801	1	49	64	2	1	15	132
5802	3	36	75	11	0	21	146
5901	3	39	64	10	1	20	137
5902	1	26	84	7	0	16	134
6001	3	49	70	1	0	4	127
6002	0	24	77	11	0	6	118
6101	1	47	56	4	1	4	113
6102	6	45	50	1	0	2	104
6201	8	63	41	2	0	3	117
6202	45	69	8	0	0	6	128
6301	37	66	3	0	0	6	112
6302	36	69	10	0	0	4	119
6401	23	64	12	0	0	2	101
6402	10	64	31	3	0	8	116
6501	10	87	20	2	0	6	125
6502	3	77	35	1	0	6	122
6601	6	84	31	1	0	3	125
6602	5	81	38	0	1	4	129
6701	5	58	38	0	0	4	105
6702	3	81	36	1	0	7	128
6801	9	104	14	0	0	6	133
6802	2	76	42	0	0	4	124
6901	4	64	58	0	0	4	130
6902	24	62	10	0	0	4	100
7001	42	52	1	0	0	1	96
7002	29	65	5	1	0	3	103
7101	9	80	15	0	0	3	107
7102	12	132	27	1	0	8	180
7201	21	109	31	0	0	1	162
7202	15	130	16	0	0	9	170
7301	100	82	2	0	0	8	192
7302	83	36	0	0	0	7	126
7401	91	26	1	0	0	2	120
7402	88	15	6	0	0	3	112
7501	68	32	6	2	1	4	113
7502	42	67	24	6	1	7	147
7601	64	71	6	0	0	4	145
7602	97	34	3	0	0	11	145
7701	104	35	1	0	1	8	149
7702	31	86	20	1		1	139

MONDO ECONOMICO OPINION POLL - CONSUMER PRICES
BREAKDOWN OF ANSWERS - PRODUCTION (1) (2)
2ND SEMESTER 1956 - 2ND SEMESTER 1977 (3)

(1) THE ANSWERS REFER TO THE FOLLOWING CLASSES:
N1: 'UP A LOT'   (5% OR MORE)
N2: 'UP A LITTLE'   (BETWEEN 2% AND 4%)
N3: 'NO CHANGE'   (BETWEEN -1% AND 1%)
N4: 'DOWN A LITTLE' (BETWEEN -4% AND -2%)
N5: 'DOWN A LOT'   (-5% OR LESS)
ND: 'DON'T KNOW'
NT IS THE TOTAL NUMBER OF ANSWERS
(2) FOR THE 2ND SEMESTER 1972 THE CLASSES ARE:
N1: 'UP A LOT'   (8% OR MORE)
N2: 'UP A LITTLE'   (BETWEEN 4% AND 7%)
N3: 'NO CHANGE'   (BETWEEN -1% AND 3%)
N4: 'DOWN A LITTLE' (-2% OR LESS)
(3) THE SEMESTERS ARE THOSE FOR WHICH EXPECTATIONS
ARE FORMED AT THE END OF THE PREVIOUS SEMESTER

TABLE D.9

```
+----------------------------------------------------------------+
I      MONDO ECONOMICO OPINION POLL - CONSUMER PRICES            I
I           BREAKDOWN OF ANSWERS - OTHER (1) (2)                 I
I         2ND SEMESTER 1956 - 2ND SEMESTER 1977 (3)             I
+----------------------------------------------------------------+
```

SEM	N1	N2	N3	N4	N5	ND	NT
5602	6	94	37	2	0	10	149
5701	67	99	12	0	0	11	189
5702	3	87	74	6	0	17	187
5801	1	100	81	7	0	17	206
5802	1	75	92	4	0	17	189
5901	2	75	72	21	0	17	187
5902	1	45	96	7	0	10	159
6001	4	71	99	4	0	4	182
6002	0	58	87	4	0	6	155
6101	3	66	90	1	0	2	162
6102	3	73	73	2	0	2	153
6201	7	94	44	0	0	6	151
6202	52	93	3	0	0	4	152
6301	57	84	1	0	0	2	144
6302	43	76	8	0	0	4	131
6401	27	104	10	1	0	3	145
6402	16	94	48	0	0	6	164
6501	13	117	31	1	0	6	168
6502	5	109	32	1	0	8	155
6601	6	112	37	1	0	4	160
6602	4	104	51	0	0	5	164
6701	6	86	56	0	0	3	151
6702	5	97	48	1	0	2	153
6801	4	114	33	0	0	6	157
6802	4	65	55	0	0	11	135
6901	3	70	64	0	0	6	143
6902	26	85	14	0	0	4	129
7001	35	86	3	1	0	4	129
7002	35	89	3	0	0	10	137
7101	14	107	13	0	0	3	137
7102	17	125	20	2	0	2	166
7201	11	134	29	1	0	6	181
7202	15	146	14	0	0	6	181
7301	94	104	4	0	0	14	216
7302	109	41	0	0	1	3	154
7401	99	29	2	0	0	6	136
7402	94	24	2	1	0	9	130
7501	73	38	7	2	2	6	128
7502	41	87	27	0	0	5	160
7601	66	82	10	1	1	8	168
7602	117	30	4	0	0	1	152
7701	115	37	2	2	1	3	160
7702	31	91	16	0		0	138

```
+----------------------------------------------------------------+
I (1) THE ANSWERS REFER TO THE FOLLOWING CLASSES:               I
I N1: 'UP A LOT'        (5% OR MORE)                            I
I N2: 'UP A LITTLE'     (BETWEEN 2% AND 4%)                     I
I N3: 'NO CHANGE'       (BETWEEN -1% AND 1%)                    I
I N4: 'DOWN A LITTLE'   (BETWEEN -4% AND -2%)                   I
I N5: 'DOWN A LOT'      (-5% OR LESS)                           I
I ND: 'DON'T KNOW'                                             I
I NT IS THE TOTAL NUMBER OF ANSWERS                            I
I (2) FOR THE 2ND SEMESTER 1972 THE CLASSES ARE:               I
I N1: 'UP A LOT'        (8% OR MORE)                            I
I N2: 'UP A LITTLE'     (BETWEEN 4% AND 7%)                     I
I N3: 'NO CHANGE'       (BETWEEN -1% AND 3%)                    I
I N4: 'DOWN A LITTLE'   (-2% OR LESS)                           I
I (3) THE SEMESTERS ARE THOSE FOR WHICH EXPECTATIONS           I
I ARE FORMED AT THE END OF THE PREVIOUS SEMESTER               I
+----------------------------------------------------------------+
```

TABLE D.10

	MONDO ECONOMICO OPINION POLL - WHOLESALE PRICES BREAKDOWN OF ANSWERS - TOTAL - NEW SERIES (1)								
	1ST SEMESTER 1978 - 2ND SEMESTER 1980 (2)								
	NUMBER OF ANSWERS								
SEM	N1	N2	N3	N4	N5	N6	N7	ND	NT
7801	5	15	75	125	44	1	0	2	267
7802	7	25	104	161	29	1	2	2	331
7901	8	27	129	140	28	2	0	2	336
7902	17	46	154	86	5	0	0	6	314
8001	42	89	97	44	3	0	0	1	276
8002	29	58	106	79	9	9	0	1	291

	2ND SEMESTER 1978 - 1ST SEMESTER 1981 (3)								
	NUMBER OF ANSWERS								
SEM	N1	N2	N3	N4	N5	N6	N7	ND	NT
7802	5	19	94	107	40	0	0	2	267
7901	8	27	122	146	19	2	2	4	330
7902	6	24	128	146	25	0	1	4	334
8001	14	46	142	99	6	2	0	4	313
8002	26	57	109	75	4	1	0	1	273
8101	19	52	104	84	28	2	0	2	291

(1) THE ANSWERS REFER TO THE FOLLOWING CLASSES:
N1: 'UP VERY VERY MUCH'   (11% OR MORE)
N2: 'UP VERY LOT'   (BETWEEN 8% AND 10%)
N3: 'UP A LOT'   (BETWEEN 5% AND 7%)
N4: 'UP A LITTLE'   (BETWEEN 2% AND 4%)
N5: 'NO CHANGE'   (BETWEEN -1% AND 1%)
N6: 'DOWN A LITTLE'   (BETWEEN -4% AND -2%)
N7: 'DOWN A LOT'   (-5% OR LESS)
ND: 'DON'T KNOW'
NT IS THE TOTAL NUMBER OF ANSWERS
(2) THE SEMESTERS ARE THOSE FOR WHICH EXPECTATIONS ARE FORMED AT THE END OF THE PREVIOUS SEMESTER
(3) THE SEMESTERS ARE THOSE FOR WHICH EXPECTATIONS ARE FORMED AT THE END OF TWO SEMESTERS BEFORE

TABLE D.11

```
+---------------------------------------------------------------------+
|          MONDO ECONOMICO OPINION POLL - WHOLESALE PRICES            |
|          BREAKDOWN OF ANSWERS - PRODUCTION - NEW SERIES (1)         |
+---------------------------------------------------------------------+
|             1ST SEMESTER 1978 - 2ND SEMESTER 1980 (2)               |
+---------------------------------------------------------------------+
|           |                 NUMBER OF ANSWERS                       |
+---------------------------------------------------------------------+
```

SEM	N1	N2	N3	N4	N5	N6	N7	ND	NT
7801	3	6	39	72	21	1	0	1	143
7802	3	11	52	82	19	1	1	1	170
7901	5	12	63	71	12	2	0	2	167
7902	8	22	80	49	2	0	0	3	164
8001	15	38	51	24	1	0	0	1	130
8002	11	25	51	42	7	5	0	1	142

```
+---------------------------------------------------------------------+
|             2ND SEMESTER 1978 - 1ST SEMESTER 1981 (3)               |
+---------------------------------------------------------------------+
|           |                 NUMBER OF ANSWERS                       |
+---------------------------------------------------------------------+
```

SEM	N1	N2	N3	N4	N5	N6	N7	ND	NT
7802	4	7	50	60	21	0	0	1	143
7901	3	12	59	85	7	1	1	2	170
7902	3	8	67	71	13	0	1	3	166
8001	5	21	77	54	3	1	0	3	164
8002	6	26	49	46	1	0	0	1	129
8101	7	26	50	40	16	1	0	2	142

```
| (1) THE ANSWERS REFER TO THE FOLLOWING CLASSES:
| N1: 'UP VERY VERY MUCH'      (11% OR MORE)
| N2: 'UP VERY LOT'         (BETWEEN 8% AND 10%)
| N3: 'UP A LOT'            (BETWEEN 5% AND 7%)
| N4: 'UP A LITTLE'         (BETWEEN 2% AND 4%)
| N5: 'NO CHANGE'           (BETWEEN -1% AND 1%)
| N6: 'DOWN A LITTLE'       (BETWEEN -4% AND -2%)
| N7: 'DOWN A LOT'          (-5% OR LESS)
| ND: 'DON'T KNOW'
| NT IS THE TOTAL NUMBER OF ANSWERS
| (2) THE SEMESTERS ARE THOSE FOR WHICH EXPECTATIONS ARE FORMED
| AT THE END OF THE PREVIOUS SEMESTER
| (3) THE SEMESTERS ARE THOSE FOR WHICH EXPECTATIONS ARE FORMED
| AT THE END OF TWO SEMESTERS BEFORE
+---------------------------------------------------------------------+
```

TABLE D.12

MONDO ECONOMICO OPINION POLL - WHOLESALE PRICES BREAKDOWN OF ANSWERS - OTHER - NEW SERIES (1)									
1ST SEMESTER 1978 - 2ND SEMESTER 1980 (2)									
	NUMBER OF ANSWERS								
SEM	N1	N2	N3	N4	N5	N6	N7	ND	NT
7801	2	9	36	53	23	0	0	1	124
7802	4	14	52	79	10	0	1	1	161
7901	3	15	66	69	16	0	0	0	169
7902	9	24	74	37	3	0	0	3	150
8001	27	51	46	20	2	0	0	0	146
8002	18	33	55	37	2	4	0	0	149
2ND SEMESTER 1978 - 1ST SEMESTER 1981 (3)									
	NUMBER OF ANSWERS								
SEM	N1	N2	N3	N4	N5	N6	N7	ND	NT
7802	1	12	44	47	19	0	0	1	124
7901	5	15	63	61	12	1	1	2	160
7902	3	16	61	75	12	0	0	1	168
8001	9	25	65	45	3	1	0	1	149
8002	20	31	60	29	3	1	1	0	144
8101	12	26	54	44	12	1	0	0	149

(1) THE ANSWERS REFER TO THE FOLLOWING CLASSES:
N1: 'UP VERY VERY MUCH' (11% OR MORE)
N2: 'UP VERY LOT' (BETWEEN 8% AND 10%)
N3: 'UP A LOT' (BETWEEN 5% AND 7%)
N4: 'UP A LITTLE' (BETWEEN 2% AND 4%)
N5: 'NO CHANGE' (BETWEEN -1% AND 1%)
N6: 'DOWN A LITTLE' (BETWEEN -4% AND -2%)
N7: 'DOWN A LOT' (-5% OR LESS)
ND: 'DON'T KNOW'
NT IS THE TOTAL NUMBER OF ANSWERS
(2) THE SEMESTERS ARE THOSE FOR WHICH EXPECTATIONS ARE FORMED AT THE END OF THE PREVIOUS SEMESTER
(3) THE SEMESTERS ARE THOSE FOR WHICH EXPECTATIONS ARE FORMED AT THE END OF TWO SEMESTERS BEFORE

TABLE D.13

```
+----------------------------------------------------------------------+
|         MONDO ECONOMICO OPINION POLL - CONSUMER PRICES               |
|         BREAKDOWN OF ANSWERS - TOTAL - NEW SERIES (1)                |
+----------------------------------------------------------------------+
|         1ST SEMESTER 1978 - 2ND SEMESTER 1980 (2)                   |
+----------------------------------------------------------------------+
|         |              NUMBER OF ANSWERS                            |
+----------------------------------------------------------------------+
| SEM  | N1  | N2  | N3  | N4  | N5 | N6 | ND | NT  |
+----------------------------------------------------------------------+
| 7801 | 16  | 29  | 120 | 93  | 9  | 0  | 0  | 267 |
| 7802 | 21  | 42  | 156 | 100 | 10 | 2  | 0  | 331 |
| 7901 | 25  | 47  | 174 | 82  | 5  | 1  | 2  | 336 |
| 7902 | 29  | 74  | 168 | 38  | 2  | 0  | 3  | 314 |
| 8001 | 60  | 104 | 88  | 21  | 1  | 0  | 2  | 276 |
| 8002 | 52  | 86  | 105 | 41  | 4  | 2  | 1  | 291 |
+----------------------------------------------------------------------+
|         2ND SEMESTER 1978 - 1ST SEMESTER 1981 (3)                   |
+----------------------------------------------------------------------+
|         |              NUMBER OF ANSWERS                            |
+----------------------------------------------------------------------+
| SEM  | N1  | N2  | N3  | N4  | N5 | N6 | ND | NT  |
+----------------------------------------------------------------------+
| 7802 | 16  | 42  | 133 | 60  | 15 | 0  | 1  | 267 |
| 7901 | 20  | 53  | 165 | 76  | 11 | 2  | 3  | 330 |
| 7902 | 16  | 55  | 154 | 97  | 5  | 1  | 6  | 334 |
| 8001 | 33  | 57  | 165 | 53  | 3  | 0  | 2  | 313 |
| 8002 | 46  | 69  | 121 | 28  | 6  | 0  | 3  | 273 |
| 8101 | 44  | 66  | 112 | 53  | 10 | 1  | 4  | 290 |
+----------------------------------------------------------------------+
| (1) THE ANSWERS REFER TO THE FOLLOWING CLASSES:                     |
| N1: 'UP VERY VERY MUCH'    (11% OR MORE)                            |
| N2: 'UP VERY LOT'          (BETWEEN 8% AND 10%)                     |
| N3: 'UP A LOT'             (BETWEEN 5% AND 7%)                      |
| N4: 'UP A LITTLE'          (BETWEEN 2% AND 4%)                      |
| N5: 'NO CHANGE'            (BETWEEN -1% AND 1%)                     |
| N6: 'DOWN A LITTLE'        (-2% OR LESS)                            |
| ND: 'DON'T KNOW'                                                    |
| NT IS THE TOTAL NUMBER OF ANSWERS                                   |
| (2) THE SEMESTERS ARE THOSE FOR WHICH EXPECTATIONS ARE FORMED       |
| AT THE END OF THE PREVIOUS SEMESTER                                 |
| (3) THE SEMESTERS ARE THOSE FOR WHICH EXPECTATIONS ARE FORMED       |
| AT THE END OF TWO SEMESTERS BEFORE                                  |
+----------------------------------------------------------------------+
```

TABLE D.14

```
+----------------------------------------------------------------------+
I         MONDO ECONOMICO OPINION POLL - CONSUMER PRICES               I
I         BREAKDOWN OF ANSWERS - PRODUCTION - NEW SERIES (1)           I
+----------------------------------------------------------------------+
I         1ST SEMESTER 1978 - 2ND SEMESTER 1980 (2)                    I
+----------------------------------------------------------------------+
I         I                    NUMBER OF ANSWERS                       I
+----------------------------------------------------------------------+
I SEM  I  N1  I  N2  I  N3  I  N4  I  N5  I  N6  I  ND  I  NT  I
+----------------------------------------------------------------------+
I 7801 I   9  I  12  I  60  I  59  I   3  I   0  I   0  I 143  I
I 7802 I   9  I  18  I  74  I  63  I   5  I   1  I   0  I 170  I
I 7901 I  13  I  17  I  86  I  47  I   1  I   1  I   2  I 167  I
I 7902 I  15  I  35  I  92  I  21  I   0  I   0  I   1  I 164  I
I 8001 I  21  I  50  I  46  I  10  I   1  I   0  I   2  I 130  I
I 8002 I  25  I  38  I  51  I  24  I   2  I   1  I   1  I 142  I
+----------------------------------------------------------------------+
I         2ND SEMESTER 1978 - 1ST SEMESTER 1981 (3)                    I
+----------------------------------------------------------------------+
I         I                    NUMBER OF ANSWERS                       I
+----------------------------------------------------------------------+
I SEM  I  N1  I  N2  I  N3  I  N4  I  N5  I  N6  I  ND  I  NT  I
+----------------------------------------------------------------------+
I 7802 I   8  I  20  I  72  I  33  I  10  I   0  I   0  I 143  I
I 7901 I   8  I  23  I  90  I  40  I   6  I   1  I   2  I 170  I
I 7902 I   6  I  26  I  76  I  48  I   4  I   1  I   5  I 166  I
I 8001 I  13  I  32  I  86  I  30  I   1  I   0  I   2  I 164  I
I 8002 I  14  I  29  I  59  I  22  I   3  I   0  I   2  I 129  I
I 8101 I  21  I  37  I  47  I  28  I   7  I   0  I   2  I 142  I
+----------------------------------------------------------------------+
I (1) THE ANSWERS REFER TO THE FOLLOWING CLASSES:                      I
I N1: 'UP VERY VERY MUCH'      (11% OR MORE)                           I
I N2: 'UP VERY LOT'            (BETWEEN 8% AND 10%)                    I
I N3: 'UP A LOT'               (BETWEEN 5% AND 7%)                     I
I N4: 'UP A LITTLE'            (BETWEEN 2% AND 4%)                     I
I N5: 'NO CHANGE'              (BETWEEN -1% AND 1%)                    I
I N6: 'DOWN A LITTLE'          (-2% OR LESS)                           I
I ND: 'DON'T KNOW'                                                     I
I NT IS THE TOTAL NUMBER OF ANSWERS                                    I
I (2) THE SEMESTERS ARE THOSE FOR WHICH EXPECTATIONS ARE FORMED        I
I AT THE END OF THE PREVIOUS SEMESTER                                  I
I (3) THE SEMESTERS ARE THOSE FOR WHICH EXPECTATIONS ARE FORMED        I
I AT THE END OF TWO SEMESTERS BEFORE                                   I
+----------------------------------------------------------------------+
```

TABLE D.15

```
+----------------------------------------------------------------+
I         MONDO ECONOMICO OPINION POLL - CONSUMER PRICES         I
I        BREAKDOWN OF ANSWERS - OTHER - NEW SERIES (1)           I
+----------------------------------------------------------------+
I            1ST SEMESTER 1978 - 2ND SEMESTER 1980 (2)           I
+----------------------------------------------------------------+
I         I                   NUMBER OF ANSWERS                  I
+---------+------+------+------+------+------+------+------+------+
I  SEM  I  N1  I  N2  I  N3  I  N4  I  N5  I  N6  I  ND  I  NT  I
+---------+------+------+------+------+------+------+------+------+
I  7801 I   7  I  17  I  60  I  34  I   6  I   0  I   0  I 124  I
I  7802 I  12  I  24  I  82  I  37  I   5  I   1  I   0  I 161  I
I  7901 I  12  I  30  I  88  I  35  I   4  I   0  I   0  I 169  I
I  7902 I  14  I  39  I  76  I  17  I   2  I   0  I   2  I 150  I
I  8001 I  39  I  54  I  42  I  11  I   0  I   0  I   0  I 146  I
I  8002 I  27  I  48  I  54  I  17  I   2  I   1  I   0  I 149  I
+---------+------+------+------+------+------+------+------+------+
I            2ND SEMESTER 1978 - 1ST SEMESTER 1981 (3)           I
+---------+------+------+------+------+------+------+------+------+
I         I                   NUMBER OF ANSWERS                  I
+---------+------+------+------+------+------+------+------+------+
I  SEM  I  N1  I  N2  I  N3  I  N4  I  N5  I  N6  I  ND  I  NT  I
+---------+------+------+------+------+------+------+------+------+
I  7802 I   8  I  22  I  61  I  27  I   5  I   0  I   1  I 124  I
I  7901 I  12  I  30  I  75  I  36  I   5  I   1  I   1  I 160  I
I  7902 I  10  I  29  I  78  I  49  I   1  I   0  I   1  I 168  I
I  8001 I  20  I  25  I  79  I  23  I   2  I   0  I   0  I 149  I
I  8002 I  32  I  40  I  62  I   6  I   3  I   0  I   1  I 144  I
I  8101 I  23  I  29  I  65  I  25  I   3  I   1  I   2  I 148  I
+---------+------+------+------+------+------+------+------+------+
I (1) THE ANSWERS REFER TO THE FOLLOWING CLASSES:                I
I N1: 'UP VERY VERY MUCH'      (11% OR MORE)                     I
I N2: 'UP VERY LOT'            (BETWEEN 8% AND 10%)             I
I N3: 'UP A LOT'               (BETWEEN 5% AND 7%)              I
I N4: 'UP A LITTLE'            (BETWEEN 2% AND 4%)              I
I N5: 'NO CHANGE'              (BETWEEN -1% AND 1%)             I
I N6: 'DOWN A LITTLE'          (-2% OR LESS)                    I
I ND: 'DON'T KNOW'                                              I
I NT IS THE TOTAL NUMBER OF ANSWERS                             I
I (2) THE SEMESTERS ARE THOSE FOR WHICH EXPECTATIONS ARE FORMED I
I AT THE END OF THE PREVIOUS SEMESTER                           I
I (3) THE SEMESTERS ARE THOSE FOR WHICH EXPECTATIONS ARE FORMED I
I AT THE END OF TWO SEMESTERS BEFORE                            I
+----------------------------------------------------------------+
```

TABLE D.16

	EXPECTED RATES OF CHANGE OF WHOLESALE PRICES VARIOUS DISTRIBUTION HYPOTHESES – TOTAL 2ND SEMESTER 1952 – 2ND SEMESTER 1980 (1)							
	MEAN				STANDARD DEVIATION			
SEM	PUC	PUM	NR1	NR2	PUC	PUM	NR1	NR2
5202	-1.48	-1.48	-2.30	-2.30	2.23	2.23	3.08	3.08
5301	-.23	-.21	-.29	-.29	2.53	2.59	2.34	2.34
5302	-.38	-.35	-.22	-.22	2.39	2.47	2.28	2.28
5401	-.50	-.50	-.52	-.49	2.09	2.09	1.75	1.69
5402	.61	.63	.56	.61	2.21	2.26	1.90	1.86
5501	1.28	1.32	1.32	1.32	2.00	2.09	1.69	1.69
5502	.60	.60	.35	.62	1.94	1.96	1.67	1.50
5601	1.37	1.42	1.33	1.33	2.10	2.20	1.82	1.82
5602	.80	.83	.75	.79	2.22	2.29	1.93	1.88
5701	3.24	3.46	3.86	3.52	1.80	2.10	2.70	1.66
5702	.20	.20	.00	.22	2.16	2.17	1.74	1.83
5801	-.09	-.07	.07	-.06	2.19	2.24	1.90	2.00
5802	-.92	-.92	-.72	-.91	2.17	2.20	1.96	1.76
5901	-.36	-.36	-.42	-.34	2.01	2.01	1.72	1.56
5902	.15	.15	.10	.16	1.80	1.82	1.64	1.34
6001	1.22	1.24	1.21	1.21	1.91	1.95	1.49	1.49
6002	.13	.13	.21	.13	1.81	1.83	1.56	1.38
6101	.56	.58	.49	.59	1.84	1.88	1.82	1.29
6102	.65	.66	1.03	.69	1.67	1.72	1.41	1.11
6201	.82	.87	1.14	1.14	1.90	2.02	1.73	1.73
6202	2.47	2.61	2.52	2.52	1.82	2.05	2.29	1.77
6301	2.50	2.64	2.51	2.51	1.76	1.98	1.77	1.77
6302	2.62	2.75	2.64	2.75	1.57	1.79	1.51	1.32
6401	2.32	2.40	2.32	2.39	1.67	1.82	1.42	1.34
6402	.71	.74	.62	.82	2.18	2.25	2.08	1.86
6501	.98	.99	.55	1.07	2.09	2.11	1.82	1.79
6502	.42	.43	.27	.45	1.82	1.83	1.64	1.34
6601	1.25	1.26	1.37	1.26	1.80	1.84	1.33	1.26
6602	1.12	1.13	.94	1.16	1.79	1.82	1.66	1.15
6701	.75	.77	1.20	1.20	1.68	1.74	1.40	1.40
6702	.77	.77	.54	.81	1.77	1.78	1.61	1.22
6801	.92	.93	1.14	.96	1.74	1.76	1.31	1.16
6802	.87	.88	.59	.59	1.63	1.66	1.62	1.62
6901	.56	.56	.72	.64	1.73	1.73	1.89	1.16
6902	2.72	2.88	2.88	2.88	1.59	1.86	1.45	1.45
7001	3.30	3.55	4.14	3.73	1.66	1.98	2.92	2.18
7002	3.14	3.37	3.37	3.40	1.57	1.91	1.77	1.47
7101	2.21	2.27	2.13	2.27	1.72	1.84	1.47	1.32
7102	1.60	1.62	1.52	1.52	1.84	1.89	1.40	1.40
7201	1.63	1.67	1.67	1.67	1.85	1.92	1.46	1.46
7202	2.19	2.25	2.23	2.23	1.70	1.82	1.35	1.34
7301	2.98	3.18	3.13	3.13	1.58	1.89	1.89	1.89
7302	6.31	6.31	6.25	5.54	3.18	3.18	3.02	2.24
7401	11.14	11.14	8.55	6.80	5.78	5.78	3.59	2.35
7402	4.44	4.44	4.70	4.79	3.31	3.31	3.54	3.68
7501	2.83	2.94	3.33	3.33	2.84	2.97	3.53	3.53
7502	1.28	1.38	1.38	1.33	2.40	2.57	2.21	2.30
7601	2.53	2.71	2.67	2.67	1.98	2.25	2.07	2.07
7602	4.75	4.75	4.84	4.74	2.40	2.40	2.31	2.13
7701	4.64	4.64	5.24	5.24	2.29	2.29	2.80	2.80
7702	2.61	2.80	2.81	2.81	2.05	2.33	2.15	2.15
7801	3.82	3.84	4.37	3.85	2.74	2.79	2.52	2.95
7802	4.24	4.26	4.30	4.48	2.74	2.80	2.99	2.71
7901	4.55	4.57	4.81	4.72	2.69	2.75	2.59	2.68
7902	5.79	5.84	6.15	6.15	2.55	2.67	2.39	2.39
8001	7.22	7.34	7.48	7.36	2.84	3.03	2.74	3.04
8002	5.84	5.92	5.95	5.95	3.36	3.50	3.59	3.59

(1) THE SEMESTERS ARE THOSE FOR WHICH EXPECTATIONS ARE FORMED AT THE END OF THE PREVIOUS SEMESTER

TABLE D.17

		MEAN				STANDARD DEVIATION		
SEM	PUC	PUM	NR1	NR2	PUC	PUM	NR1	NR2
5202	-1.64	-1.64	-2.56	-2.56	2.15	2.15	3.04	3.04
5301	-.69	-.66	-.60	-.60	2.63	2.71	2.57	2.57
5302	-.48	-.45	-.13	-.56	2.35	2.43	2.11	2.09
5401	-.70	-.70	-.76	-.76	2.08	2.08	1.84	1.84
5402	.59	.62	.56	.63	2.23	2.29	1.92	2.05
5501	.99	1.00	.95	1.02	1.96	2.00	1.54	1.61
5502	.51	.51	.57	.56	1.97	1.97	2.01	1.50
5601	1.41	1.46	1.33	1.33	2.13	2.22	1.84	1.84
5602	.67	.70	.58	.64	2.37	2.44	2.09	2.03
5701	3.45	3.68	3.79	3.73	1.73	2.02	2.05	1.62
5702	.20	.20	.20	.23	2.09	2.09	1.90	1.70
5801	-.35	-.34	-.38	-.39	2.15	2.18	2.02	1.86
5802	-1.41	-1.41	-1.41	-1.41	2.06	2.06	1.66	1.66
5901	-.38	-.38	-.39	-.39	2.00	2.00	1.65	1.65
5902	-.12	-.12	-.31	-.11	1.70	1.70	1.60	1.20
6001	1.41	1.43	1.34	1.47	1.91	1.96	1.50	1.60
6002	-.34	-.34	-.35	-.35	1.84	1.84	1.42	1.42
6101	.60	.60	.76	.68	2.08	2.08	2.29	1.56
6102	.65	.65	.68	.68	1.73	1.73	1.24	1.24
6201	.73	.79	.97	.97	2.09	2.23	2.00	2.00
6202	2.19	2.33	2.24	2.30	2.03	2.25	2.43	1.88
6301	2.24	2.37	2.29	2.29	1.95	2.17	1.90	1.90
6302	2.56	2.67	2.65	2.65	1.58	1.78	1.34	1.34
6401	2.17	2.25	2.23	2.23	1.72	1.88	1.46	1.46
6402	.69	.74	.62	.85	2.28	2.39	2.25	1.98
6501	1.09	1.11	.96	1.21	2.13	2.18	1.72	1.49
6502	.22	.22	.24	.24	1.69	1.69	1.25	1.25
6601	1.23	1.24	1.30	1.25	1.81	1.84	1.32	1.29
6602	1.04	1.04	1.50	1.09	1.87	1.87	2.20	1.31
6701	.81	.82	1.12	.85	1.71	1.75	1.36	1.14
6702	.55	.55	.64	.60	1.84	1.84	1.94	1.32
6801	.89	.91	1.12	.90	1.81	1.86	1.48	1.28
6802	.85	.87	.33	.33	1.64	1.70	1.95	1.95
6901	.61	.61	.80	.68	1.90	1.90	2.16	1.30
6902	2.85	3.03	3.03	3.03	1.55	1.84	1.43	1.29
7001	3.57	3.81	4.13	3.88	1.53	1.86	2.14	1.28
7002	3.07	3.29	3.30	3.34	1.73	2.05	1.96	1.61
7101	2.24	2.34	2.28	2.35	1.78	1.96	1.59	1.50
7102	1.59	1.62	1.55	1.55	1.85	1.90	1.42	1.42
7201	1.69	1.74	1.80	1.72	1.85	1.96	1.49	1.56
7202	2.19	2.27	2.24	2.24	1.70	1.84	1.40	1.40
7301	3.21	3.44	3.46	3.47	1.50	1.84	1.81	1.36
7302	6.68	6.68	6.96	5.51	3.22	3.22	3.21	1.87
7401	10.37	10.37	8.89	6.79	5.43	5.43	4.09	2.50
7402	4.61	4.61	4.74	4.74	3.18	3.18	3.25	3.25
7501	3.19	3.21	3.65	3.60	2.84	2.87	3.38	3.24
7502	1.36	1.46	1.42	1.42	2.35	2.52	2.27	2.27
7601	2.62	2.81	2.79	2.79	1.96	2.24	2.05	2.05
7602	4.55	4.55	4.86	4.61	2.30	2.30	2.50	2.04
7701	4.73	4.73	5.55	4.68	2.22	2.22	2.86	1.66
7702	2.47	2.65	2.66	2.66	2.09	2.36	2.16	2.16
7801	3.77	3.78	4.24	3.83	2.68	2.73	2.61	2.93
7802	4.03	4.05	4.07	4.20	2.76	2.81	2.96	2.76
7901	4.54	4.56	4.75	4.77	2.74	2.81	2.75	2.73
7902	5.67	5.72	6.10	5.56	2.51	2.62	2.30	2.82
8001	6.87	6.98	7.17	6.96	2.75	2.93	2.51	2.92
8002	5.42	5.49	5.49	5.49	3.37	3.50	3.54	3.54

(1) THE SEMESTERS ARE THOSE FOR WHICH EXPECTATIONS ARE FORMED AT THE END OF THE PREVIOUS SEMESTER

TABLE D.18

```
+-------------------------------------------------------------------------------+
I              EXPECTED RATES OF CHANGE OF WHOLESALE PRICES                     I
I              VARIOUS DISTRIBUTION HYPOTHESES - OTHER                          I
I              2ND SEMESTER 1952 - 2ND SEMESTER 1980 (1)                        I
+-------------------------------------------------------------------------------+
I        I              MEAN               I         STANDARD DEVIATION         I
+--------+----------------------------------+---------------------------------- +
I  SEM I   PUC  I   PUM  I   NR1  I   NR2  I   PUC  I   PUM  I   NR1  I   NR2  I
+--------+--------+--------+--------+--------+--------+--------+--------+--------+
I 5202 I -1.31 I -1.31 I -2.00 I -2.00 I  2.30 I  2.30 I  3.08 I  3.08 I
I 5301 I   .17 I   .18 I  -.09 I   .22 I  2.38 I  2.41 I  2.08 I  2.35 I
I 5302 I  -.29 I  -.26 I  -.23 I  -.23 I  2.42 I  2.50 I  2.37 I  2.37 I
I 5401 I  -.35 I  -.35 I  -.46 I  -.30 I  2.09 I  2.09 I  1.90 I  1.58 I
I 5402 I   .63 I   .65 I   .49 I   .67 I  2.19 I  2.24 I  1.96 I  1.85 I
I 5501 I  1.52 I  1.58 I  1.58 I  1.58 I  2.00 I  2.13 I  1.74 I  1.74 I
I 5502 I   .66 I   .67 I   .69 I   .67 I  1.92 I  1.94 I  1.53 I  1.50 I
I 5601 I  1.34 I  1.39 I  1.33 I  1.33 I  2.08 I  2.18 I  1.80 I  1.80 I
I 5602 I   .91 I   .94 I   .93 I   .93 I  2.07 I  2.14 I  1.76 I  1.76 I
I 5701 I  3.07 I  3.30 I  3.64 I  3.33 I  1.85 I  2.15 I  2.76 I  2.02 I
I 5702 I   .20 I   .20 I   .10 I   .22 I  2.21 I  2.23 I  1.79 I  1.93 I
I 5801 I   .07 I   .09 I   .12 I   .14 I  2.20 I  2.25 I  1.99 I  1.97 I
I 5802 I  -.58 I  -.57 I  -.33 I  -.61 I  2.18 I  2.22 I  1.95 I  1.81 I
I 5901 I  -.34 I  -.34 I  -.47 I  -.47 I  2.01 I  2.01 I  1.81 I  1.81 I
I 5902 I   .37 I   .38 I   .47 I   .37 I  1.86 I  1.88 I  1.58 I  1.42 I
I 6001 I  1.08 I  1.10 I  1.11 I  1.10 I  1.90 I  1.93 I  1.48 I  1.48 I
I 6002 I   .48 I   .49 I   .69 I   .50 I  1.72 I  1.74 I  1.46 I  1.23 I
I 6101 I   .54 I   .56 I   .96 I   .96 I  1.66 I  1.74 I  1.52 I  1.52 I
I 6102 I   .65 I   .68 I  1.21 I  1.21 I  1.63 I  1.71 I  1.40 I  1.40 I
I 6201 I   .88 I   .92 I  1.37 I  1.37 I  1.75 I  1.84 I  1.45 I  1.45 I
I 6202 I  2.70 I  2.84 I  2.73 I  2.85 I  1.59 I  1.83 I  1.63 I  1.36 I
I 6301 I  2.71 I  2.85 I  2.72 I  2.86 I  1.56 I  1.80 I  1.63 I  1.32 I
I 6302 I  2.69 I  2.82 I  2.67 I  2.83 I  1.57 I  1.79 I  1.62 I  1.30 I
I 6401 I  2.42 I  2.50 I  2.32 I  2.49 I  1.63 I  1.77 I  1.48 I  1.26 I
I 6402 I   .72 I   .75 I   .63 I   .79 I  2.10 I  2.16 I  1.93 I  1.76 I
I 6501 I   .90 I   .90 I  1.19 I   .98 I  2.06 I  2.06 I  2.33 I  1.65 I
I 6502 I   .58 I   .59 I   .39 I   .61 I  1.90 I  1.93 I  1.76 I  1.40 I
I 6601 I  1.26 I  1.28 I  1.42 I  1.42 I  1.80 I  1.84 I  1.34 I  1.34 I
I 6602 I  1.19 I  1.20 I  1.07 I  1.07 I  1.73 I  1.77 I  1.53 I  1.53 I
I 6701 I   .71 I   .74 I  1.24 I  1.24 I  1.66 I  1.74 I  1.40 I  1.40 I
I 6702 I   .95 I   .96 I  1.31 I  1.31 I  1.69 I  1.72 I  1.21 I  1.21 I
I 6801 I   .94 I   .94 I  1.02 I  1.03 I  1.67 I  1.67 I  1.02 I  1.02 I
I 6802 I   .89 I   .89 I   .95 I   .95 I  1.62 I  1.62 I  1.03 I  1.03 I
I 6901 I   .52 I   .52 I   .61 I   .61 I  1.56 I  1.56 I  1.04 I  1.04 I
I 6902 I  2.62 I  2.77 I  2.76 I  2.76 I  1.62 I  1.87 I  1.47 I  1.47 I
I 7001 I  3.12 I  3.35 I  3.78 I  3.44 I  1.74 I  2.05 I  2.96 I  2.16 I
I 7002 I  3.20 I  3.43 I  3.45 I  3.45 I  1.44 I  1.79 I  1.35 I  1.35 I
I 7101 I  2.18 I  2.21 I  1.96 I  2.18 I  1.68 I  1.74 I  1.35 I  1.15 I
I 7102 I  1.60 I  1.62 I  1.48 I  1.69 I  1.84 I  1.88 I  1.38 I  1.52 I
I 7201 I  1.58 I  1.61 I  1.54 I  1.54 I  1.84 I  1.89 I  1.41 I  1.41 I
I 7202 I  2.18 I  2.24 I  2.12 I  2.22 I  1.70 I  1.80 I  1.39 I  1.29 I
I 7301 I  2.79 I  2.96 I  2.82 I  2.82 I  1.64 I  1.90 I  1.88 I  1.88 I
I 7302 I  6.02 I  6.02 I  5.83 I  5.48 I  3.13 I  3.13 I  2.88 I  2.45 I
I 7401 I 11.91 I 11.91 I  6.74 I  6.74 I  6.13 I  6.13 I  2.15 I  2.15 I
I 7402 I  4.29 I  4.29 I  4.71 I  4.79 I  3.41 I  3.41 I  3.86 I  4.00 I
I 7501 I  2.54 I  2.69 I  3.00 I  3.00 I  2.85 I  3.03 I  3.57 I  3.57 I
I 7502 I  1.21 I  1.30 I  1.26 I  1.26 I  2.45 I  2.61 I  2.31 I  2.32 I
I 7601 I  2.45 I  2.62 I  2.56 I  2.56 I  2.00 I  2.26 I  2.08 I  2.08 I
I 7602 I  4.95 I  4.95 I  4.87 I  4.87 I  2.51 I  2.51 I  2.24 I  2.24 I
I 7701 I  4.56 I  4.56 I  5.02 I  4.61 I  2.36 I  2.36 I  2.75 I  2.03 I
I 7702 I  2.75 I  2.96 I  2.96 I  2.96 I  1.99 I  2.28 I  2.14 I  2.14 I
I 7801 I  3.88 I  3.90 I  3.86 I  3.82 I  2.81 I  2.86 I  2.96 I  2.69 I
I 7802 I  4.45 I  4.48 I  4.39 I  4.78 I  2.71 I  2.78 I  2.39 I  2.63 I
I 7901 I  4.56 I  4.58 I  4.67 I  4.67 I  2.64 I  2.69 I  2.61 I  2.61 I
I 7902 I  5.92 I  5.98 I  6.22 I  6.22 I  2.60 I  2.72 I  2.47 I  2.47 I
I 8001 I  7.53 I  7.66 I  7.78 I  7.73 I  2.89 I  3.08 I  2.93 I  3.11 I
I 8002 I  6.24 I  6.32 I  6.41 I  6.41 I  3.31 I  3.45 I  3.59 I  3.59 I
+-------------------------------------------------------------------------------+
I (1) THE SEMESTERS ARE THOSE FOR WHICH EXPECTATIONS ARE FORMED AT THE END       I
I OF THE PREVIOUS SEMESTER                                                       I
+-------------------------------------------------------------------------------+
```

TABLE D.19

	MEAN				STANDARD DEVIATION			
SEM	PUC	PUM	NR1	NR2	PUC	PUM	NR1	NR2

EXPECTED RATES OF CHANGE OF CONSUMER PRICES
VARIOUS DISTRIBUTION HYPOTHESES - TOTAL
2ND SEMESTER 1956 - 2ND SEMESTER 1980 (1)

SEM	PUC	PUM	NR1	NR2	PUC	PUM	NR1	NR2
5602	2.17	2.24	2.02	2.02	1.82	1.94	1.65	1.65
5701	3.68	3.89	4.04	3.93	1.68	1.95	1.93	1.55
5702	1.46	1.50	1.44	1.44	1.97	2.05	1.63	1.63
5801	1.38	1.39	.89	1.47	1.93	1.95	1.72	1.61
5802	1.03	1.05	1.05	1.05	1.94	1.99	1.56	1.56
5901	.93	.95	.75	.83	2.22	2.27	1.89	1.80
5902	.67	.69	.80	.69	1.82	1.85	1.48	1.35
6001	1.25	1.29	1.47	1.47	1.84	1.92	1.46	1.46
6002	.77	.77	.80	.80	1.87	1.87	1.46	1.46
6101	1.25	1.27	1.05	1.34	1.89	1.94	1.79	1.43
6102	1.53	1.58	1.73	1.51	1.86	1.96	1.48	1.66
6201	2.06	2.14	2.14	2.14	1.79	1.94	1.50	1.50
6202	3.74	3.96	3.99	3.99	1.57	1.85	1.43	1.43
6301	3.88	4.09	4.12	4.12	1.49	1.77	1.22	1.22
6302	3.53	3.76	3.79	3.79	1.65	1.95	1.58	1.58
6401	3.11	3.32	3.31	3.35	1.53	1.87	1.74	1.41
6402	2.21	2.33	2.33	2.34	1.85	2.07	1.68	1.67
6501	2.53	2.64	2.46	2.65	1.65	1.84	1.62	1.33
6502	2.24	2.28	2.05	2.26	1.67	1.75	1.39	1.19
6601	2.29	2.35	2.17	2.34	1.67	1.78	1.44	1.26
6602	2.08	2.12	2.11	2.11	1.75	1.84	1.29	1.29
6701	1.94	2.00	1.96	1.96	1.76	1.88	1.49	1.49
6702	2.08	2.12	1.98	2.11	1.73	1.81	1.39	1.27
6801	2.57	2.63	2.59	2.59	1.47	1.60	1.14	1.14
6802	1.85	1.88	1.85	1.85	1.74	1.82	1.35	1.35
6901	1.65	1.69	1.63	1.63	1.77	1.86	1.48	1.48
6902	3.13	3.35	3.36	3.36	1.57	1.91	1.51	1.51
7001	3.74	3.97	4.32	4.02	1.51	1.81	2.00	1.26
7002	3.47	3.71	3.88	3.76	1.45	1.80	1.88	1.29
7101	2.81	2.94	2.93	2.93	1.41	1.64	1.21	1.21
7102	2.67	2.79	2.60	2.80	1.55	1.75	1.61	1.25
7201	2.61	2.73	2.66	2.73	1.59	1.80	1.48	1.35
7202	2.88	3.00	3.00	3.00	1.31	1.54	1.12	1.12
7301	4.49	4.49	4.51	4.51	1.85	1.85	1.40	1.40
7302	6.69	6.69	5.43	5.43	3.12	3.12	1.68	1.68
7401	8.08	8.08	5.93	5.93	3.94	3.94	1.96	1.96
7402	9.60	9.60	7.23	7.06	5.22	5.22	3.31	3.16
7501	5.37	5.37	6.78	5.91	3.35	3.35	4.72	3.76
7502	2.98	3.17	3.39	3.26	2.16	2.41	2.73	2.34
7601	3.99	4.09	5.15	4.20	1.97	2.08	3.13	1.74
7602	7.82	7.82	6.07	6.07	3.92	3.92	2.33	2.33
7701	7.32	7.32	9.50	7.59	3.81	3.81	5.21	3.78
7702	5.49	5.78	5.83	5.88	2.40	2.81	2.63	2.15
7801	5.40	5.44	5.75	5.75	2.72	2.81	2.63	2.63
7802	5.57	5.62	5.80	5.87	2.78	2.89	2.79	2.66
7901	5.97	6.02	6.23	6.31	2.66	2.78	2.66	2.49
7902	6.78	6.87	7.08	6.99	2.44	2.61	2.31	2.45
8001	8.06	8.20	8.32	8.31	2.63	2.83	2.60	2.75
8002	7.29	7.40	7.55	7.55	3.04	3.20	3.39	3.02

(1) THE SEMESTERS ARE THOSE FOR WHICH EXPECTATIONS ARE FORMED AT THE END
OF THE PREVIOUS SEMESTER

TABLE D.20

EXPECTED RATES OF CHANGE OF CONSUMER PRICES VARIOUS DISTRIBUTION HYPOTHESES - PRODUCTION 2ND SEMESTER 1956 - 2ND SEMESTER 1980 (1)								
		MEAN				STANDARD DEVIATION		
SEM	PUC	PUM	NR1	NR2	PUC	PUM	NR1	NR2
5602	2.16	2.24	2.00	2.00	1.89	2.03	1.77	1.77
5701	3.60	3.83	4.05	3.88	1.62	1.92	2.08	1.44
5702	1.39	1.45	1.47	1.47	2.02	2.13	1.75	1.75
5801	1.19	1.21	.81	1.24	1.93	1.96	1.82	1.41
5802	.71	.74	.83	.83	2.03	2.11	1.80	1.80
5901	.81	.85	.71	.89	2.17	2.24	2.04	1.84
5902	.52	.53	.70	.53	1.78	1.81	1.52	1.30
6001	1.28	1.32	1.61	1.17	1.81	1.88	1.37	1.69
6002	.35	.35	.36	.36	1.86	1.86	1.44	1.44
6101	1.17	1.18	.72	1.25	2.03	2.05	1.88	1.63
6102	1.57	1.65	1.89	1.50	1.90	2.05	1.54	1.92
6201	1.93	2.03	2.03	2.03	1.91	2.07	1.68	1.68
6202	3.72	3.91	3.96	3.96	1.71	1.96	1.63	1.63
6301	3.73	3.96	3.99	3.99	1.48	1.79	1.31	1.31
6302	3.45	3.68	3.71	3.71	1.67	1.97	1.62	1.62
6401	3.11	3.33	3.35	3.35	1.63	1.95	1.58	1.58
6402	2.13	2.25	2.16	2.16	1.95	2.15	1.85	1.85
6501	2.54	2.65	2.44	2.68	1.68	1.87	1.71	1.32
6502	2.08	2.12	1.93	2.11	1.73	1.80	1.39	1.23
6601	2.27	2.34	2.18	2.33	1.70	1.83	1.48	1.31
6602	2.08	2.14	2.16	2.16	1.83	1.94	1.34	1.34
6701	1.95	2.02	1.98	1.98	1.77	1.90	1.53	1.53
6702	2.10	2.13	1.93	2.12	1.72	1.79	1.38	1.21
6801	2.78	2.88	2.86	2.86	1.35	1.54	1.11	1.11
6802	1.98	2.00	1.96	1.96	1.70	1.75	1.19	1.19
6901	1.67	1.71	1.65	1.65	1.78	1.88	1.53	1.53
6902	3.21	3.44	3.45	3.45	1.60	1.94	1.55	1.55
7001	4.17	4.29	4.32	4.32	1.62	1.77	1.22	1.22
7002	3.42	3.66	3.81	3.71	1.60	1.93	2.08	1.42
7101	2.71	2.83	2.81	2.81	1.46	1.67	1.24	1.24
7102	2.61	2.70	2.51	2.70	1.53	1.71	1.50	1.22
7201	2.66	2.81	2.81	2.81	1.64	1.90	1.51	1.51
7202	2.86	2.98	2.98	2.98	1.35	1.58	1.15	1.15
7301	4.78	4.78	4.65	4.65	1.98	1.98	1.37	1.37
7302	6.46	6.46	5.33	5.33	2.86	2.86	1.60	1.60
7401	8.18	8.18	5.85	5.85	3.95	3.95	1.82	1.82
7402	11.15	11.15	8.07	8.07	6.38	6.38	4.11	4.11
7501	5.57	5.57	6.74	6.02	3.38	3.38	4.51	3.74
7502	2.90	3.06	3.32	3.24	2.46	2.67	3.06	2.77
7601	4.17	4.23	4.31	4.31	1.84	1.92	1.63	1.63
7602	7.12	7.12	5.76	5.76	3.47	3.47	2.12	2.12
7701	7.31	7.31	5.73	5.73	3.65	3.65	1.93	1.93
7702	5.39	5.68	5.73	5.80	2.52	2.92	2.83	2.24
7801	5.24	5.27	5.76	5.76	2.71	2.77	2.52	2.52
7802	5.25	5.29	5.56	5.63	2.73	2.83	2.71	2.61
7901	5.81	5.84	6.12	5.66	2.72	2.79	2.73	3.08
7902	6.73	6.81	6.93	6.93	2.38	2.55	2.44	2.44
8001	7.73	7.88	7.93	7.95	2.54	2.76	2.63	2.56
8002	7.12	7.21	7.39	7.40	3.13	3.27	3.36	3.04

(1) THE SEMESTERS ARE THOSE FOR WHICH EXPECTATIONS ARE FORMED AT THE END OF THE PREVIOUS SEMESTER

TABLE D.21

	MEAN				STANDARD DEVIATION			
SEM	PUC	PUM	NR1	NR2	PUC	PUM	NR1	NR2
5602	2.18	2.24	2.04	2.26	1.75	1.87	1.54	1.31
5701	3.74	3.93	3.98	3.98	1.74	1.97	1.66	1.66
5702	1.51	1.54	1.39	1.39	1.94	1.99	1.53	1.53
5801	1.50	1.51	1.19	1.65	1.92	1.94	1.38	1.76
5802	1.26	1.27	1.20	1.29	1.84	1.86	1.33	1.40
5901	1.01	1.02	.78	1.22	2.25	2.28	1.75	2.35
5902	.80	.81	.87	.81	1.84	1.87	1.45	1.38
6001	1.23	1.26	1.40	1.40	1.87	1.94	1.50	1.50
6002	1.09	1.09	1.12	1.12	1.82	1.82	1.36	1.36
6101	1.30	1.33	1.61	1.23	1.79	1.85	1.31	1.57
6102	1.50	1.53	1.58	1.51	1.83	1.90	1.40	1.45
6201	2.17	2.23	2.21	2.21	1.70	1.82	1.38	1.38
6202	3.76	3.99	4.03	4.03	1.45	1.76	1.23	1.23
6301	3.99	4.18	4.22	4.22	1.49	1.74	1.11	1.11
6302	3.61	3.83	3.86	3.86	1.63	1.92	1.54	1.54
6401	3.11	3.32	3.30	3.36	1.47	1.80	1.80	1.30
6402	2.27	2.39	2.36	2.36	1.78	2.01	1.68	1.68
6501	2.52	2.63	2.50	2.63	1.62	1.81	1.54	1.33
6502	2.36	2.41	2.15	2.38	1.61	1.71	1.40	1.16
6601	2.31	2.37	2.16	2.35	1.65	1.75	1.41	1.22
6602	2.08	2.11	2.08	2.08	1.68	1.75	1.24	1.24
6701	1.93	1.99	1.95	1.95	1.76	1.87	1.46	1.46
6702	2.06	2.11	2.01	2.10	1.74	1.83	1.39	1.31
6801	2.39	2.42	2.36	2.36	1.54	1.62	1.11	1.11
6802	1.72	1.77	1.71	1.71	1.78	1.87	1.51	1.51
6901	1.63	1.66	1.62	1.62	1.77	1.83	1.43	1.43
6902	3.07	3.29	3.30	3.30	1.55	1.88	1.48	1.48
7001	3.47	3.72	3.96	3.78	1.45	1.80	2.01	1.23
7002	3.51	3.76	3.81	3.81	1.32	1.69	1.16	1.16
7101	2.89	3.02	3.02	3.02	1.35	1.60	1.17	1.17
7102	2.74	2.87	2.69	2.90	1.56	1.79	1.71	1.27
7201	2.57	2.66	2.46	2.65	1.54	1.70	1.48	1.21
7202	2.90	3.02	3.02	3.02	1.28	1.50	1.08	1.08
7301	4.27	4.34	4.38	4.38	1.75	1.82	1.40	1.40
7302	6.90	6.90	5.52	5.52	3.33	3.33	1.73	1.73
7401	8.00	8.00	5.97	5.97	3.92	3.92	2.07	2.07
7402	8.63	8.63	7.76	6.40	4.48	4.48	3.67	2.50
7501	5.20	5.20	6.78	5.81	3.32	3.32	4.87	3.77
7502	3.06	3.27	3.30	3.30	1.86	2.15	1.91	1.91
7601	3.84	3.96	4.99	4.10	2.06	2.20	3.35	1.81
7602	8.62	8.62	6.42	6.42	4.42	4.42	2.54	2.54
7701	7.34	7.34	9.05	7.76	3.94	3.94	5.15	4.13
7702	5.58	5.88	5.95	5.95	2.26	2.69	2.05	2.05
7801	5.59	5.64	5.78	5.78	2.73	2.85	2.71	2.71
7802	5.91	5.96	6.05	6.14	2.79	2.91	2.88	2.71
7901	6.13	6.20	6.36	6.36	2.62	2.75	2.55	2.55
7902	6.84	6.93	7.04	7.06	2.50	2.68	2.49	2.45
8001	8.38	8.49	8.63	8.63	2.71	2.86	2.91	2.91
8002	7.45	7.57	7.72	7.69	2.95	3.12	3.41	3.00

EXPECTED RATES OF CHANGE OF CONSUMER PRICES
VARIOUS DISTRIBUTION HYPOTHESES - OTHER
2ND SEMESTER 1956 - 2ND SEMESTER 1980 (1)

(1) THE SEMESTERS ARE THOSE FOR WHICH EXPECTATIONS ARE FORMED AT THE END
OF THE PREVIOUS SEMESTER

TABLE D.22

SEM	WPCS	MUWPUM	MUWMIX	ERWPUM	ERWMIX	SIWPUM	SIWMIX
5202	-.43	-1.48	-1.48	1.06	1.06	2.23	2.23
5301	-.14	-.21	-.23	.07	.09	2.59	2.53
5302	-.05	-.35	-.38	.29	.33	2.47	2.39
5401	.61	-.50	-.50	1.11	1.11	2.09	2.09
5402	.10	.63	.61	-.53	-.51	2.26	2.21
5501	.87	1.32	1.28	-.45	-.41	2.09	2.00
5502	-.12	.60	.60	-.72	-.71	1.96	1.94
5601	1.43	1.42	1.37	.02	.07	2.20	2.10
5602	.71	.83	.80	-.13	-.09	2.29	2.22
5701	.77	3.46	3.24	-2.70	-2.47	2.10	1.80
5702	-.39	.20	.20	-.59	-.58	2.17	2.16
5801	-.52	-.07	-.09	-.45	-.44	2.24	2.19
5802	-2.13	-.92	-.92	-1.21	-1.20	2.20	2.17
5901	-2.37	-.36	-.36	-2.01	-2.01	2.01	2.01
5902	.96	.15	.15	.80	.81	1.82	1.80
6001	.51	1.24	1.22	-.73	-.71	1.95	1.91
6002	-.12	.13	.13	-.25	-.25	1.83	1.81
6101	.25	.58	.56	-.32	-.31	1.88	1.84
6102	.05	.66	.65	-.61	-.60	1.72	1.67
6201	2.26	.87	.82	1.39	1.44	2.02	1.90
6202	1.55	2.61	2.47	-1.06	-.92	2.05	1.82
6301	3.44	2.64	2.50	.80	.93	1.98	1.76
6302	1.86	2.75	2.62	-.88	-.76	1.79	1.57
6401	2.02	2.40	2.32	-.38	-.30	1.82	1.67
6402	.60	.74	.71	-.14	-.10	2.25	2.18
6501	.85	.99	.98	-.14	-.13	2.11	2.09
6502	.97	.43	.42	.54	.54	1.83	1.82
6601	1.28	1.26	1.25	.02	.03	1.84	1.80
6602	-.62	1.13	1.12	-1.76	-1.75	1.82	1.79
6701	-.13	.77	.75	-.91	-.88	1.74	1.68
6702	.59	.77	.77	-.19	-.18	1.78	1.77
6801	.33	.93	.92	-.59	-.58	1.76	1.74
6802	-.55	.88	.87	-1.43	-1.42	1.66	1.63
6901	2.17	.56	.56	1.60	1.60	1.73	1.73
6902	3.97	2.88	2.72	1.09	1.25	1.86	1.59
7001	4.55	3.55	3.30	1.01	1.25	1.98	1.66
7002	1.43	3.37	3.14	-1.94	-1.72	1.91	1.57
7101	1.87	2.27	2.21	-.40	-.33	1.84	1.72
7102	1.28	1.62	1.60	-.34	-.32	1.89	1.84
7201	1.78	1.67	1.63	.11	.14	1.92	1.85
7202	3.23	2.25	2.19	.97	1.04	1.82	1.70
7301	8.61	3.18	3.18	5.43	5.43	1.89	1.89
7302	12.11	6.31	6.31	5.81	5.81	3.18	3.18
7401	25.88	11.14	11.14	14.74	14.74	5.78	5.78
7402	11.55	4.44	4.44	7.11	7.11	3.31	3.31
7501	1.79	2.94	2.94	-1.14	-1.14	2.97	2.97
7502	2.20	1.38	1.38	.82	.82	2.57	2.57
7601	14.13	2.71	2.71	11.42	11.42	2.25	2.25
7602	13.04	4.75	4.75	8.29	8.29	2.40	2.40
7701	8.58	4.64	4.64	3.94	3.94	2.29	2.29
7702	3.73	2.80	2.80	.92	.92	2.33	2.33
7801	4.32	3.84	4.37	.49	-.05	2.79	2.52
7802	4.12	4.26	4.30	-.14	-.19	2.80	2.99
7901	8.00	4.57	4.81	3.43	3.19	2.75	2.59
7902	9.60	5.84	6.15	3.75	3.45	2.67	2.39
8001	11.44	7.34	7.48	4.10	3.97	3.03	2.74
8002	6.10	5.92	5.95	.19	.15	3.50	3.59

| (1) THE DEFINITIONS OF THE VARIABLES ARE GIVEN IN TABLE D.28

TABLE D.23

SEM	WPCS	MUWPUM	MUWMIX	ERWPUM	ERWMIX	SIWPUM	SIWMIX

ACTUAL AND EXPECTED RATES OF CHANGE OF WHOLESALE PRICES (1)
PRODUCTION RESPONDENTS
2ND SEMESTER 1952 – 2ND SEMESTER 1980

SEM	WPCS	MUWPUM	MUWMIX	ERWPUM	ERWMIX	SIWPUM	SIWMIX
5202	-.43	-1.64	-1.64	1.21	1.21	2.15	2.15
5301	-.14	-.66	-.69	.52	.55	2.71	2.63
5302	-.05	-.45	-.48	.40	.43	2.43	2.35
5401	.61	-.70	-.70	1.31	1.31	2.08	2.08
5402	.10	.62	.59	-.52	-.49	2.29	2.23
5501	.87	1.00	.99	-.13	-.11	2.00	1.96
5502	-.12	.51	.51	-.63	-.63	1.97	1.97
5601	1.43	1.46	1.41	-.03	.02	2.22	2.13
5602	.71	.70	.67	.01	.04	2.44	2.37
5701	.77	3.68	3.45	-2.91	-2.69	2.02	1.73
5702	-.39	.20	.20	-.58	-.58	2.09	2.09
5801	-.52	-.34	-.35	-.18	-.17	2.18	2.15
5802	-2.13	-1.41	-1.41	-.72	-.72	2.06	2.06
5901	-2.37	-.38	-.38	-1.99	-1.99	2.00	2.00
5902	.96	-.12	-.12	1.08	1.08	1.70	1.70
6001	.51	1.43	1.41	-.92	-.90	1.96	1.91
6002	-.12	-.34	-.34	.22	.22	1.84	1.84
6101	.25	.60	.60	-.35	-.35	2.08	2.08
6102	.05	.65	.65	-.60	-.60	1.73	1.73
6201	2.26	.79	.73	1.46	1.52	2.23	2.09
6202	1.55	2.33	2.19	-.78	-.64	2.25	2.03
6301	3.44	2.37	2.24	1.06	1.20	2.17	1.95
6302	1.86	2.67	2.56	-.80	-.69	1.78	1.58
6401	2.02	2.25	2.17	-.23	-.15	1.88	1.72
6402	.60	.74	.69	-.13	-.09	2.39	2.28
6501	.85	1.11	1.09	-.26	-.24	2.18	2.13
6502	.97	.22	.22	.74	.74	1.69	1.69
6601	1.28	1.24	1.23	.04	.05	1.84	1.81
6602	-.62	1.04	1.04	-1.66	-1.66	1.87	1.87
6701	-.13	.82	.81	-.96	-.94	1.75	1.71
6702	.59	.55	.55	.04	.04	1.84	1.84
6801	.33	.91	.89	-.58	-.55	1.86	1.81
6802	-.55	.87	.85	-1.42	-1.40	1.70	1.64
6901	2.17	.61	.61	1.56	1.56	1.90	1.90
6902	3.97	3.03	2.85	.94	1.12	1.84	1.55
7001	4.55	3.81	3.57	.74	.99	1.86	1.53
7002	1.43	3.29	3.07	-1.87	-1.64	2.05	1.73
7101	1.87	2.34	2.24	-.47	-.37	1.96	1.78
7102	1.28	1.62	1.59	-.34	-.31	1.90	1.85
7201	1.78	1.74	1.69	.04	.09	1.96	1.85
7202	3.23	2.27	2.19	.96	1.03	1.84	1.70
7301	8.61	3.44	3.44	5.17	5.17	1.84	1.84
7302	12.11	6.68	6.68	5.43	5.43	3.22	3.22
7401	25.88	10.37	10.37	15.51	15.51	5.43	5.43
7402	11.55	4.61	4.61	6.93	6.93	3.18	3.18
7501	1.79	3.21	3.21	-1.42	-1.42	2.87	2.87
7502	2.20	1.46	1.46	.74	.74	2.52	2.52
7601	14.13	2.81	2.81	11.32	11.32	2.24	2.24
7602	13.04	4.55	4.55	8.49	8.49	2.30	2.30
7701	8.58	4.73	4.73	3.85	3.85	2.22	2.22
7702	3.73	2.65	2.65	1.08	1.08	2.36	2.36
7801	4.32	3.78	4.24	.54	.09	2.73	2.61
7802	4.12	4.05	4.07	.07	.05	2.81	2.96
7901	8.00	4.56	4.75	3.44	3.25	2.81	2.75
7902	9.60	5.72	6.10	3.88	3.49	2.62	2.30
8001	11.44	6.98	7.17	4.47	4.27	2.93	2.51
8002	6.10	5.49	5.49	.61	.61	3.50	3.54

(1) THE DEFINITIONS OF THE VARIABLES ARE GIVEN IN TABLE D.28

Ignazio Visco

TABLE D.24

SEM	WPCS	MUWPUM	MUWMIX	ERWPUM	ERWMIX	SIWPUM	SIWMIX

ACTUAL AND EXPECTED RATES OF CHANGE OF WHOLESALE PRICES (1)
OTHER RESPONDENTS
2ND SEMESTER 1952 – 2ND SEMESTER 1980

SEM	WPCS	MUWPUM	MUWMIX	ERWPUM	ERWMIX	SIWPUM	SIWMIX
5202	-.43	-1.31	-1.31	.88	.88	2.30	2.30
5301	-.14	.18	.17	-.33	-.31	2.41	2.38
5302	-.05	-.26	-.29	.21	.24	2.50	2.42
5401	.61	-.35	-.35	.96	.96	2.09	2.09
5402	.10	.65	.63	-.55	-.52	2.24	2.19
5501	.87	1.58	1.52	-.71	-.64	2.13	2.00
5502	-.12	.67	.66	-.79	-.78	1.94	1.92
5601	1.43	1.39	1.34	.04	.09	2.18	2.08
5602	.71	.94	.91	-.24	-.21	2.14	2.07
5701	.77	3.30	3.07	-2.53	-2.31	2.15	1.85
5702	-.39	.20	.20	-.59	-.58	2.23	2.21
5801	-.52	.09	.07	-.61	-.59	2.25	2.20
5802	-2.13	-.57	-.58	-1.56	-1.54	2.22	2.18
5901	-2.37	-.34	-.34	-2.03	-2.03	2.01	2.01
5902	.96	.38	.37	.58	.59	1.88	1.86
6001	.51	1.10	1.08	-.59	-.58	1.93	1.90
6002	-.12	.49	.48	-.61	-.60	1.74	1.72
6101	.25	.56	.54	-.31	-.28	1.74	1.66
6102	.05	.68	.65	-.62	-.60	1.71	1.63
6201	2.26	.92	.88	1.34	1.37	1.84	1.75
6202	1.55	2.84	2.70	-1.29	-1.15	1.83	1.59
6301	3.44	2.85	2.71	.59	.72	1.80	1.56
6302	1.86	2.82	2.69	-.95	-.82	1.79	1.57
6401	2.02	2.50	2.42	-.48	-.41	1.77	1.63
6402	.60	.75	.72	-.14	-.12	2.16	2.10
6501	.85	.90	.90	-.04	-.04	2.06	2.06
6502	.97	.59	.58	.37	.38	1.93	1.90
6601	1.28	1.28	1.26	.01	.02	1.84	1.80
6602	-.62	1.20	1.19	-1.83	-1.81	1.77	1.73
6701	-.13	.74	.71	-.87	-.84	1.74	1.66
6702	.59	.96	.95	-.37	-.37	1.72	1.69
6801	.33	.94	.94	-.61	-.61	1.67	1.67
6802	-.55	.89	.89	-1.44	-1.44	1.62	1.62
6901	2.17	.52	.52	1.64	1.64	1.56	1.56
6902	3.97	2.77	2.62	1.20	1.35	1.87	1.62
7001	4.55	3.35	3.12	1.21	1.43	2.05	1.74
7002	1.43	3.43	3.20	-2.00	-1.78	1.79	1.44
7101	1.87	2.21	2.18	-.34	-.31	1.74	1.68
7102	1.28	1.62	1.60	-.34	-.32	1.88	1.84
7201	1.78	1.61	1.58	.17	.19	1.89	1.84
7202	3.23	2.24	2.18	.99	1.04	1.80	1.70
7301	8.61	2.96	2.96	5.66	5.66	1.90	1.90
7302	12.11	6.02	6.02	6.10	6.10	3.13	3.13
7401	25.88	11.91	11.91	13.97	13.97	6.13	6.13
7402	11.55	4.29	4.29	7.26	7.26	3.41	3.41
7501	1.79	2.69	2.69	-.90	-.90	3.03	3.03
7502	2.20	1.30	1.30	.90	.90	2.61	2.61
7601	14.13	2.62	2.62	11.51	11.51	2.26	2.26
7602	13.04	4.95	4.95	8.08	8.08	2.51	2.51
7701	8.58	4.56	4.56	4.02	4.02	2.36	2.36
7702	3.73	2.96	2.96	.77	.77	2.28	2.28
7801	4.32	3.90	3.86	.42	.47	2.86	2.96
7802	4.12	4.48	4.39	-.36	-.27	2.78	2.39
7901	8.00	4.58	4.67	3.42	3.33	2.69	2.61
7902	9.60	5.98	6.22	3.62	3.38	2.72	2.47
8001	11.44	7.66	7.78	3.78	3.67	3.08	2.93
8002	6.10	6.32	6.41	-.22	-.30	3.45	3.59

(1) THE DEFINITIONS OF THE VARIABLES ARE GIVEN IN TABLE D.28

TABLE D.25

```
+------------------------------------------------------------------------+
I    ACTUAL AND EXPECTED RATES OF CHANGE OF CONSUMER PRICES (1)          I
I                        TOTAL RESPONDENTS                               I
I              2ND SEMESTER 1956 - 2ND SEMESTER 1980                     I
+--------+--------+--------+--------+--------+--------+--------+----------+
I  SEM   I  CPCS  I MUCPUM I MUCMIX I ERCPUM I ERCMIX I SICPUM I SICMIX  I
+--------+--------+--------+--------+--------+--------+--------+----------+
```

SEM	CPCS	MUCPUM	MUCMIX	ERCPUM	ERCMIX	SICPUM	SICMIX
5602	.68	2.24	2.17	-1.57	-1.50	1.94	1.82
5701	.41	3.89	3.68	-3.47	-3.26	1.95	1.68
5702	1.13	1.50	1.46	-.37	-.33	2.05	1.97
5801	2.17	1.39	1.38	.77	.78	1.95	1.93
5802	.25	1.05	1.03	-.80	-.78	1.99	1.94
5901	-1.07	.95	.93	-2.02	-2.00	2.27	2.22
5902	.88	.69	.67	.19	.20	1.85	1.82
6001	1.56	1.29	1.25	.27	.31	1.92	1.84
6002	.68	.77	.77	-.09	-.09	1.87	1.87
6101	1.09	1.27	1.25	-.18	-.16	1.94	1.89
6102	1.21	1.58	1.53	-.37	-.32	1.96	1.86
6201	2.73	2.14	2.06	.59	.66	1.94	1.79
6202	2.60	3.96	3.74	-1.35	-1.14	1.85	1.57
6301	4.90	4.09	3.88	.81	1.02	1.77	1.49
6302	2.28	3.76	3.53	-1.48	-1.26	1.95	1.65
6401	3.21	3.32	3.11	-.11	.10	1.87	1.53
6402	2.95	2.33	2.21	.62	.74	2.07	1.85
6501	2.21	2.64	2.53	-.42	-.32	1.84	1.65
6502	1.58	2.28	2.24	-.70	-.66	1.75	1.67
6601	1.14	2.35	2.29	-1.21	-1.15	1.78	1.67
6602	.81	2.12	2.08	-1.31	-1.26	1.84	1.75
6701	2.19	2.00	1.94	.19	.25	1.88	1.76
6702	1.26	2.12	2.08	-.86	-.81	1.81	1.73
6801	.57	2.63	2.57	-2.06	-1.99	1.60	1.47
6802	.14	1.88	1.85	-1.74	-1.70	1.82	1.74
6901	1.49	1.69	1.65	-.20	-.16	1.86	1.77
6902	2.16	3.35	3.13	-1.20	-.97	1.91	1.57
7001	2.72	3.97	3.74	-1.25	-1.01	1.81	1.51
7002	2.22	3.71	3.47	-1.50	-1.25	1.80	1.45
7101	2.62	2.94	2.81	-.32	-.19	1.64	1.41
7102	2.17	2.79	2.67	-.62	-.50	1.75	1.55
7201	2.66	2.73	2.61	-.07	.05	1.80	1.59
7202	3.83	3.00	2.88	.83	.95	1.54	1.31
7301	5.89	4.49	4.49	1.40	1.40	1.85	1.85
7302	5.42	6.69	6.69	-1.27	-1.27	3.12	3.12
7401	9.51	8.08	8.08	1.43	1.43	3.94	3.94
7402	12.02	9.60	9.60	2.42	2.42	5.22	5.22
7501	8.10	5.37	5.37	2.73	2.73	3.35	3.35
7502	4.78	3.17	3.17	1.60	1.60	2.41	2.41
7601	8.99	4.09	4.09	4.91	4.91	2.08	2.08
7602	9.34	7.82	7.82	1.52	1.52	3.92	3.92
7701	9.98	7.32	7.32	2.65	2.65	3.81	3.81
7702	6.20	5.78	5.78	.42	.42	2.81	2.81
7801	5.90	5.44	5.75	.47	.16	2.81	2.63
7802	5.51	5.62	5.80	-.11	-.28	2.89	2.79
7901	7.34	6.02	6.23	1.32	1.11	2.78	2.66
7902	8.31	6.87	7.08	1.44	1.24	2.61	2.31
8001	11.51	8.20	8.32	3.31	3.19	2.83	2.60
8002	9.10	7.40	7.55	1.70	1.54	3.20	3.39

```
+--------+--------+--------+--------+--------+--------+--------+----------+
I (1) THE DEFINITIONS OF THE VARIABLES ARE GIVEN IN TABLE D.28            I
+------------------------------------------------------------------------+
```

TABLE D.26

		ACTUAL AND EXPECTED RATES OF CHANGE OF CONSUMER PRICES (1) PRODUCTION RESPONDENTS 2ND SEMESTER 1956 - 2ND SEMESTER 1980					
SEM	CPCS	MUCPUM	MUCMIX	ERCPUM	ERCMIX	SICPUM	SICMIX
5602	.68	2.24	2.16	-1.57	-1.49	2.03	1.89
5701	.41	3.83	3.60	-3.42	-3.19	1.92	1.62
5702	1.13	1.45	1.39	-.32	-.26	2.13	2.02
5801	2.17	1.21	1.19	.96	.97	1.96	1.93
5802	.25	.74	.71	-.49	-.46	2.11	2.03
5901	-1.07	.85	.81	-1.92	-1.88	2.24	2.17
5902	.88	.53	.52	.34	.35	1.81	1.78
6001	1.56	1.32	1.28	.24	.28	1.88	1.81
6002	.68	.35	.35	.33	.33	1.86	1.86
6101	1.09	1.18	1.17	-.09	-.08	2.05	2.03
6102	1.21	1.65	1.57	-.44	-.36	2.05	1.90
6201	2.73	2.03	1.93	.70	.79	2.07	1.91
6202	2.60	3.91	3.72	-1.31	-1.12	1.96	1.71
6301	4.90	3.96	3.73	.94	1.17	1.79	1.48
6302	2.28	3.68	3.45	-1.40	-1.18	1.97	1.67
6401	3.21	3.33	3.11	-.12	.10	1.95	1.63
6402	2.95	2.25	2.13	.70	.82	2.15	1.95
6501	2.21	2.65	2.54	-.43	-.32	1.87	1.68
6502	1.58	2.12	2.08	-.54	-.50	1.80	1.73
6601	1.14	2.34	2.27	-1.20	-1.13	1.83	1.70
6602	.81	2.14	2.08	-1.32	-1.27	1.94	1.83
6701	2.19	2.02	1.95	.17	.24	1.90	1.77
6702	1.26	2.13	2.10	-.87	-.84	1.79	1.72
6801	.57	2.88	2.78	-2.31	-2.21	1.54	1.35
6802	.14	2.00	1.98	-1.86	-1.83	1.75	1.70
6901	1.49	1.71	1.67	-.22	-.18	1.88	1.78
6902	2.16	3.44	3.21	-1.28	-1.05	1.94	1.60
7001	2.72	4.29	4.17	-1.57	-1.45	1.77	1.62
7002	2.22	3.66	3.42	-1.44	-1.20	1.93	1.60
7101	2.62	2.83	2.71	-.21	-.10	1.67	1.46
7102	2.17	2.70	2.61	-.53	-.44	1.71	1.53
7201	2.66	2.81	2.66	-.15	.00	1.90	1.64
7202	3.83	2.98	2.86	.85	.97	1.58	1.35
7301	5.89	4.78	4.78	1.11	1.11	1.98	1.98
7302	5.42	6.46	6.46	-1.04	-1.04	2.86	2.86
7401	9.51	8.18	8.18	1.33	1.33	3.95	3.95
7402	12.02	11.15	11.15	.86	.86	6.38	6.38
7501	8.10	5.57	5.57	2.53	2.53	3.38	3.38
7502	4.78	3.06	3.06	1.71	1.71	2.67	2.67
7601	8.99	4.23	4.23	4.76	4.76	1.92	1.92
7602	9.34	7.12	7.12	2.22	2.22	3.47	3.47
7701	9.98	7.31	7.31	2.67	2.67	3.65	3.65
7702	6.20	5.68	5.68	.52	.52	2.92	2.92
7801	5.90	5.27	5.76	.64	.14	2.77	2.52
7802	5.51	5.29	5.56	.22	-.04	2.83	2.71
7901	7.34	5.84	6.12	1.50	1.22	2.79	2.73
7902	8.31	6.81	6.93	1.50	1.38	2.55	2.44
8001	11.51	7.88	7.93	3.63	3.57	2.76	2.63
8002	9.10	7.21	7.39	1.89	1.71	3.27	3.36

(1) THE DEFINITIONS OF THE VARIABLES ARE GIVEN IN TABLE D.28

TABLE D.27

```
+----------------------------------------------------------------------+
I      ACTUAL AND EXPECTED RATES OF CHANGE OF CONSUMER PRICES (1)       I
I                         OTHER RESPONDENTS                             I
I               2ND SEMESTER 1956 - 2ND SEMESTER 1980                   I
+-------+-------+--------+--------+--------+--------+--------+--------+
I  SEM  I  CPCS I MUCPUM I MUCMIX I ERCPUM I ERCMIX I SICPUM I SICMIX I
+-------+-------+--------+--------+--------+--------+--------+--------+
```

SEM	CPCS	MUCPUM	MUCMIX	ERCPUM	ERCMIX	SICPUM	SICMIX
5602	.68	2.24	2.18	-1.57	-1.51	1.87	1.75
5701	.41	3.93	3.74	-3.51	-3.33	1.97	1.74
5702	1.13	1.54	1.51	-.41	-.38	1.99	1.94
5801	2.17	1.51	1.50	.66	.67	1.94	1.92
5802	.25	1.27	1.26	-1.02	-1.01	1.86	1.84
5901	-1.07	1.02	1.01	-2.10	-2.08	2.28	2.25
5902	.88	.81	.80	.07	.08	1.87	1.84
6001	1.56	1.26	1.23	.30	.33	1.94	1.87
6002	.68	1.09	1.09	-.41	-.41	1.82	1.82
6101	1.09	1.33	1.30	-.24	-.21	1.85	1.79
6102	1.21	1.53	1.50	-.32	-.29	1.90	1.83
6201	2.73	2.23	2.17	.49	.56	1.82	1.70
6202	2.60	3.99	3.76	-1.39	-1.16	1.76	1.45
6301	4.90	4.18	3.99	.71	.91	1.74	1.49
6302	2.28	3.83	3.61	-1.55	-1.33	1.92	1.63
6401	3.21	3.32	3.11	-.11	.10	1.80	1.47
6402	2.95	2.39	2.27	.56	.69	2.01	1.78
6501	2.21	2.63	2.52	-.42	-.31	1.81	1.62
6502	1.58	2.41	2.36	-.83	-.78	1.71	1.61
6601	1.14	2.37	2.31	-1.23	-1.17	1.75	1.65
6602	.81	2.11	2.08	-1.30	-1.26	1.75	1.68
6701	2.19	1.99	1.93	.20	.26	1.87	1.76
6702	1.26	2.11	2.06	-.84	-.80	1.83	1.74
6801	.57	2.42	2.39	-1.85	-1.81	1.62	1.54
6802	.14	1.77	1.72	-1.62	-1.58	1.87	1.78
6901	1.49	1.66	1.63	-.17	-.14	1.83	1.77
6902	2.16	3.29	3.07	-1.13	-.92	1.88	1.55
7001	2.72	3.72	3.47	-1.00	-.75	1.80	1.45
7002	2.22	3.76	3.51	-1.54	-1.29	1.69	1.32
7101	2.62	3.02	2.89	-.41	-.27	1.60	1.35
7102	2.17	2.87	2.74	-.70	-.57	1.79	1.56
7201	2.66	2.66	2.57	.00	.09	1.70	1.54
7202	3.83	3.02	2.90	.81	.93	1.50	1.28
7301	5.89	4.34	4.34	1.55	1.55	1.82	1.82
7302	5.42	6.90	6.90	-1.48	-1.48	3.33	3.33
7401	9.51	8.00	8.00	1.51	1.51	3.92	3.92
7402	12.02	8.63	8.63	3.39	3.39	4.48	4.48
7501	8.10	5.20	5.20	2.89	2.89	3.32	3.32
7502	4.78	3.27	3.27	1.51	1.51	2.15	2.15
7601	8.99	3.96	3.96	5.04	5.04	2.20	2.20
7602	9.34	8.62	8.62	.72	.72	4.42	4.42
7701	9.98	7.34	7.34	2.64	2.64	3.94	3.94
7702	6.20	5.88	5.88	.32	.32	2.69	2.69
7801	5.90	5.64	5.78	.27	.13	2.85	2.71
7802	5.51	5.96	6.05	-.45	-.54	2.91	2.88
7901	7.34	6.20	6.36	1.14	.97	2.75	2.55
7902	8.31	6.93	7.04	1.38	1.28	2.68	2.49
8001	11.51	8.49	8.63	3.02	2.87	2.86	2.91
8002	9.10	7.57	7.72	1.53	1.38	3.12	3.41

```
+----------------------------------------------------------------------+
I (1) THE DEFINITIONS OF THE VARIABLES ARE GIVEN IN TABLE D.28          I
+----------------------------------------------------------------------+
```

TABLE D.28

DEFINITIONS OF VARIABLES FOR TABLES 3.2-3.7

WPCS   = average semi-annual actual rate of change of <u>wholesale</u> prices
(ratio of the average of the semester's monthly indices to
the average for the preceding semester).

CPCS   = average semi-annual actual rate of change of <u>consumer</u> prices
(ratio of the average of the semester's monthly indices to
the average for the preceding semester).

MUWPUM = expected semi-annual rate of change of <u>wholesale</u> prices (from
the answers to Mondo Economico opinion <u>poll</u>; <u>PUM</u> distribution;
the semesters are those for which expectations are formed at
the end of the preceding semester).

MUWMIX = expected semi-annual rate of change of <u>wholesale</u> prices (from
the answers to Mondo Economico opinion <u>poll</u>; <u>MIX</u> distribution;
the semesters are those for which expectations are formed at
the end of the preceding semester).

MUCPUM = expected semi-annual rate of change of <u>consumer</u> prices (from
the answers to Mondo Economico opinion <u>poll</u>; <u>PUM</u> distribution;
the semesters are those for which expectations are formed at
the end of the preceding semester).

MUCMIX = expected semi-annual rate of change of <u>consumer</u> prices (from
the answers to Mondo Economico opinion <u>poll</u>; <u>MIX</u> distribution;
the semesters are those for which expectations are formed at
the end of the preceding semester).

ERWPUM = WPCS - MUWPUM.

ERWMIX = WPCS - MUWMIX.

ERCPUM = CPCS - MUCPUM.

ERCMIX = CPCS - MUCMIX.

SIWPUM = standard deviation of individual expectations of <u>wholesale</u> price
changes; PUM distribution.

SIWMIX = standard deviation of individual expectations of <u>wholesale</u> price
changes; MIX distribution.

SICPUM = standard deviation of individual expectations of <u>consumer</u> price
changes; PUM distribution.

SICMIX = standard deviation of individual expectations of <u>consumer</u> price
changes; MIX distribution.

<u>Note</u>

Actual rates are calculated from the Istat monthly indices (source: Istat,
<u>Bollettino mensile di statistica</u>, various issues).

INDEX

273